A Prisoner in Fairyland

(The Book That 'Uncle Paul' Wrote)

Algernon Blackwood

Alpha Editions

This edition published in 2024

ISBN 9789362516565

Design and Setting By
Alpha Editions
www.alphaedis.com
Email - info@alphaedis.com

Contents

'LITTLE MOUSE THAT, LOST IN WONDER, FLICKS ITS WHISKERS AT THE THUNDER!'

"Les Pensees!
O leurs essors fougueux, leurs flammes dispersees,
Leur rouge acharnement ou leur accord vermeil!
Comme la-haut les etoiles criblaient la nue,
Elles se constellaient sur la plaine inconnue;
Elles roulaient dans l'espace, telles des feux,
Gravissaient la montagne, illuminaient la fleuve
Et jetaient leur parure universelle et neuve
De mer en mer, sur les pays silencieux."

Le Monde, EMILE VERHAEREN

CHAPTER I

Man is his own star; and the soul that can
Render an honest and a perfect man
Commands all light, all influence, all fate,
Nothing to him falls early, or too late.
Our acts our angels are, or good or ill,

Our fatal shadows that walk by us still.
                    BEAUMONT AND FLETCHER.

Minks—Herbert Montmorency—was now something more than secretary, even than private secretary: he was confidential-private-secretary, adviser, friend; and this, more because he was a safe receptacle for his employer's enthusiasms than because his advice or judgment had any exceptional value. So many men need an audience. Herbert Minks was a fine audience, attentive, delicately responsive, sympathetic, understanding, and above all— silent. He did not leak. Also, his applause was wise without being noisy. Another rare quality he possessed was that he was honest as the sun. To prevaricate, even by gesture, or by saying nothing, which is the commonest form of untruth, was impossible to his transparent nature. He might hedge, but he could never lie. And he was 'friend,' so far as this was possible between employer and employed, because a pleasant relationship of years' standing had established a bond of mutual respect under conditions of business intimacy which often tend to destroy it.

Just now he was very important into the bargain, for he had a secret from his wife that he meant to divulge only at the proper moment. He had known it himself but a few hours. The leap from being secretary in one of Henry Rogers's companies to being that prominent gentleman's confidential private secretary was, of course, a very big one. He hugged it secretly at first alone. On the journey back from the City to the suburb where he lived, Minks made a sonnet on it. For his emotions invariably sought the safety valve of verse. It was a wiser safety valve for high spirits than horse-racing or betting on the football results, because he always stood to win, and never to lose. Occasionally he sold these bits of joy for half a guinea, his wife pasting the results neatly in a big press album from which he often read aloud on Sunday nights when the children were in bed. They were signed 'Montmorency Minks'; and bore evidence of occasional pencil corrections on the margin with a view to publication later in a volume. And sometimes there were little lyrical fragments too, in a wild, original metre, influenced by Shelley and yet entirely his own. These had special pages to themselves at the end of the big book. But usually he preferred the sonnet form; it was more sober, more dignified. And just now the bumping of the Tube train shaped his emotion into something that began with

Success that poisons many a baser mind
With thoughts of self, may lift—

but stopped there because, when he changed into another train, the jerkier movement altered the rhythm into something more lyrical, and he got somewhat confused between the two and ended by losing both.

He walked up the hill towards his tiny villa, hugging his secret and anticipating with endless detail how he would break it to his wife. He felt very proud and very happy. The half-mile trudge seemed like a few yards.

He was a slim, rather insignificant figure of a man, neatly dressed, the City clerk stamped plainly over all his person. He envied his employer's burly six-foot stature, but comforted himself always with the thought that he possessed in its place a certain delicacy that was more becoming to a man of letters whom an adverse fate prevented from being a regular minor poet. There was that touch of melancholy in his fastidious appearance that suggested the atmosphere of frustrated dreams. Only the firmness of his character and judgment decreed against the luxury of longish hair; and he prided himself upon remembering that although a poet at heart, he was outwardly a City clerk and, as a strong man, must permit no foolish compromise.

His face on the whole was pleasing, and rather soft, yet, owing to this warring of opposing inner forces, it was at the same time curiously deceptive. Out of that dreamy, vague expression shot, when least expected, the hard and practical judgment of the City—or vice versa. But the whole was gentle—admirable quality for an audience, since it invited confession and assured a gentle hearing. No harshness lay there. Herbert Minks might have been a fine, successful mother perhaps. The one drawback to the physiognomy was that the mild blue eyes were never quite united in their frank gaze. He squinted pleasantly, though his wife told him it was a fascinating cast rather than an actual squint. The chin, too, ran away a little from the mouth, and the lips were usually parted. There was, at any rate, this air of incompatibility of temperament between the features which, made all claim to good looks out of the question.

That runaway chin, however, was again deceptive. It did, indeed run off, but the want of decision it gave to the countenance seemed contradicted by the prominent forehead and straight eyebrows, heavily marked. Minks knew his mind. If sometimes evasive rather than outspoken, he could on occasion be surprisingly firm. He saw life very clearly. He could certainly claim the good judgment stupid people sometimes have, due perhaps to their inability to see alternatives— just as some men's claim to greatness is born of an audacity due to their total lack of humour.

Minks was one of those rare beings who may be counted on—a quality better than mere brains, being of the heart. And Henry Rogers understood him and read him like an open book. Preferring the steady devotion to the brilliance a high salary may buy, he had watched him for many years in every sort of circumstance. He had, by degrees, here and there, shown an interest in his life. He had chosen his private secretary well. With Herbert Minks at his side he might accomplish many things his heart was set upon. And while Minks bumped down in his third-class crowded carriage to Sydenham, hunting his evasive sonnet, Henry Rogers glided swiftly in a taxi-cab to his rooms in St. James's Street, hard on the trail of another dream that seemed, equally, to keep just beyond his actual reach.

It would certainly seem that thought can travel across space between minds sympathetically in tune, for just as the secretary put his latch-key into his shiny blue door the idea flashed through him, 'I wonder what Mr. Rogers will do, now that he's got his leisure, with a fortune and—me!' And at the same moment Rogers, in his deep arm-chair before the fire, was saying to himself, 'I'm glad Minks has come to me; he's just the man I want for my big Scheme!' And then—'Pity he's such a lugubrious looking fellow, and wears those dreadful fancy waistcoats. But he's very open to suggestion. We can change all that. I must look after Minks a bit. He's rather sacrificed his career for me, I fancy. He's got high aims. Poor little Minks!'

'I'll stand by him whatever happens,' was the thought the slamming of the blue door interrupted. 'To be secretary to such a man is already success.' And again he hugged his secret and himself.

As already said, the new-fledged secretary was married and wrote poetry on the sly. He had four children. He would make an ideal helpmate, worshipping his employer with that rare quality of being interested in his ideas and aims beyond the mere earning of a salary; seeing, too, in that employer more than he, the latter, supposed. For, while he wrote verses on the sly, 'my chief,' as he now preferred to call him, lived poetry in his life.

'He's got it, you know, my dear,' he announced to his wife, as he kissed her and arranged his tie in the gilt mirror over the plush mantelpiece in the 'parlour'; 'he's got the divine thing in him right enough; got it, too, as strong as hunger or any other natural instinct. It's almost functional with him, if I may say so'—which meant 'if you can understand me'—'only, he's deliberately smothered it all these years. He thinks it wouldn't go down with other business men. And he's been in business, you see, from the word go.

He meant to make money, and he couldn't do both exactly. Just like myself——'

Minks wandered on. His wife noticed the new enthusiasm in his manner, and was puzzled by it. Something was up, she divined.

'Do you think he'll raise your salary again soon?' she asked practically, helping him draw off the paper cuffs that protected his shirt from ink stains, and throwing them in the fire. 'That seems to be the real point.'

But Herbert evaded the immediate issue. It was so delightful to watch her and keep his secret a little longer.

'And you *do* deserve success, dear,' she added; 'you've been as faithful as a horse.' She came closer, and stroked his thick, light hair a moment.

He turned quickly. Had he betrayed himself already? Had she read it from his eyes or manner?

'That's nothing,' he answered lightly. 'Duty is duty.'

'Of course, dear,' and she brought him his slippers. He would not let her put them on for him. It was not gallant to permit menial services to a woman.

'Success,' he murmured, 'that poisons many a baser mind——' and then stopped short. 'I've got a new sonnet,' he told her quickly, determined to prolong his pleasure, 'got it in the train coming home. Wait a moment, and I'll give you the rest. It's a beauty, with real passion in it, only I want to keep it cold and splendid if I can. Don't interrupt a moment.' He put the slippers on the wrong feet and stared hard into the fire.

Then Mrs. Minks knew for a certainty that something had happened. He had not even asked after the children.

'Herbert,' she said, with a growing excitement, 'why are you so full of poetry to-night? And what's this about success and poison all of a sudden?' She knew he never drank. 'I believe Mr. Rogers has raised your salary, or done one of those fine things you always say he's going to do. Tell me, dear, please tell me.' There were new, unpaid bills in her pocket, and she almost felt tempted to show them. She poked the fire fussily.

'Albinia,' he answered importantly, with an expression that brought the chin up closer to the lips, and made the eyebrows almost stern, 'Mr. Rogers will do the right thing always—when the right time comes. As a matter of fact'—here he reverted to the former train of thought —'both he and I are misfits in a practical, sordid age. We should have been born in Greece——'

'I simply love your poems, Herbert,' she interrupted gently, wondering how she managed to conceal her growing impatience so well, 'but there's not the money in them that there ought to be, and they don't pay for coals or for Ronald's flannels——'

'Albinia,' he put in softly, 'they relieve the heart, and so make me a happier and a better man. But—I should say he would,' he added, answering her distant question about the salary.

The secret was almost out. It hung on the edge of his lips. A moment longer he hugged it deliciously. He loved these little conversations with his wife. Never a shade of asperity entered into them. And this one in particular afforded him a peculiar delight.

'Both of us are made for higher things than mere money-making,' he went on, lighting his calabash pipe and puffing the smoke carefully above her head from one corner of his mouth, 'and that's what first attracted us to each other, as I have often mentioned to you. But now'—his bursting heart breaking through all control—'that he has sold his interests to a company and retired into private life—er—my own existence should be easier and less exacting. I shall have less routine, be more my own master, and also, I trust, find time perhaps for——'

'Then something *has* happened!' cried Mrs. Minks, springing to her feet.

'It has, my dear,' he answered with forced calmness, though his voice was near the trembling point.

She stood in front of him, waiting. But he himself did not rise, nor show more feeling than he could help. His poems were full of scenes like this in which the men—strong, silent fellows—were fine and quiet. Yet his instinct was to act quite otherwise. One eye certainly betrayed it.

'It has,' he repeated, full of delicious emotion.

'Oh, but Herbert——!'

'And I am no longer that impersonal factor in City life, mere secretary to the Board of a company——'

'Oh, Bertie, dear!'

'But private secretary to Mr. Henry Rogers—private and confidential secretary at——'

'Bert, darling——!'

'At 300 pounds a year, paid quarterly, with expenses extra, and long, regular holidays,' he concluded with admirable dignity and self-possession.

There was a moment's silence.

'You splendour!' She gave a little gasp of admiration that went straight to his heart, and set big fires alight there. 'Your reward has come at last! My hero!'

This was as it should be. The beginning of an epic poem flashed with tumult through his blood. Yet outwardly he kept his admirable calm.

'My dear, we must take success, like disaster, quietly.' He said it gently, as when he played with the children. It was mostly put on, of course, this false grandiloquence of the prig. His eyes already twinkled more than he could quite disguise.

'Then we can manage the other school, perhaps, for Frank?' she cried, and was about to open various flood-gates when he stopped her with a look of proud happiness that broke down all barriers of further pretended secrecy.

'Mr. Rogers,' was the low reply, 'has offered to do that for us—as a start.' The words were leisurely spoken between great puffs of smoke. 'That's what I meant just now by saying that he lived poetry in his life, you see. Another time you will allow judgment to wait on knowledge—'

'You dear old humbug,' she cried, cutting short the sentence that neither of them quite understood, 'I believe you've known this for weeks—'

'Two hours ago exactly,' he corrected her, and would willingly have prolonged the scene indefinitely had not his practical better half prevented him. For she came over, dropped upon her knees beside his chair, and, putting both arms about his neck, she kissed his foolish sentences away with all the pride and tenderness that filled her to the brim. And it pleased Minks hugely. It made him feel, for the moment at any rate, that he was the hero, not Mr. Henry Rogers.

But he did not show his emotion much. He did not even take his pipe out. It slipped down sideways into another corner of his wandering lips. And, while he returned the kiss with equal tenderness and pleasure, one mild blue eye looked down upon her soft brown hair, and the other glanced sideways, without a trace of meaning in it, at the oleograph of Napoleon on Elba that hung upon the wall. …

Soon afterwards the little Sydenham villa was barred and shuttered, the four children were sound asleep, Herbert and Albinia Minks both lost in the world of happy dreams that sometimes visit honest, simple folk whose consciences are clean and whose aims in life are commonplace but worthy.

CHAPTER II

When the creation was new and all the stars shone in their first splendour, the gods held their assembly in the sky and sang 'Oh, the picture of perfection! the joy unalloyed!'

But one cried of a sudden—'It seems that somewhere there is a break in the chain of light and one of the stars has been lost.'

The golden string of their harp snapped, their song stopped, and they cried in dismay—'Yes, that lost star was the best, she was the glory of all heavens!'

From that day the search is unceasing for her, and the cry goes on from one to the other that in her the world has lost its one joy!

Only in the deepest silence of night the stars smile and whisper among themselves—'Vain is this seeking! Unbroken perfection is over all!'

RABINDRANATH TAGORE. (Prose translation by Author from his original
Bengali.)

It was April 30th and Henry Rogers sat in his rooms after breakfast, listening to the rumble of the traffic down St. James's Street, and found the morning dull. A pile of letters lay unopened upon the table, waiting the arrival of the discriminating Mr. Minks with his shorthand note-book and his mild blue eyes. It was half-past nine, and the secretary was due at ten o'clock.

He smiled as he thought of this excellent fellow's first morning in the promoted capacity of private secretary. He would come in very softly, one eye looking more intelligent than the other; the air of the City clerk discarded, and in its place the bearing that belonged to new robes of office worn for the first time. He would bow, say 'Good morning, Mr. Rogers,' glance round with one eye on his employer and another on a possible chair, seat himself with a sigh that meant 'I have written a new poem in the night, and would love to read it to you if I dared,' then flatten out his oblong note-book and look up, expectant and receptive. Rogers would say 'Good morning, Mr. Minks. We've got a busy day before us. Now, let me see—' and would meet his glance with welcome. He would look quickly from one eye to the other- to this day he did not know which one was right to meet- and would wonder for the thousandth time how such an insignificant face could go with such an honest, capable mind. Then he smiled again as he remembered Frank, the little boy whose schooling he was paying for, and realised that Minks would bring a message of gratitude from Mrs. Minks, perhaps would hand him, with a gesture combining dignity and humbleness, a little note of thanks in a long narrow envelope of pale mauve, bearing a flourishing monogram on its back.

And Rogers scowled a little as he thought of the air of gruffness he would assume while accepting it, saying as pleasantly as he could manage, 'Oh, Mr. Minks, that's nothing at all; I'm only too delighted to be of service to the lad.' For he abhorred the expression of emotion, and his delicate sense of tact would make pretence of helping the boy himself, rather than the struggling parents.

Au fond he had a genuine admiration for Minks, and there was something lofty in the queer personality that he both envied and respected. It made him rely upon his judgment in certain ways he could not quite define. Minks seemed devoid of personal ambition in a sense that was not weakness. He was not insensible to the importance of money, nor neglectful of chances that enabled him to do well by his wife and family, but—he was after other things as well, if not chiefly. With a childlike sense of honesty he had once refused a position in a company that was not all it should have been, and the high pay thus rejected pointed to a scrupulous nicety of view that the City, of course, deemed foolishness. And Rogers, aware of this, had taken to him, seeking as it were to make this loss good to him in legitimate ways. Also the fellow belonged to leagues and armies and 'things,' quixotic some of them, that tried to lift humanity. That is, he gave of his spare time, as also of his spare money, to help. His Saturday evenings, sometimes a whole bank holiday, he devoted to the welfare of others, even though the devotion Rogers thought misdirected.

For Minks hung upon the fringe of that very modern, new-fashioned, but almost freakish army that worships old, old ideals, yet insists upon new-fangled names for them. Christ, doubtless, was his model, but it must be a Christ properly and freshly labelled; his Christianity must somewhere include the prefix 'neo,' and the word 'scientific' must also be dragged in if possible before he was satisfied. Minks, indeed, took so long explaining to himself the wonderful title that he was sometimes in danger of forgetting the brilliant truths it so vulgarly concealed. Yet never quite concealed. He must be up-to-date, that was all. His attitude to the world scraped acquaintance with nobility somewhere. His gift was a rare one. Out of so little, he gave his mite, and gave it simply, unaware that he was doing anything unusual.

This attitude of mind had made him valuable, even endeared him, to the successful business man, and in his secret heart Rogers had once or twice felt ashamed of himself. Minks, as it were, knew actual achievement because he was, forcedly, content with little, whereas he, Rogers, dreamed of so much, yet took twenty years to come within reach of what he dreamed. He was always waiting for the right moment to begin.

His reflections were interrupted by the sunlight, which, pouring in a flood across the opposite roof, just then dropped a patch of soft April glory upon the black and yellow check of his carpet slippers. Rogers got up and, opening the window wider than before, put out his head. The sunshine caught him full in the face. He tasted the fresh morning air. Tinged with the sharp sweetness of the north it had a fragrance as of fields and gardens. Even St. James's Street could not smother its vitality and perfume. He drew it with delight into his lungs, making such a to-do about it that a passer-by looked up to see what was the matter, and noticing the hanging tassel of a flamboyant dressing-gown, at once modestly lowered his eyes again.

But Henry Rogers did not see the passer-by in whose delicate mind a point of taste had thus vanquished curiosity, for his thoughts had flown far across the pale-blue sky, behind the cannon-ball clouds, up into that scented space and distance where summer was already winging her radiant way towards the earth. Visions of June obscured his sight, and something in the morning splendour brought back his youth and boyhood. He saw a new world spread about him—a world of sunlight, butterflies, and flowers, of smooth soft lawns and shaded gravel paths, and of children playing round a pond where rushes whispered in a wind of long ago. He saw hayfields, orchards, tea-things spread upon a bank of flowers underneath a hedge, and a collie dog leaping and tumbling shoulder high among the standing grass.... It was all curiously vivid, and with a sense of something about it unfading and delightfully eternal. It could never pass, for instance, whereas....

'Ain't yer forgotten the nightcap?' sang out a shrill voice from below, as a boy with a basket on his arm went down the street. He drew back from the window, realising that he was a sight for all admirers. Tossing the end of his cigarette in the direction of the cheeky urchin, he settled himself again in the arm-chair before the glowing grate-fire.

But the fresh world he had tasted came back with him. For Henry Rogers stood this fine spring morning upon the edge of a new life. A long chapter had just closed behind him. He was on the threshold of another. The time to begin had come. And the thrill of his freedom now at hand was very stimulating to his imagination. He was forty, and a rich man. Twenty years of incessant and intelligent labour had brought him worldly success. He admitted he had been lucky, where so many toil on and on till the gates of death stand up and block their way, fortunate if they have earned a competency through years where hope and disappointment wage their incessant weary battle. But he, for some reason known only to the silent Fates, had crested the difficult hill and now stood firm upon the top to see the sunrise, the dreadful gates not even yet in sight. At yesterday's Board meeting, Minks had handed him the papers for his signature; the patents had been transferred to the new company; the cheque had been paid over; and he was now a gentleman of leisure with a handsome fortune lying in his bank to await investment. He was a director in the parent, as well as the subsidiary companies, with fees that in themselves alone were more than sufficient for his simple needs.

For all his tastes *were* simple, and he had no expensive hobbies or desires; he preferred two rooms and a bath to any house that he had ever seen; pictures he liked best in galleries; horses he could hire without the trouble of owning; the few books worth reading would go into a couple of shelves; motors afflicted, even confused him—he was old-fashioned enough to love country and walk through it slowly on two vigorous legs; marriage had been put aside with a searing disappointment years ago, not forgotten, but accepted; and of travel he had enjoyed enough to realise now that its pleasures could be found reasonably near home and for very moderate expenditure indeed. And the very idea of servants was to him an affliction; he loathed their prying closeness to his intimate life and habits, destroying the privacy he loved. Confirmed old bachelor his friends might call him if they chose; he knew what he wanted. Now at last he had it. The ambition of his life was within reach.

For, from boyhood up, a single big ambition had ever thundered through his being—the desire to be of use to others. To help his fellow-kind was to be his profession and career. It had burned and glowed in him ever since he could remember, and what first revealed it in him was the sight—common enough, alas—of a boy with one leg hobbling along on crutches down the village street. Some deep power in his youthful heart, akin to the wondrous sympathy of women, had been touched. Like a shock of fire it came home to him. He, too, might lose his dearest possession thus, and be unable to climb trees, jump ditches, risk his neck along the edge of the haystack or the roof. '*That might happen to me too!*' was the terrible thing he realised, and had burst into tears....

Crutches at twelve! And the family hungry, as he later learned! Something in the world was wrong; he thought every one had enough to eat, at least, and only the old used crutches. 'The Poor was a sort of composite wretch, half criminal, who deserved to be dirty, suffering, punished; but this boy belonged to a family that worked and did its best. Something in the world-machinery had surely broken loose and caused violent disorder. For no one cared particularly. The "thorities,' he heard, looked after the Poor— "thorities in law,' as he used to call the mysterious Person he never actually saw, stern, but kindly in a grave impersonal way; and asked once if some relation- in-law or other, who was mentioned often but never seen, had, therefore, anything to do with the poor.

Dropping into his heart from who knows what far, happy star, this passion had grown instead of faded: to give himself for others, to help afflicted folk, to make the world go round a little more easily. And he had never forgotten the deep thrill with which he heard his father tell him of some wealthy man who during his lifetime had given away a million pounds— anonymously. ... His own pocket-money just then was five shillings a week, and his expectations just exactly—nothing.

But before his dreams could know accomplishment, he must have means. To be of use to anybody at all he must make himself effective. The process must be reversed, for no man could fight without weapons, and weapons were only to be had as the result of steady, concentrated effort—selfish effort. A man must fashion himself before he can be effective for others. Self-effacement, he learned, was rather a futile virtue after all.

As the years passed he saw his chances. He cut short a promising University career and entered business. His talents lay that way, as his friends declared, and unquestionably he had a certain genius for invention; for, while scores of futile processes he first discovered remained mere clever solutions of interesting problems, he at length devised improvements in the greater industries, and, patenting them wisely, made his way to practical results.

But the process had been a dangerous one, and during the long business experience the iron had entered his soul, and he had witnessed at close quarters the degrading influence of the lust of acquisition. The self-advertising humbug of most philanthropy had clouded something in him that he felt could never again grow clear and limpid as before, and a portion of his original zest had faded. For the City hardly encouraged it. One bit of gilt after another had been knocked off his brilliant dream, one jet of flame upon another quenched. The single eye that fills the body full of light was a thing so rare that its possession woke suspicion. Even of money generously given, so little reached its object; gaping pockets and grasping fingers everywhere lined the way of safe delivery. It sickened him. So few, moreover, were willing to give without acknowledgment in at least one morning paper. 'Bring back the receipt' was the first maxim even of the office-boys; and between the right hand and the left of every one were special 'private wires' that flashed the news as quickly as possible about the entire world.

Yet, while inevitable disillusion had dulled his youthful dreams, its glory was never quite destroyed. It still glowed within. At times, indeed, it ran into flame, and knew something of its original splendour. Women, in particular, had helped to keep it alive, fanning its embers bravely. For many women, he found, dreamed his own dream, and dreamed it far more sweetly. They were closer to essential realities than men were. While men bothered with fuss and fury about empires, tariffs, street-cars, and marvellous engines for destroying one another, women, keeping close to the sources of life, knew, like children, more of its sweet, mysterious secrets—the things of value no one yet has ever put completely into words. He wondered, a little sadly, to see them battling now to scuffle with the men in managing the gross machinery, cleaning the pens and regulating ink-pots. Did they really think that by helping to decide whether rates should rise or fall, or how many buttons a factory-inspector should wear upon his uniform, they more nobly helped the world go round? Did they never pause to reflect who would fill the places they thus vacated? With something like melancholy he saw them stepping down from their thrones of high authority, for it seemed to him a prostitution of their sweet prerogatives that damaged the entire sex.

'Old-fashioned bachelor, no doubt, I am,' he smiled quietly to himself, coming back to the first reflection whence his thoughts had travelled so far—the reflection, namely, that now at last he possessed the freedom he had longed and toiled for.

And then he paused and looked about him, confronted with a difficulty. To him it seemed unusual, but really it was very common.

For, having it, he knew not at first what use to make of it. This dawned upon him suddenly when the sunlight splashed his tawdry slippers with its gold. The movement to the open window was really instinctive beginning of a search, as though in the free, wonderful spaces out of doors he would find the thing he sought to do. Now, settled back in the deep arm-chair, he realised that he had not found it. The memories of childhood had flashed into him instead. He renewed the search before the dying fire, waiting for the sound of Minks' ascending footsteps on the stairs. ...

And this revival of the childhood mood was curious, he felt, almost significant, for it was symbolical of so much that he had deliberately, yet with difficulty, suppressed and put aside. During these years of concentrated toil for money, his strong will had neglected of set purpose the call of a robust imagination. He had stifled poetry just as he had stifled play. Yet really that imagination had merely gone into other channels— scientific invention. It was a higher form, married at least with action that produced poetry in steel and stone instead of in verse. Invention has ever imagination and poetry at its heart.

The acquirement of wealth demanded his entire strength, and all lighter considerations he had consistently refused to recognise, until he thought them dead. This sudden flaming mood rushed up and showed him otherwise. He reflected on it, but clumsily, as with a mind too long trained in the rigid values of stocks and shares, buying and selling, hard figures that knew not elasticity. This softer subject led him to no conclusion, leaving him stranded among misty woods and fields of flowers that had no outlet. He realised, however, clearly that this side of him was not atrophied as he thought. Its unused powers had merely been accumulating—underground.

He got no further than that just now. He poked the fire and lit another cigarette. Then, glancing idly at the paper, his eye fell upon the list of births, and by merest chance picked out the name of Crayfield. Some nonentity had been 'safely delivered of a son' at Crayfield, the village where he had passed his youth and childhood. He saw the Manor House where he was born, the bars across the night- nursery windows, the cedars on the lawn, the haystacks just beyond the stables, and the fields where the rabbits sometimes fell asleep as they sat after enormous meals too stuffed to move. He saw the old gravel-pit that led, the gardener told him, to the centre of the earth. A whiff of perfume from the laurustinus in the drive came back, the scent of hay, and with it the sound of the mowing-machine going over the lawn. He saw the pony in loose flat leather shoes. The bees were humming in the lime trees. The rooks were cawing. A blackbird whistled from the shrubberies where he once passed an entire day in hiding, after emptying an ink-bottle down the German governess's dress. He heard the old family butler in his wheezy voice calling in vain for 'Mr. 'Enery' to come in. The tone was respectful, seductive as the man could make it, yet reproachful. He remembered throwing a little stone that caught him just where the Newgate fringe met the black collar of his coat, so that his cry of delight betrayed his hiding-place. The whacking that followed he remembered too, and how his brother emerged suddenly from behind the curtain with, 'Father, may I have it instead of Henry, please?' That spontaneous offer of sacrifice, of willingness to suffer for another, had remained in his mind for a long time as a fiery, incomprehensible picture.

More dimly, then, somewhere in mist behind, he saw other figures moving—the Dustman and the Lamplighter, the Demon Chimneysweep in black, the Woman of the Haystack—outposts and sentries of a larger fascinating host that gathered waiting in the shadows just beyond. The creations of his boy's imagination swarmed up from their temporary graves, and made him smile and wonder. After twenty years of strenuous business life, how pale and thin they seemed. Yet at the same time how extraordinarily alive and active! He saw, too, the huge Net of Stars he once had made to catch them with from that night-nursery window, fastened by long golden nails made out of meteors to the tops of the cedars. ... There had been, too, a train—the Starlight Express. It almost seemed as if *they* knew, too, that a new chapter had begun, and that they called him to come back and play again. ...

Then, with a violent jump, his thoughts flew to other things, and he considered one by one the various philanthropic schemes he had cherished against the day when he could realise them. That day had come. But the schemes seemed one and all wild now, impracticable, already accomplished by others better than he could hope to accomplish them, and none of them fulfilling the first essential his practical mind demanded—knowing his money spent precisely as he wished. Dreams, long cherished, seemed to collapse one by one before him just when he at last came up with them. He thought of the woman who was to have helped him, now married to another who had money without working for it. He put the thought back firmly in its place. He knew now a greater love than that—the love for many. ...

He was embarking upon other novel schemes when there was a ring at the bell, and the charwoman, who passed with him for servant, ushered in his private secretary, Mr. Minks. Quickly readjusting the machinery of his mind, Rogers came back to the present,

'Good morning, Mr. Rogers. I trust I am punctual.'

'Good morning, Minks; yes, on the stroke of ten. We've got a busy day. Let's see now. How are you, by the by?' he added, as an afterthought, catching first one eye, then the other, and looking finally between the two.

'Very well, indeed, thank you, Mr. Rogers.' He was dressed in a black tail-coat, with a green tie neatly knotted into a spotless turn-down collar. He glanced round him for a chair, one hand already in his pocket for the note-book.

'Good,' said Rogers, indicating where he might seat himself, and reaching for the heap of letters.

The other sighed a little and began to look expectant and receptive.

'If I might give you this first, please, Mr. Rogers,' he said, suddenly pretending to remember something in his breast-pocket and handing across the table, with a slight flush upon his cheeks, a long, narrow, mauve envelope with a flourishing address. 'It was a red- letter day for Mrs. Minks when I told her of your kindness. She wished to thank you in person, but— I thought a note—I knew,' he stammered, 'you would prefer a letter. It is a tremendous help to both of us, if I may say so again.'

'Yes, yes, quite so,' said Rogers, quickly; 'and I'm glad to be of service to the lad. You must let me know from time to time how he's getting on.'

Minks subsided, flattening out his oblong notebook and examining the points of his pencil sharpened at both ends as though the fate of Empires depended on it. They attacked the pile of correspondence heartily, while the sun, watching them through the open window, danced gorgeously upon the walls and secretly put the fire out.

In this way several hours passed, for besides letters to be dictated, there were careful instructions to be given about many things. Minks was kept very busy. He was now not merely shorthand clerk, and he had to be initiated into the inner history of various enterprises in which his chief was interested. All Mr. Rogers's London interests, indeed, were to be in his charge, and, obviously aware of this, he bore himself proudly with an air of importance that had no connection with a common office. To watch him, you would never have dreamed that Herbert Minks had ever contemplated City life, much less known ten years of drudgery in its least poetic stages. For him, too, as for his employer, a new chapter of existence had begun— 'commenced' he would have phrased it—and, as confidential adviser to a man of fortune whose character he admired almost to the point of worship, he was now a person whose importance it was right the world should recognise. And he meant the world to take this attitude without delay. He dressed accordingly, knowing that of every ten people nine judge value from clothes, and hat, and boots—especially boots. His patent leather, buttoned boots were dazzling, with upper parts of soft grey leather. And his shiny 'topper' wore a band of black. Minks, so far as he knew, was not actually in mourning, but somebody for whom he ought to be in mourning might die any day, and meanwhile, he felt, the band conveyed distinction. It suited a man of letters. It also protected the hat.

'Thank'ee,' said his chief as luncheon time drew near; 'and now, if you'll get those letters typed, you might leave 'em here for me on your way home to sign. That's all we have to-day, isn't it?'

'You wanted, I think, to draft your Scheme for Disabled——' began the secretary, when the other cut him short.

'Yes, yes, but that must wait. I haven't got it clear yet in my own mind. You might think it out a bit yourself, perhaps, meanwhile, and give me your ideas, eh? Look up what others have done in the same line, for instance, and tell me where they failed. What the weakness of their schemes was, you know—and—er—so forth.'

A faint smile, that held the merest ghost of merriment, passed across the face of Minks, leaping, unobserved by his chief, from one eye to the other. There was pity and admiration in it; a hint of pathos visited those wayward lips. For the suggestion revealed the weakness the secretary had long ago divined—that the practical root of the matter did not really lie in him at all, and Henry Rogers forever dreamed of 'Schemes' he was utterly unable and unsuited to carry out. Improvements in a silk machine was one thing, but improvements in humanity was another. Like the poetry in his soul they could never know fulfilment. He had inspiration, but no constructive talent. For the thousandth time Minks wondered, glancing at his employer's face, how such calm and gentle features, such dreamy eyes and a Vandyke beard so neatly trimmed, could go with ambitions so lofty and so unusual. This sentence he had heard before, and was destined often to hear again, while achievement came no nearer.

'I will do so at the first opportunity.' He put the oblong note-book carefully in his pocket, and stood by the table in an attitude of 'any further instructions, please?' while one eye wandered to the unopened letter that was signed 'Albinia Minks, with heartfelt gratitude.'

'And, by the by, Minks,' said his master, turning as though a new idea had suddenly struck him and he had formed a hasty plan, 'you might kindly look up an afternoon train to Crayfield. Loop line from Charing Cross, you know. Somewhere about two o'clock or so. I have to—er—I think I'll run down that way after luncheon.'

Whereupon, having done this last commission, and written it down upon a sheet of paper which he placed with care against the clock, beside the unopened letter, the session closed, and Minks, in his mourning hat and lavender gloves, walked up St. James's Street apparently *en route* for the Ritz, but suddenly, as with careless unconsciousness, turning into an A.B.C. Depot for luncheon, well pleased with himself and with the world, but especially with his considerate employer.

Ten minutes later Mr. Rogers followed him on his way to the club, and just when Minks was reflecting with pride of the well-turned phrases he had dictated to his wife for her letter of thanks, it passed across the mind of its recipient that he had forgotten to read it altogether. And, truth to tell, he never yet has read it; for, returning late that evening from his sentimental journey down to Crayfield, it stood no longer where he had left it beside the clock, and nothing occurred to remind him of its existence. Apart from its joint composers, no one can ever know its contents but the charwoman, who, noticing the feminine writing, took it back to Lambeth and pored over it with a candle for full half an hour, greatly disappointed. 'Things like that,' she grumbled to her husband, whose appearance suggested that he went for bigger game, 'ain't worth the trouble of taking at all, whichever way you looks at it.' And probably she was right.

CHAPTER III

And what if All of animated nature
Be but as Instruments diversely framed
That tremble into thought, as o'er them sweeps
One infinite and intellectual Breeze,
At once the Soul of each, and God of all?
The AEolian Harp, S. T. COLERIDGE.

In the train, even before St. John's was passed, a touch of inevitable reaction had set in, and Rogers asked himself why he was going. For a sentimental journey was hardly in his line, it seemed. But no satisfactory answer was forthcoming—none, at least, that a Board or a Shareholders' Meeting would have considered satisfactory.

There was an answer in him somewhere, but he couldn't quite get down to it. The spring glory had enticed him back to childhood. The journey was symbolical of escape. That was the truth. But the part of him that knew it had lain so long in abeyance that only a whisper flitted across his mind as he sat looking out of the carriage window at the fields round Lee and Eltham. The landscape seemed hauntingly familiar, but what surprised him was the number of known faces that rose and smiled at him. A kind of dream confusion blurred his outer sight;

At Bexley, as he hurried past, he caught dimly a glimpse of an old nurse whom he remembered trying to break into bits with a hop-pole he could barely lift; and, most singular thing, on the Sidcup platform, a group of noisy schoolboys, with smudged faces and ridiculously small caps stuck on the back of their heads, had scrambled viciously to get into his compartment. They carried brown canvas satchels full of crumpled books and papers, and though the names had mostly escaped him, he remembered every single face. There was Barlow—big, bony chap who stammered, bringing his words out with a kind of whistling sneeze. Barlow had given him his first thrashing for copying his stammer. There was young Watson, who funked at football and sneaked to a master about a midnight supper. He stole pocket-money, too, and was expelled. Then he caught a glimpse of another fellow with sly face and laughing eyes; the name had vanished, but he was the boy who put jalap in the music-master's coffee, and received a penny from five or six others who thus escaped a lesson. All waved their hands to him as the train hurried away, and the last thing he saw was the station lamp where he had lit the cigar that made three of them, himself included, deadly sick. Familiar woods and a little blue-eyed stream then hid the vision … and a moment later he was standing on the platform of his childhood's station, giving up his first-class ticket (secretly ashamed that it was not third) to a station-master-ticket-collector person who simply was not real at all.

For he had no beard. He was small, too, and insignificant. The way he had dwindled, with the enormous station that used to be a mile or so in length, was severely disappointing. That STATION-MASTER with the beard ought to have lived for ever. His niche in the Temple of Fame was sure. One evening he had called in full uniform at the house and asked to see Master Henry Rogers, the boy who had got out 'WHILE-THE- TRAIN-WAS-STILL-IN-MOTION,' and had lectured him gravely with a face like death. Never again had he left a train 'whilestillinmotion,' though it was years before he discovered how his father had engineered that awful, salutary visit.

He asked casually, in a voice that hardly seemed his own, about the service back to town, and received the answer with a kind of wonder. It was so respectful. The porters had not found him out yet; but the moment they did so, he would have to run. He did not run, however. He walked slowly down the Station Road, swinging the silver-knobbed cane the office clerks had given him when he left the City. Leisurely, without a touch of fear, he passed the Water Works, where the huge iron crank of the shaft rose and fell with ominous thunder against the sky. It had once been part of that awful hidden Engine which moved the world. To go near it was instant death, and he always crossed the road to avoid it; but this afternoon he went down the cinder pathway so close that he could touch it with his stick. It was incredible that so terrible a thing could dwindle in a few years to the dimensions of a motor piston. The crank that moved up and down like a bending, gigantic knee looked almost flimsy now. …

Then the village street came into view and he suddenly smelt the fields and gardens that topped the hill beyond. The world turned gold and amber, shining beneath a turquoise sky. There was a rush of flaming sunsets, one upon another, followed by great green moons, and hosts of stars that came twinkling across barred windows to his very bedside … that grand old Net of Stars he made so cunningly. Cornhill and Lombard Street flashed back upon him for a second, then dived away and hid their faces for ever, as he passed the low grey wall beside the church where first he had seen the lame boy hobbling, and had realised that the whole world suffered.

A moment he stood here, thinking. He heard the wind sighing in the yew trees beside the dark brown porch. Rooks were cawing among the elms across the churchyard, and pigeons wheeled and fluttered about the grey square tower. The wind, the tower, the weather-stained old porch —these had not changed. This sunshine and this turquoise sky were still the same.

The village stopped at the churchyard—significant boundary. No single building ventured farther; the houses ran the other way instead, pouring down the steep hill in a cataract of bricks and roofs towards the station. The hill, once topped, and the churchyard left behind, he entered the world of fields and little copses. It was just like going through a gateway. It was a Gateway. The road sloped gently down for half-a-mile towards the pair of big iron gates that barred the drive up to the square grey house upon whose lawns he once had chased butterflies, but from whose upper windows he once had netted—stars.

The spell came over him very strongly then as he went slowly down that road. The altered scale of distance confused him; the road had telescoped absurdly; the hayfields were so small. At the turn lay the pond with yellow duckweed and a bent iron railing that divided it to keep the cows from crossing. Formerly, of course, that railing had been put to prevent children drowning in its bottomless depths; all ponds had been bottomless then, and the weeds had spread to entice the children to a watery death. But now he could have jumped across it, weed and railing too, without a run, and he looked in vain for the shores that once had been so seductively far away. They were mere dirty, muddy edges.

This general shrinkage in space was very curious. But a similar contraction, he realised, had taken place in time as well, for, looking back upon his forty years, they seemed such a little thing compared to the enormous stretch they offered when he had stood beside this very pond and looked ahead. He wondered vaguely which was the reality and which the dream. But his effort was not particularly successful, and he came to no conclusion. Those years of strenuous business life were like a few weeks, yet their golden results were in his pockets. Those years of childhood had condensed into a jumble of sunny hours, yet their golden harvest was equally in his heart. Time and space were mere bits of elastic that could stretch or shrink as thought directed, feeling chose. And now both thought and feeling chose emphatically. He stepped back swiftly. His mind seemed filled with stars and butterflies and childhood's figures of wonder. Childhood took him prisoner.

It was curious at first, though, how the acquired nature made a struggle to assert itself, and the practical side of him, developed in the busy markets of the world, protested. It was automatic rather, and at best not very persistent; it soon died away. But, seeing the gravel everywhere, he wondered if there might not be valuable clay about, what labour cost, and what the nearest stations were for haulage; and, seeing the hop-poles, he caught himself speculating what wood they were made of, and what varnish would best prevent their buried points from going rotten in this particular soil. There was a surge of practical considerations, but quickly fading. The last one was stirred by the dust of a leisurely butcher's cart. He had visions of a paste for motor-roads, or something to lay dust … but, before the dust had settled again through the sunshine about his feet, or the rumble of the cart died away into distance, the thought vanished like a nightmare in the dawn. It ran away over the switchback of the years, uphill to Midsummer, downhill to Christmas, jumping a ditch at Easter, and a hedge at that terrible thing known as "Clipse of the Moon.' The leaves of the elm trees whispered overhead. He was moving through an avenue that led towards big iron gates beside a little porter's lodge. He saw the hollies, and smelt the laurustinus. There lay the triangle of uncut grass at the cross-roads, the long, grey, wooden palings built upon moss-grown bricks; and against the sky he just caught a glimpse of the feathery, velvet cedar crests, crests that once held nails of golden meteors for his Net of Stars.

Determined to enjoy his cake and eat it at the same time as long as possible, he walked down the road a little distance, eyeing the lawns and windows of the house through narrow gaps between the boarding of the fence. He prolonged the pleasures of anticipation thus, and, besides, he wished to see if the place was occupied or empty. It looked unkempt rather, the gardens somewhat neglected, and yet there hung an air of occupancy about it all. He had heard the house had changed hands several times. But it was difficult to see clearly; the sunshine dazzled; the lilac and laburnum scattered sheets of colour through which the shadows wove themselves an obscuring veil, He kept seeing butterflies and chasing them with his sight.

'Can you tell me if this house is occupied?' he asked abruptly of an old gentleman who coughed suddenly behind him.

It was an explanation as well as a question, for the passer-by had surprised him in a remarkable attitude. He was standing on tiptoe upon the parapet of brick, pulling himself up above the fence by his hands, and his hat had fallen into the road.

'The shrubberies are so dense I can't see through them,' he added, landing upon his feet with a jump, a little breathless. He felt rather foolish. He was glad the stranger was not Minks or one of his fellow directors. 'The fact is I lived here as a boy. I'm not a burglar.'

But the old gentleman—a clergyman apparently—stood there smiling without a word as he handed him the fallen hat. He was staring rather intently into his eyes.

'Ahem!' coughed Mr. Rogers, to fill an awkward gap. 'You're very kind, sir,' and he took the hat and brushed the dust off. Something brushed off his sight and memory at the same time.

'Ahem' coughed the other, still staring. 'Please do not mention it——' adding after a second's pause, to the complete amazement of his listener, 'Mr. Rogers.'

And then it dawned upon him. Something in the charming, peace-lit face was strangely familiar.

'I say,' he exclaimed eagerly, 'this is a pleasure,' and then repeated with even greater emphasis, 'but this is a pleasure, indeed. Who ever would have thought it?' he added with delicious ambiguity. He seized the outstretched hand and shook it warmly—the hand of the old vicar who had once been his tutor too.

'You've come back to your boyhood, then. Is that it? And to see the old place and—your old friends?' asked the other with his beautiful, kindly smile that even false quantities had never been able to spoil. 'We've not forgotten you as you've forgotten us, you see,' he added; 'and the place, though empty now for years, has not forgotten you either, I'll be bound.'

They stood there in the sunshine on the dusty road talking of a hundred half-forgotten things, as the haze of memory lifted, and scenes and pictures, names and faces, details of fun and mischief rained upon him like flowers in a sudden wind of spring. The voice and face of his old tutor bridged the years like magic. Time had stood still here in this fair Kentish garden. The little man in black who came every Saturday morning with his dingy bag had forgotten to wind the clocks, perhaps. ...

'But you will like to go inside and see it all for yourself—alone,' the Vicar said at length. 'My housekeeper has the keys. I'll send a boy with them to the lodge. It won't take five minutes. And then you must come up to the Vicarage for tea—or dinner if you're kept—and stay the night. My married daughter-you remember Joan and May, of course?—is with us just now; she'll be so very glad to see you. You know the way.'

And he moved off down the country road, still vigorous at seventy, with his black straw hat and big square-toed boots, his shoulders hardly more bent than when his mischievous pupil had called every morning with Vergil and Todhunter underneath one arm, and in his heart a lust to hurry after sleepy rabbits in the field.

'My married daughter—you remember May?'

The blue-eyed girl of his boyhood passion flitted beside his disappearing figure. He remembered the last time he saw her—refusing to help her from a place of danger in the cedar branches—when he put his love into a single eloquent phrase: 'You silly ass!' then cast her adrift for ever because she said 'Thanks awfully,' and gave him a great wet kiss. But he thought a lot of her all the same, and the thoughts had continued until the uproar in the City drowned them.

Thoughts crowded thick and fast.

How vital thinking was after all! Nothing seemed able to kill its eternal pictures. The coincidence of meeting his old tutor again was like a story-book, though in reality likely enough; for his own face was not so greatly altered by the close brown beard perhaps; and the Vicar had grown smaller, that was all. Like everything else, he had shrunk, of course-like road and station-master and water-works. He had almost said, 'You, too, have shrunk'—but otherwise was the same old fluffy personality that no doubt still got sadly muddled in his sermons, gave out wrong hymns, and spent his entire worldly substance on his scattered parish. His voice was softer too. It rang in his ears still, as though there had been no break of over two decades. The hum of bees and scythes was in it just as when it came through the open study window while he construed the *Georgics*. ... But, most clearly of all, he heard two sentences—

'You have come back to your boyhood,' and 'The empty place has not forgotten you, I'll be bound.' Both seemed significant. They hummed and murmured through his mind. That old net of starlight somehow caught them in its golden meshes.

CHAPTER IV

A Spirit gripped him by the hair and carried him far away,
Till he heard as the roar of a rain-fed ford the roar of the
  Milky Way:
Till he heard the roar of the Milky Way die down and drone and
  cease.

               Tomlinson, R. KIPLING.

The boy presently came up in a cloud of dust with the key, and ran off again with a shilling in his pocket, while Henry Rogers, budding philanthropist and re-awakening dreamer, went down the hill of memories at high speed that a doctor would have said was dangerous, a philosopher morbid, and the City decreed unanimously as waste of time.

He went over the house from cellar to ceiling...

And finally he passed through a back door in the scullery and came out upon the lawn. With a shock he realised that a long time had intervened. The dusk was falling. The rustle of its wings was already in the shrubberies. He had missed the tea hour altogether. And, as he walked there, so softly that he hardly disturbed the thrushes that busily tapped the dewy grass for supper, he knew suddenly that he was not alone, but that shadowy figures hid everywhere, watching, waiting, wondering like himself. They trooped after him, invisible and silent, as he went about the old familiar garden, finding nothing changed. They were so real that once he stopped beneath the lime trees, where afternoon tea was served in summer, and where the Long Walk began its haunted, shadowy existence—stood still a moment and called to them—

'Is any one there? Come out and show yourselves....!'

And though his voice fell dead among the foliage, winning echoes from spots whence no echoes possibly could come, and rushing back upon him like a boomerang, he got the curious impression that it had penetrated into certain corners of the shrubberies where it had been heard and understood. Answers did not come. They were no more audible than the tapping of the thrushes, or the little feet of darkness that ran towards him from the eastern sky. But they were there. The troop of Presences drew closer. They had been creeping on all fours. They now stood up. The entire garden was inhabited and alive.

'He has come back!'

It ran in a muted whisper like a hush of wind. The thrill of it passed across the lawn in the dusk. The dark tunnel of the Long Walk filled suddenly to the brim. The thrushes raised their heads, peeping sideways to listen, on their guard. Then the leaves opened a little and the troop ventured nearer. The doors and windows of the silent, staring house had also opened. From the high nursery windows especially, queer shapes of shadow flitted down to join the others. For the sun was far away behind the cedars now, and that Net of Starlight dropped downwards through the air. So carefully had he woven it years ago that hardly a mesh was torn....

'He has come back again...!' the whisper ran a second time, and he looked about him for a place where he could hide.

But there was no place. Escape from the golden net was now impossible....

Then suddenly, looming against the field that held the Gravel-Pit and the sleeping rabbits, he saw the outline of the Third Class Railway Carriage his father bought as a Christmas present, still standing on the stone supports that were borrowed from a haystack.

That Railway Carriage had filled whole years with joy and wonder. They had called it the Starlight Express. It had four doors, real lamps in the roof, windows that opened and shut, and big round buffers. It started without warning. It went at full speed in a moment. It was never really still. The footboards were endless and very dangerous.

He saw the carriage with its four compartments still standing there in the hay field. It looked mysterious, old, and enormous as ever. There it still stood as in his boyhood days, but stood neglected and unused.

The memory of the thrilling journeys he had made in this Starlight Express completed his recapture, for he knew now who the troop of Presences all about him really were. The passengers, still waiting after twenty years' delay, thinking perhaps the train would never start again, were now impatient. They had caught their engine-driver again at last. Steam was up. Already the blackbirds whistled. And something utterly wild and reckless in him passionately broke its bonds with a flood of longings that no amount of years or 'Cities' could ever subdue again. He stepped out from the dozing lime trees and held his hat up like a flag.

'Take your seats,' he cried as of old, 'for the Starlight Express. Take your seats! No luggage allowed! Animals free! Passengers with special tickets may drive the engine in their turn! First stop the Milky Way for hot refreshments! Take your seats, or stay at home for ever!'

It was the old cry, still remembered accurately; and the response was immediate. The rush of travellers from the Long Walk nearly took him off his feet. From the house came streams of silent figures, families from the shrubberies, tourists from the laurels by the scullery windows, and throngs of breathless oddities from the kitchen-garden. The lawn was littered with discarded luggage; umbrellas dropped on flower-beds, where they instantly took root and grew; animals ran scuttling among them—birds, ponies, dogs, kittens, donkeys, and white mice in trailing swarms. There was not a minute to spare. One big Newfoundland brought several Persian kittens on his back, their tails behind them in the air like signals; a dignified black retriever held a baby in his mouth; and fat children by the score, with unfastened clothes and smudged faces, many of them in their nightclothes, poured along in hurrying, silent crowds, softer than clouds that hide a crescent moon in summer.

'But this is impossible,' he cried to himself. 'The multiplication tables have gone wrong. The City has driven me mad. No shareholder would stand such a thing for a minute!'

While, at the same time, that other voice in him kept shouting, ever more loudly—

'Take your seats! Take your seats! The Starlight Express is off to Fairyland! Show your tickets! Show your tickets!'

He laughed with happiness.

The throng and rush were at first so great that he recognised hardly any of the passengers; but, the first press over, he saw several bringing up the rear who were as familiar as of yesterday. They nodded kindly to him as they passed, no sign of reproach for the long delay in their friendly eyes. He had left his place beside the lime trees, and now stood at the carriage door, taking careful note of each one as he showed his ticket to the Guard. And the Guard was the blue-eyed girl. She did not clip the tickets, but merely looked at them. She looked, first at the ticket, then into the face of the passenger. The glance of the blue eyes was the passport. Of course, he remembered now—both guard and engine-driver were obliged to have blue eyes. Blue eyes furnished the motor-power and scenery and everything. It was the spell that managed the whole business—the Spell of the Big Blue eyes —blue, the colour of youth and distance, of sky and summer flowers, of childhood.

He watched these last passengers come up one by one, and as they filed past him he exchanged a word with each. How pleased they were to see him! But how ashamed he felt for having been so long away. Not one, however, reminded him of it, and—what touched him most of all—not one suspected he had nearly gone for good. All knew he would come back.

What looked like a rag-and-bone man blundered up first, his face a perfect tangle of beard and hair, and the eyebrows like bits of tow stuck on with sealing-wax. It was The Tramp—Traveller of the World, the Eternal Wanderer, homeless as the wind; his vivid personality had haunted all the lanes of childhood. And, as Rogers nodded kindly to him, the figure waited for something more.

'Ain't forgot the rhyme, 'ave yer?' he asked in a husky voice that seemed to issue from the ground beneath his broken boots. 'The rhyme we used to sing together in the Noight-Nursery when I put my faice agin' the bars, after climbin' along 'arf a mile of slippery slaites to git there.'

And Rogers, smiling, found himself saying it, while the pretty Guard fixed her blue eyes on his face and waited patiently:—

I travel far and wide,
But in my own inside!
Such places
And queer races!
I never go to them, you see,
Because they always come to me!

'Take your seat, please,' cried the Guard. 'No luggage, you know!' She pushed him in sideways, first making him drop his dirty bundle.

With a quick, light step a very thin man hurried up. He had no luggage, but carried on his shoulder a long stick with a point of gold at its tip.

'Light the lamps,' said the Guard impatiently, 'and then sit on the back buffers and hold your pole out to warn the shooting stars.'

He hopped in, though not before Rogers had passed the time of night with him first:—

I stand behind the sky, and light the stars,—
Except on cloudy nights;
And then my head
Remains in bed,
And takes along the ceiling—easier flights!

Others followed quickly then, too quickly for complete recognition. Besides, the Guard was getting more and more impatient.

'You've clean forgotten *me*,' said one who had an awful air of darkness about him; 'and no wonder, because you never saw me properly. On Sundays, when I was nicely washed up you couldn't 'ardly reckernise me. Nachural 'nuff, too!'

He shot by like a shadow, then pulled up a window with a rattle, popped his dirty head out, and called back thickly as if his mouth was full of smoke or pudding:—

The darkness suits *me* best,
For my old face
Is out of place,
Except in chimney stacks!
Upon my crown
The soot comes down
Filling my eyes with blacks.
Don't light the fire,
Or I'd—.

'Stop it!' cried the Guard, shutting the window with a snap, so that Rogers never knew whether the missing word used to be 'expire' or 'perspire'; 'and go on to your proper place on the tender.' Then she turned quickly to fix her big blue eyes upon the next comer. And how they did come, to be sure! There was the Gypsy, the Creature of the Gravel-Pit, the long-legged, long-armed thing from the Long Walk—she could make her arm stretch the whole length like elastic—the enormous Woman of the Haystack, who lived beneath the huge tarpaulin cover, the owner of the Big Cedar, and the owner of the Little Cedar, all treading fast upon one another's heels.

From the Blue Summer-house came the Laugher. Rogers remembered pretending once that he was going to faint. He had thrown himself upon the summer-house floor and kicked, and the blue-eyed girl, instead of being thrilled as both anticipated, had laughed abominably.

'Painters don't kick!' she had said with scorn, while he had answered, though without conviction, 'Men-fainters do—kick dreadfully.' And she had simply laughed till her sides ached, while he lay there kicking till his muscles were sore, in the vain hope of winning her belief.

He exchanged a glance with her now, as the Laugher slipped in past them. The eyes of the Guard were very soft. He was found out and forgiven at the same time.

Then came the very mysterious figure of authority—the Head Gardener, a composite being who included all the lesser under-gardeners as well. His sunburned face presented a resume of them all. He was the man who burned the hills of dead leaves in autumn.

'Give me of your fire, please,' whispered Rogers, something between joy and sadness in his heart, 'for there are hills of leaves that I would burn up quickly—' but the man hurried on, tossing his trowel over the Guard's head, and nearly hitting another passenger who followed too close. This was the Woman of the Haystack, an enormous, spreading traveller who utterly refused to be hurried, and only squeezed through the door because Rogers, the Guard, and several others pushed behind with all their might, while the Sweep, the Tramp, and those already in tugged breathlessly at the same time....

Last of all, just as the train was starting, came a hurrying shadowy thing with dreamy eyes, long hair like waving grass, and open hands that he spread like wings, as though he were sowing something through the air. And he was singing softly as he came fumbling along the byeways of the dusk.

'Oh, but I know *you* well,' cried Rogers, watching him come with a thrill of secret wonder, 'and I love you better than all the rest together.'

The face was hidden as he wafted silently past them. A delicious odour followed him. And something, fine as star-dust, as he scattered it all about him, sifted down before the other's sight. The Dustman entered like a ghost.

'Oh, give me of your dust!' cried Rogers again, 'for there are eyes that I would blind with it—eyes in the world that I would blind with it—your dust of dreams and beauty...!'

The man waved a shadowy hand towards him, and his own eyes filled. He closed the lids a moment; and when he opened them again he saw two monster meteors in the sky. They crossed in two big lines of glory above the house, dropping towards the cedars. The Net of Stars was being fastened. He remembered then his old Star Cave—cave where lost starlight was stored up by these sprites for future use.

He just had time to seize the little hand the Guard held out, and to drop into a seat beside her, when the train began to move. It rose soundlessly with lightning speed. It shot up to a tremendous height, then paused, hovering in the night.

The Guard turned her big blue eyes upon him.

'Where to?' she whispered. And he suddenly remembered that it was always he who decided the destination, and that this time he was at a loss what to say.

'The Star Cave, of course,' he cried, 'the cave where the lost starlight gathers.'

'Which direction?' she asked, with the yellow whistle to her lips ready to signal the driver.

'Oh, out there—to the north-west,' he answered, 'to the mountains of — across the Channel.'

But this was not precise enough. Formerly he had always given very precise directions.

'Name, please,' she urged, 'but quickly. The Interfering Sun, you know—there's no time to lose. We shall be meeting the Morning Spiders soon.'

The Morning Spiders! How it all came back! The Morning Spiders that fly over the fields in the dawn upon their private threads of gossamer and fairy cotton.

He remembered that, as children, they had never actually found this Star Cave, for the Interfering Sun had always come too soon and spoilt it all.

'Name, please, and do hurry up. We can't hover here all night,' rang in his ears.

And he made a plunge. He suddenly thought of Bourcelles, the little village in the Jura mountains, where he and his cousin had spent a year learning French. The idea flashed into him probably because it contained mountains, caves, and children. His cousin lived there now to educate his children and write his books. Only that morning he had got a letter from him.

'Bourcelles, of course, Bourcelles!' he cried, 'and steer for the slopes of Boudry where the forests dip towards the precipices of the Areuse. I'll send word to the children to meet us.'

'Splendid!' cried the Guard, and kissed him with delight. The whistle shrieked, the train turned swiftly in a tremendous sweeping curve, and vanished along the intricate star-rails into space, humming and booming as it went. It flew a mane of stars behind it through the sky.

CHAPTER V

Oh! thou art fairer than the evening air
Clad in the beauty of a thousand stars.
        Doctor Famtus, CHRISTOPHER MARLOWE.

The plop of a water-rat in the pond that occupied the rock-garden in the middle of the lawn brought him back to earth, and the Vicar's invitation to tea flashed across his mind.

'Stock Exchange and typewriters!' he exclaimed, 'how rude he'll think me!' And he rubbed something out of his eyes. He gave one long, yearning glance at the spangled sky where an inquisitive bat darted zigzag several times between himself and the Pleiades, that bunch of star-babies as yet unborn, as the blue-eyed guard used to call them.

'And I shall miss my supper and bed into the bargain!'

He turned reluctantly from his place beside the lime trees, and crossed the lawn now wet with dew. The whole house seemed to turn its hooded head and watch him go, staring with amusement in its many lidless eyes. On the front lawn there was more light, for it faced the dying sunset. The Big and Little Cedar rose from their pools of shadow, beautifully poised. Like stately dowagers in voluminous skirts of velvet they seemed to curtsey to him as he passed. Stars like clusters of sprinkled blossoms hung upon their dignified old heads. The whole place seemed aware of him. Glancing a moment at the upper nursery windows, he could just distinguish the bars through which his little hands once netted stars, and as he did so a meteor shot across the sky its flashing light of wonder. Behind the Little Cedar it dived into the sunset afterglow. And, hardly had it dipped away, when another, coming crosswise from the south, drove its length of molten, shining wire straight against the shoulder of the Big Cedar.

The whole performance seemed arranged expressly for his benefit. The Net was loosed—this Net of Stars and Thoughts—perhaps to go elsewhere. For this was taking out the golden nails, surely. It would hardly have surprised him next to see the Starlight Express he had been dreaming about dart across the heavens overhead. That cool air stealing towards him from the kitchen-garden might well have been the wind of its going. He could almost hear the distant rush and murmur of its flying mass.

'How extraordinarily vivid it all was!' he thought to himself, as he hurried down the drive. 'What detail! What a sense of reality! How carefully I must have *thought* these creatures as a boy! How thoroughly! And what a good idea to go out and see Jack's children at Bourcelles. They've never known these English sprites. I'll introduce 'em!'

He thought it out in detail, very vividly indeed. His imagination lingered over it and gave it singular reality.

Up the road he fairly ran. For Henry Rogers was a punctual man; these last twenty years he had never once been late for anything. It had been part of the exact training he had schooled himself with, and the Vicar's invitation was not one he desired to trifle with. He made his peace, indeed, easily enough, although the excuses sounded a little thin. It was something of a shock, too, to find that the married daughter after all was not the blue-eyed girl of his boyhood's passion. For it was Joan, not May, who came down the gravel path between the roses to greet him.

On the way up he had felt puzzled. Yet 'bemused,' perhaps, is the word that Herbert Minks would have chosen for one of his poems, to describe a state of mind he, however, had never experienced himself. And he would have chosen it instinctively—for onomatopoeic reasons—because it hums and drones and murmurs dreamily. 'Puzzled' was too sharp a word.

Yet Henry Rogers, who felt it, said 'puzzled' without more ado, although mind, imagination, memory all hummed and buzzed pleasantly about his ears even while he did so.

'A dream is a dream,' he reflected as he raced along the familiar dusty road in the twilight, 'and a reverie is a reverie; but that, I'd swear, went a bit further than either one or t'other. It puzzles me. Does vivid thinking, I wonder, make pictures everywhere?... And—can they last?'

For the detailed reality of the experience had been remarkable, and the actuality of those childhood's creations scarcely belonged to dream or reverie. They were certainly quite as real as the sleek Directors who sat round the long Board Room table, fidgeting with fat quill pens and pewter ink-pots; more alive even than the Leading Shareholder who rose so pompously at Annual Meetings to second the resolution that the 'Report and Balance Sheet be adopted without criticism.'

And he was conscious that in himself rose, too, a deep, passionate willingness to accept the whole experience, also 'without criticism.' Those picturesque passengers in the Starlight Express he knew so intimately, so affectionately, that he actually missed them. He felt that he had said good-bye to genuine people. He regretted their departure, and was keenly sorry he had not gone off with them—such a merry, wild, adventurous crew! He must find them again, whatever happened. There was a yearning in him to travel with that blue-eyed guard among the star-fields. He would go out to

Bourcelles and tell the story to the children. He thought very hard indeed about it all.

And now, in the Vicarage drawing-room after dinner, his bemusement increased rather than grew less. His mind had already confused a face and name. The blue-eyed May was not, after all, the girl of his boyhood's dream. His memory had been accurate enough with the passengers in the train. There was no confusion there. But this gentle married woman, who sang to her own accompaniment at her father's request, was not the mischievous, wilful creature who had teased and tortured his heart in years gone by, and had helped him construct the sprites and train and star-trips. It was, surely, the other daughter who had played that delicious role. Yet, either his memory was at fault, or the Vicar had mixed the names up. The years had played this little unimportant trick upon him anyhow. And that was clear.

But if with so-called real people such an error was possible, how could he be sure of anything? Which after all, he asked himself, was real? It was the Vicar's mistake, he learned later, for May was now a teacher in London; but the trivial incident served to point this confusion in his mind between an outer and an inner world—to the disadvantage, if anything, of the former.

And over the glass of port together, while they talked pleasantly of vanished days, Rogers was conscious that a queer, secret amusement sheltered in his heart, due to some faint, superior knowledge that this Past they spoke of had not moved away at all, but listened with fun and laughter just behind his shoulder, watching them. The old gentleman seemed never tired of remembering his escapades. He told them one after another, like some affectionate nurse or mother, Rogers thought, whose children were—to her—unique and wonderful. For he had really loved this good-for-nothing pupil, loved him the more, as mothers and nurses do, because of the trouble he had given, and because of his busy and fertile imagination. It made Rogers feel ridiculously young again as he listened. He could almost have played a trick upon him then and there, merely to justify the tales. And once or twice he actually called him 'Sir.' So that even the conversation helped to deepen this bemusement that gathered somewhat tenderly about his mind. He cracked his walnuts and watched the genial, peace-lit eyes across the table. He chuckled. Both chuckled. They spoke of his worldly success too—it seemed unimportant somehow now, although he was conscious that something in him expected, nay demanded tribute— but the former tutor kept reverting to the earlier days before achievement.

'You were indeed a boy of mischief, wonder, and mystery,' he said, his eyes twinkling and his tone almost affectionate; 'you made the whole place alive with those creatures of your imagination. How Joan helped you too—or was it May? I used to wonder sometimes—' he glanced up rather searchingly at his companion a moment—' whether the people who took the Manor House after your family left did not encounter them sometimes upon the lawn or among the shrubberies in the dusk—those sprites of yours. Eh?' He passed a neatly pared walnut across the table to his guest. 'These ghosts that people nowadays explain scientifically—what are they but thoughts visualised by vivid thinking such as yours was—creative thinking? They may be just pictures created in moments of strong passionate feeling that persist for centuries and reach other minds direct They're not seen with the outer eye; that's certain, for no two people ever see them together. But I'm sure these pictures flame up through the mind sometimes just as clearly as some folk see Grey Ladies and the rest flit down the stairs at midnight.'

They munched their walnuts a moment in silence. Rogers listened very keenly. How curious, he reflected, that the talk should lie this way. But he said nothing, hoping that the other would go on.

'And if you really believed in your things,' the older man continued presently, 'as I am sure you did believe, then your old Dustman and Sweep and Lamplighter, your Woman of the Haystack and your Net of Stars and Star Train—all these, for instance, must still be living, where you left them, waiting perhaps for your return to lead their fresh adventures.'

Rogers stared at him, choking a little over a nut he had swallowed too hurriedly.

'Yet,' mused on the other, 'it's hardly likely the family that succeeded you met them. There were no children!'

'Ah,' exclaimed the pupil impulsively, 'that's significant, yes—no children.' He looked up quickly, questioningly.

'Very, I admit.'

'Besides, the chief Magician had gone away into the City. They wouldn't answer to anybody's call, you know.'

'True again. But the Magician never forgot them quite, I'll be bound,' he added. 'They're only in hiding till his return, perhaps!' And his bright eyes twinkled knowingly.

'But, Vicar, really, you know, that is an extraordinary idea you have there-a wonderful idea. Do you really think—?'

'I only mean,' the other replied more gravely, 'that what a man thinks, and makes with thinking, is the real thing. It's in the heart that sin is first real. The act is the least important end of it— grave only because it is the inevitable result of the thinking. Action is merely delayed thinking, after all.

Don't think ghosts and bogeys, I always say to children, or you'll surely see them.'

'Ah, in *that* sense—!'

'In any sense your mind and intuition can grasp. The thought that leaves your brain, provided it be a real thought strongly fashioned, goes all over the world, and may reach any other brain tuned to its acceptance. *You* should understand that!' he laughed significantly.

'I do,' said Rogers hastily, as though he felt ashamed of himself or were acknowledging a fault in his construing of Homer. 'I understand it perfectly. Only I put all those things—imaginative things—aside when I went into business. I had to concentrate my energies upon making money.'

'You did, yes. Ah!' was the rejoinder, as though he would fain have added, 'And was that wise?'

'And I made it, Vicar; you see, I've made it.' He was not exactly nettled, but he wanted a word of recognition for his success. 'But you know why, don't you?' he added, ashamed the same moment. There was a pause, during which both looked closely at their broken nuts. From one of the men came a sigh.

'Yes,' resumed the older man presently, 'I remember your great dream perfectly well, and a noble one it was too. Its fulfilment now, I suppose, lies well within your reach? You have the means to carry it out, eh? You have indeed been truly blessed.' He eyed him again with uncommon keenness, though a smile ran from the eyes and mouth even up to the forehead and silvery hair. 'The world, I see, has not yet poisoned you. To carry it out as you once explained it to me would be indeed success. If I remember rightly,' he added, 'it was a—er—a Scheme for Disabled—'

Rogers interrupted him quickly. 'And I am full of the same big dream still,' he repeated almost shyly. 'The money I have made I regard as lent to me for investment. I wish to use it, to give it away as one gives flowers. I feel sure—'

He stopped abruptly, caught by the glow of enthusiasm that had leaped into the other's face with a strangely beautiful expression.

'You never did anything by halves, I remember,' the Vicar said, looking at him proudly. 'You were always in earnest, even in your play, and I don't mind telling you that I've often prayed for something of that zeal of yours—that zeal for others. It's a remarkable gift. You will never bury it, will you?' He spoke eagerly, passionately, leaning forward a little across the table. 'Few have it nowadays; it grows rarer with the luxury and self-seeking of the age. It struck me so in you as a boy, that even your sprites worked not for themselves but for others—your Dustman, your Sweep, your absurd Lamplighter, all were busy doing wonderful things to help their neighbours, all, too, without reward.'

Rogers flushed like a boy. But he felt the thrill of his dream course through him like great fires. Wherein was any single thing in the world worth doing, any object of life worth following, unless as means to an end, and that end helping some one else. One's own little personal dreams became exhausted in a few years, endeavours for self smothered beneath the rain of disappointments; but others, and work for others, this was endless and inexhaustible.

'I've sometimes thought,' he heard the older man going on, 'that in the dusk I saw'—his voice lowered and he glanced towards the windows where the rose trees stood like little figures, cloaked and bonneted with beauty beneath the stars—'that I saw your Dustman scattering his golden powder as he came softly up the path, and that some of it reached my own eyes, too; or that your swift Lamplighter lent me a moment his gold-tipped rod of office so that I might light fires of hope in suffering hearts here in this tiny world of my own parish. Your dreadful Head Gardener, too! And your Song of the Blue-Eyes Fairy,' he added slyly, almost mischievously, 'you remember that, I wonder?'

'H'm—a little, yes—something,' replied Rogers confusedly. 'It was a dreadful doggerel. But I've got a secretary now,' he continued hurriedly and in rather a louder voice,' a fellow named Minks, a jewel really of a secretary he is—and he, I believe, can write real—'

'It was charming enough for us all to have remembered it, anyhow,' the Vicar stopped him, smiling at his blushes,' and for May—or was it Joan? dear me, how I do forget names!—to have set it to music. She had a little gift that way, you may remember; and, before she took up teaching she wrote one or two little things like that.'

'Ah, did she really?' murmured the other. He scarcely knew what he was saying, for a mist of blue had risen before his eyes, and in it he was seeing pictures. 'The Spell of Blue, wasn't it, or something like that?' he said a moment later, 'blue, the colour of beauty in flowers, sea, sky, distance—the childhood colour par excellence?'

'But chiefly in the eyes of children, yes,' the Vicar helped him, rising at the same time from the table. 'It was the spell, the passport, the open sesame to most of your adventures. Come now, if you won't have another glass of port, and we'll go into the drawing-room, and Joan, May I mean—no, Joan, of course, shall sing it to you. For this is a very special occasion for us, you know,' he added as they passed across the threshold side by side. 'To see you is to go back with you to Fairyland.'

The piano was being idly strummed as they went in, and the player was easily persuaded to sing the little song. It floated through the open windows and across the lawn as the two men in their corners listened. She knew it by heart, as though she often played it. The candles were not lit. Dusk caught the sound and muted it enchantingly. And somehow the simple melody helped to conceal the meagreness of the childish words. Everywhere, from sky and lawn and solemn trees, the Past came softly in and listened too.

There's a Fairy that hides in the beautiful eyes
Of children who treat her well;
In the little round hole where the eyeball lies
She weaves her magical spell.

Oh, tell it to me,
Oh, how can it be,
This Spell of the Blue-Eyes Fairy.

Well,—the eyes must be blue,
And the heart must be true,
And the child must be *better* than gold;
And then, if you'll let her,
The quicker the better,
She'll make you forget that you're old,
That you're heavy and stupid, and—old!

So, if such a child you should chance to see,
Or with such a child to play,
No matter how weary and dull you be,
Nor how many tons you weigh;
You will suddenly find that you're young again,
And your movements are light and airy,
And you'll try to be solemn and stiff in vain—
It's the Spell of the Blue-Eyes Fairy!

Now I've told it to you,
And you *know* it is true—
It's the Spell of the Blue-Eyes Fairy!

'And it's the same spell,' said the old man in his corner as the last notes died away, and they sat on some minutes longer in the fragrant darkness, 'that you cast about us as a boy, Henry Rogers, when you made that wonderful Net of Stars and fastened it with your comets' nails to the big and little cedars. The one catches your heart, you see, while the other gets your feet and head and arms till you're a hopeless prisoner—a prisoner in Fairyland.'

'Only the world to-day no longer believes in Fairyland,' was the reply, 'and even the children have become scientific. Perhaps it's only buried though. The two ought to run in harness really—opposite interpretations of the universe. One might revive it—here and there perhaps. Without it, all the tenderness seems leaking out of life—'

Joan presently said good-night, but the other two waited on a little longer; and before going to bed they took a turn outside among the flower-beds and fruit-trees that formed the tangled Vicarage garden at the back. It was uncommonly warm for a night in early spring. The lilacs were in bud, and the air most exquisitely scented.

Rogers felt himself swept back wonderfully among his early years. It seemed almost naughty to be out at such an hour instead of asleep in bed. It was quite ridiculous—but he loved the feeling and let himself go with happy willingness. The story of 'Vice Versa,' where a man really became a boy again, passed through his mind and made him laugh.

And the old Vicar kept on feeding the semi-serious mood with what seemed almost intentional sly digs. Yet the digs were not intentional, really; it was merely that his listener, already prepared by his experience with the Starlight Express, read into them these searching meanings of his own. Something in him was deeply moved.

'You might make a great teacher, you know,' suggested his companion, stooping to sniff a lilac branch as they paused a moment. 'I thought so years ago; I think so still. You've kept yourself so simple.'

'How not to do most things,' laughed the other, glad of the darkness.

'How to do the big and simple things,' was the rejoinder; 'and do them well, without applause. You have Belief.'

'Too much, perhaps. I simply can't get rid of it.'

'Don't try to. It's belief that moves the world; people want teachers —that's my experience in the pulpit and the parish; a world in miniature, after all— but they won't listen to a teacher who hasn't got it. There are no great poets to-day, only great discoverers. The poets, the interpreters of discovery, are gone—starved out of life by ridicule, and by questions to which exact answers are impossible. With your imagination and belief you might help a world far larger than this parish of mine at any rate. I envy you.'

Goodness! how the kind eyes searched his own in this darkness. Though little susceptible to flattery, he was aware of something huge the words stirred in the depths of him, something far bigger than he yet had dreamed of even in his boyhood, something that made his cherished Scheme seem a little pale and faded.

'Take the whole world with you into fairyland,' he heard the low voice come murmuring in his ear across the lilacs. And there was starlight in it—that gentle, steady brilliance that steals into people while they sleep and dream, tracing patterns of glory they may recognise when they wake, yet marvelling whence it came. 'The world wants its fairyland back again, and won't be happy till it gets it.'

A bird listening to them in the stillness sang a little burst of song, then paused again to listen.

'Once give them of your magic, and each may shape his fairyland as he chooses...' the musical voice ran on.

The flowers seemed alive and walking. This was a voice of beauty. Some lilac bud was singing in its sleep. Sirius had dropped a ray across its lips of blue and coaxed it out to dance. There was a murmur and a stir among the fruit-trees too. The apple blossoms painted the darkness with their tiny fluttering dresses, while old Aldebaran trimmed them silently with gold, and partners from the Milky Way swept rustling down to lead the violets out. Oh, there was revelry to-night, and the fairy spell of the blue-eyed Spring was irresistible....

'But the world will never dance,' he whispered sadly, half to himself perhaps; 'it's far too weary.'

'It will follow a leader,' came the soft reply, 'who dances well and pipes the true old music so that it can hear. Belief inspires it always. And that Belief you have.' There was a curious vibration in his voice; he spoke from his heart, and his heart was evidently moved.

'I wonder when it came to me, then, and how?'

The Vicar turned and faced him where they stood beneath the lime trees. Their scent was pouring out as from phials uncorked by the stars.

'It came,' he caught the answer that thrilled with earnestness, 'when you saw the lame boy on the village hill and cried. As long ago as that it came.'

His mind, as he listened, became a plot of fresh-turned earth the Head Gardener filled with flowers. A mass of covering stuff the years had laid ever thicker and thicker was being shovelled away. The flowers he saw being planted there were very tiny ones. But they would grow. A leaf from some far-off rocky mount of olive trees dropped fluttering through the air and marvellously took root and grew. He felt for a moment the breath of night air that has been tamed by an eastern sun. He saw a group of men, bare-headed, standing on the slopes, and in front of them a figure of glory teaching little, simple things they found it hard to understand....

'You have the big and simple things alive in you,' the voice carried on his pictured thought among the flowers. 'In your heart they lie all waiting to be used. Nothing can smother them. Only-you must give them out.'

'If only I knew how—!'

'Keep close to the children,' sifted the strange answer through the fruit-trees; 'the world is a big child. And catch it when it lies asleep—not thinking of itself,' he whispered.

'The time is so short—'

'At forty you stand upon the threshold of life, with values learned and rubbish cleared away. So many by that time are already dead—in heart. I envy your opportunities ahead. You have learned already one foundation truth—the grandeur of toil and the insignificance of acquisition. The other foundation thing is even simpler—you have a neighbour. Now, with your money to give as flowers, and your Belief to steer you straight, you have the world before you. And—keep close to the children.'

'Before there are none left,' added Rogers under his breath. But the other heard the words and instantly corrected him—

'Children of any age, and wherever you may find them.'

And they turned slowly and made their way in silence across the soaking lawn, entering the house by the drawing-room window.

'Good-night,' the old man said, as he lit his candle and led him to his room; 'and pleasant, happy, inspiring dreams.'

He seemed to say it with some curious, heartfelt meaning in the common words. He disappeared slowly down the passage, shading the candle with one hand to pick his way, and Rogers watched him out of sight, then turned and entered his own room, closing the door as softly as possible behind him.

It had been an astonishing conversation. All his old enthusiasm was stirred. Embers leaped to flame. No woman ever had done as much. This old fellow, once merely respected tutor, had given him back his first original fire and zeal, yet somehow cleansed and purified. And it humbled him at the same time. Dead leaves, dropped year by year in his City life, were cleared away as though a mighty wind had swept him. The Gardener was burning up dead leaves; the Sweep was cleaning out the flues; the Lamplighter waving his golden signal in the sky—far ahead, it is true, but gleaming like a torch and beacon. The Starlight Express was travelling at top speed among the constellations. He stood at the beginning of the important part of life....

And now, as he lay in bed and heard the owls hooting in the woods, and smelt the flowers through the open window, his thoughts followed strongly after that old Star Train that he used to drive about the sky. He was both engine-driver and passenger. He fell asleep to dream of it.

And all the vital and enchanting thoughts of his boyhood flowed back upon him with a rush, as though they had never been laid aside. He remembered particularly one singular thing about them—that they had never seemed quite his own, but that he had either read or heard them somewhere else. As a child the feeling was always strong that these 'jolly thoughts,' as he called them, were put into him by some one else—some one who whispered to him—some one who lived close behind his ears. He had to listen very hard to catch them. It was *not* dreams, yet all night long, especially when he slept tightly, as he phrased it, this fairy whispering continued, and in the daytime he remembered what he could and made up his stories accordingly. He stole these ideas about a Star Net and a Starlight Express. One day he would be caught and punished for it. It was trespassing upon the preserves of some one else.

Yet he could never discover who this some one else was, except that it was a 'she' and lived among the stars, only coming out at night. He imagined she hid behind that little dusty constellation called the Pleiades, and that was why the Pleiades wore a veil and were so dim— lest he should find her out. And once, behind the blue gaze of the guard-girl, who was out of his heart by this time, he had known a moment of thrilling wonder that was close to awe. He saw another pair of eyes gazing out at him They were ambery eyes, as he called them— just what was to be expected from a star. And, so great was the shock, that at first he stood dead still and gasped, then dashed up suddenly close to her and stared into her face, frightening her so much that she fell backwards, and the amber eyes vanished instantly. It was the 'some one else' who whispered fairy stories to him and lived behind his ear. For a second she had been marvellously close. And he had lost her!

From that moment, however, his belief in her increased enormously, and he never saw a pair of brown-ambery eyes without feeling sure that she was somewhere close about him. The lame boy, for instance, had the same delicate tint in his sad, long, questioning gaze. His own collie had it too! For years it was an obsession with him, haunting and wonderful—the knowledge that some one who watched close beside him, filling his mind with fairy thoughts, might any moment gaze into his face through a pair of ordinary familiar eyes. And he was certain that all his star-imagination about the Net, the Starlight Express, and the Cave of Lost Starlight came first into him from this hidden 'some one else' who brought the Milky Way down into his boy's world of fantasy.

'If ever I meet her in real life,' he used to say, 'I'm done for. She is my Star Princess!'

And now, as he fell asleep, the old atmosphere of that Kentish garden drew thickly over him, shaking out clusters of stars about his bed. Dreams usually are determined by something more remote than the talk that has just preceded going to bed, but to-night it was otherwise. And two things the old Vicar had let fall—two things sufficiently singular, it seemed, when he came to think about them—influenced his night adventures. 'Catch the world when it's asleep,' and 'Keep close to the children'—these somehow indicated the route his dream should follow. For he headed the great engine straight for the village in the Jura pine woods where his cousin's children lived. He did not know these children, and had seen his cousin but rarely in recent years; yet, it seemed, they came to meet the train up among the mountain forests somewhere. For in this village, where he had gone to study French, the moods of his own childhood had somehow known continuation and development. The place had once been very dear to him, and he had known delightful adventures there, many of them with this cousin. Now he took all his own childhood's sprites out in this Starlight Express and introduced them to these transplanted children who had never made acquaintance with the English breed. They had surprising, wild adventures all together, yet in the morning he could remember very little of it all. The interfering sun melted them all down in dew. The adventures had some object, however; that was clear; though what the object was, except that it did good somewhere to. some one, was gone, lost in the deeps of sleep behind him. They scurried about the world. The sprites were very active indeed—quite fussily energetic. And his Scheme for Disabled Something-or other was not anywhere discoverable in these escapades. That seemed forgotten rather, as though they found bigger, more important things to do, and nearer home too. Perhaps the Vicar's hint about the 'Neighbour' was responsible for that. Anyhow, the dream was very vivid, even though the morning sun melted it away so quickly and completely. It seemed continuous too. It filled the entire night.

Yet the thing that Rogers took off with him to town next morning was, more than any other detail, the memory of what the old tutor had said about the living reality and persistence of figures that passionate thinking has created—that, and the value of Belief.

CHAPTER VI

Be thou my star, and thou in me be seen
To show what source divine is, and prevails.
I mark thee planting joy in constant fire.
      To Sirius, G. MEREDITH.

And he rather astonished the imperturbable Minks next day by the announcement that he was thinking of going abroad for a little holiday. 'When I return, it will be time enough to take up the Scheme in earnest,' he said. For Minks had brought a sheaf of notes embodying the results of many hours' labour, showing what others had already done in that particular line of philanthropy.

'Very good indeed, Minks, very good. I'll take 'em with me and make a careful study of the lot. I shall be only gone a week or so,' he added, noticing the other's disappointment. For the secretary had hoped to expound these notes himself at length. 'Take a week's holiday yourself,' he added. 'Mrs. Minks might like to get to the sea, perhaps. There'll only be my letters to forward. I'll give you a little cheque.' And he explained briefly that he was going out to Bourcelles to enjoy a few days' rest before they attacked great problems together. After so many years of application to business he had earned it. Crayfield, it seemed, had given him a taste for sentimental journeys. But the fact was, too, the Tramp, the Dustman, the Lamplighter, and the Starlight Express were all in his thoughts still.

And it was spring. He felt this sudden desire to see his cousin again, and make the acquaintance of his cousin's children. He remembered how the two of them had tramped the Jura forests as boys. They had met in London at intervals since. He dictated a letter to him then and there —Minks taking it down like lightning—and added a postscript in his own handwriting:—

'I feel a longing,' he wrote, 'to come out and see the little haven of rest you have chosen, and to know your children. Our ways have gone very far apart—too far—since the old days when we climbed out of the windows of *la cure* with a sheet, and tramped the mountains all night long. Do you remember? I've had my nose on the grindstone ever since, and you've worked hard too, judging by your name in publishers' lists. I hope your books are a great success. I'm ashamed I've never any time to read now. But I'm "retired" from business at last and hope to do great things. I'll tell you about a great Scheme I have in hand when we meet. I should like your advice too.

'Any room will do—sunny aspect if possible. And please give my love to your children in advance. Tell them I shall come out in the Starlight Express. Let me have a line to say if it's all right.'

In due course the line—a warm-hearted one—arrived. Minks came to Charing Cross to see him off, the gleam of the sea already in his pale-blue eyes.

'The Weather Report says "calm," Mr. Rogers,' he kept repeating. 'You'll have a good crossing, I hope and trust. I'm taking Mrs. Minks myself—'

'Yes, yes, that's good,' was the quick reply. 'Capital. And—let me see-I've got your notes with me, haven't I? I'll draft out a general plan and send it to you as soon as I get a moment. You think over it too, will you, while I'm away. And enjoy yourself at the same time. Put your children in the sea—nothing like the sea for children—sea and sun and sand and all that sort of thing.'

'Thank you very much, Mr. Rogers, and I trust—'

Somebody bumped against him, cutting short a carefully balanced sentence that was intended to be one-third good wishes, one-third weather remark, and the last third Mrs. Minks. Her letter of thanks had never been referred to. It rankled, though very slightly.

'What an absurd-looking person!' exclaimed the secretary to himself, following the aggressor with one eye, and trying to recapture the lost sentence at the same time. 'They really should not allow such people in a railway terminus,' he added aloud. The man was ragged and unkempt to the last degree—a sort of tramp; and as he bought a ticket at the third-class wicket, just beyond, he kept looking up slyly at Minks and his companion. 'The way he knocked against me almost seemed intentional,' Minks thought. The idea of pickpockets and cleverly disguised detectives ran confusedly in his mind. He felt a little flustered for some reason.

'I beg your pardon,' Mr. Rogers was saying to a man who tried to push in front of him. 'But we *must* each take our turn, you know.' The throng of people was considerable. This man looked like a dustman. He, too, was eagerly buying a ticket, but had evidently mistaken the window. 'Third-class is lower down I think,' Mr. Rogers suggested with a touch of authority.

'What a lot of foreigners there are about,' remarked Minks. 'These stations are full of suspicious characters.' The notice about loitering flashed across him.

He took the ticket Mr. Rogers handed to him, and went off to register the luggage, and when later he joined his chief at the carriage door he saw him talking to a couple of strangers who seemed anxious to get in.

'I took *this* corner seat for you, Mr. Rogers,' he explained, both to prove his careful forethought and to let the strangers know that his master was a person of some importance. They were such an extraordinary couple too! Had there been hop-pickers about he could have understood it. They were almost figures of masquerade; for while one resembled more than anything else a chimney-sweep who had forgotten to wash his face below the level of the eyes, the other carried a dirty sack across his shoulders, which apparently he had just been trying to squeeze into the rack.

They moved off when they saw Minks, but the man with the sack made a gesture with one hand, as though he scattered something into the carriage through the open door.

The secretary threw a reproachful look at a passing guard, but there was nothing he could do. People with tickets had a right to travel. Still, he resented these crowding, pushing folk. 'I'm sorry, Mr. Rogers,' he said, as though he had chosen a poor train for his honoured chief; 'there must be an excursion somewhere. There's a big fete of Vegetarians, I know, at Surbiton to-day, but I can hardly think these people——'

'Don't wait, Minks,' said the other, who had taken his seat. 'I'll let you hear from me, you know, about the Scheme and—other things. Don't wait.' He seemed curiously unobservant of these strange folk, almost absent-minded.

The guard was whistling. Minks shut the door and gave the travelling- rug a last tuck-in about his feet. He felt as though he were packing off a child. The mother in him became active. Mr. Rogers needed looking after. Another minute and he would have patted him and told him what to eat and wear. But instead he raised his hat and smiled. The train moved slowly out, making a deep purring sound like flowing water. The platform had magically thinned. Officials stood lonely among the scattered wavers of hats and handkerchiefs. As he stepped backwards to keep the carriage window in sight until the last possible moment, Minks was nearly knocked over by a man who hurried along the platform as if he still had hopes of catching the train.

'Really, sir!' gasped the secretary, stooping to pick up his newspaper and lavender glove—he wore one glove and carried the other—the collision had sent flying. But the man was already far beyond the reach of his voice. 'He must be an escaped lamplighter, or something,' he laughed good-naturedly, as he saw the long legs vanish down the platform. He leaped on to the line. Evidently he was a railway employe. He seemed to be vainly trying to catch the departing buffers. An absurd and reckless fellow, thought Minks.

But what caught the secretary's attention last, and made him wonder a little if anything unusual was happening to the world, was the curious fact that, as the last carriage glided smoothly past, he recognised four figures seated comfortably inside. Their feet were on the cushions—disgracefully. They were talking together, heads forward, laughing, even—singing. And he could have sworn that they were the two men who had watched himself and Mr. Rogers at the ticket window, and the strangers who had tried to force their way into Mr. Rogers's carriage when he came up just in time to interfere.

'They got in somehow after all, then,' he said to himself. 'Of course, I had forgotten. The Company runs third-class carriages on the continental trains now. Odd!' He mentally rubbed his eyes.

The train swept round the corner out of sight, leaving a streaming cloud of smoke and sparks behind it. It went out with a kind of rush of delight, glad to be off, and conscious of its passengers' pleasure.

'Odd.' This was the word that filled his mind as he walked home. 'Perhaps—our minds are in such intimate sympathy together—perhaps he was thinking of—of that kind of thing—er—and some of his thoughts got into my own imagination. Odd, though, very, *very* odd.'

He had once read somewhere in one of his new-fangled books that 'thoughts are things.' It had made a great impression on him. He had read about Marconi too. Later he made a more thorough study of this 'thinking business.'

And soon afterwards, having put his chief's papers in order at the flat, he went home to Mrs. Minks and the children with this other thought—that he had possibly been overworking himself, and that it was a good thing he was going to have a holiday by the sea.

He liked to picture himself as an original thinker, not afraid of new ideas, but in reality he preferred his world sober, ordinary, logical. It was merely big-sounding names he liked. And this little incident was somewhere out of joint. It was—odd.

    Success that poisons many a baser mind
    May lift——

But the sonnet had never known completion. In the space it had occupied in his mind another one abruptly sprouted. The first subject after all was banal. A better one had come to him—

    Strong thoughts that rise in a creative mind
    May flash about the world, and carry joy——

- 46 -

Then it stuck. He changed 'may' to 'shall,' but a moment later decided that 'do' was better, truer than either. After that inspiration failed him. He retired gracefully upon prose again.

'Odd,' he thought, 'very odd!'

And he relieved his mind by writing a letter to a newspaper. He did not send it in the end, for his better judgment prevented, but he had to do something by way of protest, and the only alternative was to tell his wife about it, when she would look half puzzled, half pained, and probably reply with some remark about the general cost of living. So he wrote the letter instead.

For Herbert Minks regarded himself as a man with the larger view of citizenship, a critic of public affairs, and, in a measure, therefore, an item of that public opinion which moulded governments. Hence he had a finger, though but a little finger, in the destiny of nations and in the polity—a grand word that!—of national councils. He wrote frequent letters, thus, to the lesser weekly journals; these letters were sometimes printed; occasionally—oh, joy!—they were answered by others like himself, who referred to him as 'your esteemed correspondent.' As yet, however, his following letter had never got into print, nor had he experienced the importance of that editorial decision, appended between square brackets: 'This correspondence must now cease'—so vital, that is, that the editor and the entire office staff might change their opinions unless it *did* cease.

Having drafted his letter, therefore, and carried it about with him for several hours in his breast pocket, he finally decided not to send it after all, for the explanation of his 'odd' experience, he well knew, was hardly one that a newspaper office could supply, or that public correspondence could illuminate. His better judgment always won the day in the end. Thinking *was* creative, after all.

CHAPTER VII

> ... The sun,
> Closing his benediction,
> Sinks, and the darkening air
> Thrills with a sense of the triumphing night-
> Night with her train of stars
> And her great gift of sleep.
>   W. E. HENLEY.

In a southern-facing room on the first floor of La Citadelle the English family sat after tea. The father, a spare, mild-eyed man, his thatch of brown hair well sprinkled with grey above the temples, was lighting his pipe for the tenth time-the tenth match, but the same pipeful of tobacco; and his wife, an ample, motherly woman, slightly younger than himself, was knitting on the other side of the open fireplace, in which still glowed a mass of peat ashes. From time to time she stirred them with a rickety pair of tongs, or with her foot kicked into the grate the matches he invariably threw short upon the floor. But these were adventures ill-suited to her. Knitting was her natural talent. She was always knitting.

By the open window stood two children, a boy and a girl of ten and twelve respectively, gazing out into the sunshine. It was the end of April, and though the sun was already hot, there was a sharpness in the air that told of snow still lying on the mountain heights behind the village. Across vineyard slopes and patches of agricultural land, the Lake of Neuchatel lay blue as a southern sea, while beyond it, in a line of white that the sunset soon would turn to pink and gold, stretched the whole range of Alps, from Mont Blanc to where the Eiger and the Weisshorn signalled in the east. They filled the entire horizon, already cloud-like in the haze of coming summer.

The door into the corridor opened, and a taller child came in. A mass of dark hair, caught by a big red bow, tumbled untidily down her back. She was sixteen and very earnest, but her eyes, brown like her father's, held a curious puzzled look, as though life still confused her so much that while she did her duties bravely she did not quite understand why it should be so.

'Excuse me, Mother, shall I wash up?' she said at once. She always did wash up. And 'excuse me' usually prefaced her questions.

'Please, Jane Anne,' said Mother. The entire family called her Jane Anne, although her baptismal names were rather fine. Sometimes she answered, too, to Jinny, but when it was a question of household duties it was Jane Anne, or even 'Ria.'

She set about her duties promptly, though not with any special deftness. And first she stooped and picked up the last match her father had dropped upon the strip of carpet that covered the linoleum.

'Daddy,' she said reprovingly, 'you do make such a mess.' She brushed tobacco ashes from his coat. Mother, without looking up, went on talking to him about the bills-washing, school-books, boots, blouses, oil, and peat. And as she did so a puzzled expression was visible in his eyes akin to the expression in Jane Anne's. Both enjoyed a similar mental confusion sometimes as to words and meanings and the import of practical life generally.

'We shan't want any more now, thank goodness,' he said vaguely, referring to the peat, though Mother was already far ahead, wading among boots and shirts and blouses.

'But if we get a load in now, you see, it's *cheaper*,' she said with emphasis on every alternate word, slowing up the pace to suit him.

'Mother, where *did* you put the washing-up rag?' came the voice of Jinny in plaintive accents from the tiny kitchen that lay beyond the adjoining bedroom. 'I can't find it anywhere,' she added, poking her head round the door suddenly.

'Pet lamb,' was Mother's answer, still bending over her knitting-she was prodigal of terms like this and applied them indiscriminately, for Jane Anne resembled the animal in question even less than did her father—'I saw it last on the geranium shelf—you know, where the fuchsias and the-' She hesitated, she was not sure herself. 'I'll get it, my duckie, for you,' she added, and began to rise. She was a voluminous, very stately woman. The operation took time.

'Let me,' said Daddy, drawing his mind with difficulty from the peat, and rising too. They rose together.

'It's all right, I've got it,' cried the child, who had disappeared again. 'It was in the sink. That's Jimbo; he washed up yesterday.'

'Pas vrai!' piped a little voice beside the open window, overhearing his name, 'because I only dried. It was Monkey who washed up.' They talked French and English all mixed up together.

But Monkey was too busy looking at the Alps through an old pair of opera-glasses, relic of her father's London days that served for telescope, to think reply worth while. Her baptismal names were also rather wonderful, though neither of her parents could have supplied them without a moment's reflection first. There was commotion by that window for a moment but it soon subsided again, for things that Jinny said never provoked dissension, and Jimbo and Monkey just then were busy with a Magic Horse who had wings of snow, and was making fearful leaps from the peaks of the Dent du Midi across the Blumlisalp to the Jungfrau.

'Will you please carry the samovar for me?' exclaimed Jane Anne, addressing both her parents, as though uncertain which of them would help her. 'You filled it so awfully full to-day, I can't lift it. I advertise for help.'

Her father slowly rose. 'I'll do it, child,' he said kindly, but with a patience, almost resignation, in his tone suggesting that it was absurd to expect such a thing of him. 'Then do exactly as you think best,' he let fall to his wife as he went, referring to the chaos of expenses she had been discussing with him. 'That'll be all right.' For his mind had not yet sorted the jumble of peat, oil, boots, school- books, and the rest. 'We can manage THAT at any rate; you see it's francs, not shillings,' he added, as Jane Anne pulled him by the sleeve towards the steaming samovar. He held the strings of an ever empty purse.

'Daddy, but you've *always* got a crumb in your beard,' she was saying, 'and if it isn't a crumb, it's ashes on your coat or a match on the floor.' She brushed the crumb away. He gave her a kiss. And between them they nearly upset the old nickel-plated samovar that was a present from a Tiflis Armenian to whom the mother once taught English. They looked round anxiously as though afraid of a scolding; but Mother had not noticed. And she was accustomed to the noise and laughter. The scene then finished, as it usually did, by the mother washing up, Jane Anne drying, and Daddy hovering to and fro in the background making remarks in his beard about the geraniums, the China tea, the indigestible new bread, the outrageous cost of the necessaries of life, or the book he was at work on at the moment. He often enough gave his uncertain assistance in the little menial duties connected with the preparation or removal of the tea-things, and had even been known to dry. Only washing-up he never did. Somehow his vocation rendered him immune from that. He might bring the peat in, fill the lamps, arrange and dust the scanty furniture, but washing-up was not a possibility even. As an author it was considered beneath his dignity altogether, almost improper—it would have shocked the children. Mother could do anything; it was right and natural that she should—poor soul I But Daddy's profession set him in an enclosure apart, and there were certain things in this servantless menage he could not have done without disgracing the entire family. Washing-up was one; carrying back the empty basket of tea-things to the Pension was another. Daddy wrote books. As Jane Anne put it forcibly and finally once, 'Shakespeare never washed up or carried a tea-basket in the street!'—which the others accepted as a conclusive statement of authority.

And, meantime, the two younger children, who knew how to amuse each other for hours together unaided, had left the Magic Horse in its stables for the night—an enormous snow-drift—and were sitting side by side upon the sofa conning a number of *Punch* some English aunt had sent them. The girl read out the jokes, and her brother pointed with a very dirty finger to the pictures. None of the jokes were seized by either, but Jimbo announced each one with, 'Oh! I say!' and their faces were grave and sometimes awed; and when Jimbo asked, 'But what does THAT mean?' his sister would answer, 'Don't you see, I suppose the cabman meant—' finishing with some explanation very far from truth, whereupon Jimbo, accepting it doubtfully, said nothing, and they turned another page with keen anticipation. They never appealed for outside aid, but enjoyed it in their own dark, mysterious way. And, presently, when the washing-up was finished, and the dusk began to dim the landscape and conceal the ghostly-looking Alps, they retired to the inner bedroom—for this was Saturday and there were no school tasks to be prepared—and there, seated on the big bed in the corner, they opened a book of *cantiques* used in school, and sang one hymn and song after another, interrupting one another with jokes and laughter and French and English sentences oddly mixed together. Jimbo sang the tune, and Monkey the alto. It was by no means unpleasant to listen to. And, upon the whole, it was a very grave business altogether, graver even than their attitude to "Punch." Jane Anne considered it a foolish waste of time, but she never actually said so. She smiled her grave smile and went her own puzzled way alone.

Usually at this hour the Den presented a very different appearance, the children, with slates and *cahiers*, working laboriously round the table, Jane Anne and mother knitting or mending furiously, Mere Riquette, the old cat, asleep before the fire, and a general schoolroom air pervading the place. The father, too, tea once finished, would depart for the little room he slept in and used as work-place over at the carpenter's house among the vineyards. He kept his books there, his rows of pipes and towering little heap of half- filled match-boxes, and there he wrote his clever studies that yet were unproductive of much gold and brought him little more than pleasant notices and occasional letters from enthusiastic strangers. It seemed very unremunerative labour indeed, and the family had done well to migrate from Essex into Switzerland, where, besides the excellent schools which cost barely two pounds annually per head, the children learned the language and enjoyed the air of forest and mountain into the bargain. Life, for all that, was a severe problem to them, and the difficulty of making both ends come in sight of each other, let alone meeting, was an ever-present one. That they jogged along so well was due more than the others realised to the untiring and selfless zeal of the Irish mother, a plucky, practical woman, and a noble one if ever such existed on this earth. The way she contrived would fill a book; her economies, so clever they hardly betrayed themselves, would supply a comic annual with material for years, though their comedy involved a pathos of self-denial and sleepless nights that only those similarly placed could have divined. Herself a silent, even inarticulate, woman, she never spoke of them, least of all to her husband, whose mind it was her brave desire to keep free from unnecessary worries for his work. His studies she did not understand, but his stories she read aloud with patient resignation to the children. She marked the place when the reading was interrupted with a crimson paper-knife, and often Jimbo would move it several pages farther on without any of them discovering the gap. Jane Anne, however, who made no pretence of listening to 'Daddy's muddle-stories,' was beginning to realise what went on in Mother's mind underground. She hardly seized the pathos, but she saw and understood enough to help. And she was in many ways a little second edition—a phrase the muddle-stories never knew, alas!—of her mother, with the same unselfishness that held a touch of grandeur, the same clever domestic instinct for contrivance, and the same careful ways that yet sat ill upon a boundless generosity of heart beneath. She loved to be thought older than she was, and she used the longest, biggest, grandest words she could possibly invent or find.

And the village life suited them all in all respects, for, while there was no degrading poverty anywhere, all the inhabitants, from the pasteur to the carpenter, knew the exact value of a centime; there was no question of keeping up impossible appearances, but a general frankness with regard to the fundamental values of clothing, food, and education that all shared alike and made no pretence about. Any faintest sign of snobbery, for instance, would have been drummed out of the little mountain hamlet at once by Gygi, the gendarme, who spent more time in his fields and vineyards than in his uniform. And, while every one knew that a title and large estates were a not impossible future for the famille anglaise, it made no slightest difference in the treatment of them, and indeed hardly lent them the flavour of a faintest cachet. They were the English family in La Citadelle, and that was all there was about it.

The peasants, however, rather pitied the hard-working author who 'had to write all those books,' than paid him honourable tribute for his work. It seemed so unnecessary. Vineyards produced wine a man could drink and pay for, but books——! Well, results spoke for themselves, and no one who lived in La Citadelle was millionaire.

Yet the reputation of John Frederic Campden stood high enough, for all his meagre earnings, and he was an ineffective author chiefly, perhaps, because he missed his audience. Somewhere, somehow, he fell between two stools. And his chagrin was undeniable; for though the poet's heart in him kept all its splendid fires alight, his failure chilled a little the intellect that should fashion them along effective moulds. Now, with advancing years, the increasing cost of the children's growing-up, and the failing of his wife's health a little, the burdens of life were heavier than he cared to think about.

But this evening, as the group sat round the wide peat fire, cheerful and jolly in the lamplight, there was certainly no sign of sadness. They were like a party of children in which the grave humour of the ever-knitting mother kept the balance true between fun and foolishness.

'Please, Daddy, a story at once,' Jane Anne demanded, 'but a told one, not a read-aloud one. I like a romantic effort best.'

He fumbled in his pocket for a light, and Jimbo gravely produced a box he had secretly filled with matches already used, collected laboriously from the floor during the week. Then Monkey, full of mischief, came over from the window where she had been watching them with gasps of astonishment no one had heeded through the small end of the opera-glasses. There was a dancing brilliance in her movements, and her eyes, brown like her mother's, sparkled with fun and wickedness. Taking the knee Jimbo left unoccupied, and waiting till the diversion caused by the match-box had subsided, she solemnly placed a bread-crumb in his rather tangled beard.

'Now you're full-dress,' she said, falling instantly so close against him that he could not tickle her, while Mother glanced up a second uncertain whether to criticise the impertinence or let it pass. She let it pass. None of the children had the faintest idea what it meant to be afraid of their father.

'People who waste bread,' he began, 'end by getting so thin themselves that they double up like paper and disappear.'

'But *how* thin, Daddy?' asked Jane Anne, ever literal to the death. 'And is it romantic or just silly?'

He was puzzled for a moment what to reply.

'He doesn't know. He's making up,' piped Jimbo.

'I *do* know,' came the belated explanation, as he put the crumb into the bowl of his extinguished pipe with a solemnity that delighted them, but puzzled Jane Anne, who suggested it would taste 'like toast smelt.' 'People who take bread that doesn't belong to them end by having no dinner——'

'But that isn't anything about thinness,' interrupted Jinny, still uncomforted. Some one wasted by love was in her mind perhaps.

'It is, child, because they get so frightfully thin,' he went on, 'that they end by getting thinner than the thin end of a wedge.'

The eyes of Mother twinkled, but the children still stared, waiting. They had never heard of this phrase about the wedge. Indeed Jane Anne shared with Jimbo total ignorance of the word at all. Like the audience who read his books, or rather ought to have read them, they expected something different, yet still hoped.

'It's a rhyme, and not a story though,' he added, anticipating perhaps their possible disappointment. For the recent talk about expenses had chilled his imagination too much for an instantaneous story, whereas rhymes came ever to him easily.

'All right! Let's have it anyhow,' came the verdict in sentences of French and English. And in the breathless pause that followed, even Mother looking up expectantly from her busy fingers, was heard this strange fate of the Thin Child who stole another's bread-crumb:—

He then grew thinner than the thin,
The thin end of the wedge;
He grew so pitifully thin
It set his teeth on edge;
But the edge it set his teeth upon
Was worse than getting thinner,
For it was the edge of appetite,
And his teeth were in no dinner!

There was a deep silence. Mother looked as though she expected more,— the good part yet to come. The rhyme fell flat as a pancake, for of course the children did not understand it. Its nonsense, clever enough, escaped them. True nonsense is for grown-ups only. Jane Anne stared steadily at him with a puzzled frown. Her face wore an expression like a moth.

'Thank you, Daddy, *very* much,' she said, certain as ever that the fault if any was her own, since all that Daddy said and did was simply splendid. Whereupon the others fairly screamed with delight, turning attention thereby from the dismal failure.

'She doesn't understand it, but she's always so polite!' cried Monkey.

Her mother quickly intervened. 'Never mind, Jane Anne,' she soothed her, lest her feelings should be ruffled; 'you shall never want a dinner, lovey; and when all Monkey's teeth are gone you'll still be able to munch away at something.'

But Jinny's feelings were never ruffled exactly, only confused and puzzled. She was puzzled now. Her confidence in her father's splendour was unshakable.

'And, anyhow, Mother, you'll never be a thin wedge,' she answered, meaning to show her gratitude by a compliment. She joined herself as loudly as anybody in the roar that followed this sally. Obviously, she had said a clever and amusing thing, though it was not clear to her why it was so. Her flushed face was very happy; it even wore a touch of proud superiority. Her talents were domestic rather than intellectual.

'Excuse me, Daddy,' she said gravely, in a pause that followed presently. 'But what is a wedge, exactly? And I think I'd like to copy that poetry in my book, please.' For she kept a book in which his efforts were neatly inscribed in a round copy-book handwriting, and called by Monkey 'The Muddle Book.' There his unappreciated doggerels found fame, though misunderstood most of all by the affectionate child who copied them so proudly.

The book was brought at once. Her father wrote out the nonsense verse on his knee and made a funny little illustration in the margin. 'Oh, I say!' said Jimbo, watching him, while Monkey, lapsing into French, contributed with her usual impudence, 'Pas tant mal!' They all loved the illustrations.

The general interest, then, as the way is with children, puppies, and other young Inconsistencies, centred upon the contents of the book. They eagerly turned the pages, as though they did not know its contents by heart already. They praised for the hundredth time the drawing of the Muddle Animal who

Hung its hopes upon a nail
Or laid them on the shelf;
Then pricked its conscience with its tail,
And sat upon itself.

They looked also with considerable approval upon the drawings and descriptions of the Muddle Man whose manners towards the rest of the world were cool; because

He saw things with his naked eye,
That's why his glance was chilly.

But the explanation of the disasters he caused everywhere by his disagreeable sharpness of speech and behaviour did *not* amuse them. They observed as usual that it was 'too impossible'; the drawings, moreover, did not quite convince:—

So cutting was his speaking tone
Each phrase snipped off a button,
So sharp his words, they have been known
To carve a leg of mutton;
He shaved himself with sentences,
And when he went to dances,
He made—Oh shocking tendencies!-
Deep holes with piercing glances.

But on the last page the Muddle Man behaved so badly, was so positively indecent in his conduct, that he was persuaded to disappear altogether; and his manner of extinguishing himself in the illustration delighted the children far more than the verse whose fun again escaped them:—

They observed he was indecent,
But he said it wasn't true,
For *he* pronounced it 'in descent'—
Then disappeared from view!

Mother's alleged 'second sight' was also attributed to the fact that she 'looked twice before she leaped'—and the drawing of that leap never failed to produce high spirits. For her calm and steady way of walking—sailing— had earned her the name of the frigate—and this was also illustrated, with various winds, all coloured, driving her along.

The time passed happily; some one turned the lamp out, and Daddy, regardless of expense—he had been grumbling about it ten minutes before—heaped on the bricks of peat. Riquette, a bit of movable furniture without which the room seemed incomplete, deftly slipped in between the circle of legs and feet, and curled up upon Jinny's lap. Her snoring, a wheezy noise that made Jimbo wonder 'why it didn't scrape her,' was as familiar as the ticking of the clock. Old Mere Riquette knew her rights. And she exacted them. Jinny's lap was one of these. She had a face like an old peasant woman, with a curious snub nose and irregular whiskers that betrayed recklessly the advance of age. Her snores and gentle purring filled the room now. A hush came over the whole party. At seven o'clock they must all troop over to the Pension des Glycines for supper, but there was still an hour left. And it was a magic hour. Sighs were audible here and there, as the exhausted children settled deeper into their chairs.

A change came over the atmosphere. Would nothing exciting ever happen?

'The stars are out,' said Jimbo in his soft, gentle little voice, turning his head towards the windows. The others looked too—all except Mother, whose attitude suggested suspiciously that she slept, and Riquette, who most certainly did sleep. Above the rampart of the darkened Alps swung up the army of the stars. The brighter ones were reflected in the lake. The sky was crowded. Tiny, golden pathways slid down the purple walls of the night. 'Some one in heaven is letting down the star-ladders...' he whispered.

Jimbo's sentence had marked the change of key. Enchantment was abroad —the Saturday evening spell was in the room.

And suddenly a new enormous thing stirred in their father's heart. Whence it came, or why, he knew not. Like a fire it rose in him deep down, from very far away, delightful. Was it an inspiration coming, he wondered? And why did Jimbo use that phrase of beauty about star- ladders? How did it come into the mind of a little boy? The phrase opened a new channel in the very depths of him, thence climbing up and outwards, towards the brain.... And, with a thrill of curious high wonder, he let it come. It was large and very splendid. It came with a rush—as of numerous whispering voices that flocked about him, urging some exquisite, distant sweetness in him to unaccustomed delivery. A softness of ten thousand stars trooped down into his blood. Some constellation like the Pleiades had flung their fiery tackle across the dusk upon his mind. His thought turned golden....

CHAPTER VIII

> We are the stars which sing.
> We sing with our light.
> We are the birds of fire.
> We fly across the heaven.
> Our light is a star.
> We make a road for Spirits,
> A road for the Great Spirit.
> Among us are three hunters
> Who chase a bear:
> There never was a time
> When they were not hunting;
> We look down on the mountains.
> This is the Song of the Mountains.

> *Red Indian (Algonquin) Lyric.*
>   Translator, J. D. PRINCE.

'A star-story, please,' the boy repeated, cuddling up. They all drew, where possible, nearer. Their belief in their father's powers, rarely justified, was pathetic. Each time they felt sure he would make the adventures seem real, yet somehow he never quite did. They were aware that it was invention only. These things he told about he had not experienced himself. For they badly needed a leader, these children; and Daddy just missed filling the position. He was too 'clever,' his imagination neither wild nor silly enough, for children. And he felt it. He threw off rhymes and stories for them in a spirit of bravado rather—an expression of disappointment. Yet there was passion in them too—concealed. The public missed the heart he showed them in his books in the same way.

'The stars are listening....' Jimbo's voice sounded far away, almost outside the window. Mother now snored audibly. Daddy took his courage in both hands and made the plunge.

'You know about the Star Cavern, I suppose—?' he began. It was the sudden idea that had shot into him, he knew not whence.

'No.'

'Never heard of it.'

'Where is it, please?'

'Don't interrupt. That wasn't a *real* question. Stories always begin like that.' It was Jane Anne who thus finally commanded order.

'It's not a story exactly, but a sort of adventure,' he continued, hesitating yet undaunted. 'Star Caverns are places where the unused starlight gathers. There are numbers of them about the world, and one I know of is up here in our mountains,' he pointed through the north wall towards the pine-clad Jura, 'not far from the slopes of Boudry where the forests dip towards the precipices of the Areuse—' The phrase ran oddly through him like an inspiration, or the beginning of a song he once had heard somewhere.

'Ah, beyond le Vallon Vert? I know,' whispered Jimbo, his blue eyes big already with wonder.

'Towards the precipices on the farther side,' came the explanation, 'where there are those little open spaces among the trees.'

'Tell us more exactly, please.'

'Star-rays, you see,' he evaded them, 'are visible in the sky on their way to us, but once they touch the earth they disappear and go out like a candle. Unless a chance puddle, or a pair of eyes happens to be about to catch them, you can't tell where they've gone to. They go really into these Star Caverns.'

'But in a puddle or a pair of eyes they'd be lost just the same,' came the objection.

'On the contrary,' he said; 'changed a little—increased by reflection—but not lost.'

There was a pause; the children stared, expectantly. Here was mystery.

'See how they mirror themselves whenever possible,' he went on, 'doubling their light and beauty by giving themselves away! What is a puddle worth until a Star's wee golden face shines out of it? And then—what gold can buy it? And what are your eyes worth until a star has flitted in and made a nest there?'

'Oh, like that, you mean—!' exclaimed Jane Anne, remembering that the wonderful women in the newspaper stories always had 'starry eyes.'

'Like that, yes.' Daddy continued. 'Their light puts sympathy in you, and only sympathy makes you lovely and—and—'

He stopped abruptly. He hesitated a moment. He was again most suddenly aware that this strange idea that was born in him came from somewhere else, almost from *some one* else. It was not his own idea, nor had he captured it completely yet. Like a wandering little inspiration from another mind it seemed passing through him on uncertain, feathery feet. He had suddenly lost it again. Thought wandered. He stared at Jimbo, for Jimbo somehow seemed the channel.

The children waited, then talked among themselves. Daddy so often got muddled and inattentive in this way. They were accustomed to it, expected it even.

'I always love being out at night,' said Monkey, her eyes very bright; 'it sort of excites and makes me soft and happy.'

'Excuse me, Daddy, but have you been inside one? What's it like? The Cave, I mean?' Jinny stuck to the point. She had not yet travelled beyond it.

'It all collects in there and rises to the top like cream,' he went on, 'and has a little tiny perfume like wild violets, and by walking through it you get clothed and covered with it, and come out again all soft-shiny—'

'What's soft-shiny, please?'

'Something half-primrose and half-moon. You're like a star—'

'But how—like a star?'

'Why,' he explained gently, yet a little disappointed that his adventure was not instantly accepted, 'you shine, and your eyes twinkle, and everybody likes you and thinks you beautiful—'

'Even if you're not?' inquired Jinny.

'But you *are*—'

'Couldn't we go there now? Mother's fast asleep!' suggested Jimbo in a mysterious whisper. He felt a curious excitement. This, he felt, was more real than usual. He glanced at Monkey's eyes a moment.

'Another time,' said Daddy, already half believing in the truth of his adventure, yet not quite sure of himself. 'It collects, and collects, and collects. Sometimes, here and there, a little escapes and creeps out into yellow flowers like dandelions and buttercups. A little, too, slips below the ground and fills up empty cracks between the rocks. Then it hardens, gets dirty, and men dig it out again and call it gold. And some slips out by the roof—though very, very little—and you see it flashing back to find the star it belongs to, and people with telescopes call it a shooting star, and—' It came pouring through him again.

'But when you're in it—in the Cavern,' asked Monkey impatiently; 'what happens then?'

'Well,' he answered with conviction, 'it sticks to you. It sticks to the eyes most, but a little also to the hair and voice, and nobody loves you unless you've got a bit of it somewhere on you. A girl, before any one falls in love with her, has always been there, and people who write stories and music and things—all have got some on their fingers or else nobody cares for what they write—'

'Oh, Daddy, then why don't you go there and get sticky all over with it?' Jinny burst out with sudden eagerness, ever thinking of others before herself. 'I'll go and get some for you—lots and lots.'

'I *have* been there,' he answered slowly, 'once long, long ago. But it didn't stick very well with me. It wipes off so quickly in the day- time. The sunlight kills it.'

'But you got *some*!' the child insisted. 'And you've got it still, I mean?'

'A little, perhaps, a very little.'

All felt the sadness in his voice without understanding it. There was a moment's pause. Then the three of them spoke in a single breath—

'Please show it to us—*now*,' they cried.

'I'll try,' he said, after a slight hesitation, 'but—er—it's only a rhyme, you see'; and then began to murmur very low for fear of waking Mother: he almost sang it to them. The flock of tiny voices whispered it to his blood. He merely uttered what he heard:—

> Starlight
> Runs along my mind
> And rolls into a ball of golden silk—

A little skein
Of tangled glory;
And when I want to get it out again
To weave the pattern of a verse or story,
It must unwind.

It then gets knotted, looped, and all up-jumbled,
And long before I get it straight again, unwumbled,
To make my verse or story,
The interfering sun has risen
And burst with passion through my silky prison
To melt it down in dew,
Like so much spider-gossamer or fairy-cotton.
Don't you?
I call it rotten!

A hushed silence followed. Eyes sought the fire. No one spoke for several minutes. There was a faint laughter, quickly over, but containing sighs. Only Jinny stared straight into her father's face, expecting more, though prepared at any stage to explode with unfeigned admiration.

'But that "don't you" comes in the wrong place,' she objected anxiously. 'It ought to come after "I call it rotten"——' She was determined to make it seem all right.

'No, Jinny,' he answered gravely, 'you must always put others before yourself. It's the first rule in life and literature.'

She dropped her eyes to the fire like the others. 'Ah,' she said, 'I see; of course.' The long word blocked her mind like an avalanche, even while she loved it.

'*I* call it rotten,' murmured Monkey under her breath. Jimbo made no audible remark. He crossed his little legs and folded his arms. He was not going to express an opinion until he understood better what it was all about. He began to whisper to his sister. Another longish pause intervened. It was Jinny again who broke it.

'And "wumbled,"' she asked solemnly as though the future of everybody depended on it, 'what *is* wumbled, really? There's no such thing, is there?—— In life, I mean?' She meant to add 'and literature,' but the word stopped her like a hedge.

'It's what happens to a verse or story I lose in that way,' he explained, while Jimbo and Monkey whispered more busily still among themselves about something else. 'The bit of starlight that gets lost and doesn't stick, you see—ineffective.'

'But there *is* no such word, really,' she urged, determined to clear up all she could. 'It rhymes—that's all.'

'And there *is* no verse or story,' he replied with a sigh. 'There *was*—that's all.'

There was another pause. Jimbo and Monkey looked round suspiciously. They ceased their mysterious whispering. They clearly did not wish the others to know what their confabulation was about.

'That's why your books are wumbled, is it?' she inquired, proud of an explanation that excused him, yet left his glory somehow unimpaired. Her face was a map of puzzled wrinkles.

'Precisely, Jinny. You see, the starlight never gets through properly into my mind. It lies there in a knot. My plot is wumbled. I can't disentangle it quite, though the beauty lies there right enough——'

'Oh, yes,' she interrupted, 'the beauty lies there still.' She got up suddenly and gave him a kiss.

'Never mind, Daddy,' she whispered. 'I'll get it straight for you one day. I'll unwumble it. I'll do it like a company promoter, I will.' She used words culled from newspapers.

'Thank you, child,' he smiled, returning her kiss; 'I'm sure you will. Only, you'd better let me know when you're coming. It might be dangerous to my health otherwise.'

She took it with perfect seriousness. 'Oh, but, excuse me, I'll come when you're asleep,' she told him, so low that the others could not hear. 'I'll come to you when I'm dreaming. I dream all night like a busy Highlander.'

'That's right,' he whispered, giving her a hug. 'Come when I'm asleep and all the stars are out; and bring a comb and a pair of scissors——'

'And a hay-rake,' added Monkey, overhearing.

Everybody laughed. The children cuddled up closer to him. They pitied him. He had failed again, though his failure was as much a pleasure as his complete success. They sat on his knees and played with him to make up for it, repeating bits of the rhyme they could remember. Then Mother and Riquette woke up together, and the spell was broken. The party scattered. Only Jimbo and his younger sister, retiring into a corner by themselves, continued their mysterious confabulation. Their faces were flushed with excitement. There was a curious animation in their eyes—though this may have been borrowed from the embers of the peat. Or, it may have been the stars, for they were close to the open window. Both seemed soft-shiny somehow. *They*, certainly, were not wumbled.

And several hours later, when they had returned from supper at the Pension and lay in bed, exchanging their last mysterious whispers across the darkness, Monkey said in French—

'Jimbo, I'm going to find that Cavern where the star stuff lies,' and Jimbo answered audaciously, 'I've already been there.'

'Will you show me the way, then?' she asked eagerly, and rather humbly.

'Perhaps,' he answered from beneath the bedclothes, then added, 'Of course I will.' He merely wished to emphasise the fact that he was leader.

'Sleep quickly, then, and join me—over there.' It was their game to believe they joined in one another's dreams.

They slept. And the last thing that reached them from the outer world was their mother's voice calling to them her customary warning: that the *ramoneur* was already in the chimney and that unless they were asleep in five minutes he would come and catch them by the tail. For the Sweep they looked upon with genuine awe. His visits to the village—once in the autumn and once in the spring—were times of shivery excitement.

Presently Mother rose and sailed on tiptoe round the door to peep. And a smile spread softly over her face as she noted the characteristic evidences of the children beside each bed. Monkey's clothes lay in a scattered heap of confusion, half upon the floor, but Jimbo's garments were folded in a precise, neat pile upon the chair. They looked ready to be packed into a parcel. His habits were so orderly. His school blouse hung on the back, the knickerbockers were carefully folded, and the black belt lay coiled in a circle on his coat and what he termed his 'westkit.' Beneath the chair the little pair of very dirty boots stood side by side. Mother stooped and kissed the round plush-covered head that just emerged from below the mountainous *duvet*. He looked like a tiny radish lying in a big ploughed field.

Then, hunting for a full five minutes before she discovered the shoes of Monkey, one beneath the bed and the other inside her petticoat, she passed on into the little kitchen where she cleaned and polished both pairs, and then replaced them by their respective owners. This done, she laid the table in the outer room for their breakfast at half-past six, saw that their schoolbooks and satchels were in order, gave them each a little more unnecessary tucking-up and a kiss so soft it could not have waked a butterfly, and then returned to her chair before the fire where she resumed the mending of a pile of socks and shirts, blouses and stockings, to say nothing of other indescribable garments, that lay in a formidable heap upon the big round table.

This was her nightly routine. Sometimes her husband joined her. Then they talked the children over until midnight, discussed expenses that threatened to swamp them, yet turned out each month 'just manageable somehow' and finally made a cup of cocoa before retiring, she to her self-made bed upon the sofa, and he to his room in the carpenter's house outside the village. But sometimes he did not come. He remained in the Pension to smoke and chat with the Russian and Armenian students, who attended daily lectures in the town, or else went over to his own quarters to work at the book he was engaged on at the moment. To-night he did not come. A light in an attic window, just visible above the vineyards, showed that he was working.

The room was very still; only the click of the knitting needles or the soft noise of the collapsing peat ashes broke the stillness. Riquette snored before the fire less noisily than usual.

'He's working very late to-night,' thought Mother, noticing the lighted window. She sighed audibly; mentally she shrugged her shoulders. Daddy had long ago left that inner preserve of her heart where she completely understood him. Sympathy between them, in the true sense of the word, had worn rather thin.

'I hope he won't overtire himself,' she added, but this was the habit of perfunctory sympathy. She might equally have said, 'I wish he would do something to bring in a little money instead of earning next to nothing and always complaining about the expenses.'

Outside the stars shone brightly through the fresh spring night, where April turned in her sleep, dreaming that May was on the way to wake her.

CHAPTER IX

Wrap thy form in a mantle gray,
     Star-inwrought!
Blind with thine hair the eyes of Day;
Kiss her until she be wearied out,
Then wander o'er city, and sea, and land,
Touching all with thine opiate wand-
     Come, long sought!
       To *Night*, SHELLEY.

Now, cats are curious creatures, and not without reason, perhaps, are they adored by some, yet regarded with suspicious aversion by others. They know so much they never dare to tell, while affecting that they know nothing and are innocent. For it is beyond question that several hours later, when the village and the Citadelle were lost in slumber, Mere Riquette stirred stealthily where she lay upon the hearth, opened her big green eyes, and—began to wash.

But this toilette was pretence in case any one was watching. Really, she looked about her all the time. Her sleep also had been that sham sleep of cats behind which various plots and plans mature—a questionable business altogether. The washing, as soon as she made certain no one saw her, gave place to another manoeuvre. She stretched as though her bones were of the very best elastic. Gathering herself together, she arched her round body till it resembled a toy balloon straining to rise against the pull of four thin ropes that held it tightly to the ground. Then, unable to float off through the air, as she had expected, she slowly again subsided. The balloon deflated. She licked her chops, twitched her whiskers, curled her tail neatly round her two front paws—and grinned complacently. She waited before that extinguished fire of peat as though she had never harboured a single evil purpose in all her days. 'A saucer of milk,' she gave the world to understand, c is the only thing *I* care about.' Her smile of innocence and her attitude of meek simplicity proclaimed this to the universe at large. 'That's me,' she told the darkness, 'and I don't care a bit who knows it.' She looked so sleek and modest that a mouse need not have feared her. But she did not add, 'That's what I mean the world to think,' for this belonged to the secret life cats never talk about. Those among humans might divine it who could, and welcome. They would be admitted. But the rest of the world were regarded with mere tolerant disdain. They bored.

Then, satisfied that she was unobserved, Mere Riquette abandoned all further pretence, and stalked silently about the room. The starlight just made visible her gliding shadow, as first she visited the made-up sofa-bed where the exhausted mother snored mildly beneath the book- shelves, and then, after a moment's keen inspection, turned back and went at a quicker pace into the bedroom where the children slept. There the night-light made her movements easily visible. The cat was excited. Something bigger than any mouse was coming into her life just now.

Riquette then witnessed a wonderful and beautiful thing, yet witnessed it obviously not for the first time. Her manner suggested no surprise. 'It's like a mouse, only bigger,' her expression said. And by this she meant that it was natural. She accepted it as right and proper.

For Monkey got out of herself as out of a case. She slipped from her body as a sword slips from its sheath, yet the body went on breathing in the bed just as before; the turned-up nose with the little platform at its tip did not cease from snoring, and the lids remained fastened tightly over the brilliant brown eyes, buttoned down so securely for the night. Two plaits of hair lay on the pillow; another rose and fell with the regular breathing of her little bosom. But Monkey herself stood softly shining on the floor within a paw's length.

Riquette blinked her eyes and smiled complacently. Jimbo was close behind her, even brighter than his sister, with eyes like stars.

The visions of cats are curious things, no doubt, and few may guess their furry, silent pathways as they go winding along their length of inconsequent development. For, softer than any mouse, the children glided swiftly into the next room where Mother slept beneath the book- shelves—two shining little radiant figures, hand in hand. They tried for a moment to pull out Mother too, but found her difficult to move. Somewhere on the way she stuck. They gave it up.

Turning towards the window that stood open beyond the head of the sofa-bed, they rose up lightly and floated through it out into the starry night. Riquette leaped like a silent shadow after them, but before she reached the roof of red-brown tiles that sloped down to the yard, Jimbo and Monkey were already far away. She strained her big green eyes in vain, seeing nothing but the tops of the plane trees, thick with tiny coming leaves, the sweep of vines and sky, and the tender, mothering night beyond. She pattered softly back again, gave a contemptuous glance at Mother in passing, and jumped up at once into the warm nest of sheets that gaped invitingly between the shoulder of Jimbo's body and the pillow. She shaped the opening to her taste, kneading it with both front paws, turned three times round, and then lay down. Curled in a ball, her nose buried between her back feet, she was asleep in a single moment. Her whiskers ceased to quiver.

The children were tugging at Daddy now over in the carpenter's house. His bed was short, and his body lay in a kind of knot. On the chair beside it were books and papers, and a candle that had burnt itself out. A pencil poked its nose out among the sheets, and it was clear he had fallen asleep while working.

'Wumbled!' sighed Jimbo, pointing to the scribbled notes. But Monkey was busy pulling him out, and did not answer. Then Jimbo helped her. And Daddy came out magnificently—as far as the head—then stuck like Mother. They pulled in vain. Something in his head prevented complete release.

'En voila un!' laughed Monkey. 'Quel homme!' It was her natural speech, the way she talked at school. 'It's a pity,' said Jimbo with a little sigh. They gave it up, watching him slide slowly back again. The moment he was all in they turned towards the open window. Hand in hand they sailed out over the sleeping village. And from almost every house they heard a sound of weeping. There were sighs and prayers and pleadings. All slept and dreamed—dreamed of their difficulties and daily troubles. Released in sleep, their longings rose to heaven unconsciously, automatically as it were. Even the cheerful and the happy yearned a little, even the well-to-do whom the world judged so secure—these, too, had their burdens that found release, and so perhaps relief in sleep.

'Come, and we'll help them,' Jimbo said eagerly. 'We can change all that a little. Oh, I say, what a lot we've got to do to-night.'

'Je crois bien,' laughed Monkey, turning somersaults for joy as she followed him. Her tendency to somersaults in this condition was irresistible, and a source of worry to Jimbo, who classed it among the foolish habits of what he called 'womans and things like that!'

And the sound came loudest from the huddled little building by the Church, the Pension where they had their meals, and where Jinny had her bedroom. But Jinny, they found, was already out, off upon adventures of her own. A solitary child, she always went her independent way in everything. They dived down into the first floor, and there, in a narrow bedroom whose windows stood open upon the wistaria branches, they found Madame Jequier—'Tante Jeanne,' as they knew the sympathetic, generous creature best, sister-in-law of the Postmaster—not sleeping like the others, but wide awake and praying vehemently in a wicker-chair that creaked with every nervous movement that she made. All about her were bits of paper covered with figures, bills, calculations, and the rest.

'We can't get at her,' said Monkey, her laughter hushed for a moment. 'There's too much sadness. Come on! Let's go somewhere else.'

But Jimbo held her tight. 'Let's have a try. Listen, you silly, can't you!'

They stood for several minutes, listening together, while the brightness of their near approach seemed to change the woman's face a little. She looked up and listened as though aware of something near her.

'She's praying for others as well as herself,' explained Jimbo.

'Ca vaut la peine alors,' said Monkey. And they drew cautiously nearer.... But, soon desisting, the children were far away, hovering about the mountains. They had no steadiness as yet.

'Starlight,' Jimbo was singing to himself, 'runs along my mind.'

'You're all up-jumbled,' Monkey interrupted him with a laugh, turning repeated somersaults till she looked like a catherine wheel of brightness.

'... the pattern of my verse or story...' continued Jimbo half aloud, '... a little ball of tangled glory....'

'You must unwind!' cried Monkey. 'Look out, it's the sun! It'll melt us into dew!'

But it was not the sun. Out there beyond them, towards the purple woods still sleeping, appeared a draught of starbeams like a broad, deep river of gold. The rays, coming from all corners of the sky, wove a pattern like a network.

'Jimbo!' gasped the girl, 'it's like a fishing-net. We've never noticed it before.'

'It *is* a net,' he answered, standing still as a stone, though he had not thought of it himself until she said so. He instantly dressed himself, as he always translated *il se dressait* in his funny Franco- English. *Deja* and *comme ca*, too, appeared everywhere. 'It is a net like that. I saw it already before, once.'

'Monkey,' he added, 'do you know what it really is? Oh, I say!'

'Of course I do.' She waited nevertheless for him to tell her, and he was too gallant just then in his proud excitement for personal exultation.

'It's the Star Cave—it's Daddy's Star Cave. He said it was up here "where the Boudry forests dip below the cliffs towards the Areuse." ...' He remembered the very words.

His sister forgot to turn her usual somersaults. Wonder caught them both. 'A pair of eyes, then, or a puddle! Quick!' she cried in a delighted whisper. She looked about her everywhere at once, making confused and rushing little movements of helplessness. 'Quick, quick!'

'No,' said Jimbo, with a man's calm decision, 'it's when they *can't* find eyes or puddles that they go in there. Don't interfere.'

She admitted her mistake. This was no time to press a petty advantage.

'I'll shut my eyes while you sponge up the puddles with a wedge of moss,' she began. But her brother cut her short. He was very sure of himself. He was leader beyond all question.

'You follow me,' he commanded firmly, 'and you'll get in somehow. We'll get all sticky with it. Then we'll come out again and help those crying people like Tante Jeanne and....' A list of names poured out. 'They'll think us wonderful——'

'We shall be wonderful,' whispered Monkey, obeying, yet peeping with one big brown eye.

The cataract of starbeams rushed past them in a flood of gold.

They moved towards an opening in the trees where the limestone cliffs ran into rugged shapes with pinnacles and towers. They found the entrance in the rocks. Water dripped over it, making little splashes. The lime had run into hanging pillars and a fringe of pointed fingers. Past this the river of starlight poured its brilliant golden stream. Its soft brightness shone yellow as a shower of primrose dust.

'Look out! The Interfering Sun!' gasped Monkey again, awed and confused with wonder. 'We shall melt in dew or fairy cotton. Don't you? ... I call it rotten ...!'

'You'll unwind all right,' he told her, trying hard to keep his head and justify his leadership. He, too, remembered phrases here and there. 'I'm a bit knotted, looped, and all up-jumbled too, inside. But the sun is miles away still. We're both soft-shiny still.'

They stooped to enter, plunging their bodies to the neck in the silent flood of sparkling amber.

Then happened a strange thing. For how could they know, these two adventurous, dreaming children, that Thought makes images which, regardless of space, may flash about the world, and reach minds anywhere that are sweetly tuned to their acceptance?

'What's that? Look out! *Gare!* Hold tight!' In his sudden excitement Jimbo mixed questions with commands. He had caught her by the hand. There was a new sound in the heavens above them—a roaring, rushing sound. Like the thunder of a train, it swept headlong through the sky. Voices were audible too.

'There's something enormous caught in the star-net,' he whispered.

'It's Mother, then,' said Monkey.

They both looked up, trembling with anticipation. They saw a big, dark body like a thundercloud hovering above their heads. It had a line of brilliant eyes. From one end issued a column of white smoke. It settled slowly downwards, moving softly yet with a great air of bustle and importance. Was this the arrival of a dragon, or Mother coming after them? The blood thumped in their ears, their hands felt icy. The thing dipped slowly through the trees. It settled, stopped, began to purr.

'It's a railway train,' announced Jimbo finally with authority that only just disguised amazement. 'And the passengers are getting out.' With a sigh of immense relief he said it. 'You're not in any danger, Monkey,' he added.

He drew his sister back quickly a dozen steps, and they hid behind a giant spruce to watch. The scene that followed was like the holiday spectacle in a London Terminus, except that the passengers had no luggage. The other difference was that they seemed intent upon some purpose not wholly for their own advantage. It seemed, too, they had expected somebody to meet them, and were accordingly rather confused and disappointed. They looked about them anxiously.

'Last stop; all get out here!' a Guard was crying in a kind of pleasant singing voice. 'Return journey begins five minutes before the Interfering Sun has risen.'

Jimbo pinched his sister's arm till she nearly screamed. 'Hear that?' he whispered. But Monkey was too absorbed in the doings of the busy passengers to listen or reply. For the first passenger that hurried past her was no less a person than—Jane Anne! Her face was not puzzled now. It was like a little sun. She looked utterly happy and contented, as though she had found the place and duties that belonged to her.

'Jinny!' whispered the two in chorus. But Jane Anne did not so much as turn her head. She slipped past them like a shaft of light. Her hair fell loose to her waist. She went towards the entrance. The flood rose to her neck.

'Oh! there she is!' cried a voice. 'She travelled with us instead of coming to meet us.' Monkey smiled. She knew her sister's alien, unaccountable ways only too well.

The train had settled down comfortably enough between the trees, and lay there breathing out a peaceable column of white smoke, panting a little as it did so. The Guard went down the length of it, turning out the lamps; and from the line of open doors descended the stream of passengers, all hurrying to the entrance of the cave. Each one stopped a moment in front of the Guard, as though to get a ticket clipped, but instead of producing a piece of pasteboard, or the Guard a punching instrument, they seemed to exchange a look together. Each one stared into his face, nodded, and passed on.

'What blue eyes they've got,' thought Monkey to herself, as she peered into each separate face as closely as she dared. 'I wish mine were like that!' The wind, sighing through the tree-tops, sent a shower of dew about their feet. The children started. 'What a lovely row!' Jimbo whispered. It was like footsteps of a multitude on the needles. The fact that it was so clearly audible showed how softly all these passengers moved about their business.

The Guard, they noticed then, called out the names of some of them; perhaps of all, only in the first excitement they did not catch them properly. And each one went on at once towards the entrance of the cave and disappeared in the pouring river of gold.

The light-footed way they moved, their swiftness as of shadows, the way they tossed their heads and flung their arms about—all this made the children think it was a dance. Monkey felt her own legs twitch to join them, but her little brother's will restrained her.

'If you turn a somersault here,' he said solemnly, 'we're simply lost.' He said it in French; the long word had not yet dawned upon his English consciousness. They watched with growing wonder then, and something like terror seized them as they saw a man go past them with a very familiar look about him. He went in a cloud of sparkling, black dust that turned instantly into shining gold when it reached the yellow river from the stars. His face was very dirty.

'It's *not* the *ramoneur*,' whispered Jimbo, uncertain whether the shiver he felt was his sister's or his own. 'He's much too springy.' Sweeps always had a limp.

For the figure shot along with a running, dancing leap as though he moved on wires. He carried long things over his shoulders. He flashed into the stream like a shadow swallowed by a flame. And as he went, they caught such merry words, half sung, half chanted:—,

'I'll mix their smoke with hope and mystery till they see dreams and faces in their fires——' and he was gone.

Behind him came a couple arm in arm, their movements equally light and springy, but the one behind dragging a little, as though lazily. They wore rags and torn old hats and had no collars to their shirts. The lazy one had broken boots through which his toes showed plainly. The other who dragged him had a swarthy face like the gypsies who once had camped near their house in Essex long, oh, ever so long ago.

'I'll get some too,' the slow one sang huskily as he stumbled along with difficulty 'but there's never any hurry. I'll fill their journeys with desire and make adventure call to them with love——'

'And I,' the first one answered, 'will sprinkle all their days with the sweetness of the moors and open fields, till houses choke their lungs and they come out to learn the stars by name. Ho, ho!'

They dipped, with a flying leap, into the rushing flood. Their rags and filthy slouched hats flashed radiant as they went, all bathed and cleaned in glory.

Others came after them in a continuous stream, some too outlandish to be named or recognised, others half familiar, very quick and earnest, but merry at the same time, and all intent upon bringing back something for the world. It was not for themselves alone, or for their own enjoyment that they hurried in so eagerly.

'How splendid! What a crew!' gasped Monkey. '*Quel spectacle!*' And she began a somersault.

'Be quiet, will you?' was the rejoinder, as a figure who seemed to have a number of lesser faces within his own big one of sunburned brown, tumbled by them somewhat heavily and left a smell of earth and leaves and potting-sheds about the trees behind him. 'Won't my flowers just shine and dazzle 'em? And won't the dead leaves crackle as I burn 'em up!' he chuckled as he disappeared from view. There was a rush of light as an eddy of the star-stream caught him, and something certainly went up in flame. A faint odour reached the children that was like the odour of burning leaves.

Then, with a rush, came a woman whose immensely long thin arms reached out in front of her and vanished through the entrance a whole minute before the rest of her. But they could not see the face. Some one with high ringing laughter followed, though they could not see the outline at all. It went so fast, they only heard the patter of light footsteps on the moss and needles. Jimbo and Monkey felt slightly uncomfortable as they watched and listened, and the feeling became positive uneasiness the next minute as a sound of cries and banging reached them from the woods behind. There was a great commotion going on somewhere in the train.

'I can't get out, I can't get out!' called a voice unhappily. 'And if I do, how shall I ever get in again? The entrance is so ridiculously small. I shall only stick and fill it up. Why did I ever come? Oh, why did I come at all?'

'Better stay where you are, lady,' the Guard was saying. 'You're good ballast. You can keep the train down. That's something. Steady thinking's always best, you know.'

Turning, the children saw a group of figures pushing and tugging at a dark mass that appeared to have stuck halfway in the carriage door. The pressure of many willing hands gave it a different outline every minute. It was like a thing of india-rubber or elastic. The roof strained outwards with ominous cracking sounds; the windows threatened to smash; the foot-board, supporting the part of her that had emerged, groaned with the weight already.

'Oh, what's the good of *me?*' cried the queer deep voice with petulance. 'You couldn't get a wisp of hay in there, much less all of me. I should block the whole cave up!'

'Come out a bit!' a voice cried.

'I can't.'

'Go back then!' suggested the Guard.

'But I can't. Besides I'm upside down!'

'You haven't got any upside down,' was the answer; 'so that's impossible.'

'Well, anyhow, I'm in a mess and muddle like this,' came the smothered voice, as the figures pulled and pushed with increasing energy.' And my tarpaulin skirt is all askew. The winds are at it as usual.'

'Nothing short of a gale can help you now,' was somebody's verdict, while Monkey whispered beneath her breath to Jimbo. 'She's even bigger than Mother. Quelle masse!'

Then came a thing of mystery and wonder from the sky. A flying figure, scattering points of light through the darkness like grains of shining sand, swooped down and stood beside the group.

'Oh, Dustman,' cried the guard, 'give her of your dust and put her to sleep, please. She's making noise enough to bring the Interfering Sun above the horizon before his time.'

Without a word the new arrival passed one hand above the part of her that presumably was the face. Something sifted downwards. There was a sound of gentle sprinkling through the air; a noise followed that was half a groan and half a sigh. Her struggles grew gradually less, then ceased. They pushed the bulk of her backwards through the door. Spread over many seats the Woman of the Haystack slept.

'Thank you,' said several voices with relief. 'She'll dream she's been in. That's just as good.'

'Every bit,' the others answered, resuming their interrupted journey towards the cavern's mouth.

'And when I come out she shall have some more,' answered the Dustman in a soft, thick voice; 'as much as ever she can use.'

He flitted in his turn towards the stream of gold. His feet were already in it when he paused a moment to shift from one shoulder to the other a great sack he carried. And in that moment was heard a low voice singing dreamily the Dustman's curious little song. It seemed to come from the direction of the train where the Guard stood talking to a man the children had not noticed before. Presumably he was the engine-driver, since all the passengers were out now. But it may have been the old Dustman himself who sang it. They could not tell exactly. The voice made them quite drowsy as they listened:—

    The busy Dustman flutters down the lanes,
    He's off to gather star-dust for our dreams.

    He dusts the Constellations for his sack,
    Finding it thickest on the Zodiac,
    But sweetest in the careless meteor's track;
       That he keeps only
       For the old and lonely,
       (And is very strict about it!)
    Who sleep so little that they need the best;
       The rest,—
       The common stuff,—
       Is good enough

    For Fraulein, or for Baby, or for Mother,
       Or any other
       Who likes a bit of dust,
       But yet can do without it
       If they *must*!

    The busy Dustman hurries through the sky
    The kind old Dustman's coming to *your* eye!

By the time the song was over he had disappeared through the opening.

'I'll show 'em the real stuff!' came back a voice—this time certainly his own—far inside now.

'I simply love that man,' exclaimed Monkey. 'Songs are usually such twiddly things, but that was real.' She looked as though a somersault were imminent. 'If only Daddy knew him, he'd learn how to write unwumbled stories. Oh! we *must* get Daddy out.'

'It's only the head that sticks,' was her brother's reply. 'We'll grease it.'

They remained silent a moment, not knowing what to do next, when they became aware that the big man who had been talking to the Guard was coming towards them.

'They've seen us!' she whispered in alarm. '*He's* seen us.' An inexplicable thrill ran over her.

'They saw us long ago,' her brother added contemptuously. His voice quavered.

Jimbo turned to face them, getting in front of his sister for protection, although she towered above him by a head at least. The Guard, who led the way, they saw now, was a girl—a girl not much older than Monkey, with big blue eyes. 'There they are,' the Guard said loudly, pointing; and the big man, looking about him as though he did not see very clearly, stretched out his hands towards him. 'But you must be very quick,' she added, 'the Interfering Sun—'

'I'm glad you came to meet us. I hoped you might. Jane Anne's gone in ages ago. Now we'll all go in together,' he said in a deep voice, 'and gather star-dust for our dreams...' He groped to find them. His hands grew shadowy. He felt the empty air.

His voice died away even as he said it, and the difficulty he had in seeing seemed to affect their own eyes as well. A mist rose. It turned to darkness. The river of starlight faded. The net had suddenly big holes in it. They were slipping through. Wind whispered in the trees. There was a sharp, odd sound like the plop of a water-rat in a pond....

'We must be quick,' his voice came faintly from far away. They just had time to see his smile, and noticed the gleam of two gold teeth.... Then the darkness rushed up and covered them. The stream of tangled, pouring beams became a narrow line, so far away it was almost like the streak of a meteor in the sky.... Night hid the world and everything in it....

Two radiant little forms slipped past Riquette and slid feet first into the sleeping bodies on the beds.

There came soon after a curious sound from the outer room, as Mother turned upon her sofa-bed and woke. The sun was high above the Blumlisalp, spreading a sheet of gold and silver on the lake. Birds were singing in the plane trees. The roof below the open windows shone with dew, and draughts of morning air, sweet and fresh, poured into the room. With it came the scent of flowers and forests, of fields and peaty smoke from cottage chimneys....

But there was another perfume too. Far down the sky swept some fleet and sparkling thing that made the world look different. It was delicate and many-tinted, soft as a swallow's wing, and full of butterflies and tiny winds.

For, with the last stroke of midnight from the old church tower, May had waked April; and April had run off into the mountains with the dawn. Her final shower of tears still shone upon the ground. Already May was busy drying them.

That afternoon, when school was over, Monkey and Jimbo found themselves in the attics underneath the roof together. They had abstracted their father's opera-glasses from the case that hung upon the door, and were using them as a telescope.

'What can you see?' asked Jimbo, waiting for his turn, as they looked towards the hazy mountains behind the village.

'Nothing.'

'That must be the opening, then,' he suggested, 'just air.'

His sister lowered the glasses and stared at him. 'But it can't be a real place?' she said, the doubt in her tone making her words a question. 'Daddy's never been there himself, I'm sure—from the way he told it. You only dreamed it.' 'Well, anyhow,' was the reply with conviction, 'it's there, so there must be *somebody* who believes in it.' And he was evidently going to add that he had been there, when Mother's voice was heard calling from the yard below, 'Come down from that draughty place. It's dirty, and there are dead rats in it. Come out and play in the sunshine. Try and be sensible like Jinny.'

They smuggled the glasses into their case again, and went off to the woods to play. Though their union seemed based on disagreements chiefly they were always quite happy together like this, living in a world entirely their own. Jinny went her own way apart always—ever busy with pots and pans and sewing. She was far too practical and domestic for their tastes to amalgamate; yet, though they looked down upon her a little, no one in their presence could say a word against her. For they recognised the child's unusual selflessness, and rather stood in awe of it.

And this afternoon in the woods they kept coming across places that seemed oddly familiar, although they had never visited them before. They had one of their curious conversations about the matter—queer talks they indulged in sometimes when quite alone. Mother would have squelched such talk, and Daddy muddled them with long words, while Jane Anne would have looked puzzled to the point of tears.

'I'm *sure* I've been here before,' said Monkey, looking across the trees to a place where the limestone cliffs dropped in fantastic shapes of pointed rock. 'Have you got that feeling too?'

Jimbo, with his hands in the pockets of his blue reefer overcoat and his feet stuck wide apart, stared hard at her a moment. His little mind was searching too.

'It's natural enough, I suppose,' he answered, too honest to pretend, too proud, though, to admit he had not got it.

They were rather breathless with their climb, and sat down on a boulder in the shade.

'I know all this awfully well,' Monkey presently resumed, looking about her. 'But certainly we've never come as far as this. I think my underneath escapes and comes to places by itself. I feel like that. Does yours?'

He looked up from a bundle of moss he was fingering. This was rather beyond him.

'Oh, I feel all right,' he said, 'just ordinary.' He would have given his ten francs in the savings bank, the collection of a year, to have answered otherwise. 'You're always getting tummy-aches and things,' he added kindly. 'Girls do.' It was pride that made the sharp addition. But Monkey was not hurt; she did not even notice what he said. The insult thus ignored might seem almost a compliment Jimbo thought with quick penitence.

'Then, perhaps,' she continued, more than a little thrilled by her own audacity, 'it's somebody else's thinking. Thinking skips about the world like anything, you know. I read it once in one of Daddy's books.'

'Oh, yes—like that——'

'Thinking hard *does* make things true, of course,' she insisted.

'But you can't exactly see them,' he put in, to explain his own inexperience. He felt jealous of these privileges she claimed. 'They can't last, I mean.' 'But they can't be wiped out either,' she said decidedly. 'I'm sure of that.'

Presently they scrambled higher and found among the rocks an opening to a new cave. The Jura mountains are riddled with caves which the stalactites turn into palaces and castles. The entrance was rather small, and they made no attempt to crawl in, for they knew that coming out again was often very difficult. But there was great excitement about it, and while Monkey kept repeating that she knew it already, or else had seen a picture of it somewhere, Jimbo went so far as to admit that they had certainly found it *very* easily, while suggesting that the rare good fortune was due rather to his own leadership and skill.

But when they came home to tea, full of the glory of their discovery, they found that a new excitement made the announcement fall a little flat. For in the Den, Daddy read a telegram he had just received from England to say that Cousin Henry was coming out to visit them for a bit. His room had already been engaged at the carpenter's house. He would arrive at the end of the week.

It was the first of May!

CHAPTER X

One of the great facts of the world I hold to be the registration in the Universe of every past scene and thought. F. W. M.

No place worth knowing yields itself at sight, and those the least inviting on first view may leave the most haunting pictures upon the walls of memory.

This little village, that Henry Rogers was thus to revisit after so long an interval, can boast no particular outstanding beauty to lure the common traveller. Its single street winds below the pine forest; its tiny church gathers close a few brown-roofed houses; orchards guard it round about; the music of many fountains tinkle summer and winter through its cobbled yards; and its feet are washed by a tumbling stream that paints the fields with the radiance of countless wild-flowers in the spring. But tourists never come to see them. There is no hotel, for one thing, and ticket agents, even at the railway stations, look puzzled a moment before they realise where this place with the twinkling name can hide…. Some consult books. Yet, once you get there, it is not easy to get away again. Something catches the feet and ears and eyes. People have been known to go with all their luggage on Gygi's handcart to the station—then turn aside at the last moment, caught back by the purple woods.

A traveller, glancing up at the little three-storey house with 'Poste et Telegraphe' above the door, could never guess how busy the world that came and went beneath its red-tiled roof. In spring the wistaria tree (whence the Pension borrowed its brave name, Les Glycines) hangs its blossoms between 'Poste' and 'Telegraphe,' and the perfume of invisible lilacs drenches the street from the garden at the back. Beyond, the road dips past the bee-hives of *la cure*; and Boudry towers with his five thousand feet of blue pine woods over the horizon. The tinkling of several big stone fountains fills the street.

But the traveller would not linger, unless he chanced to pass at twelve o'clock and caught the stream of people going into their mid- day dinner at the Pension. And even then he probably would not see the presiding genius, Madame Jequier, for as often as not she would be in her garden, busy with eternal bulbs, and so strangely garbed that if she showed herself at all, it would be with a shrill, plaintive explanation—'Mais il ne faut pas me regarder. Je suis invisible!' Whereupon, consistently, she would not speak again, but flit in silence to and fro, as though she were one of those spirits she so firmly believed in, and sometimes talked to by means of an old Planchette.

And on this particular morning the Widow Jequier was 'invisible' in her garden clothes as Gygi, the gendarme, came down the street to ring the *midi* bell. Her mind was black with anxiety. She was not thinking of the troop that came to *dejeuner*, their principal meal of the day, paying a franc for it, but rather of the violent scenes with unpaid tradesmen that had filled the morning-tradesmen who were friends as well (which made it doubly awkward) and often dropped in socially for an evening's music and conversation. Her pain darkened the sunshine, and she found relief in the garden which was her passion. For in three weeks the interest on the mortgages was due, and she had nothing saved to meet it. The official notice had come that morning from the Bank. Her mind was black with confused pictures of bulbs, departed *pensionnaires*, hostile bankers, and—the ghastly *charite de la Commune* which awaited her. Yet her husband, before he went into the wine-business so disastrously, had been pasteur here. He had preached from this very church whose bells now rang out the mid-day hour. The spirit of her daughter, she firmly believed, still haunted the garden, the narrow passages, and the dilapidated little salon where the ivy trailed along the ceiling.

Twelve o'clock, striking from the church-tower clock, and the voice of her sister from the kitchen window, then brought the Widow Jequier down the garden in a flying rush. The table was laid and the soup was almost ready. The people were coming in. She was late as usual; there was no time to change. She flung her garden hat aside and scrambled into more presentable garments, while footsteps already sounded on the wooden stairs that led up from the village street.

One by one the retired governesses entered, hung their cloaks upon the pegs in the small, dark hallway, and took their places at the table. They began talking among themselves, exchanging the little gossip of the village, speaking of their books and clothes and sewing, of the rooms in which they lived, scattered down the street, of the heating, of barking dogs that disturbed their sleep, the behaviour of the postman, the fine spring weather, and the views from their respective windows across the lake and distant Alps. Each extolled her own position: one had a garden; another a balcony; a third was on the top floor and so had no noisy tenant overhead; a fourth was on the ground, and had no stairs to climb. Each had her secret romance, and her secret method of cheap feeding at home. There were five or six of them, and this was their principal meal in the day; they meant to make the most of it; they always did; they went home to light suppers of tea and coffee, made in their own *appartements*. Invitations were issued and accepted. There were some who would not speak to each other. Cliques, divisions, *societes a part*, existed in the little band. And they talked many languages, learned in many lands—Russian, German, Italian, even

Armenian—for all had laboured far from their country, spending the best of their years teaching children of foreign families, many of them in important houses. They lived upon their savings. Two, at least, had less than thirty pounds a year between them and starvation, and all were of necessity careful of every centime. They wore the same dresses from one year's end to another. They had come home to die.

The Postmaster entered with the cash-box underneath one arm. He bowed gravely to the assembled ladies, and silently took his seat at the table. He never spoke; at meals his sole remarks were statements: 'Je n'ai pas de pain,' 'Il me manque une serviette,' and the like, while his black eyes glared resentfully at every one as though they had done him an injury. But his fierceness was only in the eyes. He was a meek and solemn fellow really. Nature had dressed him in black, and he respected her taste by repeating it in his clothes. Even his expression was funereal, though his black eyes twinkled.

The servant-girl at once brought in his plate of soup, and he tucked the napkin beneath his chin and began to eat. From twelve to two the post was closed; his recreation time was precious, and no minute must be lost. After dinner he took his coat off and did the heavy work of the garden, under the merciless oversight of the Widow Jequier, his sister-in-law, the cash-box ever by his side. He chatted with his tame *corbeau*, but he never smiled. In the winter he did fretwork. On the stroke of two he went downstairs again and disappeared into the cramped and stuffy bureau, whose window on the street was framed by the hanging wistaria blossoms; and at eight o'clock his day of labour ended. He carried the cash-box up to bed at 8.15. At 8.30 his wife followed him. From nine to five he slept.

Alone of all the little household the Widow Jequier scorned routine. She came and went with the uncertainty of wind. Her entrances and exits, too, were like the wind. With a scattering rush she scurried through the years— noisy, ineffective, yet somewhere fine. Her brother had finished his plate of soup, wiped his black moustaches elaborately, and turned his head towards the kitchen door with the solemn statement 'Je n'ai pas de viande,' when she descended upon the scene like a shrill-voiced little tempest.

'Bonjour Mesdames, bonjour Mademoiselle, bonjour, bonjour,' she bowed and smiled, washing her hands in the air; 'et comment allez-vous ce matin?' as the little band of hungry governesses rose with one accord and moved to take their places. Some smiled in answer; others merely bowed. She made enemies as well as friends, the Widow Jequier. With only one of them she shook hands warmly-the one whose payments were long overdue. But Madame Jequier never asked for her money; she knew the old body's tiny income; she would pay her when she could. Only last week she had sent her food and clothing under the guise of a belated little Easter present. Her heart was bigger than her body.

'La famille Anglaise n'est pas encore ici,' announced the Postmaster as though it were a funeral to come. He did not even look up. His protests passed ever unobserved.

'But I hear them coming,' said a governess, swallowing her soup with a sound of many waters. And, true enough, they came. There was a thunder on the stairs, the door into the hall flew open, voices and laughter filled the place, and Jimbo and Monkey raced in to take their places, breathless, rosy, voluble, and very hungry. Jane Anne followed sedately, bowing to every one in turn. She had a little sentence for all who cared for one. Smiles appeared on every face. Mother, like a frigate coming to anchor with a favourable wind, sailed into her chair; and behind her stumbled Daddy, looking absent-minded and pre- occupied. Money was uncommonly scarce just then—the usual Bourcelles complaint.

Conversation in many tongues, unmusically high-pitched, then at once broke loose, led ever by *la patronne* at the head of the table. The big dishes of meat and vegetables were handed round; plates were piled and smothered; knives and forks were laid between mouthfuls upon plate-edges, forming a kind of frieze all round the cloth; the gossip of the village was retailed with harmless gusto. *Dejeuner* at Les Glycines was in full swing. When the apples and oranges came round, most of the governesses took two apiece, slipping one or other into little black velvet bags they carried on their laps below the table.

Some, it was whispered, put bread there too to keep them company. But this was probably a libel. Madame Jequier, at any rate, never saw it done. She looked the other way. 'We all must live,' was her invariable answer to such foolish stories. 'One cannot sleep if one's supper is too light.' Like her body, her soul was a bit untidy—careless, that is, with loose ends. Who would have guessed, for instance, the anxiety that just now gnawed her very entrails? She was a mixture of shameless egotism, and of burning zeal for others. There was a touch of grandeur in her.

At the end of the table, just where the ivy leaves dropped rather low from their trailing journey across the ceiling, sat Miss Waghorn, her vigorous old face wrapped, apparently, in many apple skins. She was well past seventy, thin, erect, and active, with restless eyes, and hooked nose, the poor old hands knotted with rheumatism, yet the voice somehow retaining the energy of forty. Her manners were charming and old-fashioned, and she came of Quaker stock. Seven years before she arrived at the Pension for the summer, and had forgotten to leave. For she forgot most things within ten minutes of their happening. Her memory was gone; she remembered a face, as most other things as well, about twenty minutes; introductions had to be repeated every day, and sometimes at supper she would say with her gentle smile, 'We haven't met before, I think,' to some one she had held daily intercourse with for many months. 'I was born in '37,' she loved to add, 'the year of Queen Victoria's accession'; and five minutes later you might hear her ask, 'Now, guess how old I am; I don't mind a bit.' She was as proud of her load of years as an old gentleman of his thick hair. 'Say exactly what you think. And don't guess too low, mind.' Her numerous stories were self-repeaters.

Miss Waghorn's memory was a source of worry and anxiety to all except the children, who mercilessly teased her. She loved the teasing, though but half aware of it. It was their evil game to extract as many of her familiar stories as possible, one after another. They knew all the clues. There was the Cornishman—she came from Cornwall—who had seen a fairy; his adventure never failed to thrill them, though she used the same words every time and they knew precisely what was coming. She was particularly strong on family reminiscences:—her father was bald at thirty, her brother's beard was so long that he tied it round his neck when playing cricket; her sister 'had the shortest arms you ever saw.' Always of youth she spoke; it was pathetic, so determined was she to be young at seventy. Her family seemed distinguished in this matter of extremes.

But the superiority of Cornish over Devonshire cream was her *piece de resistance*. Monkey need merely whisper—Miss Waghorn's acuteness of hearing was positively uncanny—'Devonshire cream is what *I* like,' to produce a spurt of explanation and defence that lasted a good ten minutes and must be listened to until the bitter end.

Jimbo would gravely inquire in a pause—of a stranger, if possible, if not, of the table in general—

'Have you ever seen a fairy?'

'No, but I've eaten Cornish cream—it's poison, you know,' Monkey would reply. And up would shoot the keen old face, preened for the fray.

'We haven't been introduced, I think'—forgetting the formal introduction of ten minutes ago—'but I overheard, if you'll forgive my interrupting, and I can tell you all about Cornish cream. I was born in '37'—with her eager smile—'and for years it was on our table. I have made quantities of it. The art was brought first by the Phoenicians——'

'Venetians,' said Monkey.

'No, Phoenicians, dear, when they came to Cornwall for tin——'

'To put the cream in,' from the same source.

- 83 -

'No, you silly child, to get tin from the mines, of course, and——'

Then Mother or Daddy, noting the drift of things, would interfere, and the youngsters would be obliterated—until next time. Miss Waghorn would finish her recital for the hundredth time, firmly believing it to be the first. She was a favourite with everybody, in spite of the anxiety she caused. She would go into town to pay her bill at the bootmaker's, and order another pair of boots instead, forgetting why she came. Her income was sixty pounds a year. She forgot in the afternoon the money she had received in the morning, till at last the Widow Jequier seized it for her the moment it arrived. And at night she would doze in her chair over the paper novel she had been "at" for a year and more, beginning it every night afresh, and rarely getting beyond the opening chapter. For it was ever new. All were anxious, though, what she would do next. She was so full of battle.

Everybody talked at once, but forced conversation did not flourish. Bourcelles was not fashionable; no one ever had appendicitis there. Yet ailments of a milder order were the staple, inexhaustible subjects at meals. Instead of the weather, *mon estomac* was the inexhaustible tale. The girl brought in the little Cantonal newspaper, and the widow read out selections in a high, shrill voice, regardless who listened. Misfortunes and accidents were her preference. *Grand ciel* and *quelle horreur* punctuated the selections. 'There's Tante Jeanne grand-cieling as usual,' Mother would say to her husband, who, being a little deaf, would answer, 'What?' and Tante Jeanne, overhearing him, would re-read the accident for his especial benefit, while the governesses recounted personal experiences among themselves, and Miss Waghorn made eager efforts to take part in it all, or tell her little tales of fairies and Cornish cream....

One by one the governesses rose to leave; each made a comprehensive bow that included the entire company. Daddy lit a cigarette or let Jimbo light it for him, too wumbled with his thoughts of afternoon work to notice the puff stolen surreptitiously on the way. Jane Anne folded her napkin carefully, talking with Mother in a low voice about the packing of the basket with provisions for tea. Tea was included in the Pension terms; in a small clothes-basket she carried bread, milk, sugar, and butter daily across to La Citadelle, except on Sundays when she wore gloves and left the duty to the younger children who were less particular.

The governesses, charged with life for another twenty-four hours at least, flocked down the creaking stairs. They nodded as they passed the Bureau window where the Postmaster pored over his collection of stamps, or examined a fretwork pattern of a boy on a bicycle—there was no heavy garden work that day—and went out into the street. They stood in knots a moment, discussing unfavourably the food just eaten, and declaring they would stand it no longer. 'Only where else can we go?' said one, feeling automatically at her velvet bag to make sure the orange was safely in it. Upstairs, at the open window, Madame Jequier overheard them as she filled the walnut shells with butter for the birds. She only smiled.

'I wish we could help her,' Mother was saying to her husband, as they watched her from the sofa in the room behind. 'A more generous creature never lived.' It was a daily statement that lacked force owing to repetition, yet the emotion prompting it was ever new and real.

'Or a more feckless,' was his reply. 'But if we ever come into our estates, we will. It shall be the first thing.' His mind always hovered after those distant estates when it was perplexed by immediate financial difficulty, and just now he was thinking of various bills and payments falling due. It was his own sympathetic link with the widow—ways and means, and the remorseless nature of sheets of paper with columns of figures underneath the horrible word *doit*.

'So Monsieur 'Enry Rogairs is coming,' she said excitedly, turning to them a moment on her way to the garden. 'And after all these years! He will find the house the same, and the garden better—oh, wonderfully improved. But us, *helas!* he will find old, oh, how old!' She did not really mean herself, however.

She began a long 'reminiscent' chapter, full of details of the days when he and Daddy had been boys together, but in the middle of it Daddy just got up and walked out, saying, 'I must get over to my work, you know.' There was no artificiality of manners at Bourcelles. Mother followed him, with a trifle more ceremony. 'Ah, c'est partir a l'anglaise!' sighed the widow, watching them go. She was accustomed to it. She went out into her garden, full of excitement at the prospect of the new arrival. Every arrival for her meant a possible chance of help. She was as young as her latest bulb really. Courage, hope, and generosity invariably go together.

CHAPTER XI

Take him and cut him out in little stars,
And he will make the face of heaven so fine
That all the world will be in love with night
And pay no worship to the garish sun!
      Romeo and Juliet.

The announcement of Henry Rogers's coming was received—variously, for any new arrival into the Den circle was subjected to rigorous criticism. This criticism was not intentional; it was the instinctive judgment that children pass upon everything, object or person, likely to affect themselves. And there is no severer bar of judgment in the world.

'Who *is* Cousinenry? What a name! Is he stiff, I wonder?' came from Monkey, almost before the announcement had left her father's lips. 'What will he think of Tante Jeanne?' Her little torrent of questions that prejudged him thus never called for accurate answers as a rule, but this time she meant to have an answer. 'What is he exaccurately?' she added, using her own invention made up of 'exact' and 'accurate.'

Mother looked up from the typewritten letter to reply, but before she could say, 'He's your father's cousin, dear; they were here as boys twenty years ago to learn French,' Jinny burst in with an explosive interrogation. She had been reading *La Bonne Menagere* in a corner. Her eyes, dark with conjecture, searched the faces of both parents alternately. 'Excuse me, Mother, but is he a clergyman?' she asked with a touch of alarm.

'Whatever makes you think that, child?'

'Clergymen are always called the reverundhenry. He'll wear black and have socks that want mending.'

'He shouldn't punt his letters,' declared Monkey. 'He's not an author, is he?'

Jimbo, busy over school tasks, with a huge slate-pencil his crumpled fingers held like a walking-stick, watched and listened in silence. He was ever fearful, perhaps, lest his superior man's knowledge might be called upon and found wanting. Questions poured and crackled like grapeshot, while the truth slowly emerged from the explanations the parents were occasionally permitted to interject. The personality of Cousin Henry Rogers grew into life about them—gradually. The result was a curious one that Minks would certainly have resented with indignation. For Cousinenry was, apparently, a business man with pockets full of sovereigns; stern, clever, and important; the sort of man that gets into Governments and things, yet somewhere with the flavour of the clergyman about him. This clerical touch was Jane Anne's contribution to the picture; and she was certain that he wore silk socks of the most expensive description—a detail she had read probably in some chance fragments of a newspaper. For Jinny selected phrases in this way from anywhere, and repeated them on all occasions without the slightest relevancy. She practised them. She had a way of giving abrupt information and making startling statements *a propos* of nothing at all. Certain phrases stuck in her mind, it seemed, for no comprehensible reason. When excited she picked out the one that first presented itself and fired it off like a gun, the more inapt the better. And 'busy' was her favourite adjective always.

'It's like a communication from a company,' Mother was saying, as she handed back the typewritten letter.

'Is he a company promoter then?' asked Jinny like a flash, certainly ignorant what that article of modern life could mean.

'Oh, I say!' came reproachfully from Jimbo, thus committing himself for the first time to speech. He glanced up into several faces round him, and then continued the picture of Cousin Henry he was drawing on his slate. He listened all the time. Occasionally he cocked an eye or ear up. He took in everything, saying little. His opinions matured slowly. The talk continued for a long time, questions and answers.

'I think he's nice,' he announced at length in French. For intimate things, he always used that language; his English, being uncertain, was kept for matters of unimportance. 'A gentle man.'

And it was Jimbo's verdict that the children then finally adopted. Cousin Henry was *gentil*. They laughed loudly at him, yet agreed. His influence on their little conclaves, though never volubly expressed— because of that very fact, perhaps—was usually accepted. Jimbo was so decided. And he never committed himself to impulsive judgments that later had to be revised. He listened in silence to the end, then went plump for one side or the other. 'I think he'll be a nice man,' was the label, therefore, then and there attached to Mr. Henry Rogers in advance of delivery. Further than that, however, they would not go. It would have been childish to commit themselves more deeply till they saw him.

The conversation then slipped beyond their comprehension, or rather their parents used long words and circumventing phrases that made it difficult to follow. Owing to lack of space, matters of importance often had to be discussed in this way under the children's eyes, unless at night, when all were safe in bed; for French, of course, was of no avail for purposes of concealment. Long words were then made use of, dark, wumbled sentences spoken very quickly, with suggestive gestures and expressions of the eyes labelled by Monkey with, 'Look, Mother and Daddy are making faces—something's up!'

But, none the less, all listened, and Monkey, whose intuitive intelligence soaked up hidden meanings like a sponge, certainly caught the trend of what was said. She detailed it later to the others, when Jinny checked her exposition with a puzzled 'but Mother could never have said *that*,' while Jimbo looked wise and grave, as though he had understood it all along, and was even in his parents' councils.

On this occasion, however, there was nothing very vital to retail. Cousin Henry was to arrive to-morrow by the express from Paris. He was a little younger than Daddy, and would have the room above him in the carpenter's house. His meals he would take at the Pension just as they did, and for tea he would always come over to the Den. And this latter fact implied that he was to be admitted into intimacy at once, for only intimates used the Den regularly for tea, of course.

It was serious. It involved a change in all their lives. Jinny wondered if it 'would cost Daddy any more money,' or whether 'Cousinenry would bring a lot of things with him,' though not explaining whether by 'things' she meant food or presents or clothes. He was not married, so he couldn't be very old; and Monkey, suggesting that he might 'get to love' one of the retired governesses who came to the Pension for their mid-day dinner, was squelched by Jimbo with 'old governesses *never* marry; they come back to settle, and then they just die off.'

Thus was Henry Rogers predigested. But at any rate he was accepted. And this was fortunate; for a new arrival whom the children did not 'pass' had been known to have a time that may best be described as not conducive to repose of body, mind, or spirit.

The arrival of Mr. Henry Rogers in the village—in La Citadelle, that is—was a red-letter day. This, however, seems a thin description of its glory. For a more adequate description a well-worn phrase must be borrowed from the poems of Montmorency Minks—a 'Day of Festival,' for which 'coronal' invariably lay in waiting for rhyming purposes a little further down the sonnet.

Monkey that afternoon managed to get home earlier than usual from Neuchatel, a somewhat suspicious explanation as her passport. Her eyes were popping. Jimbo was always out of the village school at three. He carried a time-table in his pocket; but it was mere pretence, since he was a little walking Bradshaw, and knew every train by heart—the Geneva

Express, the Paris Rapide, the 'omnibus' trains, and the mountain ones that climbed the forest heights towards La Chaux de Fonds and Le Locle. Of these latter only the white puffing smoke was visible from the village, but he knew with accuracy their times of departure, their arrival, and the names of every station where they stopped. In the omnibus trains he even knew some of the guards personally, the engine-drivers too. He might be seen any day after school standing in the field beside the station, waiting for them to pass; *mecanicien* and *conducteur* were the commonest words in his whole vocabulary. When possible he passed the time of day with both of these important personages, or from the field he waved his hand and took his cap off. All engines, moreover, were 'powerful locomotives.' The phrase was stolen from his father—a magnificent sound it had, taking several seconds to pronounce. No day was wholly lived in vain which enabled him to turn to some one with, 'There's the Paris Rapide; it's five minutes late'; or 'That's the Geneva omnibus. You see, it has to have a very'—here a deep breath—'powerful locomotive.'

So upon this day of festival it was quite useless to talk of common things, and even the holidays acquired a very remote importance. Everybody in the village knew it. From Gygi, the solitary gendarme, to Henri Beguin, who mended boots, but had the greater distinction that he was the only man Gygi ever arrested, for periodical wild behaviour —all knew that 'Cousin Henry, father's cousin, you know,' was expected to arrive in the evening, that he was an important person in the life of London, and that he was not exactly a *pasteur*, yet shared something of a clergyman's grave splendour. Clothed in a sacerdotal atmosphere he certainly was, though it was the gravity of Jane Anne's negative description that fastened this wild ecclesiastical idea upon him.

'He's not *exactly* a clergyman,' she told the dressmaker, who for two francs every Monday afternoon sat in the kitchen and helped with the pile of indiscriminate mending,' because he has to do with rather big companies and things. But he is a serious man all the same—and most fearfully busy always.'

'We're going to meet him in the town,' said Jimbo carelessly. 'You see, the Paris Rapide doesn't stop here. We shall come back with him by the 6.20. It gets here at 6.50, so he'll be in time for supper, if it's punctual. It usually is.'

And accordingly they went to Neuchatel and met the Paris train. They met their Cousin Henry, too. Powerful locomotives and everything else were instantly forgotten when they saw their father go up to a tall thin man who jumped—yes, jumped—down the high steps on to the level platform and at once began to laugh. He had a beard like their father. 'How *will* they know which is which?' thought Jinny. They stood in everybody's way and stared.

He was so tall. Daddy looked no bigger than little Beguin beside him. He had a large, hooked nose, brown skin, and keen blue eyes that took in everything at a single glance. They twinkled absurdly for so big a man. He wore rough brown tweeds and a soft felt travelling hat. He wore also square-toed English boots. He carried in one hand a shiny brown leather bag with his initials on it like a member of the Government.

The clergyman idea was destroyed in a fraction of a second, never to revive. The company promoter followed suit. Jinny experienced an entirely new sensation in her life—something none but herself had ever felt before— something romantic. 'He's like a soldier—a General,' she said to anybody who cared to listen, and she said it so loudly that many did listen. But she did not care. She stood apart from the others, staring as though it were a railway accident. This tall figure of a cousin she could fit nowhere as yet into her limited scheme of life. She admired him intensely. Yet Daddy laughed and chatted with him as if he were nothing at all! She kept outside the circle, wondering about his socks and underclothes. His beard was much neater and better trimmed than her father's. At least no crumb or bit of cotton was in it.

But Jimbo felt no awe. After a moment's hesitation, during which the passers-by butted him this way and that, he marched straight up and looked him in the face. He reached to his watch-chain only.

'I'll be your sekrity, too,' he announced, interrupting Daddy's foolishness about 'this is my youngest lad, Rogers.' Youngest lad indeed!

And Henry Rogers then stooped and kissed the lot of them. One after the other he put his big arms round them and gave them a hug that was like the hug of a bear standing on its hind legs. They took it, each in his own way, differently. Jimbo proudly; Monkey, with a smacking return kiss that somehow conveyed the note of her personality— impudence; but Jane Anne, with a grave and outraged dignity, as though in a public railway station this kind of behaviour was slightly inappropriate. She wondered for days afterwards whether she had been quite correct. He was a cousin, but still he was—a man. And she wondered what she ought to call him. 'Mr. Rogers' was not quite right, yet 'Mr. Cousin Henry' was equally ill-chosen. She decided upon a combination of her own, a kind of code-word that was affectionate yet distant: 'Cousinenry.' And she used it with an explosive directness that was almost challenge—he could accept which half he chose.

But all accepted him at once without fear. They felt, moreover, a secret and very tender thing; there was something in this big, important man that made them know he would love them for themselves; and more—that something in him had need of them. Here lay the explanation of their instant confidence and acceptance.

'What a jolly bunch you are, to be sure!' he exclaimed. 'And you're to be my secretary, are you?' he added, taking Jimbo by the shoulders. 'How splendid!'

'*I'm* not,' said Monkey, with a rush of laughter already too long restrained. Her manner suggested a somersault, only prevented by engines and officials.

But Jimbo was a little shocked. This sort of thing disgraced them.

'Oh, I say!' he exclaimed reproachfully.

'Daddy, isn't she awful?' added Jane Anne under her breath, a sentence of disapproval in daily use. Her life seemed made up of apologising for her impudent sister.

'The 6.20 starts at 6.20, you know,' Jimbo announced. 'The Lausanne Express has gone. Are your "baggages" registered?' And the party moved off in a scattered and uncertain manner to buy tickets and register the luggage. They went back second class—for the first time in their lives. It was Cousin Henry who paid the difference. That sealed his position finally in their eyes. He was a millionaire. All London people went first or second class.

But Jimbo and his younger sister had noticed something else about the new arrival besides his nose and eyes and length. Even his luxurious habit of travelling second class did not impress them half as much as this other detail in his appearance. They referred to it in a whispered talk behind the shelter of the *conducteur's* back while tickets were being punched.

'You know,' whispered Monkey, her eyes popping, 'I've seen Cousin Henry before somewhere. I'm certain.' She gave a little gasp.

Jimbo stared, only half believing, yet undeniably moved. Even his friend, the Guard, was temporarily neglected. 'Where?' he asked; 'do you mean in a picture?'

'No,' she answered with decision, 'out here, I think. In the woods or somewhere.' She seemed vague. But her very vagueness helped him to believe. She was not inventing; he was sure of that.

The *conducteur* at that moment passed away along the train, and Cousin Henry looked straight at the pair of them. Through the open window dusk fluttered down the sky with spots of gold already on its wings.

'What jolly stars you've got here,' he said, pointing. 'They're like diamonds. Look, it's a perfect network far above the Alps. By gum— what beauties!'

And as he said it he smiled. Monkey gave her brother a nudge that nearly made him cry out. He wondered what she meant, but all the same he returned the nudge significantly. For Cousin Henry, when he smiled, had plainly shown—two teeth of gold.

The children had never seen gold-capped teeth.

'I'd like one for my collection,' thought Jimbo, meaning a drawer that included all his loose possessions of small size. But another thing stirred in him too, vague, indefinite, far away, something he had, as it were, forgotten.

CHAPTER XII

O star benignant and serene,
  I take the good to-morrow,
That fills from verge to verge my dream,
  With all its joy and sorrow!
The old sweet spell is unforgot
  That turns to June December;
And, though the world remember not,
  Love, we would remember.
Life and Death, W. E. HENLEY.

And Rogers went over to unpack. It was soon done. He sat at his window in the carpenter's house and enjoyed the peace. The spell of evening stole down from the woods. London and all his strenuous life seemed very far away. Bourcelles drew up beside him, opened her robe, let down her forest hair, and whispered to him with her voice of many fountains....

She lies just now within the fringe of an enormous shadow, for the sun has dipped behind the blue-domed mountains that keep back France. Small hands of scattered mist creep from the forest, fingering the vineyards that troop down towards the lake. A dog barks. Gygi, the gendarme, leaves the fields and goes home to take his uniform from its peg. Pere Langel walks among his beehives. There is a distant tinkling of cow-bells from the heights, where isolated pastures gleam like a patchwork quilt between the spread of forest; and farther down a train from Paris or Geneva, booming softly, leaves a trail of smoke against the background of the Alps where still the sunshine lingers.

But trains, somehow, do not touch the village; they merely pass it. Busy with vines, washed by its hill-fed stream, swept by the mountain winds, it lies unchallenged by the noisy world, remote, un-noticed, half forgotten. And on its outskirts stands the giant poplar that guards it—*la sentinelle* the peasants call it, because its lofty crest, rising to every wind, sends down the street first warning of any coming change. They see it bend or hear the rattle of its leaves. The *coup de Joran*, most sudden and devastating of mountain winds, is on the way from the precipice of the Creux du Van. It comes howling like artillery down the deep Gorges de l'Areuse. They run to fasten windows, collect the washing from roof and garden, drive the cattle into shelter, and close the big doors of the barns. The children clap their hands and cry to Gygi, 'Plus vite! Plus vite!' The lake turns dark. Ten minutes later it is raging with an army of white horses like the sea.

Darkness drapes the village. It comes from the whole long line of Jura, riding its troop of purple shadows—slowly curtaining out the world. For the carpenter's house stands by itself, apart. Perched upon a knoll beside his little patch of vineyard, it commands perspective. From his upper window Rogers saw and remembered....

High up against the fading sky ridges of limestone cliff shine out here and there, and upon the vast slopes of Boudry—*l'immense geant de Boudry*—lies a flung cloak of forest that knows no single seam. The smoke from *bucheron* fires, joining the scarves of mist, weaves across its shoulder a veil of lace-like pattern, and at its feet, like some great fastening button, hides the village of the same name, where Marat passed his brooding youth. Its evening lights are already twinkling. They signal across the vines to the towers of Colombier, rising with its columns of smoke and its poplars against the sheet of darkening water—Colombier, in whose castle *milord marechal Keith* had his headquarters as Governor of the Principality of Neuchatel under the King of Prussia. And, higher up, upon the flank of wooded mountains, is just visible still the great red-roofed farm of Cotendard, built by his friend Lord Wemyss, another Jacobite refugee, who had strange parties there and entertained Jean Jacques Rousseau in his exile. La Citadelle in the village was the wing of another castle he began to build, but left unfinished.

White in the gathering dusk, Rogers saw the strip of roadway where passed the gorgeous coach—*cette fameuse diligence du milord marshal Keith*—or more recent, but grimmer memory, where General Bourbaki's division of the French army, 80,000 strong, trailed in unspeakable anguish, hurrying from the Prussians. At Les Verrieres, upon the frontier, they laid down their arms, and for three consecutive days and nights the pitiful destitute procession passed down that strip of mountain road in the terrible winter of 1870-71.

Some among the peasants still hear that awful tramping in their sleep: the kindly old *vigneron* who stood in front of his chalet from dawn to sunset, giving each man bread and wine; and the woman who nursed three soldiers through black small-pox, while neighbours left food upon the wall before the house.... Memories of his boyhood crowded thick and fast. The spell of the place deepened about him with the darkness. He recalled the village postman—fragment of another romance, though a tattered and discredited one. For this postman was the descendant of that audacious pale-frenier who married Lord Wemyss' daughter, to live the life of peasants with her in a yet tinier hamlet higher up the slopes. If you asked him, he would proudly tell you, with his bullet-shaped, close-cropped head cocked impertinently on one side, how his brother, now assistant in a Paris shop, still owned the title of baron by means of which his reconciliated lordship sought eventually to cover up the unfortunate escapade. He would hand you English letters—and Scotch ones too!—with an air of covert insolence that was the joy of half the village. And on Sundays he was to be seen, garbed in knickerbockers, gaudy stockings, and sometimes high, yellowish spats, walking with his peasant girl along the very road his more spirited forbear covered in his runaway match....

The night stepped down more quickly every minute from the heights. Deep-noted bells floated upwards to him from Colombier, bringing upon the evening wind some fragrance of these faded boyhood memories. The stars began to peep above the peaks and ridges, and the mountains of the Past moved nearer. A veil of gossamer rose above the tree-tops, hiding more and more of the landscape; he just could see the slim new moon dip down to drink from her own silver cup within the darkening lake. Workmen, in twos and threes, came past the little house from their toil among the vines, and fragments of the Dalcroze songs rose to his ear— songs that the children loved, and that he had not heard for nearly a quarter of a century. Their haunting refrains completed then the spell, for all genuine spells are set to some peculiar music of their own. These Dalcroze melodies were exactly right.... The figures melted away into the single shadow of the village street. The houses swallowed them, voices, footsteps, and all.

And his eye, wandering down among the lights that twinkled against the wall of mountains, picked out the little ancient house, nestling so close beside the church that they shared a wall in common. Twenty-five years had passed since first he bowed his head beneath the wistaria that still crowned the Pension doorway. He remembered bounding up the creaking stairs. He felt he could still bound as swiftly and with as sure a step, only—he would expect less at the top now. More truly put, perhaps, he would expect less for himself. That ambition of his life was over and done with. It was for others now that his desires flowed so strongly. Mere personal aims lay behind him in a faded heap, their seductiveness exhausted.... He was a man with a Big Scheme now— a Scheme to help the world....

The village seemed a dull enough place in those days, for the big Alps beckoned beyond, and day and night he longed to climb them instead of reading dull French grammar. But now all was different. It dislocated his sense of time to find the place so curiously unchanged. The years had played some trick upon him. While he himself had altered, developed, and the rest, this village had remained identically the same, till it seemed as if no progress of the outer world need ever change it. The very people were so little altered—hair grown a little whiter, shoulders more rounded, steps here and there a trifle slower, but one and all following the old routine he knew so well as a boy.

Tante Jeanne, in particular, but for wrinkles that looked as though a night of good sound sleep would smooth them all away, was the same brave woman, still 'running' that Wistaria Pension against the burden of inherited debts and mortgages. 'We're still alive,' she had said to him, after greetings delayed a quarter of a century, 'and if we haven't got ahead much, at least we haven't gone back!' There was no more hint of complaint than this. It stirred in him a very poignant sense of admiration for the high courage that drove the ageing fighter forward still with hope and faith. No doubt she still turned the kitchen saucer that did duty for planchette, unconsciously pushing its blunted pencil towards the letters that should spell out coming help. No doubt she still wore that marvellous tea-gown garment that did duty for so many different toilettes, even wearing it when she went with goloshes and umbrella to practise Sunday's hymns every Saturday night on the wheezy church harmonium. And most likely she still made underskirts from the silk of discarded umbrellas because she loved the sound of frou-frou thus obtained, while the shape of the silk exactly adapted itself to the garment mentioned. And doubtless, too, she still gave away a whole week's profits at the slightest call of sickness in the village, and then wondered how it was the Pension did not pay...!

A voice from below interrupted his long reverie.

'Ready for supper, Henry?' cried his cousin up the stairs. 'It's past seven. The children have already left the Citadelle.'

And as the two middle-aged dreamers made their way along the winding street of darkness through the vines, one of them noticed that the stars drew down their grand old network, fastening it to the heights of Boudry and La Tourne. He did not mention it to his companion, who was wumbling away in his beard about some difficult details of his book, but the thought slipped through his mind like the trail of a flying comet: 'I'd like to stay a long time in this village and get the people straight a bit,'—which, had he known it, was another thought carefully paraphrased so that he should not notice it and feel alarm: 'It will be difficult to get away from here. My feet are in that net of stars. It's catching about my heart.'

Low in the sky a pale, witched moon of yellow watched them go....

'The Starlight Express is making this way, I do believe,' he thought. But perhaps he spoke the words aloud instead of thinking them.

'Eh! What's that you said, Henry?' asked the other, taking it for a comment of value upon the plot of a story he had referred to.

'Oh, nothing particular,' was the reply. 'But just look at those stars above La Tourne. They shine like beacons burning on the trees.' Minks would have called them 'braziers.'

'They are rather bright, yes,' said the other, disappointed. 'The air here is so very clear.' And they went up the creaking wooden stairs to supper in the Wistaria Pension as naturally as though the years had lifted them behind the mountains of the past in a single bound— twenty-five years ago.

CHAPTER XIII

Near where yonder evening star
  Makes a glory in the air,
Lies a land dream—found and far
  Where it is light always.
There those lovely ghosts repair
  Who in sleep's enchantment are,
In Cockayne dwell all things fair—
  (But it is far away).
Cockayne Country, Agnes Duclaux.

The first stage in Cousinenry's introduction took place, as has been seen, at a railway station; but further stages were accomplished later. For real introductions are not completed by merely repeating names and shaking hands, still less by a hurried kiss. The ceremony had many branches too— departments, as it were. It spread itself, with various degrees, over many days as opportunity offered, and included Gygi, the gendarme, as well as the little troop of retired governesses who came to the Pension for their mid-day dinner. Before two days were passed he could not go down the village street without lifting his cap at least a dozen times. Bourcelles was so very friendly; no room for strangers there; a new-comer might remain a mystery, but he could not be unknown. Rogers found his halting French becoming rapidly fluent again. And every one knew so much about him— more almost than he knew himself.

At the Den next day, on the occasion of their first tea together, he realised fully that introduction—to the children at any rate— involved a kind of initiation.

It seemed to him that the room was full of children, crowds of them, an intricate and ever shifting maze. For years he had known no dealings with the breed, and their movements now were so light and rapid that it rather bewildered him. They were in and out between the kitchen, corridor, and bedroom like bits of a fluid puzzle. One moment a child was beside him, and the next, just as he had a suitable sentence ready to discharge at it, the place was vacant. A minute later 'it' appeared through another door, carrying the samovar, or was on the roof outside struggling with Riquette.

'Oh, there you are!' he exclaimed. 'How you do dart about, to be sure!'

And the answer, if any, was invariably of the cheeky order—

'One can't keep still here; there's not room enough.'

Or, worse still—

'I must get past you somehow!' This, needless to say, from Monkey, who first made sure her parents were out of earshot.

But he liked it, for he recognised this proof that he was accepted and made one of the circle. These were tentative invitations to play. It made him feel quite larky, though at first he found his machinery of larking rather stiff. The wheels required oiling. And his first attempt to chase Miss Impudence resulted in a collision with Jane Anne carrying a great brown pot of home-made jam for the table. There was a dreadful sound. He had stepped on the cat at the same time.

His introduction to the cat was the immediate result, performed solemnly by Jimbo, and watched by Jinny, still balancing the jar of jam, with an expression of countenance that was half amazement and half shock. Collisions with creatures of his size and splendour were a new event to her.

'I must advertise for help if it occurs again!' she exclaimed.

'That's Mere Riquette, you know,' announced Jimbo formally to his cousin, standing between them in his village school blouse, hands tucked into his belt.

'I heard her, yes.' From a distance the cat favoured him with a single comprehensive glance, then turned away and disappeared beneath the sofa. She, of course, reserved her opinion.

'It didn't REALLY hurt her. She always squeals like that.'

'Perhaps she likes it,' suggested Rogers.

'She likes better tickling behind the ear,' Jimbo thought, anxious to make him feel all right, and then plunged into a description of her general habits—how she jumped at the door handles when she wanted to come in, slept on his bed at night, and looked for a saucer in a particular corner of the kitchen floor. This last detail was a compliment. He meant to imply that Cousin Henry might like to see to it himself sometimes, although it had always been his own special prerogative hitherto.

'I shall know in future, then,' said Rogers earnestly, showing, by taking the information seriously, that he possessed the correct instinct.

'Oh yes, it's quite easy. You'll soon learn it,' spoken with feet wide apart and an expression of careless importance, as who should say, 'What a sensible man you are! Still, these *are* little things one has to be careful about, you know.'

Mother poured out tea, somewhat laboriously, as though the exact proportions of milk, hot water, and sugar each child took were difficult to remember. Each had a special cup, moreover. Her mind, ever crammed with a thousand domestic details which she seemed to carry all at once upon the surface, ready for any sudden question, found it difficult to concentrate upon the teapot. Her mind was ever worrying over these. Her husband was too vague to be of practical help. When any one spoke to her, she would pause in the middle of the operation, balancing a cup in one hand and a milk jug in the other, until the question was properly answered, every t crossed and every i dotted. There was no mistaking what Mother meant—provided you had the time to listen. She had that careful thoroughness which was no friend of speed. The result was that hands were stretched out for second cups long before she had completed the first round. Her own tea began usually when everybody else had finished—and lasted—well, some time.

'Here's a letter I got,' announced Jimbo, pulling a very dirty scrap of paper from a pocket hidden beneath many folds of blouse. 'You'd like to see it.' He handed it across the round table, and Rogers took it politely. 'Thank you very much; it came by this morning's post, did it?'

'Oh, no,' was the reply, as though a big correspondence made the date of little importance. 'Not by *that* post.' But Monkey blurted out with the jolly laughter that was her characteristic sound, 'It came ages ago. He's had it in his pocket for weeks.'

Jimbo, ignoring the foolish interruption, watched his cousin's face, while Jinny gave her sister a secret nudge that every one could see.

'Darling Jimbo,' was what Rogers read, 'I have been to school, and did strokes and prickings and marched round. I am like you now. A fat kiss and a hug, your loving——' The signature was illegible, lost amid several scratchy lines in a blot that looked as if a beetle had expired after violent efforts in a pool of ink.

'Very nice indeed, very well put,' said Rogers, handing it gravely back again, while some one explained that the writer, aged five, had just gone to a kindergarten school in Geneva. 'And have you answered it?'

'Oh, yes. I answered it the same day, you see.' It was, perhaps, a foolish letter for a man to have in his pocket. Still—it was a letter.

'Good! What a capital secretary you'll make me.' And the boy's flush of pleasure almost made the dish of butter rosy.

'Oh, take another; take a lot, please,' Jimbo said, handing the cakes that Rogers divined were a special purchase in his honour; and while he did so, managed to slip one later on to the plates of Monkey and her sister, who sat on either side of him. The former gobbled it up at once, barely keeping back her laughter, but Jinny, with a little bow, put hers carefully aside on the edge of her plate, not knowing quite the 'nice' thing to do with it. Something in the transaction seemed a trifle too familiar perhaps. She stole a glance at mother, but mother was filling the cups and did not notice. Daddy could have helped her, only he would say 'What?' in a loud voice, and she would have to repeat her question for all to hear. Later, she ate the cake in very small morsels, a little uncomfortably.

It was a jolly, merry, cosy tea, as teas in the Den always were. Daddy wumbled a number of things in his beard to which no one need reply unless they felt like it. The usual sentences were not heard to-day: 'Monkey, what a mouthful! You *must* not shovel in your food like that!' or, 'Don't *gurgle* your tea down; swallow it quietly, like a little lady'; or, 'How often have you been told *not* to drink with your mouth full; this is not the servants' hall, remember!' There were no signs of contretemps of any kind, nothing was upset or broken, and the cakes went easily round, though not a crumb was left over.

But the entire time Mr. Rogers was subjected to the keenest scrutiny imaginable. Nothing he did escaped two pairs of eyes at least. Signals were flashed below as well as above the table. These signals were of the kind birds know perhaps—others might be aware of their existence if they listened very attentively, yet might not interpret them. No Comanche ever sent more deft communications unobserved to his brother across a camp fire.

Yet nothing was done visibly; no crumb was flicked; and the table hid the pressure of the toe which, fortunately, no one intercepted. Monkey, at any rate, had eyes in both her feet, and Jimbo knew how to keep his counsel without betrayal. But inflections of the voice did most of the work—this, with flashes of brown and blue lights, conveyed the swift despatches.

'My underneath goes out to him,' Monkey telegraphed to her brother while she asked innocently for 'jam, please, Jimbo'; and he replied, 'Oh, he's all right, I think, but better not go too fast,' as he wiped the same article from his chin and caught her big brown eye upon him. 'He'll be our Leader,' she conveyed later by the way she stirred her cup of tea-hot-water-milk, 'when once we've got him "out" and taught him'; and Jimbo offered and accepted his own resignation of the coveted, long-held post by the way he let his eyelid twiddle in answer to her well-directed toe-nudge out of sight.

This, in a brief resume, was the purport of the give and take of numerous despatches between them during tea, while outwardly Mother— and

Father, too, when he thought about it—were delighted with their perfect company manners.

Jane Anne, outside all this flummery, went her own way upon an even keel. She watched him closely too, but not covertly. She stared him in the face, and imitated his delicate way of eating. Once or twice she called him 'Mr. Rogers,' for this had a grown-up flavour about it that appealed to her, and 'Cousin Henry' did not come easily to her at first. She could not forget that she had left the *ecole secondaire* and was on her way to a Geneva Pension where she would attend an *ecole menagere*. And the bursts of laughter that greeted her polite 'Mr. Rogers, did you have a nice journey, and do you like Bourcelles?'—in a sudden pause that caught Mother balancing cup and teapot in mid-air—puzzled her a good deal. She liked his quiet answer though—'Thank you, Miss Campden, I think both quite charming.' He did not laugh. He understood, whatever the others might think. She had wished to correct the levity of the younger brother and sister, and he evidently appreciated her intentions. He seemed a nice man, a very nice man.

Tea once over, she carried off the loaded tray to the kitchen to do the washing-up. Jimbo and Monkey had disappeared. They always vanished about this time, but once the unenvied operation was safely under way, they emerged from their hiding-places again. No one ever saw them go. They were gone before the order, 'Now, children, help your sister take the things away,' was even issued. By the time they re-appeared Jinny was halfway through it and did not want to be disturbed.

'Never mind, Mother,' she said, 'they're chronic. They're only little busy Highlanders!' For 'chronic' was another catch-word at the moment, and sometimes by chance she used it appropriately. The source of 'busy Highlanders' was a mystery known only to herself. And resentment, like jealousy, was a human passion she never felt and did not understand. Jane Anne was the spirit of unselfishness incarnate. It was to her honour, but made her ineffective as a personality.

Daddy lit his big old meerschaum—the 'squelcher' Jinny called it, because of its noise—and mooned about the room, making remarks on literature or politics, while Mother picked a work-basket cleverly from a dangerously overloaded shelf, and prepared to mend and sew. The windows were wide open, and framed the picture of snowy Alps, now turning many-tinted in the slanting sunshine. (Riquette, gorged with milk, appeared from the scullery and inspected knees and chairs and cushions that seemed available, selecting finally the best arm-chair and curling up to sleep. Rogers smoked a cigarette, pleased and satisfied like the cat.) A hush fell on the room. It was the hour of peace between tea and the noisy Pension supper that later broke the spell. So quiet was it that the mouse began to nibble in the bedroom walls, and even peeped through the cracks it knew between the boards. It came out, flicked its whiskers, and then darted in again like lightning. Jane Anne, rinsing out the big teapot in the scullery, frightened it. Presently she came in softly, put the lamp ready for her mother's needle, in case of need later, gave a shy queer look at 'Mr. Rogers' and her father, both of whom nodded absent-mindedly to her, and then went on tip-toe out of the room. She was bound for the village shop to buy methylated spirits, sugar, blotting-paper, and—a 'plaque' of Suchard chocolate for her Cousinenry. The forty centimes for this latter was a large item in her savings; but she gave no thought to that. What sorely perplexed her as she hurried down the street was whether he would like it 'milk' or 'plain.' In the end she bought both.

Down the dark corridor of the Citadelle, before she left, she did not hear the muffled laughter among the shadows, nor see the movement of two figures that emerged together from the farther end.

'He'll be on the sofa by now. Shall we go for him?' It was the voice of Monkey.

'Leave it to me.' Jimbo still meant to be leader so far as these two were concerned at any rate. Let come later what might.

'Better get Mother out of the way first, though.'

'Mother's nothing. She's sewing and things,' was the reply. He understood the conditions thoroughly. He needed no foolish advice.

'He's awfully easy. You saw the two gold teeth. It's him, I'm sure.'

'Of course he's easy, only a person doesn't want to be pulled about after tea,' in the tone of a man who meant to feel his way a bit.

Clearly they had talked together more than once since the arrival at the station. Jimbo made up for ignorance by decision and sublime self-confidence. He answered no silly questions, but listened, made up his mind, and acted. He was primed to the brim—a born leader.

'Better tell him that we'll come for him to-night,' the girl insisted. 'He'll be less astonished then. You can tell he dreams a lot by his manner. Even now he's only half awake.'

The conversation was in French—school and village French. Her brother ignored the question with 'va te cacher!' He had no doubts himself.

'Just wait a moment while I tighten my belt,' he observed. 'You can tell it by his eyes,' he added, as Monkey urged him forward to the door. 'I know a good dreamer when I see one.'

Then fate helped them. The door against their noses opened and Daddy came out, followed by his cousin. All four collided.

'Oh, is the washing-up finished?' asked Monkey innocently, quick as a flash.

'How you startled me!' exclaimed Daddy. 'You really must try to be less impetuous. You'd better ask Mother about the washing,' he repeated, 'she's in there sewing.' His thoughts, it seemed, were just a trifle confused. Plates and linen both meant washing, and sometimes hair and other stuff as well.

'There's no light, you see, yet,' whispered Jimbo. A small lamp usually hung upon the wall. Jane Anne at that moment came out carrying it and asking for a match.

'No starlight, either,' added Monkey quickly, giving her cousin a little nudge. 'It's all upwumbled, or whatever Daddy calls it.'

The look he gave her might well have suppressed a grown-up person— 'grande personne,' as Jimbo termed it, translating literally—but on Monkey it had only slight effect. Her irrepressible little spirit concealed springs few could regulate. Even avoir-dupois increased their resiliency the moment it was removed. But Jimbo checked her better than most. She did look a trifle ashamed—for a second.

'Can't you wait?' he whispered. 'Daddy'll spoil it if you begin it here. How you do fidget!'

They passed all together out into the yard, the men in front, the two children just behind, walking warily.

Then came the separation, yet none could say exactly how it was accomplished. For separations are curious things at the best of times, the forces that effect them as mysterious as wind that blows a pair of butterflies across a field. Something equally delicate was at work. One minute all four stood together by the fountain, and the next Daddy was walking downhill towards the carpenter's house alone, while the other three were already twenty metres up the street that led to the belt of forest.

Jimbo, perhaps, was responsible for the deft manoeuvring. At any rate, he walked beside his big cousin with the air of a successful aide-de- camp. But Monkey, too, seemed flushed with victory, rolling along—her rotundity ever suggested rolling rather than the taking of actual steps—as if she led a prisoner.

'Don't bother your cousin, children,' their father's voice was heard again faintly in the distance. Then the big shoulder of La Citadelle hid him from view and hearing.

And so the sight was seen of these three, arm in arm, passing along the village street in the twilight. Gygi saw them go and raised his blue, peaked cap; and so did Henri Favre, standing in the doorway of his little shop, as he weighed the possible value of the new customer for matches, chocolate, and string—the articles English chiefly bought; and likewise Alfred Sandoz, looking a moment through the window of his cabaret, the Guillaume Tell, saw them go past like shadows towards the woods, and observed to his carter friend across the table, 'They choose queer times for expeditions, these English, *ouah!*'

'It's their climate makes them like that,' put in his wife, a touch of pity in her voice. Her daughter swept the Den and lit the *fourneau* for *la famille anglaise* in the mornings, and the mother, knowing a little English, spelt out the weather reports in the *Daily Surprise* she sometimes brought.

Meanwhile the three travellers had crossed the railway line, where Jimbo detained them for a moment's general explanation, and passed the shadow of the sentinel poplar. The cluster of spring leaves rustled faintly on its crest. The village lay behind them now. They turned a moment to look back upon the stretch of vines and fields that spread towards the lake. From the pool of shadow where the houses nestled rose the spire of the church, a strong dark line against the fading sunset. Thin columns of smoke tried to draw it after them. Lights already twinkled on the farther shore, five miles across, and beyond these rose dim white forms of the tremendous ghostly Alps. Dusk slowly brought on darkness.

Jimbo began to hum the song of the village he had learned in school—

P'tit Bourcelles sur sa colline
De partout a gentille mine;
On y pratique avec success
L'exploitation du francais,

and the moment it was over, his sister burst out with the question that had been buzzing inside her head the whole time—

'How long are you going to stay?' she said, as they climbed higher along the dusty road.

'Oh, about a week,' he told her, giving the answer already used a dozen times. 'I've just come out for a holiday—first holiday I've had for twenty years. Fancy that! Pretty long time, eh?'

They simply didn't believe that; they let it pass—politely.

'London's stuffy, you know, just now,' he added, aware that he was convicted of exaggeration. 'Besides, it's spring.'

'There are millions of flowers here,' Jimbo covered his mistake kindly, 'millions and millions. Aren't there, Monkey?'

'Oh, billions.'

'Of course,' he agreed.

'And more than anywhere else in the whole world.'

'It looks like that,' said Cousin Henry, as proudly as they said it themselves. And they told him how they picked clothes-baskets full of the wild lily of the valley that grew upon the Boudry slopes, hepaticas, periwinkles, jonquils, blue and white violets, as well as countless anemones, and later, the big yellow marguerites.

'Then how long are you going to stay—*really*?' inquired Monkey once again, as though the polite interlude were over. It was a delicate way of suggesting that he had told an untruth. She looked up straight into his face. And, meeting her big brown eyes, he wondered a little—for the first time—how he should reply.

'Daddy came here meaning to stay only six months—first.'

'When I was littler,' Jimbo put in.

'——and stayed here all this time—four years.'

'I hope to stay a week or so—just a little holiday, you know,' he said at length, giving the answer purposely. But he said it without conviction, haltingly. He felt that they divined the doubt in him. They guessed his thought along the hands upon his arm, as a horse finds out its rider from the touch upon the reins. On either side big eyes watched and judged him; but the brown ones put a positive enchantment in his blood. They shone so wonderfully in the dusk.

'Longer than that, I think,' she told him, her own mind quite made up. 'It's not so easy to get away from.'

'You mean it?' he asked seriously. 'It makes one quite nervous.'

'There's such a lot to do here,' she said, still keeping her eyes fixed upon his face till he felt the wonder in him become a little unmanageable. 'You'll never get finished in a week.'

'My secretary,' he stammered, 'will help me,' and Jimbo nodded, fastening both hands upon his arm, while Monkey indulged in a little gust of curious laughter, as who should say 'He who laughs last, laughs best.'

They entered the edge of the forest. Hepaticas watched them with their eyes of blue. Violets marked their tread. The frontiers of the daylight softly closed behind them. A thousand trees opened a way to let them pass, and moss twelve inches thick took their footsteps silently as birds. They came presently to a little clearing where the pines stood in a circle and let in a space of sky. Looking up, all three saw the first small stars in it. A wild faint scent of coming rain was in the air—those warm spring rains that wash the way for summer. And a signal flashed unseen from the blue eyes to the brown.

'This way,' said Jimbo firmly. 'There's an armchair rock where you can rest and get your wind a bit,' and, though Rogers had not lost his wind, he let himself be led, and took the great grey boulder for his chair. Instantly, before he had arranged his weight among the points and angles, both his knees were occupied.

'By Jove,' flashed through his mind. 'They've brought me here on purpose. I'm caught!'

A tiny pause followed.

'Now, look here, you little Schemers, I want to know what——'

But the sentence was never finished. The hand of Monkey was already pointing upwards to the space of sky. He saw the fringe of pine tops fencing it about with their feathery, crested ring, and in the centre shone faint, scattered stars. Over the fence of mystery that surrounds common objects wonder peeped with one eye like a star.

'Cousinenry,' he heard close to his ear, so soft it almost might have been those tree-tops whispering to the night, 'do you know anything about a Star Cave—a place where the starlight goes when there are no eyes or puddles about to catch it?'

A Star Cave! How odd! His own boyhood's idea. He must have mentioned it to his cousin perhaps, and *he* had told the children. And all that was in him of nonsense, poetry, love rose at a bound as he heard it. He felt them settle themselves more comfortably upon his knees. He forgot to think about the points and angles. Here surely a gateway was opening before his very feet, a gateway into that world of fairyland the old clergyman had spoken about. A great wave of tenderness swept him—a flood strong and deep, as he had felt it long ago upon the hill of that Kentish village. The golden boyhood's mood rushed over him once more with all its original splendour. It took a slightly different form, however. He knew better how to direct it for one thing. He pressed the children closer to his side.

'A what?' he asked, speaking low as they did. 'Do I know a what?'

'A cave where lost starlight collects,' Monkey repeated, 'a Star Cave.'

And Jimbo said aloud the verses he had already learned by heart. While his small voice gave the words, more than a little mixed, a bird high up among the boughs woke from its beauty sleep and sang. The two sounds mingled. But the singing of the bird brought back the scenery of the Vicarage garden, and with it the strange, passionate things the old clergyman had said. The two scenes met in his mind, passed in and out of one another like rings of smoke, interchanged, and finally formed a new picture all their own, where flowers danced upon a carpet of star-dust that glittered in mid-air.

He knew some sudden, deep enchantment of the spirit. The Fairyland the world had lost spread all about him, and—he had the children close. The imaginative faculty that for years had invented ingenious patents, woke in force, and ran headlong down far sweeter channels—channels that fastened mind, heart, and soul together in a single intricate network of soft belief. He remembered the dusk upon the Crayfield lawns.

'Of course I know a Star Cave,' he said at length, when Jimbo had finished his recitation, and Monkey had added the details their father had told them. 'I know the very one your Daddy spoke about. It's not far from where we're sitting. It's over there.' He pointed up to the mountain heights behind them, but Jimbo guided his hand in the right direction—towards the Boudry slopes where the forests dip upon the precipices of the Areuse.

'Yes, that's it—exactly,' he said, accepting the correction instantly; 'only *I* go to the top of the mountains first so as to slide down with the river of starlight.'

'We go straight,' they told him in one breath.

'Because you've got more star-stuff in your eyes than I have, and find the way better,' he explained.

That touched their sense of pity. 'But you can have ours,' they cried, 'we'll share it.'

'No,' he answered softly, 'better keep your own. I can get plenty now. Indeed, to tell the truth—though it's a secret between ourselves, remember—that's the real reason I've come out here. I want to get a fresh supply to take back to London with me. One needs a fearful lot in London——'

'But there's no sun in London to melt it,' objected Monkey instantly.

'There's fog though, and it gets lost in fog like ink in blotting- paper. There's never enough to go round. I've got to collect an awful lot before I go back.'

'That'll take more than a week,' she said triumphantly.

They fastened themselves closer against him, like limpets on a rock.

'I told you there was lots to do here,' whispered Monkey again. 'You'll never get it done in a week.'

'And how will you take it back?' asked Jimbo in the same breath. The answer went straight to the boy's heart.

'In a train, of course. I've got an express train here on purpose——'

'The "Rapide"?' he interrupted, his blue eyes starting like flowers from the earth.

'Quicker far than that. I've got——'

They stared so hard and so expectantly, it was almost like an interruption. The bird paused in its rushing song to listen too.

'——a Starlight Express,' he finished, caught now in the full tide of fairyland. 'It came here several nights ago. It's being loaded up as full as ever it can carry. I'm to drive it back again when once it's ready.'

'Where is it now?'

'Who's loading it?'

'How fast does it go? Are there accidents and collisions?'

'How do you find the way?'

'May I drive it with you?'

'Tell us exactly everything in the world about it—at once!'

Questions poured in a flood about him, and his imagination leaped to their answering. Above them the curtain of the Night shook out her million stars while they lay there talking with bated breath together. On every single point he satisfied them, and himself as well. He told them all—his visit to the Manor House, the sprites he found there still alive and waiting as he had made them in his boyhood, their songs and characters, the Dustman, Sweep, and Lamplighter, the Laugher, and the Woman of the Haystack, the blue-eyed Guard——

'But now her eyes are brown, aren't they?' Monkey asked, peering very close into his face. At the same moment she took his heart and hid it deep away among her tumbling hair.

'I was coming to that. They're brown now, of course, because in this different atmosphere brown eyes see better than blue in the dark. The colours of signals vary in different countries.

'And I'm the *mecanicien*,' cried Jimbo. 'I drive the engine.'

'And I'm your stoker,' he agreed, 'because here we burn wood instead of coal, and I'm director in a wood-paving company and so know all about it.'

They did not pause to dissect his logic—but just tore about full speed with busy plans and questionings. He began to wonder how in the world he would satisfy them—and satisfy himself as well!—when the time should come to introduce them to Express and Cave and Passengers. For if he failed in that, the reality of the entire business must fall to the ground. Yet the direct question did not come. He wondered more and more. Neither child luckily insisted on immediate tangible acquaintance. They did not even hint about it. So far the whole thing had gone splendidly and easily, like floating a new company with the rosiest prospectus in the world; but the moment must arrive when profits and dividends would have to justify mere talk. Concrete results would be demanded. If not forthcoming, where would his position be?

Yet, still the flood of questions, answers, explanations flowed on without the critical sentence making its appearance. He had led them well—so far. How in the world, though, was he to keep it up, and provide definite result at the end?

Then suddenly the truth dawned upon him. It was not he who led after all; it was they. He was being led. They knew. They understood. The reins of management lay in their small capable hands, and he had never really held them at all. Most cleverly, with utmost delicacy, they had concealed from him his real position. They were Directors, he the merest shareholder, useful only for 'calls.' The awkward question that he feared would never come, but instead he would receive instructions. 'Keep close to the children; they will guide you.' The words flashed back. He was a helpless prisoner; but had only just discovered the fact. He supplied the funds; they did the construction. Their plans and schemes netted his feet in fairyland just as surely as the weight of their little warm, soft bodies fastened him to the boulder where he sat. He could not move. He could not go further without their will and leadership.

But his captivity was utterly delightful to him....

The sound of a deep bell from the Colombier towers floated in to them between the trees. The children sprang from his knees. He rose slowly, a little cramped and stiff.

'Half-past six,' said Jimbo. 'We must go back for supper.'

He stood there a moment, stretching, while the others waited, staring up at him as though he were a tree. And he felt like a big tree; they were two wild-flowers his great roots sheltered down below.

And at that moment, in the little pause before they linked up arms and started home again, the Question of Importance came, though not in the way he had expected it would come.

'Cousinenry, do you sleep very tightly at night, please?' Monkey asked it, but Jimbo stepped up nearer to watch the reply.

'Like a top,' he said, wondering.

Signals he tried vainly to intercept flashed between the pair of them.

'Why do you ask?' as nothing further seemed forthcoming.

'Oh, just to know,' she explained. 'It's all right.'

'Yes, it's quite all right like that,' added Jimbo. And without more ado they took his arms and pulled him out of the forest.

And Henry Rogers heard something deep, deep down within himself echo the verdict.

'I think it is all right.'

On the way home there were no puddles, but there were three pairs of eyes—and the stars were uncommonly thick overhead. The children asked him almost as many questions as there were clusters of them between the summits of Boudry and La Tourne. All three went floundering in that giant Net. It was so different, too, from anything they had been accustomed to. Their father's stories, answers, explanations, and the like, were ineffective because they always felt he did not quite believe them himself even while he gave them. He did not think he believed them, that is. But Cousin Henry talked of stars and star- stuff as though he had some in his pocket at the moment. And, of course, he had. For otherwise they would not have listened. He could not have held their attention.

They especially liked the huge, ridiculous words he used, because such words concealed great mysteries that pulsed with wonder and exquisitely wound them up. Daddy made things too clear. The bones of impossibility were visible. They saw thin nakedness behind the explanations, till the sense of wonder faded. They were not babies to be fed with a string of one-syllable words!

Jimbo kept silence mostly, his instinct ever being to conceal his ignorance; but Monkey talked fifteen to the dozen, filling the pauses with long 'ohs' and bursts of laughter and impudent observations. Yet her cheeky insolence never crossed the frontier where it could be resented. Her audacity stopped short of impertinence.

'There's a point beyond which—' her cousin would say gravely, when she grew more daring than usual; and, while answering 'It'll stick into you, then, not into me,' she yet withdrew from the borders of impertinence at once.

'What is star-stuff really then?' she asked.

'The primordial substance of the universe,' he answered solemnly, no whit ashamed of his inaccuracy.

'Ah yes!' piped Jimbo, quietly. *Ecole primaire* he understood. This must be something similar.

'But what does it do, I mean, and why is it good for people to have it in them—on them—whatever it is?' she inquired.

'It gives sympathy and insight; it's so awfully subtle and delicate,' he answered. 'A little of it travels down on every ray and soaks down into you. It makes you feel inclined to stick to other people and understand them. That's sympathy.'

'*Sympathie*,' said Jimbo for his sister's benefit apparently, but in reality because he himself was barely treading water.

'But sympathy,' the other went on, 'is no good without insight—which means seeing things as others see them—from inside. That's insight—'

'Inside sight,' she corrected him.

'That's it. You see, the first stuff that existed in the universe was this star-stuff—nebulae. Having nothing else to stick to, it stuck to itself, and so got thicker. It whirled in vortices. It grew together in sympathy, for sympathy brings together. It whirled and twirled round itself till it got at last into solid round bodies—worlds— stars. It passed, that is, from mere dreaming into action. And when the rays soak into you, they change your dreaming into action. You feel the desire to do things—for others.'

'Ah! yes,' repeated Jimbo, 'like that.'

'You must be full of vorty seas, then, because you're so long,' said Monkey, 'but you'll never grow into a solid round body——'

He took a handful of her hair and smothered the remainder of the sentence.

'The instant a sweet thought is born in your mind,' he continued, 'the heavenly stables send their starry messengers to harness it for use. A ray, perhaps, from mighty Sirius picks it out of your heart at birth.'

'Serious!' exclaimed Jimbo, as though the sun were listening.

'Sirius—another sun, that is, far bigger than our own—a perfect giant, yet so far away you hardly notice him.'

The boy clasped his dirty fingers and stared hard. The sun *was* listening.

'Then what I *think* is known—like that—all over the place?' he asked. He held himself very straight indeed.

'Everywhere,' replied Cousinenry gravely. 'The stars flash your thoughts over the whole universe. None are ever lost. Sooner or later they appear in visible shape. Some one, for instance, must have thought this flower long ago'—he stooped and picked a blue hepatica at their feet—'or it couldn't be growing here now.'

Jimbo accepted the statement with his usual gravity.

'Then I shall always think enormous and tremendous things—powerful locomotives, like that and—and——'

'The best is to think kind little sweet things about other people,' suggested the other. 'You see the results quicker then.'

'Mais oui,' was the reply, 'je pourrai faire ca au meme temps, n'est- ce pas?'

'Parfaitemong,' agreed his big cousin.

'There's no room in her for inside sight,' observed Monkey as a portly dame rolled by into the darkness. 'You can't tell her front from her back.' It was one of the governesses.

'We'll get her into the cave and change all that,' her cousin said reprovingly. 'You must never judge by outside alone. Puddings should teach you that.'

But no one could reprove Monkey without running a certain risk.

'We don't have puddings here,' she said, 'we have dessert—sour oranges and apples.'

She flew from his side and vanished down the street and into the Citadelle courtyard before he could think of anything to say. A shooting star flashed at the same moment behind the church tower, vanishing into the gulf of Boudry's shadow. They seemed to go at the same pace together.

'Oh, I say!' said Jimbo sedately, 'you must punish her for that, you know. Shall I come with you to the carpenter's?' he added, as they stood a moment by the fountain. 'There's just ten minutes to wash and brush your hair for supper.'

'I think I can find my way alone,' he answered, 'thank you all the same.'

'It's nothing,' he said, lifting his cap as the village fashion was, and watching his cousin's lengthy figure vanish down the street.

'We'll meet at the Pension later,' the voice came back, 'and in the morning I shall have a lot of correspondence to attend to. Bring your shorthand book and lots of pencils, mind.'

'How many?'

'Oh, half a dozen will do.'

The boy turned in and hurried after his sister. But he was so busy collecting all the pencils and paper he could find that he forgot to brush his hair, and consequently appeared at the supper table with a head like a tangled blackberry bush. His eyes were bright as stars.

CHAPTER XIV

O pure one, take thy seat in the barque of the Sun,
  And sail thou over the sky.
    Sail thou with the imperishable stars,
    Sail thou with the unwearied stars.
      Pyramid Texts, Dynasty VI.

But Henry Rogers ran the whole two hundred yards to his lodgings in the carpenter's house. He ran as though the entire field of brilliant stars were at his heels. There was bewilderment, happiness, exhilaration in his blood. He had never felt so light-hearted in his life. He felt exactly fifteen years of age—and a half. The half was added to ensure a good, safe margin over the other two.

But he was late for supper too—later than the children, for first he jotted down some notes upon the back of an envelope. He wrote them at high speed, meaning to correct them later, but the corrections were never made. Later, when he came to bed, the envelope had been tidied away by the careful housewife into the dustbin. And he was ashamed to ask for them. The carpenter's wife read English.

'Pity,' he said to himself. 'I don't believe Minks could have done it better!'

The energy that went to the making of those 'notes' would have run down different channels a few years ago. It would have gone into some ingenious patent. The patent, however, might equally have gone into the dustbin. There is an enormous quantity of misdirected energy pouring loose about the world!

The notes had run something like this—

O children, open your arms to me,
Let your hair fall over my eyes;
Let me sleep a moment—and then awake
In your Gardens of sweet Surprise!
For the grown-up folk
Are a wearisome folk,
And they laugh my fancies to scorn,
My fun and my fancies to scorn.

O children, open your hearts to me,
And tell me your wonder-thoughts;
Who lives in the palace inside your brain?

Who plays in its outer courts?
Who hides in the hours To-morrow holds?
Who sleeps in your yesterdays?
Who tiptoes along past the curtained folds
Of the shadow that twilight lays?

O children, open your eyes to me,
And tell me your visions too;
Who squeezes the sponge when the salt tears flow
To dim their magical blue?
Who draws up their blinds when the sun peeps in?
Who fastens them down at night?
Who brushes the fringe of their lace-veined lids?
Who trims their innocent light?

Then, children, I beg you, sing low to me,
And cover my eyes with your hands;
O kiss me again till I sleep and dream
That I'm lost in your fairylands;
For the grown-up folk
Are a troublesome folk,
And the book of their childhood is torn,
Is blotted, and crumpled, and torn!

Supper at the Pension dissipated effectively the odd sense of enchantment to which he had fallen a victim, but it revived again with a sudden rush when Jimbo and his sister came up at half-past eight to say good-night. It began when the little fellow climbed up to plant a resounding kiss upon his lips, and it caught him fullest when Monkey's arms were round his neck, and he heard her whisper in his ear—

'Sleep as tightly as you can, remember, and don't resist. We'll come later to find you.' Her brown eyes were straight in front of his own. Goodness, how they shone! Old Sirius and Aldebaran had certainly left a ray in each.

'Hope you don't get any longer when you're asleep!' she added, giving him a sly dig in the ribs—then was gone before he could return it, or ask her what she meant by 'we'll find you later.'

'And don't say a word to Mother,' was the last thing he heard as she vanished down the stairs.

Slightly confused, he glanced down at the aged pumps he happened to have on, and noticed that one bow was all awry and loose. He stooped to fidget with it, and Mother caught him in the act.

'I'll stitch it on for you,' she said at once. 'It won't take a minute. One of the children can fetch it in the morning.'

But he was ashamed to add to her endless sewing. Like some female Sisyphus, she seemed always pushing an enormous needle through a mountain of clothes that grew higher each time she reached the top.

'I always wear it like that,' he assured her gravely, his thoughts still busy with two other phrases—' find you' and 'sleep tightly.' What in the world could they mean? Did the children really intend to visit him at night? They seemed so earnest about it. Of course it was all nonsense. And yet——!

'You mustn't let them bother you too much,' he heard their mother saying, her voice sounding a long way off. 'They're so wildly happy to have some one to play with.'

'That's how I like them,' he answered vaguely, referring half to the pumps and half to the children. 'They're no trouble at all, believe me.'

'I'm afraid we've spoilt them rather——'

'But—not at all,' he murmured, still confused. 'They're only a little loose—er—lively, I mean. That's how they should be.'

And outside all heard their laughing voices dying down the street as they raced along to the Citadelle for bed. It was Monkey's duty to see her brother safely in. Ten minutes later Mother would follow to tell them tuck-up stories and hear their prayers.

'Excuse me! Have you got a hot-water bottle?' asked a sudden jerky voice, and he turned with a start to see Jane Anne towering beside him.

'I'm sorry,' he answered, 'but I don't carry such things about with me.' He imagined she was joking, then saw that it was very serious.

She looked puzzled a moment. 'I meant—would you like one? Everybody uses them here.' She thought all grown-ups used hot-water bottles.

He hesitated a second. The child looked as though she would produce one from her blouse like any conjurer. As yet, however, the article in question had not entered his scheme of life. He declined it with many thanks.

'I can get you a big one,' she urged. But even that did not tempt him.

'Will you have a cold-water bandage then—for your head—or anything?'

She seemed so afflicted with a desire to do something for him that he almost said 'Yes'; only the fear that she might offer next a beehive or a gramophone restrained him.

'Thank you *so* much, but really I can manage without it—to-night.'

Jane Anne made no attempt to conceal her disappointment. What a man he was, to be sure! And what a funny place the world was!

'It's Jinny's panacea,' said Mother, helping herself with reckless uncertainty to a long word. 'She's never happy unless she's doing for somebody,' she added ambiguously. 'It's her *metier* in life.'

'Mother, what *are* you saying?' said the child's expression. Then she made one last attempt. She remembered, perhaps, the admiring way he had watched her brother and sister's antics in the Den before. She was not clever on her feet, but at least she could try.

'Shall I turn head over heels for you, then?'

He caught her mother's grave expression just in time to keep his laughter back. The offer of gymnastics clearly involved sacrifice somewhere.

'To-morrow,' he answered quickly. 'Always put off till to-morrow what you're too old to do to-day.'

'Of course; I see—yes.' She was more perplexed than ever, as he meant that she should be. His words were meaningless, but they helped the poignant situation neatly. She could not understand why all her offers were refused like this. There must be something wrong with her selection, perhaps. She would think of better ones in future. But, oh, what a funny place the world was!

'Good-night, then, Mr.—Cousin Rogers,' she said jerkily with resignation. 'Perhaps to-morrow—when I'm older——'

'If it comes.' He gravely shook the hand she held out primly, keeping a certain distance from him lest he should attempt to kiss her.

'It always comes; it's a chronic monster,' she laughed, saying the first thing that came into her queer head. They all laughed. Jane Anne went out, feeling happier. At least, she had amused him. She marched off with the air of a grenadier going to some stern and difficult duty. From the door she flung back at him a look of speechless admiration, then broke into a run, afraid she might have been immodest or too forward. They heard her thumping overhead.

And presently he followed her example. The Pension sitting-room emptied. Unless there was something special on hand—a dance, a romp, a game, or some neighbours who dropped in for talk and music—it was rarely occupied after nine o'clock. Daddy had already slipped home—he had this mysterious way of disappearing when no one saw him go. At this moment, doubtless, a wumbled book absorbed him over at the carpenter's. Old Miss

Waghorn sat in a corner nodding over her novel, and the Pension cat, Borelle, was curled up in her sloping, inadequate lap.

The big, worn velvet sofa in the opposite corner was also empty. On romping nights it was the *train de Moscou*, where Jimbo sold tickets to crowded passengers for any part of the world. To-night it was a mere dead sofa, uninviting, dull.

He went across the darkened room, his head scraping acquaintance with the ivy leaves that trailed across the ceiling. He slipped through the little hall. In the kitchen he heard the shrill voice of Mme. Jequier talking very loudly about a dozen things at once to the servant-girl, or to any one else who was near enough to listen. Luckily she did not see him. Otherwise he would never have escaped without another offer of a hot-water bottle, a pot of home-made marmalade, or a rug and pillow for his bed. He made his way downstairs into the street unnoticed; but just as he reached the bottom his thundering tread betrayed him. The door flew open at the top.

'Bon soir, bonne nuit,' screamed the voice; 'wait a moment and I'll get the lamp. You'll break your neck. Is there anything you want—a hot-water bottle, or a box of matches, or some of my marmalade for your breakfast? Wait, and I'll get it in a moment——' She would have given the blouse off her back had he needed, or could have used it.

She flew back to the kitchen to search and shout. It sounded like a quarrel; but, pretending not to hear, he made good his escape and passed out into the street. The heavy door of the Post Office banged behind him, cutting short a stream of excited sentences. The peace and quiet of the night closed instantly about his steps.

By the fountain opposite the Citadelle he paused to drink from the pipe of gushing mountain water. The open courtyard looked inviting, but he did not go in, for, truth to tell, there was a curious excitement in him—an urgent, keen desire to get to sleep as soon as possible. Not that he felt sleepy—quite the reverse in fact, but that he looked forward to his bed and to 'sleeping tightly.'

The village was already lost in slumber. No lights showed in any houses. Yet it was barely half-past nine. Everywhere was peace and stillness. Far across the lake he saw the twinkling villages. Behind him dreamed the forests. A deep calm brooded over the mountains; but within the calm, and just below the surface in himself, hid the excitement as of some lively anticipation. He expected something. Something was going to happen. And it was connected with the children. Jimbo and Monkey were at the bottom of it. They had said they would come for him—to 'find him later.' He wondered—quite absurdly he wondered.

He passed his cousin's room on tiptoe, and noticed a light beneath the door. But, before getting into bed, he stood a moment at the open window and drew in deep draughts of the fresh night air. The world of forest swayed across his sight. The outline of the Citadelle merged into it. A point of light showed the window where the children already slept. But, far beyond, the moon was loading stars upon the trees, and a rising wind drove them in glittering flocks along the heights....

Blowing out the candle, he turned over on his side to sleep, his mind charged to the brim with wonder and curious under-thrills of this anticipation. He half expected—what? Reality lay somewhere in the whole strange business; it was not merely imaginative nonsense. Fairyland was close.

And the moment he slept and began to dream, the thing took a lively and dramatic shape. A thousand tiny fingers, soft and invisible, drew him away into the heart of fairyland. There was a terror in him lest he should—stick. But he came out beautifully and smoothly, like a thread of summer grass from its covering sheath.

'I *am* slippery after all, then—slippery enough,' he remembered saying with surprised delight, and then——

CHAPTER XV

Look how the floor of heaven
Is thick inlaid with patines of bright gold.
There's not the smallest orb which thou beholdest
But in his motion like an angel sings,
Still quiring to the young-eyed cherubims.
Merchant of Venice.

——there came to him a vivid impression of sudden light in the room, and he knew that something very familiar was happening to him, yet something that had not happened consciously for thirty years and more —since his early childhood in the night-nursery with the bars across the windows.

He was both asleep and awake at the same time. Some part of him, rather, that never slept was disengaging itself—with difficulty. He was getting free. Stimulated by his intercourse with the children, this part of him that in boyhood used to be so easily detached, light as air, was getting loose. The years had fastened it in very tightly. Jimbo and Monkey had got at it. And Jimbo and Monkey were in the room at this moment. They were pulling him out.

It was very wonderful; a glory of youth and careless joy rushed through him like a river. Some sheath or vesture melted off. It seemed to tear him loose. How in the world could he ever have forgotten it— let it go out of his life? What on earth could have seemed good enough to take its place? He felt like an eagle some wizard spell had imprisoned in a stone, now released and shaking out its crumpled wings. A mightier spell had set him free. The children stood beside his bed!

'I can manage it alone,' he said firmly. 'You needn't try to help me.'

No sound was audible, but they instantly desisted. This thought, that took a dozen words to express ordinarily, shot from him into them the instant it was born. A gentle pulsing, like the flicker of a flame, ran over their shining little forms of radiance as they received it. They shifted to one side silently to give him room. Thus had he seen a searchlight pass like lightning from point to point across the sea.

Yet, at first, there was difficulty; here and there, in places, he could not get quite loose and free.

'He sticks like Daddy,' he heard them think. 'In the head it seems, too.'

There was no pain in the sensation, but a certain straining as of unaccustomed muscles being stretched. He felt uncomfortable, then embarrassed, then—exhilarated. But there were other exquisite sensations too. Happiness, as of flooding summer sunshine, poured through him.

'He'll come with a rush. Look out!' felt Jimbo—'felt' expressing 'thought' and 'said' together, for no single word can convey the double operation thus combined in ordinary life.

The reality of it caught him by the throat.

'This,' he exclaimed, 'is real and actual. It is happening to me now!'

He looked from the pile of clothes taken off two hours ago—goodness, what a mass!—to the children's figures in the middle of the room. And one was as real as the other. The moods of the day and evening, their play and nonsense, had all passed away. He had crossed a gulf that stood between this moment and those good-nights in the Pension. This was as real as anything in life; more real than death. Reality—he caught the obvious thought pass thickly through the body on the bed— is what has been experienced. Death, for that reason, is not real, not realised; dinner is. And this was real because he had been through it, though long forgotten it. Jimbo stood aside and 'felt' directions.

'Don't push,' he said.

'Just think and wish,' added Monkey with a laugh.

It was her laugh, and perhaps the beauty of her big brown eyes as well, that got him finally loose. For the laughter urged some queer, deep yearning in him towards a rush of exquisite accomplishment. He began to slip more easily and freely. The brain upon the bed, oddly enough, remembered a tradition of old Egypt—that Thoth created the world by bursting into seven peals of laughter. It touched forgotten springs of imagination and belief. In some tenuous, racy vehicle his thought flashed forth. With a gliding spring, like a swooping bird across a valley, he was suddenly—out.

'I'm out!' he cried.

'All out!' echoed the answering voices.

And then he understood that first vivid impression of light. It was everywhere, an evenly distributed light. He saw the darkness of the night as well, the deep old shadows that draped the village, woods, and mountains. But in themselves was light, a light that somehow enabled them to see everything quite clearly. Solid things were all transparent.

Light even radiated from objects in the room. Two much-loved books upon the table shone beautifully—his Bible and a volume of poems; and, fairer still, more delicate than either, there was a lustre on the table that had so brilliant a halo it almost corruscated. The sparkle in it was like the sparkle in the children's eyes. It came from the bunch of violets, gentians, and hepaticas, already faded, that Mother had placed there days ago on his arrival. And overhead, through plaster, tiles, and rafters he saw—the stars.

'We've already been for Jinny,' Jimbo informed him; 'but she's gone as usual. She goes the moment she falls asleep. We never can catch her up or find her.'

'Come on,' cried Monkey. 'How slow you both are! We shan't get anywhere at this rate.' And she made a wheel of coloured fire in the air. 'I'm ready,' he answered, happier than either. 'Let's be off at once.'

Through his mind flashed this explanation of their elder sister's day-expression—that expression of a moth she had, puzzled, distressed, only half there, as the saying is. For if she went out so easily at night in this way, some part of her probably stayed out altogether. She never wholly came back. She was always dreaming. The entire instinct of the child, he remembered, was for others, and she thought of herself as little as did the sun—old tireless star that shines for all.

'She's soaked in starlight,' he cried, as they went off headlong. 'We shall find her in the Cave. Come on, you pair of lazy meteors.'

He was already far beyond the village, and the murmur of the woods rose up to them. They entered the meshes of the Star Net that spun its golden threads everywhere about them, linking up the Universe with their very hearts.

'There are no eyes or puddles to-night. Everybody sleeps. Hooray, hooray!' they cried together.

There were cross-currents, though. The main, broad, shining stream poured downwards in front of them towards the opening of the Cave, a mile or two beyond, where the forests dipped down among the precipices of the Areuse; but from behind—from some house in the slumbering village—came a golden tributary too, that had a peculiar and astonishing brightness of its own. It came, so far as they could make out, from the humped outline of La Citadelle, and from a particular room there, as though some one in that building had a special source of supply. Moreover, it scattered itself over the village in separate swift rivulets that dived and dipped towards particular houses here and there. There seemed a constant coming and going, one stream driving straight into the Cave, and another pouring out again, yet neither mingling. One stream brought supplies, while the other directed their distribution. Some one, asleep or awake—they could not tell—was thinking golden thoughts of love and sympathy for the world.

'It's Mlle. Lemaire,' said Jimbo. 'She's been in bed for thirty years——' His voice was very soft.

'The Spine, you know,' exclaimed Monkey, a little in the rear.

'——and even in the daytime she looks white and shiny,' added the boy. 'I often go and talk with her and tell her things.' He said it proudly. 'She understands everything—better even than Mother.' Jimbo had told most. It was all right. His leadership was maintained and justified. They entered the main stream and plunged downwards with it towards the earth—three flitting figures dipped in this store of golden brilliance.

A delicious and wonderful thing then happened. All three remembered.

'This was where we met you first,' they told him, settling down among the trees together side by side. 'We saw your teeth of gold. You came in that train——'

'I was thinking about it—in England,' he exclaimed, 'and about coming out to find you here.'

'The Starlight Express,' put in Jimbo.

'——and you were just coming up to speak to us when we woke, or you woke, or somebody woke—and it all went,' said Monkey.

'That was when I stopped thinking about it,' he explained.

'It all vanished anyhow. And the next time was'—she paused a moment—'you—we saw your two gold teeth again somewhere, and half recognised you——'

It was the daylight world that seemed vague and dreamlike now, hard to remember clearly.

'In another train—' Jimbo helped her, 'the Geneva omnibus that starts at—at——' But even Jimbo could not recall further details.

'You're wumbled,' said Rogers, helping himself and the others at the same time. 'You want some starlight to put you in touch again. Come on; let's go in. We shall find all the others inside, I suspect, hard at it.'

'At what?' asked two breathless voices.

'Collecting, of course—for others. Did you think they ate the stuff, just to amuse themselves?'

'They glided towards the opening, cutting through the little tributary stream that was pouring out on its way down the sky to that room in La Citadelle. It was brighter than the main river, they saw, and shone with a peculiar brilliance of its own, whiter and swifter than the rest. Designs, moreover, like crystals floated on the crest of every wave.

'That's the best quality,' he told them, as their faces shone a moment in its glory. 'The person who deserves it must live entirely for others. That he keeps only for the sad and lonely. The rest, the common stuff, is good enough for Fraulein or for baby, or for mother, or any other——' The words rose in him like flowers that he knew.

'Look out, *mon vieux*!' It was Monkey's voice. They just had time to stand aside as a figure shot past them and disappeared into the darkness above the trees. A big bundle, dripping golden dust, hung down his back.

'The Dustman!' they cried with excitement, easily recognising his energetic yet stooping figure; and Jimbo added, 'the dear old Dustman!' while Monkey somersaulted after him, returning breathless a minute later with, 'He's gone; I couldn't get near him. He went straight to La Citadelle——'

And then collided violently with the Lamplighter, whose pole of office caught her fairly in the middle and sent her spinning like a conjurer's plate till they feared she would never stop. She kept on laughing the whole time she spun—like a catherine wheel that laughs instead of splutters. The place where the pole caught her, however—it was its lighted end—shines and glows to this day: the centre of her little heart.

'Do let's be careful,' pleaded Jimbo, hardly approving of these wild gyrations. He really did prefer his world a trifle more dignified. He was ever the grave little gentleman.

They stooped to enter by the narrow opening, but were stopped again— this time by some one pushing rudely past them to get in. From the three points of the compass to which the impact scattered them, they saw a shape of darkness squeeze itself, sack and all, to enter. An ordinary man would have broken every bone in his body, judging by the portion that projected into the air behind. But he managed it somehow, though the discomfort must have been intolerable, they all thought. The darkness dropped off behind him in flakes like discarded clothing; he turned to gold as he went in; and the contents of his sack—he poured it out like water—shone as though he squeezed a sponge just dipped in the Milky Way.

'What a lot he's collected,' cried Rogers from his point of vantage where he could see inside. 'It all gets purified and clean in there. Wait a moment. He's coming out again—off to make another collection.'

And then they knew the man for what he was. He shot past them into the night, carrying this time a flat and emptied sack, and singing like a blackbird as he went:—

Sweeping chimneys and cleaning flues,
That is the work I love;
Brushing away the blacks and the blues,
And letting in light from above!
I twirl my broom in your tired brain
When you're tight in sleep up-curled,
Then scatter the stuff in a soot-like rain
Over the edge of the world.

The voice grew fainter and fainter in the distance—

For I'm a tremendously busy Sweep,
Catching the folk when they're all asleep,
And tossing the blacks on the Rubbish Heap
Over the edge of the world...!

The voice died away into the wind among the high branches, and they heard it no more.

'There's a Sweep worth knowing,' murmured Rogers, strong yearning in him.

'There are no blacks or blues in *my* brain,' exclaimed Monkey, 'but Jimbo's always got some on his face.'

The impudence passed ignored. Jimbo took his cousin's hand and led him to the opening. The 'men' went in first together; the other sex might follow as best it could. Yet somehow or other Monkey slipped between their legs and got in before them. They stood up side by side in the most wonderful place they had ever dreamed of.

And the first thing they saw was—Jane Anne.

'I'm collecting for Mother. Her needles want such a chronic lot, you see.' Her face seemed full of stars; there was no puzzled expression in the eyes now. She looked beautiful. And the younger children stared in sheer amazement and admiration.

'I have no time to waste,' she said, moving past them with a load in her spread apron that was like molten gold; 'I have to be up and awake at six to make your porridge before you go to school. I'm a busy monster, I can tell you!' She went by them like a flash, and out into the night.

Monkey felt tears in her somewhere, but they did not fall. Something in her turned ashamed—for a moment. Jimbo stared in silence. 'What a girl!' he thought. 'I'd like to be like that!' Already the light was sticking to him.

'So this is where she always comes,' said Monkey, soon recovering from the temporary attack of emotion. 'She's better out than in; she's safest when asleep! No wonder she's so funny in the daytime.'

Then they turned to look about them, breathing low as wild-flowers that watch a rising moon.

The place was so big for one thing—far bigger than they had expected. The storage of lost starlight must be a serious affair indeed if it required all this space to hold it. The entire mountain range was surely hollow. Another thing that struck them was the comparative dimness of this huge interior compared with the brilliance of the river outside. But, of course, lost things are ever dim, and those worth looking for dare not be too easily found.

A million tiny lines of light, they saw, wove living, moving patterns, very intricate and very exquisite. These lines and patterns the three drew in with their very breath. They swallowed light—the tenderest light the world can know. A scent of flowers—something between a violet and a wild rose—floated over all. And they understood these patterns while they breathed them in. They read them. Patterns in Nature, of course, are fairy script. Here lay all their secrets sweetly explained in golden writing, all mysteries made clear. The three understood beyond their years; and inside-sight, instead of glimmering, shone. For, somehow or other, the needs of other people blazed everywhere, obliterating their own. It was most singular.

Monkey ceased from somersaulting and stared at Jimbo.

'You've got two stars in your face instead of eyes. They'll never set!' she whispered. 'I love you because I understand every bit of you.'

'And you,' he replied, as though he were a grande personne, 'have got hair like a mist of fire. It will never go out!'

'Every one will love me now,' she cried, 'my underneath is gold.'

But her brother reproved her neatly:—

'Let's get a lot—simply an awful lot'—he made a grimace to signify quantity—'and pour it over Daddy's head till it runs from his eyes and beard. He'll write real fairy stories then and make a fortune.'

And Cousin Henry moved past them like a burning torch. They held their breath to see him. Jane Anne, their busy sister, alone excelled him in brightness. Her perfume, too, was sweeter.

'He's an old hand at this game,' Monkey said in French.

'But Jinny's never done anything else since she was born,' replied her brother proudly.

And they all three fell to collecting, for it seemed the law of the place, a kind of gravity none could disobey. They stooped—three semi- circles of tender brilliance. Each lost the least desire to gather for himself; the needs of others drove them, filled them, made them eager and energetic.

'Riquette would like a bit,' cried Jimbo, almost balancing on his head in his efforts to get it all at once, while Monkey's shining fingers stuffed her blouse and skirts with sheaves of golden gossamer that later she meant to spread in a sheet upon the pillow of Mademoiselle Lemaire.

'She sleeps so little that she needs the best,' she sang, realising for once that her own amusement was not the end of life. 'I'll make her nights all wonder.'

Cousinenry, meanwhile, worked steadily like a man who knows his time is short. He piled the stuff in heaps and pyramids, and then compressed it into what seemed solid blocks that made his pockets bulge like small balloons. Already a load was on his back that bent him double.

'Such a tiny bit is useful,' he explained, 'if you know exactly how and where to put it. This compression is my own patent.'

'Of course,' they echoed, trying in vain to pack it up as cleverly as he did.

Nor were these three the only gatherers. The place was full of movement. Jane Anne was always coming back for more, deigning no explanations. She never told where she had spent her former loads. She gathered an apron full, sped off to spend and scatter it in places she knew of, and then came bustling in again for more. And they always knew her whereabouts because of the whiter glory that she radiated into the dim yellow world about them.

And other figures, hosts of them, were everywhere—stooping, picking, loading one another's backs and shoulders. To and fro they shot and glided, like Leonids in autumn round the Earth. All were collecting, though the supply seemed never to grow less. An inexhaustible stream poured in through the narrow opening, and scattered itself at once in all directions as though driven by a wind. How could the world let so much escape it, when it was what the world most needed every day. It ran naturally into patterns, patterns that could be folded and rolled up like silken tablecloths. In silence, too. There was no sound of drops falling. Sparks fly on noiseless feet. Sympathy makes no bustle.

'Even on the thickest nights it falls,' a voice issued from a robust patch of light beside them that stooped with huge brown hands all knotted into muscles; 'and it's a mistake to think different.' His voice rolled on into a ridiculous bit of singing:—

It comes down with the rain drops,
It comes down with the dew,
There's always 'eaps for every one—
For 'im and me and you.

They recognised his big face, bronzed by the sun, and his great neck where lines drove into the skin like the rivers they drew with blunt pencils on their tedious maps of Europe. It was several faces in one. The Head Gardener was no stranger to their imaginations, for they remembered him of old somewhere, though not quite sure exactly where. He worked incessantly for others, though these 'others' were only flowers and cabbages and fruit-trees. He did his share in the world, he and his army of queer assistants, the under-gardeners.

Peals of laughter, too, sounded from time to time in a far away corner of the cavern, and the laughter sent all the stuff it reached into very delicate, embroidered patterns. For it was merry and infectious laughter, joy somewhere in it like a lamp. It bordered upon singing; another touch would send it rippling into song. And to that far corner, attracted by the sound, ran numberless rivulets of light, weaving a lustrous atmosphere about the Laugher that, even while it glowed, concealed the actual gatherer from sight. The children only saw that the patterns were even more sweet and dainty than their own. And they understood. Inside-sight explained the funny little mystery. Laughter is magical—brings light and help and courage. They laughed themselves then, and instantly saw their own patterns wave and tremble into tiny outlines that they could squeeze later even into the darkest, thickest head.

Cousinenry, meanwhile, they saw, stopped for nothing. He was singing all the time as he bent over his long, outstretched arms. And it was the singing after all that made the best patterns—better even than the laughing. He knew all the best tricks of this Star Cave. He remained their leader.

And the stuff no hands picked up ran on and on, seeking a way of escape for itself. Some sank into the ground to sweeten the body of the old labouring earth, colouring the roots of myriad flowers; some soaked into the rocky walls, tinting the raw materials of hills and woods and mountain tops. Some escaped into the air in tiny drops that, meeting in moonlight or in sunshine, instantly formed wings. And people saw a brimstone butterfly—all wings and hardly any body. All went somewhere for some useful purpose. It was not in the nature of star-stuff to keep still. Like water that must go down-hill, the law of its tender being forced it to find a place where it could fasten on and shine. It never could get wholly lost; though, if the place it settled on was poor, it might lose something of its radiance. But human beings were obviously what most attracted it. Sympathy must find an outlet; thoughts are bound to settle somewhere.

And the gatherers all sang softly—'Collect for others, never mind yourself!'

Some of it, too, shot out by secret ways in the enormous roof. The children recognised the exit of the separate brilliant stream they had encountered in the sky—the one especially that went to the room of pain and sickness in La Citadelle. Again they understood. That unselfish thinker of golden thoughts knew special sources of supply. No wonder that her atmosphere radiated sweetness and uplifting influence. Her patience, smiles, and courage were explained. Passing through the furnace of her pain, the light was cleansed and purified. Hence the delicate, invariable radiation from her presence, voice, and eyes. From the bed of suffering she had not left for thirty years she helped the world go round more sweetly and more easily, though few divined those sudden moments of beauty they caught flashing from her halting words, nor guessed their source of strength.

'Of course,' thought Jimbo, laughing, 'I see now why I like to go and tell her everything. She understands all before I've said it. She's simply stuffed with starlight—bursting with inside-sight.'

'That's sympathy,' his cousin added, hearing the vivid thought. And he worked away like an entire ant-heap. But he was growing rather breathless now. 'There's too much for me,' he laughed as though his mouth were full. 'I can't manage it all!' He was wading to the waist, and his coat and trousers streamed with runnels of orange-coloured light.

'Swallow it then!' cried Monkey, her hair so soaked that she kept squeezing it like a sponge, both eyes dripping too.

It was their first real experience of the joy of helping others, and they hardly knew where to begin or end. They romped and played in the stuff like children in sand or snow—diving, smothering themselves, plunging, choking, turning somersaults, upsetting each other's carefully reared loads, and leaping over little pyramids of gold. Then, in a flash, their laughter turned the destroyed heaps into wonderful new patterns again; and once more they turned sober and began to work.

But their cousin was more practical. 'I've got all I can carry comfortably,' he sang out at length. 'Let's go out now and sow it among the sleepers. Come on!'

A field of stars seemed to follow him from the roof as he moved with difficulty towards the opening of the cave.

Some one shot out just in front of him. 'My last trip!' The words reached them from outside. His bulging figure squeezed somehow through the hole, layers of light scraping off against the sides. The children followed him. But no one stuck. All were beautifully elastic; the starlight oiled and greased their daring, subtle star-bodies. Laden to the eyes, they sped across the woods that still slept heavily. The tips of the pines, however, were already opening a million eyes. There was a faint red glimmer in the east. Hours had passed while they were collecting.

'The Interfering Sun is on the way. Look out!' cried some one, shooting past them like an unleashed star. 'I must get just a little more—my seventeenth journey to-night!' And Jane Anne, the puzzled look already come back a little into her face, darted down towards the opening. The waking of the body was approaching.

'What a girl!' thought Jimbo again, as they hurried after their grown- up cousin towards the village.

And here, but for the leadership of Cousin Henry, they must have gone astray and wasted half their stores in ineffective fashion. Besides, the east was growing brighter, and there was a touch of confusion in their little star-bodies as sleep grew lighter and the moment of the body's waking drew nearer.

Ah! the exquisite adjustment that exists between the night and day bodies of children! It is little wonder that with the process of growing-up there comes a coarsening that congeals the fluid passages of exit, and finally seals the memory centres too. Only in a few can this delicate adjustment be preserved, and the sources of inspiration known to children be kept available and sweet—in the poets, dreamers, and artists of this practical, steel-girdled age.

'This way,' called Cousinenry. 'Follow me.' They settled down in a group among Madame Jequier's lilacs. 'We'll begin with the Pension des Glycines. Jinny is already busy with La Citadelle.'

They perched among the opening blossoms. Overhead flashed by the Sweep, the Dustman, and the Laugher, bound for distant ports, perhaps as far as England. The Head Gardener lumbered heavily after them to find his flowers and trees. Starlight, they grasped, could be no separate thing. The rays started, indeed, from separate points, but all met later in the sky to weave this enormous fairy network in which the currents and cross-currents and criss-cross-currents were so utterly bewildering. Alone, the children certainly must have got lost in the first five minutes.

Their cousin gathered up the threads from Monkey's hair and Jimbo's eyes, and held them in one hand like reins. He sang to them a moment while they recovered their breath and forces:—

The stars in their courses
Are runaway horses
That gallop with Thoughts from the Earth;
They collect them, and race
Back through wireless space,
Bringing word of the tiniest birth;
Past old Saturn and Mars,
And the hosts of big stars,
Who strain at their leashes for joy.
Kind thoughts, like fine weather,
  Bind sweetly together
  God's suns—with the heart of a boy.

So, beware what you think;
It is written in ink
That is golden, and read by His Stars!

'Hadn't we better get on?' cried Monkey, pulling impatiently at the reins he held.

'Yes,' echoed Jimbo. 'Look at the sky. The "rapide" from Paris comes past at six o'clock.'

CHAPTER XVI

Aus den Himmelsaugen droben
Fallen zitternd goldne Funken
Durch die Nacht, und meine Seele
Dehnt sich liebeweit und weiter.

O ihr Himmelsaugen droben,
Weint euch aus in meine Seele,
Dass von lichten Sternentranen
Uberfliesset meine Seele!
                    Heine.

They rose, fluttered a moment above the lilac bushes, and then shot forward like the curve of a rainbow into the sleeping house. The next second they stood beside the bed of the Widow Jequier.

She lay there, so like a bundle of untidy sticks that, but for the sadness upon the weary face, they could have burst out laughing. The perfume of the wistaria outside the open window came in sweetly, yet could not lighten the air of heavy gloom that clothed her like a garment. Her atmosphere was dull, all streaked with greys and black, for her mind, steeped in anxiety even while she slept, gave forth cloudy vapours of depression and disquietude that made impossible the approach of—light. Starlight, certainly, could not force an entrance, and even sunlight would spill half its radiance before it reached her heart. The help she needed she thus deliberately shut out. Before going to bed her mood had been one of anxious care and searching worry. It continued, of course, in sleep.

'Now,' thought their leader briskly, 'we must deal with this at once'; and the children, understanding his unspoken message, approached closer to the bed. How brilliant their little figures were—Jimbo, a soft, pure blue, and Monkey tinged faintly here and there with delicate clear orange. Thus do the little clouds of sunset gather round to see the sun get into bed. And in utter silence; all their intercourse was silent—thought, felt, but never spoken.

For a moment there was hesitation. Cousinenry was uncertain exactly how to begin. Tante Jeanne's atmosphere was so very thick he hardly knew the best way to penetrate it. Her mood had been so utterly black and rayless. But his hesitation operated like a call for help that flew instantly about the world and was communicated to the golden threads that patterned the outside sky. They quivered, flashed the message automatically; the enormous network repeated it as far as England, and the answer came. For thought is instantaneous, and desire is prayer. Quick as lightning came the telegram. Beside them stood a burly figure of gleaming gold.

'I'll do it,' said the earthy voice. 'I'll show you 'ow. For she loves 'er garden. Her sympathy with trees and flowers lets me in. Always send for *me* when she's in a mess, or needs a bit of trimmin' and cleanin' up.'

The Head Gardener pushed past them with his odour of soil and burning leaves, his great sunburned face and his browned, stained hands. These muscular, big hands he spread above her troubled face; he touched her heart; he blew his windy breath of flowers upon her untidy hair; he called the names of lilac, wistaria, roses, and laburnum....

The room filled with the little rushing music of wind in leaves; and, as he said 'laburnum,' there came at last a sudden opening channel through the fog that covered her so thickly. Starlight, that was like a rivulet of laburnum blossoms melted into running dew, flowed down it. The Widow Jequier stirred in her sleep and smiled. Other channels opened. Light trickled down these, too, drawn in and absorbed from the store the Gardener carried. Then, with a rush of scattering fire, he was gone again. Out into the enormous sky he flew, trailing golden flame behind him. They heard him singing as he dived into the Network —singing of buttercups and cowslips, of primroses and marigolds and dandelions, all yellow flowers that have stored up starlight.

And the atmosphere of Tante Jeanne first glowed, then shone; it changed slowly from gloom to glory. Golden channels opened everywhere, making a miniature network of their own. Light flashed and corruscated through it, passing from the children and their leader along the tiny pipes of sympathy the Gardener had cleared of rubbish and decay. Along the very lines of her face ran tiny shining rivers; flooding across her weary eyelids, gilding her untidy hair, and pouring down into her heavy heart. She ceased fidgeting; she smiled in her sleep; peace settled on her face; her fingers on the coverlet lost their touch of strain. Finally she turned over, stretched her old fighting body into a more comfortable position, sighed a moment, then settled down into a deep and restful slumber. Her atmosphere was everywhere 'soft-shiny' when they left her to shoot next into the attic chamber above, where Miss Waghorn lay among her fragments of broken memory, and the litter of disordered images that passed with her for 'thinking.'

And here, again, although their task was easier, they needed help to show the right way to begin. Before they reached the room Jimbo had wondered how they would 'get at' her. That wonder summoned help. The tall, thin figure was already operating beside the bed as they entered. His length seemed everywhere at once, and his slender pole, a star hanging from the end, was busy touching articles on walls and floor and furniture. The disorder everywhere was the expression of her dishevelled mind, and though he could not build the ruins up again, at least he could trace the outlines of an ordered plan that she might use when she left her body finally and escaped from the rebellious instrument in death. And now that escape was not so very far away. Obviously she was already loose. She was breaking up, as the world expresses it.

And the children, watching with happy delight, soon understood his method. Each object that he touched emitted a tiny light. In her mind he touched the jumble of wandering images as well. On waking she would find both one and the other better assorted. Some of the lost things her memory ever groped for she would find more readily. She would see the starlight on them.

'See,' said their leader softly, as the long thin figure of the Lamplighter shot away into the night, 'she sleeps so lightly because she is so old—fastened so delicately to the brain and heart. The fastenings are worn and loose now. Already she is partly out!'

'That's why she's so muddled in the daytime,' explained Jimbo, for his sister's benefit.

'Exaccurately, I knew it already!' was the reply, turning a somersault like a wheel of twirling meteors close to the old lady's nose.

'Carefully, now!' said their leader. 'And hurry up! There's not much we can do here, and there's heaps to do elsewhere. We must remember Mother and Daddy—before the Interfering Sun is up, you know.'

They flashed about the attic chamber, tipping everything with light, from the bundle of clothes that strewed the floor to the confused interior of the black basket-trunk where she kept her money and papers. There were no shelves in this attic chamber; no room for cupboards either; it was the cheapest room in the house. And the old woman in the bed sometimes opened her eyes and peered curiously, expectantly, about her. Even in her sleep she looked for things. Almost, they felt, she seemed aware of their presence near her, she knew that they were there; she smiled.

A moment later they were in mid-air on their way to the Citadelle, singing as they went:—

> He keeps that only
> For the old and lonely,
> Who sleep so little that they need the best.
>   The rest—
>   The common stuff—

Is good enough
For Fraulein, or for baby, or for mother,
  Or any other
  Who likes a bit of dust,
  And yet can do without it—
    If they must...

Already something of the Dawn's faint magic painting lay upon the world. Roofs shone with dew. The woods were singing, and the flowers were awake. Birds piped and whistled shrilly from the orchards. They heard the Mer Dasson murmuring along her rocky bed. The rampart of the Alps stood out more clearly against the sky.

'We must be *very* quick,' Cousin Henry flashed across to them, 'quicker than an express train.'

'That's impossible,' cried Jimbo, who already felt the call of waking into his daily world. 'Hark! There's whistling already....'

The next second, in a twinkling, he was gone. He had left them. His body had been waked up by the birds that sang and whistled so loudly in the plane tree outside his window. Monkey and her guide raced on alone into the very room where he now sat up and rubbed his eyes in the Citadelle. He was telling his mother that he had just been 'dreaming extraordinary.' But Mother, sleeping like a fossil monster in the Tertiary strata, heard him not.

'He often goes like that,' whispered Monkey in a tone of proud superiority. 'He's only a little boy really, you see.'

But the sight they then witnessed was not what they expected.

For Mademoiselle Lemaire herself was working over Mother like an engine, and Mother was still sleeping like the dead. The radiance that emanated from the night-body of this suffering woman, compared to their own, was as sunlight is to candle-light. Its soft glory was indescribable, its purity quite unearthly, and the patterns that it wove lovely beyond all telling. Here they surprised her in the act, busy with her ceaseless activities for others, working for the world by *thinking* beauty. While her pain-racked body lay asleep in the bed it had not left for thirty years, nor would ever leave again this side of death, she found her real life in loving sympathy for the pain of others everywhere. For thought is prayer, and prayer is the only true effective action that leaves no detail incomplete. She *thought* light and glory into others. Was it any wonder that she drew a special, brilliant supply from the Starlight Cavern, when she had so much to give? For giving-out involved drawing-in to fill the emptied spaces. Her pure and endless sources of supply were all explained.

'I've been working on her for years,' she said gently, looking round at their approach, 'for her life is so thickly overlaid with care, and the care she never quite knows how to interpret. We were friends, you see, in childhood.... You'd better hurry on to the carpenter's house. You'll find Jinny there doing something for her father.' She did not cease her working while she said it, this practical mind so familiar with the methods of useful thinking, this loving heart so versed in prayer while her broken body, deemed useless by the world, lay in the bed that was its earthly prison-house. '*He* can give me all the help I need,' she added.

She pointed, and they saw the figure of the Sweep standing in the corner of the room among a pile of brimming sacks. His dirty face was beaming. They heard him singing quietly to himself under his breath, while his feet and sooty hands marked time with a gesture of quaintest dancing:—

> *Such* a tremendously busy Sweep,
> Catching the world when it's all asleep,
> And tossing the blacks on the Rubbish Heap
>   Over the edge of the world!

'Come,' whispered Cousin Henry, catching at Monkey's hair, 'we can do something, but we can't do *that*. She needs no help from us!'

They sped across to the carpenter's house among the vineyards.

'What a splendour!' gasped the child as they went. 'My starlight seems quite dim beside hers.'

'She's an old hand at the game,' he replied, noticing the tinge of disappointment in her thought. 'With practice, you know——'

'And Mummy must be pretty tough,' she interrupted with a laugh, her elastic nature recovering instantly.

'——with practice, I was going to say, your atmosphere will get whiter too until it simply shines. That's why the saints have halos.'

But Monkey did not hear this last remark, she was already in her father's bedroom, helping Jinny.

Here there were no complications, no need for assistance from a Sweep, or Gardener, or Lamplighter. It was a case for pulling, pure and simple. Daddy was wumbled, nothing more. Body, mind, and heart were all up-jumbled. In making up the verse about the starlight he had merely told the truth—about himself. The poem was instinctive and inspirational confession. His atmosphere, as he lay there, gently snoring in his beauty sleep, was clear and sweet and bright, no darkness in it of grey or ugliness; but its pattern was a muddle, or rather there were several patterns that scrambled among each other for supremacy. Lovely patterns hovered just outside him, but none of them got really in. And the result was chaos. Daddy was not clear-headed; there was no concentration. Something of the perplexed confusion that afflicted his elder daughter in the daytime mixed up the patterns inextricably. There was no main pathway through his inner world.

And the picture proved it. It explained why Jinny pulled in vain. His night-body came out easily as far as the head, then stuck hopelessly. He looked like a knotted skein of coloured wools. Upon the paper where he had been making notes before going to sleep—for personal atmosphere is communicated to all its owner touches—lay the same confusion. Scraps of muddle, odds and ends of different patterns, hovered in thick blots of colour over the paragraphs and sentences. His own uncertainty was thus imparted to what he wrote, and his stories brought no conviction to his readers. He was too much the Dreamer, or too much the Thinker, which of the two was not quite clear. Harmony was lacking.

'That's probably what I'M like, too,' thought his friend, but so softly that the children did not hear it. That Scheme of his passed vaguely through his mind.

Then he cried louder—a definite thought:—

'There's no good tugging like that, my dears. Let him slip in again. You'll only make him restless, and give him distorted dreams.'

'I've tugged like this every night for months,' said Jinny, 'but the moment I let go he flies back like elastic.'

'Of course. We must first untie the knots and weave the patterns into one. Let go!'

Daddy's night-body flashed back like a sword into its sheath. They stood and watched him. He turned a little in his sleep, while above him the lines twined and wriggled like phosphorus on moving water, yet never shaped themselves into anything complete. They saw suggestions of pure beauty in them here and there that yet never joined together into a single outline; it was like watching the foam against a steamer's sides in moonlight—just failing of coherent form.

'They want combing out,' declared Jane Anne with a brilliant touch of truth. 'A rake would be best.'

'Assorting, sifting, separating,' added Cousinenry, 'but it's not easy.' He thought deeply for a moment. 'Suppose you two attend to the other things,' he said presently, 'while I take charge of the combing- out.'

They knew at once his meaning; it was begun as soon as thought, only they could never have thought of it alone; none but a leader with real sympathy in his heart could have discovered the way.

Like Fairies, lit internally with shining lanterns, they flew about their business. Monkey picked up his pencils and dipped their points into her store of starlight, while Jinny drew the cork out of his ink- pot and blew in soft-shiny radiance of her own. They soaked his books in it, and smoothed his paper out with their fingers of clean gold. His note-books, chair, and slippers, his smoking-coat and pipes and tobacco-tins, his sponge, his tooth-brush and his soap—everything from dressing-gown to dictionary, they spread thickly with their starlight, and continued until the various objects had drunk in enough to make them shine alone.

Then they attacked the walls and floor and ceiling, sheets and bed- clothes. They filled the tin-bath full to the very brim, painted as well the windows, door-handles, and the wicker chair in which they knew he dozed after dejeuner. But with the pencils, pens, and ink-pots they took most trouble, doing them very thoroughly indeed. And his enormous mountain-boots received generous treatment too, for in these he went for his long lonely walks when he thought out his stories among the woods and valleys, coming home with joy upon his face—'I got a splendid idea to-day—a magnificent story—if only I can get it on to paper before it's gone…!' They understood his difficulty now: the 'idea' was wumbled before he could fashion it. He could not get the pattern through complete.

And his older friend, working among the disjointed patterns, saw his trouble clearly too. It was not that he lacked this sympathy that starlight brings, but that he applied it without discernment. The receiving instrument was out of order, some parts moving faster than others. Reason and imagination were not exaccurately adjusted. He gathered plenty in, but no clear stream issued forth again; there was confusion in delivery. The rays were twisted, the golden lines caught into knots and tangles. Yet, ever just outside him, waiting to be taken in, hovered these patterns of loveliness that might bring joy to thousands. They floated in beauty round the edges of his atmosphere, but the moment they sank in to reach his mind, there began the distortion that tore their exquisite proportions and made designs mere disarrangement. Inspiration, without steady thought to fashion it, was of no value.

He worked with infinite pains to disentangle the mass of complicated lines, and one knot after another yielded and slipped off into rivulets of gold, all pouring inwards to reach heart and brain. It was exhilarating, yet disappointing labour. New knots formed themselves so easily, yet in the end much surely had been accomplished. Channels had been cleared; repetition would at length establish habit.

But the line of light along the eastern horizon had been swiftly growing broader meanwhile. It was brightening into delicate crimson. Already the room was clearer, and the radiance of their bodies fading into a paler glory. Jane Anne grew clumsier, tumbling over things, and butting against her more agile sister. Her thoughts became more muddled. She said things from time to time that showed it—hints that waking was not far away.

'Daddy's a wumbled Laplander, you know, after all. Hurry up!' The foolish daylight speech came closer.

'Give his ink-pot one more blow,' cried Monkey. Her body always slept at least an hour longer than the others. She had more time for work.

Jane Anne bumped into the washhand-stand. She no longer saw quite clearly.

'I'm a plenipotentiary, that's what I am. I'm afraid of nothing. But the porridge has to be made. I must get back....'

She vanished like a flash, just as her brother had vanished half an hour before.

'We'll go on with it to-morrow night,' signalled Cousin Henry to his last remaining helper. 'Meet me here, remember, when...the moon...is high enough to...cast...a...shadow....'

The opening and shutting of a door sounded through his sleep. He turned over heavily. Surely it was not time to get up yet. That could not be hot water coming! He had only just fallen asleep. He plunged back again into slumber.

But Monkey had disappeared.

'What a spanking dream I've had...!' Her eyes opened, and she saw her school-books on the chair beside the bed. Mother was gently shaking her out of sleep. 'Six o'clock, darling. The bath is ready, and Jinny's nearly got the porridge done. It's a lovely morning!'

'Oh, Mummy, I——'

But Mummy lifted her bodily out of bed, kissed her sleepy eyes awake, and half carried her over to the bath. 'You can tell me all about that later,' she said with practical decision; 'when the cold water's cleared your head. You're always fuzzy when you wake.'

Another day had begun. The sun was blazing high above the Blumlisalp. The birds sang in chorus. Dew shone still on the fields, but the men were already busy in the vineyards.

And presently Cousin Henry woke too and stared lazily about his room. He looked at his watch.

'By Jove,' he murmured. 'How one does sleep in this place! And what a dream to be sure—I who never dream!'

He remembered nothing more. From the moment he closed his eyes, eight hours before, until this second, all was a delicious blank. He felt refreshed and wondrously light-hearted, at peace with all the world. There was music in his head. He began to whistle as he lay among the blankets for half an hour longer. And later, while he breakfasted alone downstairs, he remembered that he ought to write to Minks. He owed Minks a letter. And before going out into the woods he wrote it. 'I'm staying on a bit,' he mentioned at the end. 'I find so much to do here, and it's such a rest. Meanwhile I can leave everything safely in your hands. But as soon as I get a leisure moment I'll send you the promised draft of my Scheme for Disabled, etc., etc.'

But the Scheme got no further somehow. New objections, for one thing, kept cropping up in his mind. It would take so long to build the place, and find the site, satisfy County Councils, and all the rest. The Disabled, moreover, were everywhere; it was invidious to select one group and leave the others out. Help the world, yes—but what was 'the world'? There were so many worlds. He touched a new one every day and every hour. Which needed his help most? Bourcelles was quite as important, quite as big and hungry as any of the others. 'That old Vicar knew a thing or two,' he reflected later in the forest, while he gathered a bunch of hepaticas and anemones to take to Mlle. Lemaire. 'There are "neighbours" everywhere, the world's simply chock full of 'em. But what a pity that we die just when we're getting fit and ready to begin. Perhaps we go on afterwards, though. I wonder...!'

CHAPTER XVII

The stars ran loose about the sky,
Wasting their beauty recklessly,
  Singing and dancing,
  Shooting and prancing,
Until the Pole Star took command,
Changing each wild, disordered band
Into a lamp to guide the land—
    A constellation.

And so, about my mind and yours,
Thought dances, shoots, and wastes its powers,
  Coming and going,
  Aimlessly flowing,
Until the Pole Star of the Will
Captains them wisely, strong, and still,
Some dream for others to fulfil
    With consecration.
            Selected Poems, Montmorency Minke.

There was a certain air of unreality somewhere in the life at Bourcelles that
ministered to fantasy. Rogers had felt it steal over him from the beginning.
It was like watching a children's play in which the scenes were laid
alternately in the Den, the Pension, and the Forest. Side by side with the
grim stern facts of existence ran the coloured spell of fairy make-believe. It
was the way they mingled, perhaps, that ministered to this spirit of fantasy.

There were several heroines for instance—Tante Jeanne, Mademoiselle
Lemaire, and Mother; each played her role quite admirably. There were the
worthy sterling men who did their duty dumbly, regardless of
consequences—Daddy, the Postmaster, and the picturesque old clergyman
with failing powers. There was the dark, uncertain male character, who
might be villain, yet who might prove extra hero—the strutting postman of
baronial ancestry; there was the role of quaint pathetic humour Miss
Waghorn so excellently filled, and there were the honest rough-and-tumble
comedians—half mischievous, half malicious—the retired governesses.
Behind them all, brought on chiefly in scenes of dusk and moonlight, were
the Forest Elves who, led by Puck, were responsible for the temporary
confusion that threatened disaster, yet was bound to have a happy ending—
the children. It was all a children's play set in the lovely scenery of
mountain, forest, lake, and old-world garden.

Numerous other characters also flitted in and out. There was the cat, the bird, the donkey as in pantomime; goblin caves and haunted valleys and talking flowers; and the queer shadowy folk who came to the Pension in the summer months, then vanished into space again. Links with the outside world were by no means lacking. As in the theatre, one caught now and again the rumble of street traffic and the roar of everyday concerns. But these fell in by chance during quiet intervals, and served to heighten contrast only.

And so many of the principal roles were almost obviously assumed, interchangeable almost; any day the players might drop their wigs, rub off the paint, and appear otherwise, as they were in private life. The Widow Jequier's husband, for instance, had been a *pasteur* who had gone later into the business of a wine-merchant. She herself was not really the keeper of a Pension for Jeune Filles, but had drifted into it owing to her husband's disastrous descent from pulpit into cellar— understudy for some one who had forgotten to come on. The Postmaster, too, had originally been a photographer, whose funereal aspect had sealed his failure in that line. His customers could never smile and look pleasant. The postman, again, was a baron in disguise—in private life he had a castle and retainers; and even Gygi, the gendarme, was a make-believe official who behind the scenes was a *vigneron* and farmer in a very humble way. Daddy, too, seemed sometimes but a tinsel author dressed up for the occasion, and absurdly busy over books that no one ever saw on railway bookstalls. While Mademoiselle Lemaire was not in fact and verity a suffering, patient, bed-ridden lady, but a princess who escaped from her disguise at night into glory and great beneficent splendour.

Mother alone was more real than the other players. There was no make-believe about Mother. She thundered across the stage and stood before the footlights, interrupting many a performance with her stubborn common-sense and her grip upon difficult grave issues. 'This performance will finish at such and such an hour,' was her cry. 'Get your wraps ready. It will be cold when you go out. And see that you have money handy for your 'bus fares home!' Yes, Mother was real. She knew some facts of life at least. She knitted the children's stockings and did the family mending.

Yet Rogers felt, even with her, that she was merely waiting. She knew the cast was not complete as yet. She waited. They all waited—for some one. These were rehearsals; Rogers himself had dropped in also merely as an understudy. Another role was vacant, and it was the principal role. There was no one in the company who could play it, none who could understudy it even. Neither Rogers nor Daddy could learn the lines or do the 'business.' The part was a very important one, calling for a touch of genius to be filled adequately. And it was a feminine role. For here was a Fairy Play without a Fairy Queen. There was not even a Fairy Princess!

This idea of a representation, all prepared specially for himself, induced a very happy state of mind; he felt restful, calm, at peace with all the world. He had only to sit in his stall and enjoy. But it brought, too, this sense of delicate bewilderment that was continually propounding questions to which he found no immediate answer. With the rest of the village, he stood still while Time flowed past him. Later, with Minks, he would run after it and catch it up again. Minks would pick out the lost clues. Minks stood on the banks—in London—noting the questions floating by and landing them sometimes with a rod and net. His master would deal with them by and by; but just now he could well afford to wait and enjoy himself. It was a holiday; there was no hurry; Minks held the fort meanwhile and sent in reports at intervals.

And the sweet spring weather continued; days were bright and warm; the nights were thick with stars. Rogers postponed departure on the flimsiest reasons. It was no easy thing to leave Bourcelles. 'Next week the muguet will be over in the vallon vert. We must pick it quickly together for Tante Anna.' Jinny brought every spring flower to Mademoiselle Lemaire in this way the moment they appeared. Her room was a record of their sequence from week to week. And Jimbo knew exactly where to find them first; his mind was a time-table of flowers as well as of trains, dates of arrival, and stations where they grew. He knew it all exaccurately. This kind of fact with him was never wumbled. 'Soon the sabot de Venus will be in flower at the Creux du Van, but it takes time to find it. It's most awfully rare, you see. You'll have to climb beyond the fontaine froide. That's past the Ferme Robert, between Champ du Moulin and Noiraigue. The snow ought to be gone by now. We'll go and hunt for it. I'll take you in—oh, in about deux semaines—comme ca.' Alone, those dangerous cliffs were out of bounds for him, but if he went with Cousinenry, permission could not be refused. Jimbo knew what he was about. And he took for granted that his employer would never leave Bourcelles again. 'Thursday and Saturday would be the best days,' he added. They were his half- holidays, but he did not say so. Secretaries, he knew, did not have half-holidays comme ca. 'Je suis son vrai secretaire,' he had told Mademoiselle Lemaire, who had confirmed it with a grave mais oui. No one but Mother heard the puzzled question one night when he was being tucked into bed; it was asked with just a hint of shame upon a very puckered little face—'But, Mummy, what really *is* a sekrity?'

And so Rogers, from day to day, stayed on, enjoying himself and resting. The City would have called it loafing, but in the City the schedule of values was a different one. Meanwhile the bewilderment he felt at first gradually disappeared. He no longer realised it, that is. While still outside, attacked by it, he had realised the soft entanglement. Now he was in it, caught utterly, a prisoner. He was no longer mere observer. He was part and parcel of it. 'What does a few weeks matter out of a whole strenuous life?' he argued. 'It's all to the good, this holiday. I'm storing up strength and energy for future use. My Scheme can wait a little. I'm thinking things out meanwhile.'

He often went into the forest alone to think his things out, and 'things' always meant his Scheme ... but the more he thought about it the more distant and impracticable seemed that wondrous Scheme. He had the means, the love, the yearning, all in good condition, waiting to be put to practical account. In his mind, littered more and more now with details that Minks not infrequently sent in, this great Scheme by which he had meant to help the world ran into the confusion of new issues that were continually cropping up. Most of these were caused by the difficulty of knowing his money spent exactly as he wished, not wasted, no pound of it used for adornment, whether salaries, uniforms, fancy stationery, or unnecessary appearances, whatever they might be. Whichever way he faced it, and no matter how carefully thought out were the plans that Minks devised, these leakages cropped up and mocked him. Among a dozen propositions his original clear idea went lost, and floundered. It came perilously near to wumbling itself away altogether.

For one thing, there were rivals on the scene—his cousin's family, the education of these growing children, the difficulties of the Widow Jequier, some kind of security he might ensure to old Miss Waghorn, the best expert medical attendance for Mademoiselle Lemaire ... and his fortune was after all a small one as fortunes go. Only his simple scale of personal living could make these things possible at all. Yet here, at least, he would know that every penny went exaccurately where it was meant to go, and accomplished the precise purpose it was intended to accomplish.

And the more he thought about it, the more insistent grew the claims of little Bourcelles, and the more that portentous Scheme for Disabled Thingumabobs faded into dimness. The old Vicar's words kept singing in his head: 'The world is full of Neighbours. Bring them all back to Fairyland.' He thought things out in his own way and at his leisure. He loved to wander alone among the mountains... thinking in this way. His thoughts turned to his cousin's family, their expenses, their difficulties, the curious want of harmony somewhere. For the conditions in which the *famille anglaise* existed, he had soon discovered, were those of muddle pure and simple, yet of muddle on so large a scale that it was fascinating and even exhilarating. It must be lovely, he reflected, to live so carelessly. They drifted. Chance forces blew them hither and thither as gusts of wind blow autumn leaves. Five years in a place and then—a gust that blew them elsewhere. Thus they had lived five years in a London suburb, thinking it permanent; five years in a lonely Essex farm, certain they would never abandon country life; and five years, finally, in the Jura forests.

Neither parent, though each was estimable, worthy, and entirely of good repute, had the smallest faculty for seeing life whole; each studied closely a small fragment of it, the fragment limited by the Monday and the Saturday of next week, or, in moments of optimistic health, the fragment that lies between the first and thirty-first of a single month. Of what lay beyond, they talked; oh, yes, they talked voluminously and with detail that sounded impressive to a listener, but somehow in circles that carried them no further than the starting- point, or in spirals that rose higher with each sentence and finally lifted them bodily above the solid ground. It was merely talk— ineffective—yet the kind that makes one feel it has accomplished something and so brings the false security of carelessness again. Neither one nor other was head of the house. They took it in turns, each slipping by chance into that onerous position, supported but uncoveted by the other. Mother fed the children, mended everything, sent them to the dentist when their teeth ached badly, but never before as a preventative, and—trusted to luck.

'Daddy,' she would say in her slow gentle way, 'I do wish we could be more practical sometimes. Life is such a business, isn't it?' And they would examine in detail the grain of the stable door now that the horse had escaped, then close it very carefully.

'I really must keep books,' he would answer, 'so that we can see exactly how we stand,' having discovered at the end of laborious calculation concerning the cost of the proposed Geneva schooling for Jinny that they had reckoned in shillings instead of francs. And then, with heads together, they selected for their eldest boy a profession utterly unsuited to his capacities, with coaching expenses far beyond their purses, and with the comforting consideration that 'there's a pension attached to it, you see, for when he's old.'

Similarly, having planned minutely, and with personal sacrifice, to save five francs in one direction, they would spend that amount unnecessarily in another. They felt they had it to spend, as though it had been just earned and already jingled in their pockets. Daddy would announce he was walking into Neuchatel to buy tobacco. 'Better take the tram,' suggested Mother, 'it's going to rain. You save shoe leather, too,' she added laughingly. 'Will you be back to tea?' He thought not; he would get a cup of tea in town. 'May I come, too?' from Jimbo. 'Why not?' thought Mother. 'Take him with you, he'll enjoy the trip.' Monkey and Jane Ann, of course, went too. They *all* had tea in a shop, and bought chocolate into the bargain. The five francs melted into—nothing, for tea at home was included in their Pension terms. Saving is in the mind. There was no system in their life.

'It would be jolly, yes, if you could earn a little something regular besides your work,' agreed Mother, when he thought of learning a typewriter to copy his own books, and taking in work to copy for others too.

'I'll do it,' he decided with enthusiasm that was forgotten before he left the room ten minutes later.

It was the same with the suggestion of teaching English. He had much spare time, and could easily have earned a pound a week by giving lessons, and a pound a week is fifty pounds a year—enough to dress the younger children easily. The plan was elaborated laboriously. 'Of course,' agreed Daddy, with genuine interest. 'It's easily done. I wonder we never thought of it before.' Every few months they talked about it, but it never grew an inch nearer to accomplishment. They drifted along, ever in difficulty, each secretly blaming the other, yet never putting their thoughts into speech. They did not quite understand each other's point of view.

'Mother really might have foreseen *that*!' when Jimbo, growing like a fairy beanstalk, rendered his recent clothes entirely useless. 'Boys must grow. Why didn't she buy the things a size or two larger?'

'It's rather thoughtless, almost selfish, of Daddy to go on writing these books that bring in praise without money. He could write anything if he chose. At least, he might put his shoulder to the wheel and teach, or something!'

And so, not outwardly in spoken words or quarrels, but inwardly, owing to that deadliest of cancers, want of sympathy, these two excellent grown-up children had moved with the years further and further apart. Love had not died, but want of understanding, not attended to in time, had frayed the edges so that they no longer fitted well together. They have blown in here, thought Rogers as he watched them, like seeds the wind has brought. They have taken root and grown a bit. They think they're here for ever, but presently a wind will rise and blow them off again elsewhere. And thinking it is their own act, they will look wisely at each other, as children do, and say, 'Yes, it *is* time now to make a move. The children are getting big. Our health, too, needs a change.' He wondered, smiling a little, in what vale or mountain top the wind would let them down. And a big decision blazed up in his heart. 'I'm not very strong in the domestic line,' he exclaimed, 'but I think I can help them a bit. They're neighbours at any rate. They're all children too. Daddy's no older than Jimbo, or Mother than Jane Anne!'

* * *

In the spaces of the forest there was moss and sunshine. It was very still. The primroses and anemones had followed the hepaticas and periwinkles. Patches of lily of the valley filled the air with fragrance. Through openings of the trees he caught glimpses of the lake, deep as the Italian blue of the sky above his head. White Alps hung in the air beyond its farther shore line. Below him, already far away, the village followed slowly, bringing its fields and vineyards with it, until the tired old church called halt. And then it lay back, nestling down to sleep, very small, very cosy, mere handful of brown roofs among the orchards. Only the blue smoke of occasional peat fires moved here and there, betraying human occupation.

The peace and beauty sank into his heart, as he wandered higher across Mont Racine's velvet shoulder. And the contrast stirred memories of his recent London life. He thought of the scurrying busy-bodies in the 'City,' and he thought of the Widow Jequier attacking life so restlessly in her garden at that very minute. That other sentence of the old Vicar floated though his mind: 'the grandeur of toil and the insignificance of acquisition.'... Far overhead two giant buzzards circled quietly, ceaselessly watching from the blue. A brimstone butterfly danced in random flight before his face. Two cuckoos answered one another in the denser forest somewhere above him. Bells from distant village churches boomed softly through the air, voices from a world forgotten.

And the contrast brought back London. He thought of the long busy chapter of his life just finished. The transition had been so abrupt. As a rule periods fade into one another gradually in life, easily, divisions blurred; it is difficult on looking back to say where the change began. One is well into the new before the old is realised as left behind. 'How did I come to this?' the mind asks itself. 'I don't remember any definite decision. Where was the boundary crossed?' It has been imperceptibly accomplished.

But here the change had been sudden and complete, no shading anywhere. He had leaped a wall. Turmoil and confusion lay on that side; on this lay peace, rest and beauty. Strain and ugliness were left behind, and with them so much that now seemed false, unnecessary, vain. The grandeur of toil, and the insignificance of acquisition—the phrase ran through his mind with the sighing of the pine trees; it was like the first line of a song. The Vicar knew the song complete. Even Minks, perhaps, could pipe it too. Rogers was learning it. 'I must help them somehow,' he thought again. 'It's not a question of money merely. It's that they want welding together more— more harmony—more sympathy. They're separate bits of a puzzle now, whereas they might be a rather big and lovely pattern. ...'

He lay down upon the moss and flung his hat away. He felt that Life stood still within him, watching, waiting, asking beautiful, deep, searching questions. It made him slightly uncomfortable. Henry Rogers, late of Threadneedle Street, took stock of himself, not of set intention, yet somehow deliberately. He reviewed another Henry Rogers who had been unable to leap that wall. The two peered at one another gravely.

The review, however, took no definite form; precise language hardly came to help with definite orders. A vague procession of feelings, half sad, half pleasurable, floated past his closing eyes. ... Perhaps he slept a moment in the sunshine upon that bed of moss and pine needles. ...

Such curious thoughts flowed up and out and round about, dancing like the brimstone butterflies out of reach before he could seize them, calling with voices like the cuckoos, themselves all the time just out of sight. Who ever saw a cuckoo when it's talking? Who ever foretold the instant when a butterfly would shoot upwards and away? Such darting, fragile thoughts they were, like hints, suggestions. Still, they *were* thoughts.

Minks, dragging behind him an enormous Scheme, emerged from the dark vaults of a Bank where gold lay piled in heaps. Minks was looking for him, yet smiling a little, almost pityingly, as he strained beneath the load. It was like a comic opera. Minks was going down the noisy, crowded Strand. Then, suddenly, he paused, uncertain of the way. From an upper window a shining face popped out and issued clear directions —as from a pulpit. 'That way—towards the river,' sang the voice—and far down the narrow side street flashed a gleam of flowing water with orchards on the farther bank. Minks instantly turned and went down it with his load so fast that the scenery changed before the heavy traffic could get out of the way. Everything got muddled up with fields and fruit-trees; the Scheme changed into a mass of wild- flowers; a lame boy knocked it over with his crutch; gold fell in a brilliant, singing shower, and where each sovereign fell there sprang up a buttercup or dandelion. Rogers rubbed his eyes ... and realised that the sun was rather hot upon his face. A dragon fly was perched upon his hat three feet away. ...

The tea hour at the Den was close, and Jimbo, no doubt, was already looking for him at the carpenter's house. Rogers hurried home among the silent forest ways that were sweet with running shadows and slanting sunshine. Oh, how fragrant was the evening air! And how the lily of the valley laughed up in his face! Normally, at this time, he would be sitting in a taxi, hurrying noisily towards his Club, thoughts full of figures, politics, philanthropy cut to line and measure—a big Scheme standing in squares across the avenue of the future. Now, moss and flowers and little children took up all the available space. ... How curiously out of the world Bourcelles was, to be sure. Newspapers had no meaning any longer. Picture-papers and smart weekly Reviews, so necessary and important in St.

James's Street, here seemed vulgar, almost impertinent—ridiculous even. Big books, yes; but not pert, topical comments issued with an absurd omnipotence upon things merely ephemeral. How the mind accumulated rubbish in a city! It seemed incredible. He surely had climbed a wall and dropped down into a world far bigger, though a world the 'city' would deem insignificant and trivial. Yet only because it had less detail probably! A loved verse flashed to him across the years:—

'O to dream, O to awake and wander
  There, and with delight to take and render,
    Through the trance of silence,
      Quiet breath!

Lo! for there among the flowers and grasses,
  Only the mightier movement sounds and passes;
    Only winds and rivers,
      Life and death.'

Bourcelles was important as London, yes, while simple as the nursery. The same big questions of life and death, of battle, duty, love, ruled the peaceful inhabitants. Only the noisy shouting, the clatter of superfluous chattering and feverish striving had dropped away. Hearts and minds wore fewer clothes among these woods and vineyards. There was no nakedness though … there were flowers and moss, blue sky and peace and beauty. … Thought ran into confused, vague pictures. He could not give them coherence, shape, form. …

He crossed the meadows and entered the village through the Pension garden. The Widow Jequier gave him a spray of her Persian lilac on the way. 'It's been growing twenty-five years for you,' she said, 'only do not look at *me*. I'm in my garden things—invisible.' He remembered with a smile Jane Anne's description—that 'the front part of the house was all at the back.'

Tumbling down the wooden stairs, he crossed the street and made for the Citadelle, where the children opened the door for him even before he rang. Jimbo and Monkey, just home from school, pulled him by both arms towards the tea-table. They had watched for his coming.

'The samovar's just boiling,' Mother welcomed him. Daddy was on the sofa by the open window, reading manuscript over to himself in a mumbling voice; and Jane Anne, apron on, sleeves tucked up, face flushed, poked her head in from the kitchen:

'Excuse me, Mother, the cupboard's all in distress. I can't find the marmalade anywhere.'

'But it's already on the table, child.'

She saw her Cousin and popped swiftly back again from view. One heard fragments of her sentences—'wumbled ... chronic ... busy monster. ... 'And two minutes later *la famille anglaise* was seriously at tea.

CHAPTER XVIII

What art thou, then? I cannot guess;
  But tho' I seem in star and flower
  To feel thee some diffusive power,
I do not therefore love thee less.
        Love and Death, TENNYSON.

In the act of waking up on the morning of the Star Cave experience, Henry Rogers caught the face of a vivid dream close against his own— but in rapid motion, already passing. He tried to seize it. There was a happy, delightful atmosphere about it. Examination, however, was impossible; the effort to recover the haunting dream dispersed it. He saw the tip, like an express train flying round a corner; it flashed and disappeared, fading into dimness. Only the delightful atmosphere remained and the sense that he had been somewhere far away in very happy conditions. People he knew quite well, had been there with him; Jimbo and Monkey; Daddy too, as he had known him in his boyhood. More than this was mere vague surmise; he could not recover details. Others had been also of the merry company, familiar yet unrecognisable. Who in the world were they? It all seemed oddly real.

'How I do dream in this place, to be sure,' he thought; 'I, who normally dream so little! It was like a scene of my childhood— Crayfield or somewhere.' And he reflected how easily one might be persuaded that the spirit escaped in sleep and knew another order of experience. The sense of actuality was so vivid.

He lay half dozing for a little longer, hoping to recover the adventures. The flying train showed itself once or twice again, but smaller, and much, much farther away. It curved off into the distance. A deep cutting quickly swallowed it. It emerged for the last time, tiny as a snake upon a chess-board of far-off fields. Then it dipped into mist; the snake shot into its hole. It was gone. He sighed. It had been so lovely. Why must it vanish so entirely? Once or twice during the day it returned, touched him swiftly on the heart and was gone again. But the waking impression of a dream is never the dream itself. Sunshine destroys the sense of enormous wonder.

'I believe I've been dreaming all night long, and going through all kinds of wild adventures.'

He dressed leisurely, still hunting subconsciously for fragments of that happy dreamland. Its aroma still clung about him. The sunshine poured into the room. He went out on to the balcony and looked at the Alps through his Zeiss field-glasses. The brilliant snow upon the Diablerets danced and sang into his blood; across the broken teeth of the Dent du Midi trailed thin strips of early cloud. Behind him rose great Boudry's massive shoulders, a pyramid of incredible deep blue. And the limestone precipices of La Tourne stood dazzlingly white, catching the morning sunlight full in their face.

The air had the freshness of the sea. Men were singing at their work among the vineyards. The tinkle of cow-bells floated to him from the upper pastures upon Mont Racine. Little sails like sea-gulls dipped across the lake. Goodness, how happy the world was at Bourcelles! Singing, radiant, careless of pain and death. And, goodness, how he longed to make it happier still!

Every day now this morning mood had been the same. Desire to do something for others ran races with little practical schemes for carrying it out. Selfish considerations seemed to have taken flight, all washed away while he slept. Moreover, the thought of his Scheme had begun to oppress him; a touch of shame came with it, almost as though an unworthy personal motive were somewhere in it. Perhaps after all—he wondered more and more now—there had been an admixture of personal ambition in the plan. The idea that it would bring him honour in the eyes of the world had possibly lain there hidden all along. If so, he had not realised it; the depravity had been unconscious. Before the Bourcelles standard of simplicity, artificial elements dropped off automatically, ashamed. ... And a profound truth, fished somehow out of that vanished dreamland, spun its trail of glory through his heart. Kindness that is thanked-for surely brings degradation—a degradation almost as mean as the subscription acknowledged in a newspaper, or the anonymous contribution kept secret temporarily in order that its later advertisement may excite the more applause. Out flashed this blazing truth: kind acts must be instinctive, natural, thoughtless. One hand must be in absolute ignorance of the other's high adventures. ... And when the carpenter's wife brought up his breakfast tray, with the bunch of forest flowers standing in a tumbler of water, she caught him pondering over another boyhood's memory—that friend of his father's who had given away a million anonymously.

... In his heart plans shaped themselves with soft, shy eyes and hidden faces.... He longed to get *la famille anglaise* straight ... for one thing. ...

It was an hour later, while he still sat dreaming in the sunshine by the open window, that a gentle tap came at the door, and Daddy entered. The visit was a surprise. Usually, until time for *dejeuner*, he kept his room, busily unwumbling stories. This was unusual. And something had happened to him; he looked different. What was it that had changed? Some veil had cleared away; his eyes were shining. They greeted one another, and Rogers fell shyly to commonplaces, while wondering what the change exactly was.

But the other was not to be put off. He was bursting with something. Rogers had never seen him like this before.

'You've stopped work earlier than usual,' he said, providing the opening. He understood his diffidence, his shyness in speaking of himself. Long disappointments lay so thinly screened behind his unfulfilled enthusiasm.

But this time the enthusiasm swept diffidence to the winds. It had been vitally stirred.

'Early indeed,' he cried. 'I've been working four hours without a break, man. Why, what do you think?—I woke at sunrise, a thing I never do, with—with a brilliant idea in my head. Brilliant, I tell you. By Jove, if only I can carry it out as I see it——!'

'You've begun it already?'

'Been at it since six o'clock, I tell you. It was in me when I woke— idea, treatment, everything complete, all in a perfect pattern of Beauty.'

There was a glow upon his face, his hair was untidy; a white muffler with blue spots was round his neck instead of collar. One end stuck up against his chin. The safety pin was open.

'By Jove! I am delighted!' Rogers had seen him excited before over a 'brilliant idea,' but the telling of it always left him cold. It touched the intellect, yet not the heart. It was merely clever. This time, however, there was a new thing in his manner. 'How did you get it?' he repeated. Methods of literary production beyond his own doggerels were a mystery to him. 'Sort of inspiration, eh?'

'Woke with it, I tell you,' continued his cousin, twisting the muffler so that it tickled his ear now instead of his chin. 'It must have come to me in sleep——' 'In sleep,' exclaimed the other; 'you dreamt it, then?'

'Kind of inspiration business. I've heard of that sort of thing, but never experienced it——' The author paused for breath.

'What is it? Tell me.' He remembered how ingenious details of his patents had sometimes found themselves cleared up in the morning after refreshing slumber. This might be something similar. 'Let's hear it,' he added; 'I'm interested.'

His cousin's recitals usually ended in sad confusion, so that all he could answer by way of praise was—' You ought to make something good out of that. I shall like to read it when you've finished it.' But this time, he felt, there was distinctly a difference. There were new conditions.

The older man leaned closer, his face alight, his manner shyly, eagerly confidential. The morning sunshine blazed upon his untidy hair. A bread crumb from breakfast still balanced in his beard.

'It's difficult to tell in a few words, you see,' he began, the enthusiasm of a boy in his manner, 'but—I woke with the odd idea that this little village might be an epitome of the world. All the emotions of London, you see, are here in essence—the courage and cowardice, the fear and hope, the greed and sacrifice, the love and hate and passion—everything. It's the big world in miniature. Only—with one difference.'

'That's good,' said Rogers, trying to remember when it was he had told his cousin this very thing. Or had he only *thought* it? 'And what *is* the difference?'

'The difference,' continued the other, eyes sparkling, face alight, 'that here the woods, the mountains and the stars are close. They pour themselves in upon the village life from every side—above, below, all round. Flowers surround it; it dances to the mountain winds; at night it lies entangled in the starlight. Along a thousand imperceptible channels an ideal simplicity from Nature pours down into it, modifying the human passions, chastening, purifying, uplifting. Don't you see? And these sweet, viewless channels— who keeps them clean and open? Why, God bless you———. The children! *My* children!'

'By Jingo, yes; *your* children.'

Rogers said it with emphasis. But there was a sudden catch at his heart; he was conscious of a queer sensation he could not name. This was exactly what he had felt himself—with the difference that his own thought had been, perhaps, emotion rather than a reasoned-out idea. His cousin put it into words and gave it form. A picture—had he seen it in a book perhaps?—flashed across his mind. A child, suspiciously like Monkey, held a pen and dipped it into something bright and flowing. A little boy with big blue eyes gathered this shining stuff in both hands and poured it in a golden cataract upon the eyelids of a sleeping figure. And the figure had a beard. It was a man ... familiar. ... A touch of odd excitement trembled through his undermind ... thrilled ... vanished. ...

All dived out of sight again with the swiftness of a darting swallow. His cousin was talking at high speed. Rogers had lost a great deal of what he had been saying.

'… it may, of course, have come from something you said the other night as we walked up the hill to supper—you remember?—something about the brilliance of our stars here and how they formed a shining network that hung from Boudry and La Tourne. It's impossible to say. The germ of a true inspiration is never discoverable. Only, I remember, it struck me as an odd thing for *you* to say. I was telling you about my idea of the scientist who married—no, no, it wasn't that, it was my story of the materialist doctor whom circumstances compelled to accept a position in the Community of Shakers, and how the contrast produced an effect upon his mind of—of— you remember, perhaps? It was one or the other; I forget exactly,'—then suddenly— 'No, no, I've got it—it was the analysis of the father's mind when he found——'

'Yes, yes,' interrupted Rogers. 'We were just passing the Citadelle fountain. I saw the big star upon the top of Boudry, and made a remark about it.' His cousin was getting sadly wumbled. He tried to put severity and concentration into his voice.

'That's it,' the other cried, head on one side and holding up a finger, 'because I remember that my own thought wandered for a moment — thought will, you know, in spite of one's best effort sometimes—and you said a thing that sent a little shiver of pleasure through me for an instant— something about a Starlight Train—and made me wonder where you got the idea. That's it. I do believe you've hit the nail on the head. Isn't it curious sometimes how a practical mind may suggest valuable material to the artist? I remember, several years ago——'

'Starlight Express, wasn't it?' said his friend with decision in his voice. He thumped the table vigorously with one fist. 'Keep to the point, old man. Follow it out. Your idea is splendid.'

'Yes, I do believe it is.' Something in his voice trembled.

One sentence in particular Rogers heard, for it seemed plucked out of the talk he had with the children in the forest that day two weeks ago.

'You see, all light meets somewhere. It's all one, I mean. And so with minds. They all have a common meeting-place. Sympathy is the name for that place—that state—they feel with each other, see flash-like from the same point of view for a moment. And children are the conduits. They do not think things out. They feel them, eh?' He paused an instant.

'For you see, along these little channels that the children—my children, as I think I mentioned—keep sweet and open, there might troop back into the village—Fairyland. Not merely a foolish fairyland of make-believe and dragons and princesses imprisoned in animals, but a fairyland the whole world needs—the sympathy of sweet endeavour, love, gentleness and sacrifice for others. The stars would bring it— starlight don't you see? One might weave starlight in and out everywhere—use it as the symbol of sympathy—and—er—so on—'

Rogers again lost the clue. Another strangely familiar picture, and then another, flashed gorgeously before his inner vision; his mind raced after them, yet never caught them up. They were most curiously familiar. Then, suddenly, he came back and heard his cousin still talking. It was like a subtle plagiarism. Too subtle altogether, indeed, it was for him. He could only stare and listen in amazement.

But the recital grew more and more involved. Perhaps, alone in his work-room, Daddy could unwumble it consistently. He certainly could not tell it. The thread went lost among a dozen other things. The interfering sun had melted it all down in dew and spider gossamer and fairy cotton. ...

'I must go down and work,' he said at length, rising and fumbling with the door handle. He seemed disappointed a little. He had given out his ideas so freely, perhaps too freely. Rogers divined he had not sympathised enough. His manner had been shamefully absent-minded. The absent-mindedness was really the highest possible praise, but the author did not seem to realise it.

'It's glorious, my dear fellow, glorious,' Rogers added emphatically. 'You've got a big idea, and you can write it too. You will.' He said it with conviction. 'You touch my heart as you tell it. I congratulate you. Really I do.'

There was no mistaking the sincerity of his words and tone. The other came back a step into the room again. He stroked his beard and felt the crisp, hard crumb. He picked it out, examining it without surprise. It was no unfamiliar thing, perhaps; at any rate, it was an excuse to lower his eyes. Shyness returned upon him.

'Thank you,' he said gently; 'I'm glad you think so. You see, I sometimes feel—perhaps—my work has rather suffered from—been a little deficient in—the human touch. One must reach people's hearts if one wants big sales. So few have brains. Not that I care for money, or could ever write for money, for that brings its own punishment in loss of inspiration. But of course, with a family to support. ... I *have* a family, you see.' He raised his eyes and looked out into the sunshine. 'Well, anyhow, I've begun this thing. I shall send it in short form to the X. *Review*. It may attract attention there. And later I can expand it into a volume.' He hesitated, examined the crumb closely again, tossed it away, and looked up at his cousin suddenly full in the face. The high enthusiasm flamed back into his eyes again. 'Bring the world back to Fairyland, you see!' he concluded with vehemence, 'eh?'

'Glorious!' Surely thought ran about the world like coloured flame, if this was true.

The author turned towards the door. He opened it, then stopped on the threshold and looked round like a person who has lost his way.

'I forgot,' he added, 'I forgot another thing, one of the chief almost. It's this: there must be a Leader—who shall bring it back. Without the Guide, Interpreter, Pioneer, how shall the world listen or understand, even the little world of Bourcelles?'

'Of course, yes—some big figure—like a priest or prophet, you mean? A sort of Chairman, President, eh?'

'Yes,' was the reply, while the eyes flashed fires that almost recaptured forgotten dreams, 'but hardly in the way you mean, perhaps. A very simple figure, *I* mean, unconscious of its mighty role. Some one with endless stores of love and sympathy and compassion that have never found an outlet yet, but gone on accumulating and accumulating unexpressed.'

'I see, yes.' Though he really did not 'see' a bit. 'But who is there like that here? You'll have to invent him.' He remembered his own thought that some principal role was vacant in his Children's Fairy Play. How queer it all was! He stared. 'Who is there?' he repeated.

'No one—now. I shall bring her, though.'

'*Her*!' exclaimed Rogers with surprise. 'You mean a woman?'

'A childless woman,' came the soft reply. 'A woman with a million children—all unborn.' But Rogers did not see the expression of the face. His cousin was on the landing. The door closed softly on the words. The steps went fumbling down the stairs, and presently he heard the door below close too. The key was turned in it.

'A childless woman!' The phrase rang on long after he had gone. What an extraordinary idea! 'Bring her here' indeed! Could his cousin mean that some such woman might read his story and come to claim the position, play the vacant role? No, nothing so literal surely. The idea was preposterous. He had heard it said that imaginative folk, writers, painters, musicians, all had a touch of lunacy in them somewhere. He shrugged his shoulders. And what a job it must be, too, the writing of a book! He had never realised it before. A real book, then, meant putting one's heart into sentences, telling one's inmost secrets, confessing one's own ideals with fire and lust and passion. That was the difference perhaps between literature and mere facile invention. His cousin had never dared do this before; shyness prevented; his intellect wove pretty patterns that had no heat of life in them. But now he had discovered a big idea, true as the sun, and able, like the sun, to warm thousands of readers, all ready for it without knowing it. ...

Rogers sat on thinking in the bright spring sunshine, smoking one cigarette after another. For the idea his cousin had wumbled over so fubsily had touched his heart, and for a long time he was puzzled to find the reason. But at length he found it. In that startling phrase 'a childless woman' lay the clue. A childless woman was like a vessel with a cargo of exquisite flowers that could never make a port. Sweetening every wind, she yet never comes to land. No harbour welcomes her. She sails endless seas, charged with her freight of undelivered beauty; the waves devour her glory, her pain, her lovely secret all unconfessed. To bring such a woman into port, even imaginatively in a story, or subconsciously in an inner life, was fulfilment of a big, fine, wholesome yearning, sacred in a way, too.

'By George!' he said aloud. He felt strange, great life pour through him. He had made a discovery ... in his heart ... deep, deep down.

Something in himself, so long buried it was scarcely recognisable, stirred out of sight and tried to rise. Some flower of his youth that time had hardened, dried, yet never killed, moved gently towards blossoming. It shone. It was still hard a little, like a crystal, glistening down there among shadows that had gathered with the years. And then it suddenly melted, running in a tiny thread of gold among his thoughts into that quiet sea which so rarely in a man may dare the relief of tears. It was a tiny yellow flower, like a daisy that had forgotten to close at night, so that some stray starbeam changed its whiteness into gold.

Forgotten passion, and yearning long denied, stirred in him with that phrase. His cousin's children doubtless had prepared the way. A faded Dream peered softly into his eyes across the barriers of the years. For every woman in the world was a mother, and a childless woman was the grandest, biggest mother of them all. And he had longed for children of his own; he, too, had remained a childless father. A vanished face gazed up into his own. Two vessels, making the same fair harbour, had lost their way, yet still sailed, perhaps, the empty seas. Yet the face he did not quite recognise. The eyes, instead of blue, were amber. ...

And did this explain a little the spell that caught him in this Jura village, perhaps? Were these children, weaving a network so cunningly about his feet, merely scouts and pilots? Was his love for the world of suffering folk, after all, but his love for a wife and children of his own transmuted into wider channels? Denied the little garden he once had planned for it, did it seek to turn the whole big world into a garden? Suppression was impossible; like murder, it must out. A bit of it had even flamed a passage into work and patents and 'City' life. For love is life, and life is ever and everywhere one. He thought and thought and thought. A man begins by loving himself; then, losing himself, he loves a woman; next, that love spreads itself over a still bigger field, and he loves his family, his wife and children, and their families again in turn. But, that expression denied, his love inevitably, irrepressibly seeking an outlet, finds it in a Cause, a Race, a Nation, perhaps in the entire world. The world becomes his 'neighbour.' It was a great Fairy Story. ...

Again his thoughts returned to that one singular sentence ... and he realised what his cousin meant. Only a childless Mother, some woman charged to the brim with this power of loving to which ordinary expression had been denied, could fill the vacant role in his great Children's Play. No man could do it. He and his cousin were mere 'supers' on this stage. His cousin would invent her for his story. He would make her come. His passion would create her. That was what he meant.

Rogers smiled to himself, moving away from the window where the sunshine grew too fierce for comfort. What a funny business it all was, to be sure! And how curiously every one's thinking had intermingled! The children had somehow divined his own imaginings in that Crayfield garden; their father had stolen the lot for his story. It was most extraordinary. And then he remembered Minks, and all his lunatic theories about thought and thought-pictures. The garden scene at Crayfield came back vividly, the one at Charing Cross, in the orchard, too, with the old Vicar, when they had talked beneath the stars. Who among them all was the original sponsor? And which of them had set the ball a-rolling? It was stranger than the story of creation. ... It *was* the story of creation.

Yet he did not puzzle very long. Actors in a play are never puzzled; it is the bewildered audience who ask questions. And Henry Rogers was on the stage. The gauzy curtain hung between him and the outside point of view. He was already deeply involved in Fairyland. ... His feet were in the Net of Stars. ... He was a prisoner.

And that woman he had once dreamed might mother his own children— where was she? Until a few years ago he had still expected, hoped to meet her. One day they would come together. She waited somewhere. It was only recently he had let the dream slip finally from him, abandoned with many another personal ambition.

Idly he picked up a pencil, and before he was aware of it the words ran into lines. It seemed as though his cousin's mood, thought, inspiration, worked through him.

Upon what flowering shore,
'Neath what blue skies

- 160 -

She stands and waits,
It is not mine to know;
Only I know that shore is fair,
Those skies are blue.

Her voice I may not hear,
Nor see her eyes,
Yet there are times
When in the wind she speaks.
When stars and flowers
Tell me of her eyes.
When rivers chant her name.

If ever signs were sure,
I know she waits;
If not, what means this sweetness in the wind,
The singing in the rain, the love in flowers?
What mean these whispers in the air,
This calling from the hills and from the sea?
These tendernesses of the Day and Night?
Unless she waits!

What in the world was this absurd sweetness running in his veins?

He laughed a little. A slight flush, too, came and went its way. The tip of
the pencil snapped as he pressed too heavily on it. He had drawn it through
the doggerel with impatience, for he suddenly realised that he had told a
deep, deep secret to the paper. It had stammered its way out before he was
aware of it. This was youth and boyhood strong upon him, the moods of
Crayfield that he had set long ago on one side—deliberately. The mood that
wrote the Song of the Blue Eyes had returned, waking after a sleep of a
quarter of a century.

'What rubbish!' he exclaimed; 'I shall be an author next!' He tore it up and,
rolling the pieces into a ball, played catch with it. 'What waste of energy! Six
months ago that energy would have gone into something useful, a patent—
perhaps an improvement in the mechanism of—of—' he hesitated, then
finished the sentence with a sigh of yearning and another passing flush—'a
perambulator!'

He tossed it out of the window and, laughing, leaned out to watch it fall. It
bounced upon a head of tousled hair beneath, then flew off sideways in the
wind and rattled away faintly among the vines. The head was his cousin's.

'What are you up to?' cried the author, looking up. 'I'm not a waste- paper
basket.' There was a cigarette ash in his beard.

'Sending you ideas, he answered. 'I'm coming myself now. Look out!' He was in high spirits again. He believed in that Fairy Princess.

'All right; I've put you in already. Everybody will wonder who Cousinenry is. ...' The untidy head of hair popped in again.

'Hark!' cried Rogers, trying to look round the corner of the house. He edged himself out at a dangerous angle. His ears had caught another sound. There was music in the air.

CHAPTER XIX

The sweet spring winds came laughing down the street, bearing a voice that mingled with their music.

Daddy! Daddy! vite; il y a un paquet!' sounded in a child's excited cry. 'It arrives this afternoon. It's got the Edinburgh postmark. Here is the notice. *C'est enorme!'*

The figure of Jimbo shot round the corner, dancing into view. He waved a bit of yellow paper in his hand. A curious pang tore its way into the big man's heart as he saw him—a curious, deep, searching pain that yet left joy all along its trail. Positively moisture dimmed his eyes a second.

But Jimbo belonged to some one else.

Daddy's wumbled head projected instantly again from the window beneath.

'A box?' he asked, equally excited. 'A box from Scotland? Why, we had one only last month. Bless their hearts! How little they know what help and happiness. ... 'The rest of the sentence disappeared with the head; and a moment later Jimbo was heard scampering up the stairs. Both men went out to meet him.

The little boy was breathless with excitement, yet the spirit of the man of affairs worked strongly in him. He deliberately suppressed hysterics. He spoke calmly as might be, both hands in his trouser- pockets beneath the blouse of blue cotton that stuck out like a ballet skirt all round. The belt had slipped down. His eyes were never still. He pulled one hand out, holding the crumpled paper up for inspection.

'It's a *paquet,*' he said, '*comme ca.*' He used French and English mixed, putting the latter in for his cousin's benefit. He had little considerate ways like that. It's coming from Scotland, *et puis ca pese soixante-quinze kilos.* Oh, it's big. It's enormous. The last one weighed,' he hesitated, forgetful, 'much, much less,' he finished. He paused, looking like a man who has solved a problem by stating it.

'One hundred and fifty pounds,' exclaimed his father, just as eager as the boy. 'Let me look,' and he held his hand out for the advice from the railway. 'What *can* be in it?'

'Something for everybody,' said Jimbo decidedly. 'All the village knows it. It will come by the two o'clock train from Bale, you know.' He gave up the paper unwillingly. It was his badge of office. 'That's the paper about it,' he added again.

Daddy read out slowly the advice of consignment, with dates and weights and address of sender and recipient, while Jimbo corrected the least mistake. He knew it absolutely by heart.

'There'll be dresses and boots for the girls this time,' he announced, 'and something big enough for Mother to wear, too. You can tell——'

'How can you tell?' asked Daddy, laughing slyly, immensely pleased about it all.

'Oh, by the weight of the *paquet, comme ca*,' was the reply. 'It weighs 75 kilos. That means there must be something for Mummy in it.'

The author turned towards his cousin, hiding his smile. 'It's a box of clothes,' he explained, 'from my cousins in Scotland, Lady X you know, and her family. Things they give away—usually to their maids and what-not. Awfully good of them, isn't it? They pay the carriage too,' he added. It was an immense relief to him.

'Things they can't wear,' put in Jimbo, 'but *very* good things— suits, blouses, shirts, collars, boots, gloves, and—oh, *toute sorte de choses comme ca*.'

'Isn't it nice of 'em,' repeated Daddy. It made life easier for him— ever so much easier. 'A family like that has such heaps of things. And they always pay the freight. It saves me a pretty penny I can tell you. Why, I haven't bought the girls a dress for two years or more. And Edward's dressed like a lord, I tell you,' referring to his eldest boy now at an expensive tutor's. 'You can understand the excitement when a box arrives. We call it the Magic Box.'

Rogers understood. It had puzzled him before why the children's clothes, Daddy's and Mummy's as well for that matter, were such an incongruous assortment of village or peasant wear, and smart, well-cut garments that bore so obviously the London mark.

'They're very rich indeed,' said Jimbo. 'They have a motor car. These are the only things that don't fit them. There's not much for me usually; I'm too little yet. But there's lots for the girls and the others.' And 'the others,' it appeared, included the Widow Jequier, the Postmaster and his wife, the carpenter's family, and more than one household in the village who knew the use and value of every centimetre of ribbon. Even the retired governesses got their share. No shred or patch was ever thrown away as useless. The assortment of cast-off clothing furnished Sunday Bests to half the village for weeks to come. A consignment of bullion could not have given half the pleasure and delight that the arrival of a box produced.

But *midi* was ringing, and *dejeuner* had to be eaten first. Like a meal upon the stage, no one ate sincerely; they made a brave pretence, but the excitement was too great for hunger. Every one was in the secret—the Postmaster (he might get another hat out of it for himself) had let it out with a characteristic phrase: 'Il y a un paquet pour la famille anglaise!' Yet all feigned ignorance. The children exchanged mysterious glances, and afterwards the governesses hung about the Post Office, simulating the purchase of stamps at two o'clock. But every one watched Daddy's movements, for he it was who would say the significant words.

And at length he said them. 'Now, we had better go down to the station,' he observed casually, 'and see if there is anything for us.' His tone conveyed the impression that things often arrived in this way; it was an everyday affair. If there was nothing, it didn't matter much. His position demanded calmness.

'Very well,' said Jimbo. 'I'll come with you.' He strutted off, leading the way.

'And I, and I,' cried Monkey and Jane Anne, for it was a half-holiday and all were free. Jimbo would not have appeared to hurry for a kingdom.

'I think I'll join you, too,' remarked Mother, biting her lips, 'only please go slowly.' There were hills to negotiate.

They went off together in a party, and the governesses watched them go. The Widow Jequier put her head out of the window, pretending she was feeding the birds. Her sister popped out opportunely to post a letter. The Postmaster opened his *guichet* window and threw a bit of string into the gutter; and old Miss Waghorn, just then appearing for her daily fifteen minutes' constitutional, saw the procession and asked him, 'Who in the world all those people were?' She had completely forgotten them. 'Le barometre a monte,' he replied, knowing no word of English, and thinking it was her usual question about the weather. He reported daily the state of the barometer. 'Vous n'aurez pas besoin d'un parapluie.' 'Mercy,' she said, meaning *merci*.

The train arrived, and with it came the box. They brought it up themselves upon the little hand-cart—*le char.* It might have weighed a ton and contained priceless jewels, the way they tugged and pushed, and the care they lavished on it. Mother puffed behind, hoping there would be something to fit Jimbo this time.

'Shall we rest a moment?' came at intervals on the hill, till at last Monkey said, 'Sit on the top, Mummy, and we'll pull you too.' And during the rests they examined the exterior, smelt it, tapped it, tried to see between the cracks, and ventured endless and confused conjectures as to its probable contents.

They dragged the hand-cart over the cobbles of the courtyard, and heaved the box up the long stone staircase. It was planted at length on the floor beside the bed of Mlle. Lemaire, that she might witness the scene from her prison windows. Daddy had the greatest difficulty in keeping order, for tempers grow short when excitement is too long protracted. The furniture was moved about to make room. Orders flew about like grape-shot. Everybody got in everybody else's way. But finally the unwieldy packing-case was in position, and a silence fell upon the company.

'My gum, we've put it upside down,' said Daddy, red in the face with his exertions. It was the merest chance that there was no wisp of straw yet in his beard.

'Then the clothes will all be inside out,' cried Monkey, 'and we shall have to stand on our heads.'

'You silly,' Jane Anne rebuked her, yet half believing it was true, while Jimbo, holding hammer and chisel ready, looked unutterable contempt. 'Can't you be serious for a moment?' said his staring blue eyes.

The giant chest was laboriously turned over, the two men straining every muscle in the attempt. Then, after a moment's close inspection again to make quite sure, Daddy spoke gravely. Goodness, how calm he was!

'Jimbo, boy, pass me the hammer and the chisel, will you?'

In breathless silence the lid was slowly forced open and the splintered pieces gingerly removed. Sheets of dirty brown paper and bundles of odorous sacking came into view.

'Perhaps that's all there is,' suggested Jinny.

'Ugh! What a whiff!' said Monkey.

'Fold them up carefully and put them in a corner,' ordered Mother. Jane Anne religiously obeyed. Oh dear, how slow she was about it!

Then everybody came up very close, heads bent over, hands began to stretch and poke. You heard breathing—nothing more.

'Now, wait your turn,' commanded Mother in a dreadful voice, 'and let your Father try on everything first.' And a roar of laughter made the room echo while Daddy extracted wonder after wonder that were packed in endless layers one upon another.

Perhaps what would have struck an observer most of all would have been the strange seriousness against which the comedy was set. The laughter was incessant, but it was a weighty matter for all that. The bed- ridden woman, who was sole audience, understood that; the parents understood it too.

Every article of clothing that could be worn meant a saving, and the economy of a franc was of real importance. The struggles of *la famille anglaise* to clothe and feed and educate themselves were no light affair. The eldest boy, now studying for the consular service, absorbed a third of their entire income. The sacrifices involved for his sake affected each one in countless ways. And for two years now these magic boxes had supplied all his suits and shirts and boots. The Scotch cousins luckily included a boy of his own size who had extravagant taste in clothes. A box sometimes held as many as four excellent suits. Daddy contented himself with one a year — ordered ready-made from the place they called Chasbakerinhighholborn.' Mother's clothes were 'wropp in mystery' ever. No one ever discovered where they came from or how she made them. She did. It seemed always the same black dress and velvet blouse.

Gravity and laughter, therefore, mingled in Daddy's face as he drew out one paper parcel after another, opened it, tried the article on himself, and handed it next to be tried on similarly by every one in turn.

And the first extraction from the magic box was a curious looking thing that no one recognised. Daddy unfolded it and placed it solemnly on his head. He longed for things for himself, but rarely found them. He tried on everything, hoping it might 'just do,' but in the end yielded it with pleasure to the others. He rarely got more than a pair of gloves or a couple of neckties for himself. The coveted suits just missed his size.

Grave as a judge he balanced the erection on his head. It made a towering heap. Every one was puzzled. 'It's a motor cap,' ventured some one at length in a moment of intuition.

'It's several!' cried Monkey. She snatched the bundle and handed it to Mother. There were four motor caps, neatly packed together. Mother put on each in turn. They were in shades of grey. They became her well.

'You look like a duchess,' said Daddy proudly. 'You'd better keep them all.'

'I think perhaps they'll do,' she said, moving to the glass, 'if no one else can wear them.' She flushed a little and looked self- conscious.

'They want long pins,' suggested Jinny. 'They'll keep the rain off too, like an umbrella.' She laughed and clapped her hands. Mother pinned one on and left it there for the remainder of the afternoon. The unpacking of the case continued.

The next discovery was gloves. The lid of the box looked like a counter in a glove shop. There were gloves of leather and chamois, gauntlets, driving-gloves, and gloves of suede, yellow, brown, and grey. All had been used a little, but all were good. 'They'll wash,' said Jane Anne. They were set aside in a little heap apart. No one coveted them. It was not worth while. In the forests of Bourcelles gloves were at a discount, and driving a pleasure yet unknown. Jinny, however a little later put on a pair of ladies' suede that caught her fancy, and wore them faithfully to the end of the performance, just to keep her mother's motor cap in countenance.

The main contents of the box were as yet unbroached, however, and when next an overcoat appeared, with velvet collar and smart, turned-up cuffs, Daddy beamed like a boy and was into it before any one could prevent. He went behind a screen. The coat obviously did not fit him, but he tugged and pulled and wriggled his shoulders with an air of 'things that won't fit must be made to fit.'

'You'll bust the seams! You'll split the buttons! See what's in the pockets!' cried several voices, while he shifted to and fro like a man about to fight.

'It may stretch,' he said hopefully. 'I think I can use it. It's just what I want.' He glanced up at his wife whose face, however, was relentless.

'Maybe,' replied the practical mother, 'but it's more Edward's build, perhaps.' He looked fearfully disappointed, but kept it on. Edward got the best of every box. He went on with the unpacking, giving the coat sly twitches from time to time, as he pulled out blouses, skirts, belts, queer female garments, boots, soft felt hats—the green Homburg he put on at once, as who should dare to take it from him—black and brown Trilbys, shooting-caps, gaiters, flannel shirts, pyjamas, and heaven knows what else besides.

The excitement was prodigious, and the floor looked like a bargain sale. Everybody talked at once; there was no more pretence of keeping order Mlle. Lemaire lay propped against her pillows, watching the scene with feelings between tears and laughter. Each member of the family tried on everything in turn, but yielded the treasures instantly at a word from Mother—'That will do for so and so; this will fit Monkey; Jimbo, you take this,' and so on.

The door into the adjoining bedroom was for ever opening and shutting, as the children disappeared with armfuls and reappeared five minutes later, marvellously apparelled. There was no attempt at sorting yet. Blouses and flannel trousers lay upon the floor with boots and motor veils. Every one had something, and the pile set aside for Edward grew apace. Only Jimbo was disconsolate. He was too small for everything; even the ladies' boots were too narrow and too pointed for his little feet. From time to time he rummaged with the hammer and chisel (still held *very* tightly) among the mass of paper at the bottom. But, as usual, there was nothing but gaudy neckties that he could use. And these he did not care about. He said no word, but stood there watching the others and trying to laugh, only keeping the tears back with the greatest difficulty.

From his position in the background Rogers took it all in. He moved up and slipped a ten-franc piece into the boy's hand. 'Secretaries don't wear clothes like this,' he whispered. 'We'll go into town to-morrow and get the sort of thing you want.'

Jimbo looked up and stared. He stood on tip-toe to kiss him. 'Oh, thank you so much,' he said, fearful lest the others should see; and tucked the coin away into a pocket underneath his cotton blouse. A moment later he came back from the corner where he had hid himself to examine it. 'But, Cousin Henry,' he whispered, utterly astonished, 'it's gold.' He had thought the coin was a ten-centime piece such as Daddy sometimes gave him. He could not believe it. He had never seen gold before. He ran up and told his parents. His sisters were too excited to be told just then. After that he vanished into the passage without being noticed, and when he returned five minutes later his eyes were suspiciously red. But no one heard him say a word about getting nothing out of the box. He stood aside, with a superior manner and looked quietly on. 'It's very nice for the girls,' his expression said. His interest in the box had grown decidedly less. He could buy an entire shop for himself now.

'Mother, Daddy, everybody,' cried an excited voice, 'will you look at me a minute, please! It all fits me perfectly,' and Jinny emerged from the bedroom door. She had been trying on. A rough brown dress of Harris tweed became her well; she wore a motor veil about her head, and another was tied round her neck; a white silk blouse, at least one size too large for her, bulged voluminously from beneath the neat tweed jacket. She wore her suede gloves still. 'And there's an outside pocket in the skirt, you see.' She pulled it up and showed a very pointed pair of brown boots; they were much too long; they looked ridiculous after her square village boots. 'I can waggle my toes in them,' she explained, strutting to and fro to be admired. 'I'm a fashionable monster now!'

But she only held the centre of the stage a minute, for Monkey entered at her heels, bursting with delight in a long green macintosh thrown over another tweed skirt that hid her feet and even trailed behind. A pair of yellow spats were visible sometimes that spread fan-shaped over her boots and climbed half-way up the fat legs.

'It all fits me exaccurately,' was her opinion. The sisters went arm in arm about the room, dancing and laughing.

'We're busy blackmailers,' cried Jinny, using her latest acquisition which she practised on all possible occasions. 'We're in Piccadilly, going to see the Queen for tea.'

They tripped over Monkey's train and one of the spats came off in the struggle for recovery. Daddy, in his Homburg hat, looked round and told them sternly to make less noise. Behind a screen he was getting surreptitiously into a suit that Mother had put aside for Edward. He tried on several in this way, hopeful to the last.

'I think this will fit me all right,' he said presently, emerging with a grave expression on his puckered face. He seemed uncertain about it. He was solemn as a judge. 'You could alter the buttons here and there, you know,' and he looked anxiously at his wife. The coat ran up behind, the waistcoat creased badly owing to the strain, and the trousers were as tight as those of a cavalry officer. Anywhere, and any moment, he might burst out into unexpected revelation. 'A little alteration,' he suggested hopefully, 'and it would be all right—don't you think?' And then he added 'perhaps.'

He turned and showed himself. Even the roar of laughter that greeted his appearance did not quite convince him. He looked like a fat, impoverished bookmaker.

'I think it will fit Edward better,' said Mother again without pity, for she did not like to see her husband look foolish before the children. He disappeared behind the screen, but repeated the performance with two other suits. 'This striped one seems a little looser,' he said; or, 'If you'd let out the trousers at the bottom, I think they would do.' But in the end all he got from the box was two pairs of pink silk pyjamas, the Homburg hat, several pairs of gloves, spats, and gaiters, and half a dozen neckties that no one else would wear. He made his heap carefully in the corner of the room, and later, when the mess was all cleared up and everybody went off with their respective treasures, he entirely forgot them in his pleasure and admiration of the others. He left them lying in the corner. Riquette slept on them that night, and next morning Jimbo brought them over for him to the carpenter's house. And Edward later magnanimously yielded up two flannel shirts because he had so many left over from the previous box. Also a pair of pumps.

'I've not done so badly after all,' was his final matured opinion. 'Poor mother! She got nothing but motor caps.' Jimbo, however, had made a final discovery of value for himself—of some value, at least. When the empty case was overturned as a last hope, he rummaged among the paper with his hammer and chisel, and found four pairs of golf stockings! The legs fitted him admirably, but the feet were much too big. There was some discussion as to whether they had belonged to a very thin-legged boy with big feet or to a girl who had no calves. Luckily, the former was decided upon, for otherwise they would have given no pleasure to Jimbo. Even as it was, he adopted them chiefly because it pleased his parents. Mother cut off the feet and knitted new ones a little smaller. But there was no mystery about those stockings. No special joy went with them. He had watched Mother knitting too often for that; she could make stockings half asleep.

Two hours later, while Jane Ann and Mother prepared the tea in the Den, Daddy, Jimbo, and Cousin Henry went in a procession to the carpenter's house carrying the piles of clothing in their arms to the astonishment of half the village. They were to be re-sorted there in privacy by the 'men,' where the 'children' could not interfere. The things they could not use were distributed later among the governesses; the Pension and the village also, got their share. And the Postmaster got his hat—a black Trilby. He loved its hue.

And for days afterwards the children hoarded their treasures with unholy joy. What delighted them as much as anything, perhaps, were the coronets upon the pyjamas and the shirts. They thought it was a London or Edinburgh laundry mark. But Jimbo told them otherwise: 'It means that Daddy's Cousin is a Lord-and-Waiting, and goes to see the King.' This explanation was generally accepted.

The relief to the parents, however, as they sat up in the Den that night and discussed how much this opportune Magic Box had saved them, may be better imagined than described. The sum ran into many, many francs. Edward had suits now for at least two years. 'He's stopped growing,' said his mother; 'thank goodness,' said his father.

And to the long list he prayed for twice a day Jimbo added of his accord, 'Ceux qui ont envoye la grosse caisse.'

CHAPTER XX

Break up the heavens, O Lord! and far,
Thro' all yon starlight keen,
Draw me, thy bride, a glittering star,
In raiment white and clean.

He lifts me to the golden doors;
The flashes come and go;
All heaven bursts her starry floors,
And strews her lights below.
   St. Agnes' Eve, Tennyson.

Miss Waghorn, of late, had been unusually trying, and especially full of complaints. Her poor old memory seemed broken beyond repair. She offered Madame Jequier her weekly payment twice within ten minutes, and was quite snappy about it when the widow declined the second tender.

'But you had the receipt in your hand wizin ten minutes ago, Mees Wag'orn. You took it upstairs. The ink can hardly be now already yet dry.' But nothing would satisfy her that she had paid until they went up to her room together and found it after much searching between her Bible and her eternal novel on the writing-table.

'Forgive me, Madame, but you do forget sometimes, don't you?' she declared with amusing audacity. 'I like to make quite sure—— especially where money is concerned.' On entering the room she had entirely forgotten why they came there. She began complaining, instead, about the bed, which had not yet been made. A standing source of grumbling, this; for the old lady would come down to breakfast many a morning, and then go up again before she had it, thinking it was already late in the day. She worried the *pensionnaires* to death, too. It was their duty to keep the salon tidy, and Miss Waghorn would flutter into the room as early as eight o'clock, find the furniture still unarranged, and at once dart out again to scold the girls. These interviews were amusing before they became monotonous, for the old lady's French was little more than 'nong pas' attached to an infinitive verb, and the girls' Swiss-German explanations of the alleged neglect of duty only confused her. 'Nong pas faire la chambre,' she would say, stamping her foot with vexation. 'You haven't done the room, though it's nearly dejooner time!' Or else—'Ten minutes ago it was tidy. Look at it now!' while she dragged them in and forced them to put things straight, until some one in authority came and explained gently her mistake. 'Oh, excuse me, Madame,' she would say then, 'but they do forget *so* often.' Every one was very patient with her as a rule.

And of late she had been peculiarly meddlesome, putting chairs straight, moving vases, altering the lie of table-cloths and the angle of sofas, opening windows because it was 'so stuffy,' and closing them a minute later with complaints about the draught, forcing occupants of arm-chairs to get up because the carpet was caught, fiddling with pictures because they were crooked either with floor or ceiling, and never realising that in the old house these latter were nowhere parallel. But her chief occupation was to prevent the children crossing their legs when they sat down, or pulling their dresses lower, with a whispered, 'You *must* not cross your legs like that; it isn't ladylike, dear.'

She had been very exasperating and interfering. Tempers had grown short. Twice running she had complained about the dreadful noise the *pensionnaires* made at seven o'clock in the morning. 'Nong pas creer comme ca!' she called, running down the passage in her dressing-gown and bursting angrily into their rooms without knocking—to find them empty. The girls had left the day before.

But to-day (the morning after the Star Cave adventure) the old lady was calmer, almost soothed, and at supper she was composed and gentle. Sleep, for some reason, had marvellously refreshed her. Attacks that opened as usual about Cornish Cream or a Man with a long Beard, she repelled easily and quietly. 'I've told you that story before, my dear; I know I have.' It seemed her mind and memory were more orderly somehow. And the Widow Jequier explained how sweet and good-natured she had been all day—better than for years. 'When I took her drops upstairs at eleven o'clock I found her tidying her room; she was sorting her bills and papers. She read me a letter she had written to her nephew to come out and take her home—well written and quite coherent. I've not known her mind so clear for months. Her memory, too. She said she had slept so well. If only it would last, *helas*!'

'There *are* days like that,' she added presently, 'days when everything goes right and easily. One wakes up happy in the morning and sees only the bright side of things. Hope is active, and one has new courage somehow.' She spoke with feeling, her face was brighter, clearer, her mind less anxious. She had planned a visit to the Bank Manager about the mortgages. It had come as an inspiration. It might be fruitless, but she was hopeful, and so knew a little peace. 'I wonder why it is,' she added, 'and what brings these changes into the heart so suddenly.'

'Good sleep and sound digestion,' Mrs. Campden thought. She expressed her views deliberately like this in order to counteract any growth of fantasy in the children.

'But it is strange,' her husband said, remembering his new story; 'it may be much deeper than that. While the body sleeps the spirit may get into touch with helpful forces——' His French failed him. He wumbled painfully.

'Thought-forces possibly from braver minds,' put in Rogers. 'Who knows? Sleep and dreaming have never really been explained.' He recalled a theory of Minks.

'*I* dream a great deal,' Miss Waghorn observed, eager to take part. 'It's delightful, dreaming—if only one could remember!' She looked round the table with challenge in her eager old eyes. But no one took her up. It involved such endless repetition of well-known stories. The Postmaster might have said a word—he looked prepared—but, not understanding English, he went on with his salad instead.

'Life is a dream,' observed Monkey, while Jinny seemed uncertain whether she should laugh or take it seriously.

The Widow Jequier overheard her. There was little she did not overhear.

'Coquine!' she said, then quoted with a sentimental sigh:—

La vie est breve,
Un peu d'amour.
Un peu de rive
Et puis—bonjour!

She hung her head sideways a moment for effect. There was a pause all down the long table.

'I'm sure dreams have significance,' she went on. 'There's more in dreaming than one thinks. They come as warnings or encouragement. All the saints had dreams. I always pay attention to mine.'

'Madame, *I* dream a great deal,' repeated Miss Waghorn, anxious not to be left out of a conversation in which she understood at least the key-word *reve*; 'a very great deal, I may say.'

Several looked up, ready to tell nightmares of their own at the least sign of encouragement. The Postmaster faced the table, laying down his knife and fork. He took a deep breath. This time he meant to have his say. But his deliberation always lost him openings.

I don't,' exclaimed Jinny, bluntly, five minutes behind the others. 'When I'm in bed, I sleep.' The statement brought laughter that confused her a little.

She loved to define her position. She had defined it. And the Postmaster had lost his chance. Mlle. Sandoz, a governess who was invited to supper as payment for a music lesson given to his boy, seized the opening.

'Last night I dreamed that a bull chased me. Now what did *that* mean, I wonder?'

'That there was no danger since it was only a dream!' said the Postmaster sharply, vexed that he had not told his own.

But no one applauded, for it was the fashion to ignore his observations, unless they had to do with stamps and weights of letters, parcels, and the like. A clatter of voices rose, as others, taking courage, decided to tell experiences of their own; but it was the Postmaster's wife in the hall who won. She had her meals outside with the kitchen maid and her niece, who helped in the Post Office, and she always tried to take part in the conversation from a distance thus. She plunged into a wordy description of a lengthy dream that had to do with clouds, three ravens, and a mysterious face. All listened, most of them in mere politeness, for as cook she was a very important personage who could furnish special dishes on occasion— but her sister listened as to an oracle. She nodded her head and made approving gestures, and said, 'Aha, you see,' or 'Ah, voila!' as though that helped to prove the importance of the dream, if not its actual truth. And the sister came to the doorway so that no one could escape. She stood there in her apron, her face hot and flushed still from the kitchen.

At length it came to an end, and she looked round her, hoping for a little sympathetic admiration, or at least for expressions of wonder and interest. All waited for some one else to speak. Into the pause came her husband's voice, 'Je n'ai pas de sel.'

There was no resentment. It was an everyday experience. The spell was broken instantly. The cook retired to her table and told the dream all over again with emphatic additions to her young companions. The Postmaster got his salt and continued eating busily as though dreams were only fit for women and children to talk about. And the English group began whispering excitedly of their Magic Box and all it had contained. They were tired of dreams and dreaming.

Tante Jeanne made a brave effort to bring the conversation back to the key of sentiment and mystery she loved, but it was not a success.

'At any rate I'm certain one's mood on going to bed decides the kind of dream that comes,' she said into the air. 'The last thought before going to sleep is very important. It influences the adventures of the soul when it leaves the body every night.'

For this was a tenet of her faith, although she always forgot to act upon it. Only Miss Waghorn continued the train of ideas this started, with a coherence that surprised even herself. Somehow the jabber about dreams, though in a language that only enabled her to catch its general drift, had interested her uncommonly. She seemed on the verge of remembering something. She had listened with patience, a look of peace upon her anxious old face that was noticed even by Jane Anne. 'It smoothed her out,' was her verdict afterwards, given only to herself though. 'Everything is a sort of long unfinished dream to her, I suppose, at *that* age.'

While the *famille anglaise* renewed noisily their excitement of the Magic Box, and while the talk in the hall went on and on, re-hashing the details of the cook's marvellous experience, and assuming entirely new proportions, Miss Waghorn glanced about her seeking whom she might devour—and her eye caught Henry Rogers, listening as usual in silence.

'Ah,' she said to him, 'but *I* look forward to sleep. I might say I long for it.' She sighed very audibly. It was both a sigh for release and a faint remembrance that last night her sleep had been somehow deep and happy, strangely comforting.

'It is welcome sometimes, isn't it?' he answered, always polite and rather gentle with her.

'Sleep unravels, yes,' she said, vaguely as to context, yet with a querulous intensity. It was as if she caught at the enthusiasm of a connected thought somewhere. 'I might even say it unties,' she added, encouraged by his nod, 'unties knots—if you follow me.'

'It does, Miss Waghorn. Indeed, it does.' Was this a precursor of the Brother with the Beard, he wondered? 'Untied knots' would inevitably start her off. He made up his mind to listen to the tale with interest for the twentieth time if it came. But it didn't come.

'I am very old and lonely, and *I* need the best,' she went on happily, half saying it to herself.

Instantly he took her up—without surprise too. It was like a dream.

'Quite so. The rest, the common stuff——'

'Is good enough——' she chimed in quickly—

'For Fraulein, or for baby, or for mother,' he laughed.

'Or any other,' chuckled Miss Waghorn.

'Who needs a bit of sleep——'

'But yet can do without it——' she carried it on.

Then both together, after a second's pause—

'If they must——' and burst out laughing.

Goodness, how did *she* know the rhyme? Was it everywhere? Was thought running loose like wireless messages to be picked up by all who were in tune for acceptance?

'Well, I never!' he heard her exclaim, 'if that's not a nursery rhyme of my childhood that I've not heard for sixty years and more! I declare,' she added with innocent effrontery, 'I've not heard it since I was ten years old. And I was born in '37—the year——'

'Just fancy!' he tried to stop her.

'Queen Victoria came to the throne.'

'Strange,' he said more to himself than to any one else. She did not contradict him.

'You or me?' asked Monkey, who overheard.

'All of us,' he answered. 'We all think the same things. It's a dream, I believe; the whole thing is a dream.'

'It's a fact though,' said Miss Waghorn with decision, 'and now I must go and write my letters, and then finish a bit of lace I'm doing. You will excuse me?' She rose, made a little bow, and left the table.

Mother watched her go. 'What *has* come over the old lady?' she thought. 'She seems to be getting back her mind and memory too. How very odd!'

In the afternoon Henry Rogers had been into Neuchatel. It seemed he had some business there of a rather private nature. He was very mysterious about it, evading several offers to accompany him, and after supper he retired early to his own room in the carpenter's house. And, since he now was the principal attraction, a sort of magnet that drew the train of younger folk into his neighbourhood, the Pension emptied, and the English family, deprived of their leader, went over to the Den.

'Partir a l'anglaise,' laughed the Widow Jequier, as she saw them file away downstairs; and then she sighed. Some day, when the children were older and needed a different education, they would all go finally. Down these very stairs they would go into the street. She loved them for themselves, but, also, the English family was a permanent source of income to her, and the chief. They stayed on in the winter, when boarders were few and yet living expenses doubled. She sighed, and fluttered into her tiny room to take her finery off, finery that had once been worn in Scotland and had reached her by way of Cook and *la petite vitesse* in the Magic Box.

And presently she fluttered out again and summoned her sister. The Postmaster had gone to bed; the kitchen girl was washing up the last dishes; Miss Waghorn would hardly come down again. The salon was deserted.

'Come, Anita,' she cried, yet with a hush of excitement in her voice, 'we will have an evening of it. Bring the *soucoupe* with you, while I prepare the little table.' In her greasy kitchen apron Anita came. Zizi, her boy, came with her. Madame Jequier, with her flowing garment that was tea-gown, garden-dress, and dressing-gown all in one, looked really like a witch, her dark hair all askew and her eyes shining with mysterious anticipation. 'We'll ask the spirits for help and guidance,' she said to herself, lest the boy should overhear. For Zizi often helped them with their amateur planchette, only they told him it was electricity: *le magnetisme, le fluide,* was the term they generally made use of. Its vagueness covered all possible explanations with just the needed touch of confusion and suggestion in it.

They settled down in a corner of the room, where the ivy from the ceiling nearly touched their heads. The small round table was produced; the saucer, with an arrow pencilled on its edge, was carefully placed upon the big sheet of paper which bore the letters of the alphabet and the words *oui* and *non* in the corners. The light behind them was half veiled by ivy; the rest of the old room lay in comparative darkness; through the half-opened door a lamp shone upon the oil-cloth in the hall, showing the stains and the worn, streaked patches where the boards peeped through. The house was very still.

They began with a little prayer—to *ceux qui ecoutent,*—and then each of them placed a finger on the rim of the upturned saucer, waiting in silence. They were a study in darkness, those three pointing fingers.

'Zizi, tu as beaucoup de fluide ce soir, oui?' whispered the widow after a considerable interval.

'Oh, comme d'habitude,' he shrugged his shoulders. He loved these mysterious experiments, but he never claimed much *fluide* until the saucer moved, jealous of losing his reputation as a storehouse of this strange, human electricity.

Yet behind this solemn ritual, that opened with prayer and invariably concluded with hope renewed and courage strengthened, ran the tragic element that no degree of comedy could kill. In the hearts of the two old women, ever fighting their uphill battle with adversity, burned the essence of big faith, the faith that plays with mountains. Hidden behind the curtain, an indulgent onlooker might have smiled, but tears would have wet his eyes before the smile could have broadened into laughter. Tante Jeanne, indeed, *had* heard that the subconscious mind was held to account for the apparent intelligence that occasionally betrayed itself in the laboriously spelled replies; she even made use of the word from time to time to baffle Zizi's too importunate inquiries. But after *le subconscient* she always tacked on *fluide*, *magnetisme*, or *electricite* lest he should be frightened, or she should lose her way. And of course she held to her belief that spirits produced the phenomena. A subconscious mind was a cold and comfortless idea.

And, as usual, the saucer told them exactly what they had desired to know, suggested ways and means that hid already in the mind of one or other, yet in stammered sentences that included just enough surprise or turn of phrase to confirm their faith and save their self-respect. It was their form of prayer, and with whole hearts they prayed. Moreover, they acted on what was told them. Had they discovered that it was merely the content of their subconscious mind revealing thus its little hopes and fears, they would have lost their chief support in life. God and religion would have suffered a damaging eclipse. Big scaffolding in their lives would have collapsed.

Doubtless, Tante Jeanne did not knowingly push the saucer, neither did the weighty index finger of the concentrated cook deliberately exert muscular pressure. Nor, similarly, was Zizi aware that the weight of his entire hand helped to urge the dirty saucer across the slippery surface of the paper in whatever direction his elders thus indicated. But one and all knew 'subconsciously' the exact situation of consonants and vowels—that *oui* lay in the right-hand corner and *non* in the left. And neither Zizi nor his mother dared hint to their leader not to push, because she herself monopolised that phrase, saying repeatedly to them both, 'mais il ne faut *pas* pousser! Legerement avec les doigts, toujours tres legerement! Sans ca il n'y a pas de valeur, tu comprends!' Zizi inserted an occasional electrical question. It was discreetly ignored always.

They asked about the Bank payments, the mortgages, the future of their much-loved old house, and of themselves; and the answers, so vague concerning any detailed things to come, were very positive indeed about the Bank. They were to go and interview the Manager three days from now. They had already meant to go, only the date was undecided; the corroboration of the spirits was required to confirm it. This settled it. Three days from to-night!

'Tu vois!' whispered Tante Jeanne, glancing mysteriously across the table at her sister. 'Three days from now! That explains your dream about the three birds. Aha, tu vois!' She leaned back, supremely satisfied. And the sister gravely bowed her head, while Zizi looked up and listened intently, without comprehension. He felt a little alarm, perhaps, to-night.

For this night there *was* indeed something new in the worn old ritual. There was a strange, uncalculated element in it all, unexpected, and fearfully thrilling to all three. Zizi for the first time had his doubts about its being merely electricity.

'C'est d'une puissance extraordinaire,' was the widow's whispered, eager verdict.

'C'est que j'ai enormement de fluide ce soir,' declared Zizi, with pride and confidence, yet mystified. The other two exchanged frequent glances of surprise, of wonder, of keen expectancy and anticipation. There was certainly a new 'influence' at work to-night. They even felt a touch of faint dread. The widow, her ruling passion strong even before the altar, looked down anxiously once or twice at her disreputable attire. It was vivid as that—this acute sense of another presence that pervaded the room, not merely hung about the little table. She could be 'invisible' to the Pension by the magic of old- established habit, but she could not be so to the true Invisibles. And they saw her in this unbecoming costume. She forgot, too, the need of keeping Zizi in the dark. He must know some day. What did it matter when?

She tidied back her wandering hair with her free hand, and drew the faded garment more closely round her neck.

'Are you cold?' asked her sister with a hush in her voice; 'you feel the cold air—all of a sudden?'

'I do, *maman*,' Zizi answered. 'It's blowing like a wind across my hand. What is it?' He was shivering. He looked over his shoulder nervously.

There was a heavy step in the hall, and a figure darkened the doorway. All three gave a start.

'J'ai sommeil,' announced the deep voice of the Postmaster. This meant that the boy must come to bed. It was the sepulchral tone that made them jump perhaps. Zizi got up without a murmur; he was glad to go, really. He slept in the room with his parents. His father, an overcoat thrown over his night things, led him away without another word. And the two women resumed their seance. The saucer moved more easily and swiftly now that Zizi had gone. 'C'est done *toi* qui as le fluide,' each said to the other.

But in the excitement caused by this queer, new element in the proceedings, the familiar old routine was forgotten. Napoleon and Marie Antoinette were brushed aside to make room for this important personage who suddenly descended upon the saucer from an unknown star with the statement—it took half an hour to spell—'Je viens d'une etoile tres eloignee qui n'a pas encore de nom.'

'There *is* a starry light in the room. It was above your head just now,' whispered the widow, enormously excited. 'I saw it plainly.' She was trembling.

'That explains the clouds in my dream,' was the tense reply, as they both peered round them into the shadows with a touch of awe. 'Now, give all your attention. This has an importance, but, you know, an importance—' She could not get the degree of importance into any words. She looked it instead, leaving the sentence eloquently incomplete.

For, certainly, into the quaint ritual of these two honest, troubled old women there crept then a hint of something that was uncommon and uplifting. That it came through themselves is as sure as that it spelt out detailed phrases of encouragement and guidance with regard to their coming visit to the Bank. That they both were carried away by it into joy and the happiness of sincere relief of mind is equally a fact. That their receptive mood attuned them to overhear subconsciously messages of thought that flashed across the night from another mind in sympathy with their troubles—a mind hard at work that very moment in the carpenter's house—was not known to them; nor would it have brought the least explanatory comfort even if they had been told of it. They picked up these starry telegrams of unselfish thinking that flamed towards them through the midnight sky from an eager mind elsewhere busily making plans for their benefit. And, reaching them subconsciously, their deep subconsciousness urged the dirty saucer to the spelling of them, word by word and letter by letter. The flavour of their own interpretation, of course, crept in to mar, and sometimes to obliterate. The instruments were gravely imperfect. But the messages came through. And with them came the great feeling that the Christian calls answered prayer. They had such absolute faith. They had belief.

'Go to the Bank. Help awaits you there. And I shall go with you to direct and guide.' This was the gist of that message from 'une etoile tres eloignee.'

They copied it out in violet ink with a pen that scratched like the point of a pin. And when they stole upstairs to bed, long after midnight, there was great joy and certainty in their fighting old hearts. There was a perfume of flowers, of lilacs and wistaria in the air, as if the whole garden had slipped in by the back door and was unable to find its way out again. They dreamed of stars and starlight.

CHAPTER XXI

La vie est un combat qu'ils ont change en fete. *Lei Elus*, E. VERHAIREN.

The excitement a few days later spread through the village like a flame. People came out of their way to steal a glance at the Pension that now, for the first time in their—memory, was free of debt. Gygi, tolling the bell at *midi*, forgot to stop, as he peered through the narrow window in the church tower and watched the Widow Jequier planting and digging recklessly in her garden. Several came running down the street, thinking it was a warning of fire.

But the secret was well kept; no one discovered who had worked the miracle. Pride sealed the lips of the beneficiaries themselves, while the inhabitants of the Citadelle, who alone shared the knowledge, kept the facts secret, as in honour bound. Every one wondered, however, for every one knew the sum ran into several thousand francs; and a thousand francs was a fortune; the rich man in the corner house, who owned so many vineyards, and was reputed to enjoy an income of ten thousand francs a year, was always referred to as 'le million naire.' And so the story spread that Madame Jequier had inherited a fortune, none knew whence. The tradespeople treated her thereafter with a degree of respect that sweetened her days till the end of life.

She had come back from the Bank in a fainting condition, the sudden joy too much for her altogether. A remote and inaccessible air pervaded her, for all the red of her inflamed eyes and tears. She was aloof from the world, freed at last from the ceaseless, gnawing anxiety that for years had eaten her life out. The spirits had justified themselves, and faith and worship had their just reward. But this was only the first, immediate effect: it left her greater than it found her, this unexpected, huge relief—brimming with new sympathy for others. She doubled her gifts. She planned a wonderful new garden. That very night she ordered such a quantity of bulbs and seedlings that to this day they never have been planted.

Her interview with Henry Rogers, when she called at the carpenter's house in all her finery, cannot properly be told, for it lay beyond his powers of description. Her sister accompanied her; the Postmaster, too, snatched fifteen minutes from his duties to attend. The ancient tall hat, worn only at funerals as a rule, was replaced by the black Trilby that had been his portion from the Magic Box, as he followed the excited ladies at a reasonable distance. 'You had better show yourself,' his wife suggested; 'Monsieur

Rogairs would like to see you with us—to know that you are there.' Which meant that he was not to interfere with the actual thanksgiving, but to countenance the occasion with his solemn presence. And, indeed, he did not go upstairs. He paced the road beneath the windows during the interview, looking exactly like a professional mourner waiting for the arrival of the hearse.

'My dear old friend—friends, I mean,' said Rogers in his fluent and very dreadful French, 'if you only knew what a pleasure it is to *me*—It is *I* who should thank you for giving me the opportunity, not you who should thank me.' The sentence broke loose utterly, wandering among intricacies of grammar and subjunctive moods that took his breath away as he poured it out. 'I was only afraid you would think it unwarrantable interference. I am delighted that you let me do it. It's such a little thing to do.'

Both ladies instantly wept. The Widow came closer with a little rush. Whether Rogers was actually embraced, or no, it is not stated officially.

'It is a loan, of course, it is a loan,' cried the Widow.

'It is a present,' he said firmly, loathing the scene.

'It's a part repayment for all the kindness you showed me here as a boy years and years ago.' Then, remembering that the sister was not known to him in those far-away days, he added clumsily, 'and since—I came back.... And now let's say no more, but just keep the little secret to ourselves. It is nobody's business but our own.'

'A present!' gasped both ladies to one another, utterly overcome; and finding nothing else to embrace, they flung their arms about each other's necks and praised the Lord and wept more copiously than ever.... 'Grand ciel' was heard so frequently, and so loudly, that Madame Michaud, the carpenter's wife, listening on the stairs, made up her mind it was a quarrel, and wondered if she ought to knock at the door and interfere.

'I see your husband in the road,' said Rogers, tapping at the window. 'I think he seems waiting for you. Or perhaps he has a telegram for me, do you think?' He bowed and waved his hand, smiling as the Postmaster looked up in answer to the tapping and gravely raised his Trilby hat.

'There now, he's calling for you. Do not keep him waiting—I'm sure—' he didn't know what to say or how else to get them out. He opened the door. The farewells took some time, though they would meet an hour later at *dejeuner* as usual.

'At least you shall pay us no more *pension*,' was the final sentence as they flounced downstairs, so happy and excited that they nearly tumbled over each other, and sharing one handkerchief to dry their tears.

'Then I shall buy my own food and cook it here,' he laughed, and somehow managed to close his door upon the retreating storm. Out of the window he saw the procession go back, the sombre figure of the Postmaster twenty yards behind the other two.

And then, with joy in his heart, though a sigh of relief upon his lips—there may have been traces of a lump somewhere in his throat as well, but if so, he did not acknowledge it—he turned to his letters, and found among them a communication from Herbert Montmorency Minks, announcing that he had found an ideal site, and that it cost so and so much per acre—also that the County Council had made no difficulties. There was a hint, moreover—a general flavour of resentment and neglect at his master's prolonged absence—that it would not be a bad thing for the great Scheme if Mr. Rogers could see his way to return to London 'before very long.'

'Bother the fellow!' thought he; 'what a nuisance he is, to be sure!'

And he answered him at once. 'Do not trouble about a site just yet,' he wrote; 'there is no hurry for the moment.' He made a rapid calculation in his head. He had paid those mortgages out of capital, and the sum represented just about the cost of the site Minks mentioned. But results were immediate. There was no loss, no waste in fees and permits and taxes. Each penny did its work.

'There's the site gone, anyhow,' he laughed to himself. 'The foundation will go next, then the walls. But, at any rate, they needed it. The Commune Charity would have had 'em at the end of the month. They're my neighbours after all. And I must find out from them who else in the village needs a leg up. For these people are worth helping, and I can see exactly where every penny goes.'

Bit by bit, as it would seem, the great Scheme for Disabled Thingumagigs was being undermined.

CHAPTER XXII

And those who were good shall be happy.
  They shall sit in a golden chair;
They shall splash at a ten-league canvas
  With brushes of comets' hair.
They shall have real saints to paint from—
  Magdalene, Peter, and Paul;
They shall work for an age at a sitting
  And never get tired at all.

And only the Master shall praise them,
  And only the Master shall blame;
And no one shall work for money,
  And no one shall work for fame;
But each for the joy of the working,
  And each in his separate star,
Shall draw the thing as he sees it
  For the God of things as they are,
                    R. KIPLING.

And meanwhile, as May ran laughing to meet June, an air of coloured
wonder spread itself about the entire village. Rogers had brought it with
him from that old Kentish garden somehow. His journey there had opened
doors into a region of imagination and belief whence fairyland poured back
upon his inner world, transfiguring common things. And this
transfiguration he unwittingly put into others too. Through this very
ordinary man swept powers that usually are left behind with childhood. The
childhood aspect of the world invaded all who came in contact with him,
enormous, radiant, sparkling, charged with questions of wonder and
enchantment. And every one felt it according to their ability of
reconstruction. Yet he himself had not the least idea that he did it all. It was
a reformation, very tender, soft, and true.

For wonder, of course, is the basis of all inquiry. Interpretation varies, facts
remain the same; and to interpret is to recreate. Wonder leads to worship. It
insists upon recreation, prerogative of all young life. The Starlight Express
ran regularly every night, Jimbo having constructed a perfect time-table that
answered all requirements, and was sufficiently elastic to fit instantly any
scale that time and space demanded. Rogers and the children talked of little
else, and their adventures in the daytime seemed curiously fed by details of
information gleaned elsewhere.

But where? The details welled up in one and all, though whence they came remained a mystery. 'I believe we dream a lot of it,' said Jimbo. 'It's a lot of dreams we have at night, comme ça.' He had made a complete map of railway lines, with stations everywhere, in forests, sky, and mountains. He carried stations in his pocket, and just dropped one out of the carriage window whenever a passenger shouted, 'Let's stop here.' But Monkey, more intellectual, declared it was 'all Cousinenry's invention and make-up,' although she asked more questions than all the others put together. Jinny, her sister, stared and listened with her puzzled, moth-like expression, while Mother watched and marvelled cautiously from a distance. In one and all, however, the famished sense of wonder interpreted life anew. It named the world afresh—the world of common things. It subdued the earth unto itself. What a mind creates it understands. Through the familiar these adventurers trace lines of discovery into the unfamiliar. They understood. They were up to their waists in wonder. There was still disorder, of course, in their great reconstruction, but that was where the exciting fun came in; for disorder involves surprise. Any moment out might pop the unexpected—event or person.

Cousin Henry was easily leader now. While Daddy remained absorbed with his marvellous new story, enthusiastic and invisible, they ran about the world at the heels of this 'busy engineer,' as Jane Ann entitled him. He had long ago told them, with infinite and exaccurate detail, of his journey to the garden and his rediscovery of the sprites, forgotten during his twenty years of business life. And these sprites were as familiar to them now as those of their own childhood. They little knew that at night they met and talked with them. Daddy had put them all into the Wumble Book, achieving mediocre success with the rhymes, but amply atoning with the illustrations. The Woman of the Haystack was evidently a monster pure and simple, till Jinny announced that she merely had 'elephantitis,' and thus explained her satisfactorily. The Lamplighter, with shining feet, taking enormous strides from Neuchatel to a London slum, putting fire into eyes and hearts *en route*, thrilled them by his radiant speed and ubiquitous activity, while his doggerel left them coldly questioning. For the rhymes did *not* commend themselves to their sense of what was proper in the use of words. His natural history left them unconvinced, though the anatomy of the drawing fascinated them.

> He walked upon his toes
> As softly as a saying does,
> For so the saying goes.

That he 'walked upon his toes' was all right, but that he 'walked softly as a saying' meant nothing, even when explained that 'thus the saying goes.'

'Poor old Daddy,' was Jinny's judgment; 'he's got to write something. You see, he is an author. Some day he'll get his testimonial.'

It was Cousin Henry who led them with a surer, truer touch. He always had an adventure up his sleeve—something their imaginations could accept and recreate. Each in their own way, they supplied interpretations as they were able.

Every walk they took together furnished the germ of an adventure.

'But I'm not exciting to-day,' he would object thirsting for a convincing compliment that should persuade him to take them out. Only the compliment never came quite as he hoped.

'Everybody's exciting somewhere,' said Monkey, leading the way and knowing he would follow. 'We'll go to the Wind Wood.'

Jimbo took his hand then, and they went. Corners of the forest had names now, born of stories and adventures he had placed there—the Wind Wood, the Cuckoo Wood, where Daddy could not sleep because 'the beastly cuckoo made such a noise'; the Wood where Mother Fell, and so on. No walk was wholly unproductive.

And so, one evening after supper, they escaped by the garden, crossed the field where the standing hay came to their waists, and climbed by forest paths towards the Wind Wood. It was a spot where giant pines stood thinly, allowing a view across the lake towards the Alps. The moss was thick and deep. Great boulders, covered with lichen, lay about, and there were fallen trees to rest the back against. Here he had told them once his vision of seeing the wind, and the name had stuck; for the story had been very vivid, and every time they felt the wind or heard it stirring in the tree-tops, they expected to see it too. There were blue winds, black winds, and winds— violent these—of purple and flaming scarlet.

They lay down, and Cousinenry made a fire. The smoke went up in thin straight lines of blue, melting into the sky. The sun had set half an hour before, and the flush of gold and pink was fading into twilight. The glamour of Bourcelles dropped down upon all three. They ought to have been in bed—hence the particular enjoyment.

'Are you getting excited now?' asked Monkey, nestling in against him.

'Hush!' he said, 'can't you hear it coming?'

'The excitement?' she inquired under her breath.

'No, the Night. Keep soft and silent—if you can.'

'Tell us, please, at once,' both children begged him instantly, for the beauty of the place and hour demanded explanation, and explanation, of course, must be in story or adventure form. The fire crackled faintly; the smell crept out like incense; the lines of smoke coiled upwards, and seemed to draw the tree-stems with them. Indeed they formed a pattern together, big thick trunks marking the uprights at the corners, and wavy smoke lines weaving a delicate structure in between them. It was a kind of growing, moving scaffolding. Saying nothing, Cousin Henry pointed to it with his finger. He traced its general pattern for them in the air.

'That's the Scaffolding of the Night beginning,' he whispered presently, feeling adventure press upon him.

'Oh, I say,' said Jimbo, sitting up, and pretending as usual more comprehension than he actually possessed. But his sister instantly asked, 'What is it—the Scaffolding of the Night? A sort of cathedral, you mean?'

How she divined his thought, and snatched it from his mind always, this nimble-witted child! His germ developed with a bound at once.

'More a palace than a cathedral,' he whispered. 'Night is a palace, and has to be built afresh each time. Twilight rears the scaffolding first, then hangs the Night upon it. Otherwise the darkness would simply fall in lumps, and lie about in pools and blocks, unfinished—a ruin instead of a building. Everything must have a scaffolding first. Look how beautifully it's coming now,' he added, pointing, 'each shadow in its place, and all the lines of grey and black fitting exaccurately together like a skeleton. Have you never noticed it before?'

Jimbo, of course, *had* noticed it, his manner gave them to understand, but had not thought it worth while mentioning until his leader drew attention to it.

'Just as trains must have rails to run on,' he explained across Cousinenry's intervening body to Monkey, 'or else there'd be accidents and things all the time.'

'And night would be a horrid darkness like a plague in Egypt,' she supposed, adroitly defending herself and helping her cousin at the same time. 'Wouldn't it?' she added, as the shadows drew magically nearer from the forest and made the fire gradually grow brighter. The children snuggled closer to their cousin's comforting bulk, shivering a little. The woods went whispering together. Night shook her velvet skirts out.

'Yes, everything has its pattern,' he answered, 'from the skeleton of a child or a universe to the outline of a thought. Even a dream must have its scaffolding,' he added, feeling their shudder and leading it towards fun and beauty. 'Insects, birds, and animals all make little scaffoldings with their wee emotions, especially kittens and butterflies. Engine-drivers too,' for he felt Jimbo's hand steal into his own and go to sleep there, 'but particularly little beasties that live in holes under stones and in fields.

When a little mouse in wonder
Flicks its whiskers at the thunder,

it makes a tiny scaffolding behind which it hides in safety, shuddering. Same with Daddy's stories. Thinking and feeling does the trick. Then imagination comes and builds it up solidly with bricks and wall-papers....'

He told them a great deal more, but it cannot be certain that they heard it all, for there were other Excitements about besides their cousin—the fire, the time, the place, and above all, this marvellous coming of the darkness. They caught words here and there, but Thought went its own independent way with each little eager mind. He had started the machinery going, that was all. Interpretation varied; facts remained the same. And meanwhile twilight brought the Scaffolding of Night before their eyes.

'You can see the lines already,' he murmured sleepily, 'like veins against the sunset.... Look!'

All saw the shadowy slim rafters slip across the paling sky, mapping its emptiness with intricate design. Like an enormous spider's web of fine dark silk it bulged before the wind. The trellis-work, slung from the sky, hung loose. It moved slowly, steadily, from east to west, trailing grey sheets of dusk that hung from every filament. The maze of lines bewildered sight. In all directions shot the threads of coming darkness, spun from the huge body of Night that still hid invisible below the horizon.

'They're fastening on to everything ... look!' whispered Cousin Henry, kicking up a shower of sparks with his foot. 'The Pattern's being made before your eyes! Don't you see the guy ropes?'

And they saw it actually happen. From the summits of the distant Alps ran filmy lines of ebony that knotted themselves on to the crests of the pines beside them. There were so many no eye could follow them. They flew and darted everywhere, dropping like needles from the sky itself, sewing the tent of darkness on to the main supports, and threading the starlight as they came. Night slowly brought her beauty and her mystery upon the world. The filmy pattern opened. There was a tautness in the lines that made one feel they would twang with delicate music if the wind swept its hand more rapidly across them. And now and again all vibrated, each line making an ellipse between its fastened ends, then gradually settling back to its thin, almost invisible bed. Cables of thick, elastic darkness steadied them.

How much of it all the children realised themselves, or how much flashed into them from their cousin's mind, is of course a thing not even a bat can tell.

'Is that why bats fly in such a muddle? Like a puzzle?'

'Of course,' he said. The bats were at last explained.

They built their little pictures for themselves. No living being can lie on the edge of a big pine forest when twilight brings the darkness without the feeling that everything becomes too wonderful for words. The children as ever fed his fantasy, while he thought he did it all himself. Dusk wore a shroud to entangle the too eager stars, and make them stay.

'I never noticed it before,' murmured Monkey against his coat sleeve. 'Does it happen every night like this?'

'You only see it if you look very closely,' was the low reply. 'You must think hard, very hard. The more you think, the more you'll see.'

'But really,' asked Jimbo, 'it's only—*crepuscule, comme ca*, isn't it?' And his fingers tightened on his leader's hand.

'Dusk, yes,' answered Cousin Henry softly, 'only dusk. But people everywhere are watching it like ourselves, and thinking feather thoughts. You can see the froth of stars flung up over the crest of Night. People are watching it from windows and fields and country roads everywhere, wondering what makes it so beautiful. It brings yearnings and long, long desires. Only a few like ourselves can see the lines of scaffolding, but everybody who thinks about it, and loves it, makes it more real for others to see, too. Daddy's probably watching it too from his window.'

'I wonder if Jinny ever sees it,' Monkey asked herself.

But Jimbo knew. 'She's in it,' he decided. 'She's always in places like that; that's where she lives.'

The children went on talking to each other under their breath, and while they did so Cousin Henry entered their little wondering minds. Or, perhaps, they entered his. It is difficult to say. Not even an owl, who is awfully wise about everything to do with night and darkness, could have told for certain. But, anyhow, they all three saw more or less the same thing. The way they talked about it afterwards proves that. Their minds apparently merged, or else there was one big mirror and two minor side-reflections of it. It was their cousin's interpretation, at any rate, that they remembered later. They brought the material for his fashioning.

'Look!' cried Monkey, sitting up, 'there are millions and millions now—lines everywhere—pillars and squares and towers. It's like a city. I can see lamps in every street——'

'That's stars,' interrupted Jimbo. The stars indeed were peeping here and there already. 'I feel up there,' he added, 'my inside, I mean—up among the stars and lines and sky-things.'

'That's the mind wandering,' explained the eldest child of the three. 'Always follow a wandering mind. It's quite safe. Mine's going presently too. We'll all go off together.'

Several little winds, released by darkness, passed them just then on their way out of the forest. They gathered half a dozen sparks from the fire to light them on their way, and brought cool odours with them from the deepest recesses of the trees—perfumes no sunlight ever finds. And just behind them came a big white moth, booming and whirring softly. It darted to and fro to find the trail, then vanished, so swiftly that no one saw it go.

'He's pushing it along,' said Jimbo.

'Or fastening the lines,' his sister thought, 'you see he hovers in one place, then darts over to another.'

'That's fastening the knots,' added Jimbo.

'No; he's either an Inspector or a Pathfinder,' whispered Cousin Henry, 'I don't know exactly which. They show the way the scaffolding goes. Moths, bats, and owls divide the work between them somehow.' He sat up suddenly to listen, and the children sat up with him. 'Hark!' he added, 'do you hear that?'

Sighings and flutterings rose everywhere about them, and overhead the fluffy spires of the tree-tops all bent one way as the winds went foraging across the night. Majestically the scaffolding reared up and towered through the air, while sheets of darkness hung from every line, and trailed across the earth like gigantic sails from some invisible vessel. Loose and enormous they gradually unfolded, then suddenly swung free and dropped with a silent dip and rush. Night swooped down upon the leagues of Jura forest. She spread her tent across the entire range.

The threads were fastened everywhere now, and the uprights all in place. Moths were busy in all directions, showing the way, while bats by the dozen darted like black lightning from corner to corner, making sure that every spar and beam was fixed and steady. So exquisitely woven was the structure that it moved past them overhead without the faintest sound, yet so frail and so elastic that the whirring of the moths sent ripples of quivering movement through the entire framework.

'Hush!' murmured Rogers, 'we're properly inside it now. Don't think of anything in particular. Just follow your wandering minds and wait.' The children lay very close against him. He felt their warmth and the breathing of their little bosoms. All three moved sympathetically within the rhythm of the dusk. The 'inside' of each went floating up into the darkening sky.

The general plan of the scaffolding they clearly made out as they passed among its myriad, mile-long rafters, but the completed temple, of course, they never saw. Black darkness hides that ever. Night's secret mystery lies veiled finally in its innermost chamber, whence it steals forth to enchant the mind of men with its strange bewilderment. But the Twilight Scaffolding they saw clearly enough to make a map of it. For Daddy afterwards drew it from their description, and gave it an entire page in the Wumble Book, Monkey ladling on the colour with her camel's-hair brush as well as she could remember.

It was a page to take the breath away, the big conception blundering clumsily behind the crude reconstruction. Great winds formed the base, winds of brown and blue and purple, piled mountainously upon each other in motionless coils, and so soft that the upright columns of the structure plunged easily and deeply into them. Thus the framework could bend and curve and sway, moving with steady glide across the landscape, yet never collapsing nor losing its exquisite proportions. The forests shored it up, its stays and bastions were the Jura precipices; it rested on the shoulders of the hills. From vineyard, field, and lake vast droves of thick grey shadows trooped in to curtain the lower halls of the colossal edifice, as chamber after chamber disappeared from view and Night clothed the structure from the ground-floors upwards. And far overhead a million tiny scarves, half sunset and half dusk, wove into little ropes that lashed the topmost spars together, dovetailing them neatly, and fastening them at last with whole clusters of bright thin stars.

'Ohhhhh!' breathed Jimbo with a delicious shudder of giddiness. 'Let's climb to the very tip and see all the trains and railway stations in the world!'

'Wait till the moon comes up and puts the silver rivets in,' the leader whispered. 'It'll be safer then. My weight, you know—'

'There she is!' interrupted Monkey with a start, 'and there's no such thing as weight—'

For the moon that instant came up, it seemed with a rush, and the line of distant Alps moved forward, blocked vividly against the silvery curtain that she brought. Her sight ran instantly about the world. Between the trees shot balls of yellowish white, unfolding like ribbon as they rolled. They splashed the rocks and put shining pools in the hollows among the moss. Spangles shone on Monkey's hair and eyes; skins and faces all turned faintly radiant. The lake, like a huge reflector, flashed its light up into the heavens. The moon laid a coating of her ancient and transfiguring paint upon the enormous structure, festooning the entire sky. 'She's put the silver rivets in,' said Jimbo.

'Now we can go,' whispered Rogers, 'only, remember, it's a giddy business, rather.'

All three went fluttering after it, floating, rising, falling, like fish that explore a sunken vessel in their own transparent medium. The elastic structure bore them easily as it swung along. Its enormous rhythm lulled their senses with a deep and drowsy peace, and as they climbed from storey to storey it is doubtful if the children caught their leader's words at all. There were no echoes—the spaces were too vast for that—and they swung away from spar to spar, and from rafter to rafter, as easily as acrobats on huge trapezes. Jimbo and Monkey shot upwards into space.

'I shall explore the lower storeys first,' he called after them, his words fluttering in feathers of sound far up the vault. 'Keep the fire in sight to guide you home again ...' and he moved slowly towards the vast ground-floor chambers of the Night. Each went his independent way along the paths of reverie and dream. He found himself alone.

For he could not soar and float as they did; he kept closer to the earth, wandering through the under chambers of the travelling building that swung its way over vineyards, woods, and village roofs. He kept more in touch with earth than they did. The upper sections where the children climbed went faster than those lower halls and galleries, so that the entire framework bent over, breaking ever into a crest of foaming stars. But in these under halls where he stood and watched there was far less movement. From century to century these remained the same. Between the bases of the mighty columns he watched the wave of darkness drown the world, leading it with a rush of silence towards sleep. For the children Night meant play and mischief; for himself it meant graver reverie....

These were the chambers, clearly, of ancestral sleep and dream: they seemed so familiar and well known. Behind him blinked the little friendly fire in the forest, link with the outer world he must not lose. He would find the children there when he went back, lively from their scamper among the stars; and, meanwhile, he was quite content to wander down these corridors in the floor of Night and taste their deep repose. For years he had not visited or known them. The children had led him back, although he did not realise it. He believed, on the contrary, that it was he who led and they who followed. For true leadership is ever inspired, making each follower feel that he goes first and of his own free will....

'Jimbo, you flickery sprite, where are you now?' he called, suddenly noticing how faint the little fire had grown with distance.

A lonely wind flew down upon him with a tiny shout:

'Up here, at the very top, with Daddy. He's making notes in a tower- room all by himself!'

Rogers could not believe his ears. Daddy indeed!

'Is Monkey with you? And is she safe?'

'She's helping Daddy balance. The walls aren't finished, and he's on a fearful ledge. He's after something or other for his story, he says.'

It seemed impossible. Daddy skylarking on the roof of Night, and making notes! Yet with a moment's reflection the impossibility vanished; surprise went after it; it became natural, right, and true. Daddy, of course, sitting by his window in the carpenter's house, had seen the Twilight Scaffolding sweep past and had climbed into it. Its beauty had rapt him out and away. In the darkness his mind wandered, too, gathering notes subconsciously for his wonderful new story.

'Come down here to me,' he cried, as a man cries in his sleep, making no audible sound. 'There's less risk among the foundations.' And down came Daddy with an immediate rush. He arrived in a bundle, then straightened up. The two men stood side by side in these subterraneans of the night.

'You!' whispered Rogers, trying to seize his hand, while the other evaded him, hiding behind a shadow.

'Don't touch me,' he murmured breathlessly. 'You'll scatter my train of thought. Think of something else at once, please....' He moved into thicker shadows, half disappearing. 'I'm after something that suddenly occurred to me for my story.'

'What is it? I'll think it with you,' his cousin called after him. 'You'll see it better if I do. Tell me.'

'A train that carries Thought, as this darkness carries stars—a starlight express,' was the quick reply, 'and a cavern where lost starlight gathers till it's wanted-sort of terminus of the railway. They belong to the story somewhere if only I can find them and fit them in. Starlight binds all together as thought and sympathy bind minds....'

Rogers thought hard about them. Instantly his cousin vanished.

'Thank you,' ran a faint whisper among the pillars; 'I'm on their trail again now. I must go up again. I can see better from the top,' and the voice grew fainter and higher and further off with each word till it died away completely into silence. Daddy went chasing his inspiration through the scaffolding of reverie and dream.

'We did something for him the other night after all, then,' thought Rogers with delight.

'Of course,' dropped down a wee, faint answer from above, as the author heard him thinking; 'you did a lot. I'm partly out at last. This is where all the Patterns hide. Awake, I only get their dim reflections, broken and distorted. This is reality, not that. Ha, ha! If only I can get it through, my lovely, beautiful pattern—'

'You will, you will,' cried the other, as the voice went fluttering through space. 'Ask the children. Jimbo and Monkey are up there somewhere. They're the safest guides.'

Rogers gave a gulp and found that he was coughing. His feet were cold. A shudder ran across the feathery structure, making it tremble from the foundations to the forest of spires overhead. Jimbo came sliding down a pole of gleaming ebony. In a hammock of beams and rafters, swinging like a network of trapezes, Monkey swooped down after him, head first as usual. For the moon that moment passed behind a cloud, and the silver rivets started from their shadowy sockets. Clusters of star nails followed suit. The palace bent and tottered like a falling wave. Its pillars turned into trunks of pine trees; its corridors were spaces through the clouds; its chambers were great dips between the mountain summits.

'It's going too fast for sight,' thought Rogers; 'I can't keep up with it. Even the children have toppled off.' But he still heard Daddy's laughter echoing down the lanes of darkness as he chased his pattern with yearning and enthusiasm.

The huge structure with its towers and walls and platforms slid softly out of sight. The moonlight sponged its outlines from the sky. The scaffolding melted into darkness, moving further westwards as night advanced. Already it was over France and Italy, sweeping grandly across the sea, bewildering the vessels in its net of glamour, and filling with wonder the eyes of the look-out men at the mast heads.

'The fire's going out,' a voice was saying. Rogers heard it through a moment's wild confusion as he fell swiftly among a forest of rafters, beams, and shifting uprights.

'I'll get more wood.'

The words seemed underground. A mountain wind rose up and brought the solid world about him. He felt chilly, shivered, and opened his eyes.

There stood the solemn pine trees, thick and close; moonlight flooded the spaces between them and lit their crests with silver.

'This is the Wind Wood,' he remarked aloud to reassure himself.

Jimbo was bending over the fire, heaping on wood. Flame leaped up with a shower of sparks. He saw Monkey rubbing her eyes beside him.

'I've had a dream of falling,' she was saying, as she snuggled down closer into his side.

'*I* didn't,' Jimbo said. 'I dreamed of a railway accident, and everybody was killed except one passenger, who was Daddy. It fell off a high bridge. We found Daddy in the *fourgon* with the baggages, writing a story and laughing—making an awful row.'

'What did *you* dream, Cousinenry?' asked Monkey, peering into his eyes in the firelight.

'That my feet were cold, because the fire had gone out,' he answered, trying in vain to remember whether he had dreamed anything at all. 'And—that it's time to go home. I hear the curfew ringing.'

Some one whistled softly. They ought to have been in bed an hour ago.

It was ten o'clock, and Gygi was sounding the *couvre feu* from the old church tower. They put the fire out and walked home arm in arm, separating with hushed good-nights in the courtyard of the Citadelle. But Rogers did not hear the scolding Mother gave them when they appeared at the Den door, for he went on at once to his own room in the carpenter's house, with the feeling that he had lived always in Bourcelles, and would never leave it again. His Scheme had moved bodily from London to the forest.

And on the way upstairs he peeped a moment into his cousin's room, seeing a light beneath the door. The author was sitting beside the open window with the lamp behind him and a note-book on his knees. Moonlight fell upon his face. He was sound asleep.

'I won't wake him,' thought his cousin, going out softly again. 'He's dreaming—dreaming of his wonderful new story probably.'

CHAPTER XXII

Even as a luminous haze links star to star,
I would supply all chasms with music, breathing
Mysterious motions of the soul, no way
To be defined save in strange melodies.
    Paracelsus, R. BROWNING.

Daddy's story, meanwhile, continued to develop itself with wonder and enthusiasm. It was unlike anything he had ever written. His other studies had the brilliance of dead precious stones, perhaps, but this thing moved along with a rushing life of its own. It grew, fed by sources he was not aware of. It developed of itself—changed and lived and flashed. Some creative fairy hand had touched him while he slept perhaps. The starry sympathy poured through him, and he thought with his feelings as well as with his mind.

At first he was half ashamed of it; the process was so new and strange; he even attempted to conceal his method, because he could not explain or understand it. 'This is emotional, not intellectual,' he sighed to himself; 'it must be second childhood. I'm old. They'll call it decadent!' Presently, however, he resigned himself to the delicious flow of inspiration, and let it pour out till it flowed over into his daily life as well. Through his heart it welled up and bubbled forth, a thing of children, starlight, woods, and fairies.

Yet he was shy about it. He would talk about the story, but would not read it out. 'It's a new *genre* for me,' he explained shyly, 'an attempt merely. We'll see what comes of it. My original idea, you see, has grown out of hand rather. I wake every morning with something fresh, as though'—he hesitated a moment, glancing towards his wife— 'as if it came to me in sleep,' he concluded. He felt her common sense might rather despise him for it.

'Perhaps it does,' said Rogers.

'Why not?' said Mother, knitting on the sofa that was her bed at night.

She had put her needles down and was staring at her husband; he stared at Rogers; all three stared at each other. Something each wished to conceal moved towards utterance and revelation. Yet no one of them wished to be the first to mention it. A great change had come of late upon Bourcelles. It no longer seemed isolated from the big world outside as before; something had linked it up with the whole surrounding universe, and bigger, deeper currents of life flowed through it. And with the individual life of each it was the same. All dreamed the same enormous, splendid dream, yet dared not tell it—yet.

Both parents realised vaguely that it was something their visitor had brought, but what could it be exactly? It was in his atmosphere, he himself least of all aware of it; it was in his thought, his attitude to life, yet he himself so utterly unconscious of it. It brought out all the best in everybody, made them feel hopeful, brighter, more courageous. Yes, certainly, *he*, brought it. He believed in them, in the best of them—they lived up to it or tried to. Was that it? Was it belief and vision that he brought into their lives, though unconsciously, because these qualities lay so strongly in himself? Belief is constructive. It is what people *are* rather than what they preach that affects others. Two strangers meet and bow and separate without a word, yet each has changed; neither leaves the other quite as he was before. In the society of children, moreover, one believes everything in the world—for the moment. Belief is constructive and creative; it is doubt and cynicism that destroy. In the presence of a child these latter are impossible. Was this the explanation of the effect he produced upon their little circle—the belief and wonder and joy of Fairyland?

For a moment something of this flashed through Daddy's mind. Mother, in her way, was aware of something similar. But neither of them spoke it. The triangular staring was its only evidence. Mother resumed her knitting. She was not given to impulsive utterance. Her husband once described her as a solid piece of furniture. She was.

'You see,' said Daddy bravely, as the moment's tension passed, 'my original idea was simply to treat Bourcelles as an epitome, a miniature, so to speak, of the big world, while showing how Nature sweetened and kept it pure as by a kind of alchemy. But that idea has grown. I have the feeling now that the Bourcelles we know is a mere shadowy projection cast by a more real Bourcelles behind. It is only the dream village we know in our waking life. The real one—er—we know only in sleep.' There!—it was partly out!

Mother turned with a little start. 'You mean when we sleep?' she asked. She knitted vigorously again at once, as though ashamed of this sudden betrayal into fantasy. 'Why not?' she added, falling back upon her customary non-committal phrase. Yet this was not the superior attitude he had dreaded; she was interested. There was something she wanted to confess, if she only dared. Mother, too, had grown softer in some corner of her being. Something shone through her with a tiny golden radiance.

'But this idea is not my own,' continued Daddy, dangerously near to wumbling. 'It comes *through* me only. It develops, apparently, when I'm asleep,' he repeated. He sat up and leaned forward. 'And, I believe,' he added, as on sudden reckless impulse, 'it comes from you, Henry. Your mind, I feel, has brought this cargo of new suggestion and discharged it into me—into every one—into the whole blessed village. Man, I think you've bewitched us all!'

Mother dropped a stitch, so keenly was she listening. A moment later she dropped a needle too, and the two men picked it up, and handed it back together as though it weighed several pounds.

'Well,' said Rogers slowly, 'I suppose all minds pour into one another somewhere—in and out of one another, rather—and that there's a common stock or pool all draw upon according to their needs and power to assimilate. But I'm not conscious, old man, of driving anything deliberately into you—'

'Only you think and feel these things vividly enough for me to get them too,' said Daddy. Luckily 'thought transference' was not actually mentioned, or Mother might have left the room, or at least have betrayed an uneasiness that must have chilled them.

'As a boy I imagined pretty strongly,' in a tone of apology, 'but never since. I was in the City, remember, twenty years—'

'It's the childhood things, then,' Daddy interrupted eagerly. 'You've brought the great childhood imagination with you—the sort of gorgeous, huge, and endless power that goes on fashioning of its own accord just as dreams do—'

'I *did*, indulge in that sort of thing as a boy, yes,' was the half- guilty reply; 'but that was years and years ago, wasn't it?'

'They have survived, then,' said Daddy with decision. 'The sweetness of this place has stimulated them afresh. The children'—he glanced suspiciously at his wife for a moment—'have appropriated them too. It's a powerful combination. After a pause he added, 'I might develop that idea in my story—that you've brought back the sweet creations of childhood with you and captured us all—a sort of starry army.'

'Why not?' interpolated Mother, as who should say there was no harm in *that*. 'They certainly have been full of mischief lately.'

'Creation *is* mischievous,' murmured her husband. 'But since you have come,' he continued aloud,—'how can I express it exactly?—the days have seemed larger, fuller, deeper, the forest richer and more mysterious, the sky much closer, and the stars more soft and intimate. I dream of them, and they all bring me messages that help my story. Do you know what I mean? There were days formerly, when life seemed empty, thin, peaked, impoverished, its scale of values horribly reduced, whereas now—since you've been up to your nonsense with the children—some tide stands at the full, and things are always happening.'

'Well, really, Daddy!' said the expression on Mother's face and hands and knitting-needles, 'you *are* splendid to-day'; but aloud she only repeated her little hold-all phrase, 'Why not?'

Yet somehow he recognised that she understood him better than usual. Her language had not changed—things in Mother worked slowly, from within outwards as became her solid personality—but it held new meaning. He felt for the first time that he could make her understand, and more—that she was ready to understand. That is, he felt new sympathy with her. It was very delightful, stimulating; he instantly loved her more, and felt himself increased at the same time.

'I believe a story like that might even sell,' he observed, with a hint of reckless optimism. 'People might recognise a touch of their own childhood in it, eh?'

He longed for her to encourage him and pat him on the back.

'True,' said Mother, smiling at him, 'for every one likes to keep in touch with their childhood—if they can. It makes one feel young and hopeful—jolly; doesn't it? Why not?'

Their eyes met. Something, long put aside and buried under a burden of exaggerated care, flashed deliciously between them. Rogers caught it flying and felt happy. Bridges were being repaired, if not newly built.

'Nature, you see, is always young really,' he said; 'it's full of children. The very meaning of the word, eh, John?' turning to his cousin as who should say, 'We knew our grammar once.'

'*Natura*, yes—something about to produce.' They laughed in their superior knowledge of a Latin word, but Mother, stirred deeply though she hardly knew why, was not to be left out. Would the bridge bear her, was perhaps her thought.

'And of the feminine gender,' she added slyly, with a touch of pride. The bridge creaked, but did not give way. She said it very quickly. She had suddenly an air of bouncing on her sofa.

'Bravo, Mother,' said her husband, looking at her, and there was a fondness in his voice that warmed and blessed and melted down into her. She had missed it so long that it almost startled her. 'There's the eternal old magic, Mother; you're right. And if I had more of you in me—more of the creative feminine—I should do better work, I'm sure. You must give it to me.'

She kept her eyes upon her needles. The others, being unobservant 'mere men,' did not notice that the stitches she made must have produced queer kind of stockings if continued. 'We'll be collaborators,' Daddy added, in the tone of a boy building on the sands at Margate.

'I will,' she said in a low voice, 'if only I know how.'

'Well,' he answered enthusiastically, looking from one to the other, delighted to find an audience to whom he could talk of his new dream, 'you see, this is really a great jolly fairy-tale I'm trying to write. I'm blessed if I know where the ideas come from, or how they pour into me like this, but—anyhow it's a new experience, and I want to make the most of it. I've never done imaginative work before, and—though it is a bit fantastical, mean to keep in touch with reality and show great truths that emerge from the commonest facts of life. The critics, of course, will blame me for not giving 'em the banal thing they expect from me, but what of that?' He was dreadfully reckless.

'I see,' said Mother, gazing open-mindedly into his face; 'but where does *my* help come in, please?'

She leaned back, half-sighing, half-smiling. 'Here's my life'—she held up her needles—'and that's the soul of prosaic dulness, isn't it?'

'On the contrary,' he answered eagerly, 'it's reality. It's courage, patience, heroism. You're a spring-board for my fairy-tale, though I'd never realised it before. I shall put you in, just as you are. You'll be one of the earlier chapters.'

'Every one'll skip me, then, I'm afraid.'

'Not a bit,' he laughed gaily; 'they'll feel you all through the book. Their minds will rest on you. You'll be a foundation. "Mother's there," they'll say, "so it's all right. This isn't nonsense. We'll read on." And they will read on.'

'I'm all through it, then?'

'Like the binding that mothers the whole book, you see,' put in Rogers, delighted to see them getting on so well, yet amazed to hear his cousin talk so openly with her of his idea.

Daddy continued, unabashed and radiant. Hitherto, he knew, his wife's attitude, though never spoken, had been very different. She almost resented his intense preoccupation with stories that brought in so little cash. It would have been better if he taught English or gave lessons in literature for a small but regular income. He gave too much attention to these unremunerative studies of types she never met in actual life. She was proud of the reviews, and pasted them neatly in a big book, but his help and advice on the practical details of the children's clothing and education were so scanty. Hers seemed ever the main burden.

Now, for the first time, though she distrusted fantasy and deemed it destructive of action, she felt something real. She listened with a kind of believing sympathy. She noticed, moreover, with keen pleasure, that her attitude fed him. He talked so freely, happily about it all. Already her sympathy, crudely enough expressed, brought fuel to his fires. Some one had put starlight into her.

'He's been hungry for this all along,' she reflected; 'I never realised it. I've thought only of myself without knowing it.'

'Yes, I'll put you in, old Mother,' he went on, 'and Rogers and the children too. In fact, you're in it already,' he chuckled, 'if you want to know. Each of you plays his part all day long without knowing it.' He changed his seat, going over to the window-sill, and staring down upon them as he talked on eagerly. 'Don't you feel,' he said, enthusiasm growing and streaming from him, 'how all this village life is a kind of dream we act out against the background of the sunshine, while our truer, deeper life is hidden somewhere far below in half unconsciousness? Our daily doings are but the little bits that emerge, tips of acts and speech that poke up and out, masquerading as complete? In that vaster sea of life we lead below the surface lies my big story, my fairy-tale—when we sleep.' He paused and looked down questioningly upon them. 'When we sleep,' he repeated impressively, struggling with his own thought. 'You, Mother, while you knit and sew, slip down into that enormous under-sea and get a glimpse of the coloured pictures that pass eternally behind the veil. I do the same when I watch the twilight from my window in reverie. Sunshine obliterates them, but they go just the same. *You* call it day- dreaming. Our waking hours are the clothes we dress the spirit in after its nightly journeys and activities. Imagination does not create so much as remember. Then, by transforming, it reveals.'

Mother sat staring blankly before her, utterly lost, while her husband flung these lumps of the raw material of his story at her—of its atmosphere, rather. Even Rogers felt puzzled, and hardly followed what he heard. The intricacies of an artistic mind were indeed bewildering. How in the world would these wild fragments weave together into any intelligible pattern?

'You mean that we travel when we sleep,' he ventured, remembering a phrase that Minks had somewhere used, 'and that our real life is out of the body?' His cousin was taking his thought—or was it originally Minks's?—wholesale.

Mother looked up gratefully. 'I often dream I'm flying,' she put in solemnly. 'Lately, in particular, I've dreamed of stars and funny things like that a lot.'

Daddy beamed his pleasure. 'In my fairy-tale we shall all see stars,' he laughed, 'and we shall all get "out." For our thoughts will determine the kind of experience and adventure we have when the spirit is free and unhampered. And contrariwise, the kind of things we do at night—in sleep, in dream—will determine our behaviour during the day. There's the importance of thinking rightly, you see. Out of the body is eternal, and thinking is more than doing—it's more complete. The waking days are brief intervals of test that betray the character of our hidden deeper life. We are judged in sleep. We last for ever and ever. In the day, awake, we stand before the easel on which our adventures of the night have painted those patterns which are the very structure of our outer life's behaviour. When we sleep again we re- enter the main stream of our spirit's activity. In the day we forget, of course—as a rule, and most of us—but we follow the pattern just the same, unwittingly, because we can't help it. It's the mould we've made.'

'Then your story,' Rogers interrupted, 'will show the effect in the daytime of what we do at night? Is that it?' It amazed him to hear his cousin borrowing thus the entire content of his own mind, sucking it out whole like a ripe plum from its skin.

'Of course,' he answered; 'and won't it be a lark? We'll all get out in sleep and go about the village together in a bunch, helping, soothing, cleaning up, and putting everybody straight, so that when they wake up they'll wonder why in the world they feel so hopeful, strong, and happy all of a sudden. We'll put thoughts of beauty into them—beauty, you remember, which "is a promise of happiness."'

'Ah!' said Mother, seizing at his comprehensible scrap with energy. 'That *is* a story.'

'If I don't get it wumbled in the writing down,' her husband continued, fairly bubbling over. 'You must keep me straight, remember, with your needles—your practical aspirations, that is. I'll read it out to you bit by bit, and you'll tell me where I've dropped a stitch or used the wrong wool, eh?'

'Mood?' she asked.

'No, wool,' he said, louder.

There was a pause.

'But you see my main idea, don't you—that the sources of our life lie hid with beauty very very far away, and that our real, big, continuous life is spiritual—out of the body, as I shall call it. The waking-day life uses what it can bring over from this enormous under-running sea of universal consciousness where we're all together, splendid, free, untamed, and where thinking is creation and we feel and know each other face to face? See? Sympathy the great solvent? All linked together by thought as stars are by their rays. Ah! You get my idea— the great Network?'

He looked straight into his wife's eyes. They were opened very wide. Her mouth had opened a little, too. She understood vaguely that he was using a kind of shorthand really. These cryptic sentences expressed in emotional stenography mere odds and ends that later would drop into their proper places, translated into the sequence of acts that are the scaffolding of a definite story. This she firmly grasped—but no more.

'It's grand-a wonderful job,' she answered, sitting back upon the sofa with a sigh of relief, and again bouncing a little in the process, so that Rogers had a horrible temptation to giggle. The tension of listening had been considerable. 'People, you mean, will realise how important thinking is, and that sympathy——er——' and she hesitated, floundering.

'Is the great way to grow,' Rogers quickly helped her, 'because by feeling with another person you add his mind to yours and so get bigger. And '— turning to his cousin—' you're taking starlight as the symbol of sympathy? You told me that the other day, I remember.' But the author did not hear or did not answer; his thought was far away in his dream again.

The situation was saved. All the bridges had borne well. Daddy, having relieved his overcharged mind, seemed to have come to a full stop. The Den was full of sunlight. A delightful feeling of intimacy wove the three humans together. Mother caught herself thinking of the far-off courtship days when their love ran strong and clear. She felt at one with her husband, and remembered him as lover. She felt in touch with him all over. And Rogers was such a comfortable sort of person. Tact was indeed well named—sympathy so delicately adjusted that it involved feeling-with to the point of actual touch.

Daddy came down from his perch upon the window-sill, stretched his arms, and drew a great happy sigh.

'Mother,' he added, rising to go out, 'you shall help me, dearie. We'll write this great fairy-tale of mine together, eh?' He stooped and kissed her, feeling love and tenderness and sympathy in his heart.

'You brave old Mother!' he laughed; 'we'll send Eddie to Oxford yet, see if we don't. A book like that might earn 100 pounds or even 200 pounds.'

Another time she would have answered, though not bitterly, 'Meanwhile I'll go on knitting stockings,' or 'Why not? we shall see what we shall see'—

something, at any rate, corrective and rather sober, quenching. But this time she said nothing. She returned the kiss instead, without looking up from her needles, and a great big thing like an unborn child moved near her heart. He had not called her 'dearie' for so long a time, it took her back to their earliest days together at a single, disconcerting bound. She merely stroked his shoulder as he straightened up and left the room. Her eyes then followed him out, and he turned at the door and waved his hand. Rogers, to her relief, saw him to the end of the passage, and her handkerchief was out of sight again before he returned. As he came in she realised even more clearly than before that he somehow was the cause of the changing relationship. He it was who brought this something that bridged the years—made old bridges safe to use again. And her love went out to him. He was a man she could open her heart to even.

Patterns of starry beauty had found their way in and were working out in all of them. But Mother, of course, knew nothing of this. There was a tenderness in him that won her confidence. That was all she felt. 'Oh, dear,' she thought in her odd way, 'what a grand thing a man is to be sure, when he's got that!' It was like one of Jane Anne's remarks.

As he came in she had laid the stocking aside and was threading a needle for darning and buttons, and the like.

'"Threading the eye of a yellow star," eh?' he laughed, 'and always at it. You've stirred old Daddy up this time. He's gone off to his story, simply crammed full. What a help and stimulus you must be to him!'

'I,' she said, quite flabbergasted; 'I only wish it were true—again.' The last word slipped out by accident; she had not meant it.

But Rogers ignored it, even if he noticed it.

'I never can help him in his work. I don't understand it enough. I don't understand it at all.' She was ashamed to hedge with this man. She looked him straight in the eye.

'But he feels your sympathy,' was his reply. 'It's not always necessary to understand. That might only muddle him. You help by wishing, feeling, sympathising—believing.'

'You really think so?' she asked simply. 'What wonderful thoughts you have I One has read, of course, of wives who inspired their husbands' work; but it seemed to belong to books rather than to actual life.'

Rogers looked at her thoughtful, passionate face a moment before he answered. He realised that his words would count with her. They approached delicate ground. She had an absurd idea of his importance in their lives; she exaggerated his influence; if he said a wrong thing its effect upon her would be difficult to correct.

'Well,' he said, feeling mischief in him, 'I don't mind telling *you* that I should never have understood that confused idea of his story but for one thing.'

'What was that?' she asked, relieved to feel more solid ground at last.

'That I saw the thing from his own point of view,' he replied; 'because I have had similar thoughts all my life. I mean that he's bagged it all unconsciously out of my own mind; though, of course,' he hastened to add, 'I could never, never have made use of it as he will. I could never give it shape and form.'

Mother began to laugh too. He caught the twinkle in her eyes. She bounced again a little on the springy sofa as she turned towards him, confession on her lips at last.

'And I do believe you've felt it too, haven't you?' he asked quickly, before she could change her mind.

'I've felt something—yes,' she assented; 'odd, unsettled; new things rushing everywhere about us; the children mysterious and up to all sorts of games and wickedness; and bright light over everything, like- like a scene in a theatre, somehow. It's exhilarating, but I can't quite make it out. It can't be right to feel so frivolous and jumpy- about at my age, can it?'

'You feel lighter, eh?

She burst out laughing. Mother was a prosaic person; that is, she had strong common-sense; yet through her sober personality there ran like a streak of light some hint of fairy lightness, derived probably from her Celtic origin. Now, as Rogers watched her, he caught a flash of that raciness and swift mobility, that fluid, protean elasticity of temperament which belonged to the fairy kingdom. The humour and pathos in her had been smothered by too much care. She accepted old age before her time. He saw her, under other conditions, dancing, singing, full of Ariel tricks and mischief—instead of eternally mending stockings and saving centimes for peat and oil and washerwomen. He even saw her feeding fantasy—poetry—to Daddy like a baby with a spoon. The contrast made him laugh out loud.

'You've lived here five years,' he went on, 'but lived too heavily. Care has swamped imagination. I did the same-in the City-for twenty years. It's all wrong. One has to learn to live carelessly as well as carefully. When I came here I felt all astray at first, but now I see more clearly. The peace and beauty have soaked into me.' He hesitated an instant, then continued. Even if she didn't grasp his meaning now with her brains, it would sink down into her and come through later.

'The important things of life are very few really. They stand out vividly here. You've both vegetated, fossilised, atrophied a bit. I discovered it in my own case when I went back to Crayfield and—'

He told her about his sentimental journey, and how he found all the creations of his childhood's imagination still so alive and kicking in a forgotten backwater of his mind that they all hopped out and took objective form—the sprites, the starlight express, the boundless world of laughter, fun and beauty.

'And, without exactly knowing it, I suppose I've brought them all out here,' he continued, seeing that she drank it in thirstily, 'and— somehow or other—you all have felt it and responded. It's not my doing, of course,' he added; 'it's simply that I'm the channel as it were, and Daddy, with his somewhat starved artist's hunger of mind, was the first to fill up. It's pouring through him now in a story, don't you see; but we're all in it—'

'In a way, yes, that's what I've felt,' Mother interrupted. 'It's all a kind of dream here, and I've just waked up. The unchanging village, the forests, the Pension with its queer people, the Magic Box—'

'Like a play in a theatre,' he interrupted, 'isn't it?'

'Exactly,' she laughed, yet half-seriously.

'While your husband is the dramatist that writes it down in acts and scenes. You see, his idea is, perhaps, that life as we know it is never a genuine story, complete and leading to a climax. It's all in disconnected fragments apparently. It goes backwards and forwards, up and down, in and out in a wumbled muddle, just anyhow, as it were. The fragments seem out of their proper place, the first ones often last, and *vice versa*. It seems inconsequential, because we only see the scraps that break through from below, from the true inner, deeper life that flows on steadily and dramatically out of sight. That's what he means by "out of the body" and "sleep" and "dreaming." The great pattern is too big and hidden for us to see it whole, just as when you knit I only see the stitches as you make them, although the entire pattern is in your mind complete. Our daily, external acts are the stitches we show to others and that everybody sees. A spiritual person sees the whole.'

'Ah!' Mother interrupted, 'I understand now. To know the whole pattern in my mind you'd have to get in sympathy with my thought below. Is that it?'

'Sometimes we look over the fence of mystery, yes, and see inside—see the entire stage as it were.'

'It *is* like a great play, isn't it?' she repeated, grasping again at the analogy with relief. 'We give one another cues, and so on——'

'While each must know the whole play complete in order to act his part properly—be in sympathy, that is, with all the others. The tiniest details so important, too,' he added, glancing significantly at the needles on her lap. 'To act your own part faithfully you must carry all the others in your mind, or else—er—get your own part out of proportion.'

'It will be a wonderful story, won't it?' she said, after a pause in which her eyes travelled across the sunshine towards the carpenter's house where her husband, seen now in a high new light, laboured steadily.

There was a clatter in the corridor before he could reply, and Jimbo and Monkey flew in with a rush of wings and voices from school. They were upon him in an instant, smelling of childhood, copy-books, ink, and rampagious with hunger. Their skins and hair were warm with sunlight. 'After tea we'll go out,' they cried, 'and show you something in the forest—oh, an enormous and wonderful thing that nobody knows of but me and Jimbo, and comes over every night from France and hides inside a cave, and goes back just before sunrise with a sack full of thinkings——'

'Thoughts,' corrected Jimbo.

'——that haven't reached the people they were meant for, and then——'

'Go into the next room, wash yourselves and tidy up,' said Mother sternly, 'and then lay the table for tea. Jinny isn't in yet. Put the charcoal in the samovar. I'll come and light it in a moment.'

They disappeared obediently, though once behind the door there were sounds that resembled a pillow-fight rather than tidying-up; and when Mother presently went after them to superintend, Rogers sat by the window and stared across the vineyards and blue expanse of lake at the distant Alps. It was curious. This vague, disconnected, rambling talk with Mother had helped to clear his own mind as well. In trying to explain to her something he hardly understood himself, his own thinking had clarified. All these trivial scenes were little bits of rehearsal. The Company was still waiting for the arrival of the Star Player who should announce the beginning of the real performance. It was a woman's role, yet Mother certainly could not play it. To get the family really straight was equally beyond his powers. 'I really must have more common-sense,' he reflected uneasily; 'I am getting out of touch with reality somewhere. I'll write to Minks again.'

Minks, at the moment, was the only definite, positive object in the outer world he could recall. 'I'll write to him about——' His thought went wumbling. He quite forgot what it was he had to say to him—'Oh, about lots of things,' he concluded, 'his wife and children and—and his own future and so on.'

The Scheme had melted into air, it seemed. People lost in Fairyland, they say, always forget the outer world of unimportant happenings. They live too close to the source of things to recognise their clownish reflections in the distorted mirrors of the week-day level.

Yes, it was curious, very curious. Did Thought, then, issue primarily from some single source and pass thence along the channels of men's minds, each receiving and interpreting according to his needs and powers? Was the Message—the Prophet's Vision—merely the more receipt of it than most? Had, perhaps, this whole wonderful story his cousin wrote originated, not in his, Rogers's mind, nor in that of Minks, but in another's altogether—the mind of her who was destined for the principal role? Thrills of absurd, electric anticipation rushed through him—very boyish, wildly impossible, yet utterly delicious.

Two doors opened suddenly—one from the kitchen, admitting Monkey with a tray of cups and saucers, steam from the hissing samovar wrapping her in a cloud, the other from the corridor, letting in Jane Anne, her arms full of packages. She had been shopping for the family in Neuchatel, and was arrayed in garments from the latest Magic Box. She was eager and excited.

'Cousinenry,' she cried, dropping half the parcels in her fluster, 'I've had a letter!' It was in her hand, whereas the parcels had been merely under her arms. 'The postman gave it me himself as I came up the steps. I'm a great correspondencer, you know.' And she darted through the steam to tell her mother. Jimbo passed her, carrying the tea-pot, the sugar-basin dangerously balanced upon spoons and knives and butter-dish. He said nothing, but glanced at his younger sister significantly. Rogers saw the entire picture through the cloud of steam, shot through with sunlight from the window. It was like a picture in the clouds. But he intercepted that glance and knew then the writer of the letter.

'But did you get the mauve ribbon, child?' asked Mother.

Instead of answer, the letter was torn noisily open. Jinny never had letters. It was far more important than ribbons.

'And how much change have you left out of the five francs? Daddy will want to know.'

Jimbo and Monkey were listening carefully, while pretending to lay the table. Mother's silence betrayed that she was reading the letter with interest and curiosity equal to those of its recipient. 'Who wrote it? Who's it from? I must answer it at once,' Jinny was saying with great importance. 'What time does the post go, I wonder? I mustn't miss it.'

'The post-mark,' announced Mother, 'is Bourcelles. It's very mysterious.' She tapped the letter with one hand, like the villain in the theatre. Rogers heard her and easily imagined the accompanying stage gesture. 'The handwriting on the envelope is like Tante Anna,' he heard, 'but the letter itself is different. It's all capitals, and wrongly spelt.' Mlle. Lemaire was certainly not the writer.

Jimbo and Monkey were busy hanging the towel out of the window, signal to Daddy that tea was ready. But as Daddy was already coming down the street at a great pace, apparently excited too, they waved it instead. Rogers suddenly remembered that Jimbo that morning had asked him for a two-centime stamp. He made no remark, however, merely wondering what was in the letter itself.

'It's a joke, of course,' Mother was heard to say in an odd voice.

'Oh no, Mother, for how could anybody know? It's what I've been dreaming about for nights and nights. It's so aromantic, isn't it?'

The louder hissing of the samovar buried the next words, and at that moment Daddy came into the room. He was smiling and his eyes were bright. He glanced at the table and sat down by his cousin on the sofa.

'I've done a lot of work since you saw me,' he said happily, patting him on the knee, 'although in so short a time. And I want my cup of tea. It came so easily and fluently for a wonder; I don't believe I shall have to change a word—though usually I distrust this sort of rapid composition.'

'Where are you at now?' asked Rogers. 'We're all "out,"' was the reply, 'and the Starlight Express is just about to start and—Mother, let me carry that for you,' he exclaimed, turning round as his wife appeared in the doorway with more tea-things. He got up quickly, but before he could reach her side Jinny flew into his arms and kissed him.

'Did you get my tobacco, Jinny?' he asked. She thrust the letter under his nose. What was tobacco, indeed, compared to an important letter! 'You can keep the change for yourself.'

He read it slowly with a puzzled expression, while Mother and the children watched him. Riquette jumped down from her chair and rubbed herself against his leg while he scratched himself with his boot, thinking it was the rough stocking that tickled him.

'Eh? This is very queer,' he muttered, slapping the open sheet just as his wife had done, and reading it again at arm's-length. 'Somebody'— he looked suspiciously round the room—'has been reading my notes or picking out my thoughts while I'm asleep, eh?'

'But it's a real letter,' objected Jinny; 'it's correspondence, isn't it, Daddy?'

'It is certainly a correspondence,' he comforted her, and then, reading it aloud, he proceeded to pin it on the wall above the mantelpiece:—

'The Starlight Xpress starts to-night, Be reddy and punctuel. Sleep titely and get out.'

That was all. But everybody exchanged glances.

'Odd,' thought Mother, again remembering her dreams.

Jimbo upset the milk-jug. Usually there would have been a rumpus over this. To-day it seemed like something happening far away—something that had not really happened at all.

'We must all be ready then,' said Rogers, noticing vaguely that Mother's sleeve had smeared the butter as she mopped up the mess.

Daddy was making a note on his shirt sleeve:—

> The Sweep, the Laugher and the Tramp,
> The running man who lights the lamp,
> The Woman of the Haystack, too,
> The Gardener and Man of Dust
> Are passengers because they must
> Follow the Guard with eyes of blue.
> Over the forests and into the Cave
> That is the way we must all behave—

'Please, Daddy, will you move? It's dripping on to your boot.'

They all looked down; the milk had splashed from the cloth and fallen upon the toe of his big mountain boots. It made a pretty, white star. Riquette was daintily lapping it up with her long pink Tongue. Ray by ray the star set in her mysterious interior.

'Riquette must come too,' said Rogers gravely. 'She's full of white starlight now.'

And Jimbo left his chair and went seriously over to the book-shelf above Mother's sofa-bed to arrange the signals. For between the tightly-wedged books he had inserted all the available paper-knives and book-markers he could find to represent railway-signals. They stuck out at different angles. He altered several, putting some up, some down, and some at right angles.

'The line's all clear for to-night,' he announced to Daddy with a covert significance he hardly grasped himself, then coming back to home-made jam and crusty village bread.

Jane Anne caught her father's answering glance-mysterious, full of unguessed meanings. 'Oh, excuse me, Mother,' she said, feeling the same thing in herself and a little frightened; 'but I do believe they're conspiring, aren't they?'

And Mother gave a sudden start, whose cause she equally failed to analyse. 'Hush, dear,' she said. 'Don't criticise your elders, and when you do, don't use long words you cannot possibly understand.'

And everybody understood something none of them understood-while tea went on as usual to the chatter of daily details of external life.

CHAPTER XXIV

All we have willed or hoped or dreamed of good shall exist;
Not its semblance, but itself; no beauty, nor good, nor power
Whose voice has gone forth, but each survives for the melodist
When eternity affirms the conception of an hour.
The high that proved too high, the heroic for earth too hard,
The passion that left the ground to lose itself in the sky,
Are music sent up to God by the lover and the bard;
Enough that he heard it once: we shall hear it by and by.
        Abt Vogler, R. BROWNING.

Some hours later, as Rogers undressed for bed in his room beneath the roof, he realised abruptly that the time had come for him to leave. The weeks had flown; Minks and the Scheme required him; other matters needed attention too. What brought him to the sudden decision was the fact that he had done for the moment all he could find to do, beginning with the Pension mortgages and ending with little Edouard Tissot, the *vigneron's* boy who had curvature of the spine and could not afford proper treatment. It was a long list. He was far from satisfied with results, yet he had done his best, in spite of many clumsy mistakes. In the autumn he might return and have a further try. Finances were getting muddled, too, and he realised how small his capital actually was when the needs of others made claims upon it. Neighbours were as plentiful as insects.

He had made all manner of schemes for his cousin's family as well, yet seemed to have accomplished little. Their muddled life defied disentanglement, their difficulties were inextricable. With one son at a costly tutor, another girl in a Geneva school, the younger children just outgrowing the local education, the family's mode of living so scattered, meals in one place, rooms in several others,—it was all too unmethodical and dispersed to be covered by their small uncertain income. Concentration was badly needed. The endless talks and confabulations, which have not been reported here because their confusion was interminable and unreportable, landed every one in a mass of complicated jumbles. The solution lay beyond his power, as equally beyond the powers of the obfuscated parents. He would return to England, settle his own affairs, concoct some practical scheme with the aid of Minks, and return later to discuss its working out. The time had come for him to leave.

And, oddly enough, what made him see it were things the children had said that very evening when he kissed them all good-night. England had been mentioned.

'You're here for always now,' whispered Monkey, 'because you love me and can't get away. I've tied you with my hair, you know.'

'You'll have no sekrity in London,' said Jimbo. 'Who'll stick your stamps on?'

'The place will seem quite empty if you go,' Jane Anne contributed, not wishing to make her contribution too personal, lest she should appear immodest. 'You've made a memorandum of agreement.' This meant he had promised rashly once to stay for ever. The phrase lent an official tone besides.

He fell asleep, devising wonderful plans, as usual, for the entire world, not merely a tiny section of it. The saviour spirit was ever in his heart. It failed to realise itself because the mind was unequal to the strain of wise construction; but it was there, as the old vicar had divined. He had that indestructible pity to which no living thing is outcast.

But to-night he fell asleep so slowly, gradually, that he almost watched the dissolving of consciousness in himself. He hovered a long time about the strange, soft frontiers. He saw the barriers lower themselves into the great dim plains. Inch by inch the outer world became remote, obscure, lit dubiously by some forgotten sun, and inch by inch the profound recesses of nightly adventure coaxed him down. He realised that he swung in space between the two. The room and house were a speck in the universe above him, his brain the mere outlet of a tunnel up which he climbed every morning to put his horns out like a snail, and sniff the outer world. Here, in the depths, was the workroom where his life was fashioned. Here glowed the mighty, hidden furnaces that shaped his tools. Drifting, glimmering figures streamed up round him from the vast under-world of sleep, called unconscious. 'I *am* a spirit,' he heard, not said or thought, 'and no spirit can be unconscious for eight hours out of every twenty-four...!'

Slowly the sea of dreamless sleep, so-called, flowed in upon him, down, round, and over; it submerged the senses one by one, beginning with hearing and ending with sight. But, as each physical sense was closed, its spiritual counterpart—the power that exists apart from its limited organ—opened into clear, divine activity, free as life itself....

How ceaseless was this movement of Dreams, never still, always changing and on the dance, incessantly renewing itself in kaleidoscopic patterns. There was perpetual metamorphosis and rich transformation; many became one, one many; the universe was a single thing, charged with stimulating emotional shocks as each scrap of interpretation passed in and across the mind....

He was falling into deeper and deeper sleep, into that eternal region where he no longer thought, but knew... Immense processions of shifting imagery absorbed him into themselves, spontaneous, unfamiliar, self-multiplying, and as exquisitely baffling as God and all His angels....

The subsidence of the external world seemed suddenly complete.

So deeply was he sunk that he reached that common pool of fluid essence upon which all minds draw according to their needs and powers. Relations were established, wires everywhere connected. The central switchboard clicked all round him; brains linked with brains, asleep or not asleep. He was so deep within himself that, as the children and the Story phrased it, he was 'out.' The air grew light and radiant.

'Hooray! I'm out!' and he instantly thought of his cousin.

'So am I!' That wumbled author shot immediately into connection with him. 'And so is Mother—for the first time. Come on: we'll all go together.'

It was unnecessary to specify where, for that same second they found themselves in the room of Mlle. Lemaire. At this hour of the night it was usually dark, except for the glimmer of the low-turned lamp the sufferer never quite extinguished.

From dusk till dawn her windows in La Citadelle shone faintly for all to see who chanced to pass along the village street. 'There she lies, poor aching soul, as she has lain for twenty years, thinking good of some one, or maybe praying!' For the glimmer was visible from very far, and familiar as a lighthouse to wandering ships at sea. But, had they known her inner happiness, they would not have said 'poor soul!' They would have marvelled. In a Catholic canton, perhaps, they would have crossed themselves and prayed. Just now they certainly would have known a singular, exalted joy. Caught in fairyland, they would have wondered and felt happy.

For the room was crowded to the doors. Walls, windows, ceiling, had melted into transparency to let in the light of stars; and, caught like gold-fish in the great network of the rays, shone familiar outlines everywhere— Jimbo, Monkey, Jinny, the Sweep, the Tramp, the Gypsy, the Laugher up against the cupboard, the Gardener by the window where the flower-pots stood, the Woman of the Haystack in the corridor, too extensive to slip across the threshold, and, in the middle of the room, motionless with pleasure-Mother!

'Like gorgeous southern butterflies in a net, I do declare!' gasped Daddy, as he swept in silently with his companion, their colours mingling harmoniously at once with the rest.

And Mother turned.

'You're out, old girl, at last!' he cried.

'God bless my soul, I am!' she answered. Their sentences came both together, and their blues and yellows swam into each other and made a lovely green. 'It's what I've been trying to do all these years without knowing it. What a glory! I understand now—understand myself and you. I see life clearly as a whole. Hooray, hooray!' She glided nearer to him, her face was beaming.

'Mother's going to explode,' said Monkey in a whisper. But, of course, everybody 'heard' it; for the faintest whisper of thought sent a ripple through that sea of delicate colour. The Laugher bent behind the cupboard to hide her face, and the Gardener by the window stooped to examine his flower-pots. The Woman of the Haystack drew back a little into the corridor again, preparatory to another effort to squeeze through. But Mother, regardless of them all, swam on towards her husband, wrapped in joy and light as in a garment. Hitherto, in her body, the nearest she had come to coruscating was once when she had taken a course of sulphur baths. This was a very different matter. She fairly glittered.

'We'll never go apart again,' Daddy was telling her. 'This inner sympathy will last, you know. *He* did it. It's him we have to thank,' and he pointed at his cousin. 'It's starlight, of course, he has brought down into us.'

But Rogers missed the compliment, being busy in a corner with Monkey and Jimbo, playing at mixing colours with startling results. Mother swam across to her old friend, Mlle. Lemaire. For a quarter of a century these two had understood one another, though never consciously been 'out' together. She moved like a frigate still, gliding and stately, but a frigate that has snapped its hawsers and meant to sail the skies.

'Our poor, stupid, sleeping old bodies,' she smiled.

But the radiant form of the other turned to her motionless cage upon the bed behind her. 'Don't despise them,' she replied, looking down upon the worn-out prison-house, while a little dazzle of brilliance flashed through her atmosphere. 'They are our means of spreading this starlight about the world and giving it to others. Our brains transmit it cunningly; it flashes from our eyes, and the touch of our fingers passes it on. We gather it here, when we are "out," but we can communicate it best to others when we are "in."'

There was sound of confusion and uproar in the room behind as some one came tumbling in with a rush, scattering the figures in all directions as when a gust of wind descends upon a bed of flowers.

'In at last!' cried a muffled voice that sounded as though a tarpaulin smothered it, and the Woman of the Haystack swept into the room with a kind of clumsy majesty. The Tramp and Gypsy, whose efforts had at length dislodged her awkward bulk, came rolling after. They had been pushing steadily from behind all this time, though no one had noticed them slip out.

'*We* can do more than the smaller folk,' she said proudly, sailing up to Mother. 'We can't be overlooked, for one thing'; and arm-in-arm, like a pair of frigates then, they sailed about the room, magnificent as whales that swim in a phosphorescent sea. The Laugher straightened up to watch them, the Gardener turned his head, and Rogers and the children paused a moment in their artificial mixing, to stare with wonder.

'I'm in!' said the Woman.

'I'm out!' said Mother.

And the children felt a trifle envious. Instantly their brilliance dimmed a little. The entire room was aware of it.

'Think always of the world in gold and silver,' shot from Mlle. Lemaire. The dimness passed as she said it.

'It was my doing,' laughed Monkey, turning round to acknowledge her wickedness lest some one else should do it for her and thus increase her shame.

'Sweep! Sweep!' cried Rogers.

But this thought-created sprite was there before the message flashed. With his sack wide open, he stood by Monkey, full of importance. A moment he examined her. Then, his long black fingers darting like a shuttle, he discovered the false colouring that envy had caused, picked it neatly out—a thread of dirty grey—and, winding it into a tiny ball, tossed it with contempt into his sack.

'Over the edge of the world you go,
With the mud and the leaves and the dirty snow!'

he sang, skipping off towards the door. The child's star-body glowed and shone again, pulsing all over with a shimmering, dancing light that was like moonshine upon running water.

'Isn't it time to start now?' inquired Jinny; and as she said it all turned instinctively towards the corner of the room where they were assembled.

They gathered round Mlle. Lemaire. It was quite clear who was leader now. The crystal brilliance of her whiteness shone like a little oval sun. So sparkling was her atmosphere, that its purity scarcely knew a hint of colour even. Her stream of thought seemed undiluted, emitting rays in all directions till it resembled a wheel of sheer white fire. The others fluttered round her as lustrous moths about an electric light.

'Start where?' asked Mother, new to this great adventure.

Her old friend looked at her, so that she caught a darting ray full in the face, and instantly understood.

'First to the Cave to load up,' flashed the answer; 'and then over the sleeping world to mix the light with everybody's dreams. Then back again before the morning spiders are abroad with the interfering sun.'

She floated out into the corridor, and all the others fell into line as she went. The draught of her going drew Mother into place immediately behind her. Daddy followed close, their respective colours making it inevitable, and Jinny swept in after him, bright and eager as a little angel. She tripped on the edge of something he held tightly in one hand, a woven maze of tiny glittering lines, exquisitely inter-threaded—a skeleton of beauty, waiting to be filled in and clothed, yet already alive with spontaneous fire of its own. It was the Pattern of his story he had been busy with in the corner.

'I won't step on it, Daddy,' she said gravely.

'It doesn't matter if you do. You're in it,' he answered, yet lifted it higher so that it flew behind him like a banner in the night.

The procession was formed now. Rogers and the younger children came after their sister at a little distance, and then, flitting to and fro in darker shades, like a fringe of rich embroidery that framed the moving picture, came the figures of the sprites, born by Imagination out of Love in an old Kentish garden years and years ago. They rose from the tangle of the ancient building. Climbing the shoulder of a big, blue wind, they were off and away!

It was a jolly night, a windy night, a night without clouds, when all the lanes of the sky were smooth and swept, and the interstellar spaces seemed close down upon the earth.

'Kind thoughts, like fine weather,
 Link sweetly together God's stars
 With the heart of a boy,'

sang Rogers, following swiftly with Jimbo and his sister. For all moved along as easily as light across the surfaces of polished glass. And the sound of Rogers's voice seemed to bring singing from every side, as the gay procession swept onwards. Every one contributed lines of their own, it seemed, though there was a tiny little distant voice, soft and silvery, that intruded from time to time and made all wonder where it came from. No one could see the singer. At first very far away, it came nearer and nearer.

DADDY. 'The Interfering Sun has set!
GARDENER. Now Sirius flings down the Net!
LAMPLIGHTER. See, the meshes flash and quiver,
        As the golden, silent river

SWEEP. Clears the dark world's troubled dream.
DUSTMAN. Takes it sleeping,
        Gilds its weeping
      With a star's mysterious beam.
Tiny, distant Voice. Oh, think Beauty!
        It's your duty!
      In the Cave you work for others,
      All the stars are little brothers;

ROGERS. Think their splendour,

        Strong and tender;
DADDY. Think their glory
        In the Story
MOTHER. Of each day your nights redeem?
Voice (nearer). Every loving, gentle thought
        Of this fairy brilliance wrought,
JANE ANNE. Every wish that you surrender,
MONKEY. Every little impulse tender,
JIMBO. Every service that you render
TANTE ANNA. Brings its tributary stream!
TRAMP AND GYFSY. In the fretwork
        Of the network
      Hearts lie patterned and a-gleam!

WOMAN OF THE Think with passion
   HAYSTACK. That shall fashion
        Life's entire design well-planned;
Voice (still nearer). While the busy Pleiades,
ROGERS. Sisters to the Hyades,
Voice (quite close). Seven by seven,
        Across the heaven,
ROGERS. Light desire
        With their fire!
Voice (in his ear). Working cunningly together in a soft and

tireless band,
Sweetly linking
All our thinking,
In the Net of Sympathy that brings back
Fairyland!'

Mother kept close to her husband; she felt a little bewildered, and uncertain in her movements; it was her first conscious experience of being out. She wanted to go in every direction at once; for she knew everybody in the village, knew all their troubles and perplexities, and felt the call from every house.

'Steady,' he told her; 'one thing at a time, you know.' Her thoughts, he saw, had turned across the sea to Ireland where her strongest ties were. Ireland seemed close, and quite as accessible as the village. Her friend of the Haystack, on the other hand, seemed a long way off by comparison.

'That's because Henry never realised her personality very clearly,' said Daddy, seeing by her colour that she needed explanation. 'When creating all these Garden Sprites, he didn't *think* her sharply, vividly enough to make her effective. He just felt that a haystack suggested the elderly spread of a bulky and untidy old woman whose frame had settled beneath too many clothes, till she had collapsed into a field and stuck there. But he left her where he found her. He assigned no duties to her. She's only half alive. As a rule, she merely sits—just "stays put"—until some one moves her.'

Mother turned and saw her far in the rear, settling down comfortably upon a flat roof near the church. She rather envied her amiable disposition. It seemed so safe. Every one else was alive with such dangerous activity.

'Are we going *much* further—?' she began, when Monkey rushed by, caught up the sentence, and discharged herself with impudence into Daddy.

'Which is right, "further" or "farther"?' she asked with a flash of light.

'Further, of course,' said unsuspecting Mother.

'But "further" sounds "farther,"' she cried, with a burst of laughter that died away with her passage of meteoric brilliance—into the body of the woods beyond.

'But the other Sprites, you see, are real and active,' continued Daddy, ignoring the interruption as though accustomed to it, because he thought out clearly every detail. 'They're alive enough to haunt a house or garden till sensitive people become aware of them and declare they've seen a ghost.'

'And *we*?' she asked. 'Who thought us out so wonderfully?'

'That's more than I can tell,' he answered after a little pause. 'God knows that, for He thought out the entire universe to which we belong. I only know that we're real, and all part of the same huge, single thing.' He shone with increased brightness as he said it. 'There's no question about *our* personalities and duties and the rest. Don't you feel it too?'

He looked at her as he spoke. Her outline had grown more definite. As she began to understand, and her bewilderment lessened, he noted that her flashing lines burned more steadily, falling into a more regular, harmonious pattern. They combined, moreover, with his own, and with the starlight too, in some exquisite fashion he could not describe. She put a hand out, catching at the flying banner of his Story that he trailed behind him in the air. They formed a single design, all three. His happiness became enormous.

'I feel joined on to everything,' she replied, half singing it in her joy. 'I feel tucked into the universe everywhere, and into you, dear. These rays of starlight have sewn us together.' She began to tremble, but it was the trembling of pure joy and not of alarm....

'Yes,' he said, 'I'm learning it too. The moment thought gets away from self it lets in starlight and makes room for happiness. To think with sympathy of others is to grow: you take in their experience and add it to your own— development; the heart gets soft and deep and wide till you feel the entire universe buttoning its jacket round you. To think of self means friction and hence reduction.'

'And your Story,' she added, glancing up proudly at the banner that they trailed. 'I have helped a little, haven't I?'

'It's nearly finished,' he flashed back; 'you've been its inspiration and its climax. All these years, when we thought ourselves apart, you've been helping really underground—that's true collaboration.'

'Our little separation was but a *reculer pour mieux sauter*. See how we've rushed together again!'

A strange soft singing, like the wind in firs, or like shallow water flowing over pebbles, interrupted them. The sweetness of it turned the night alive.

'Come on, old Mother. Our Leader is calling to us. We must work.'

They slid from the blue wind into a current of paler air that happened to slip swiftly past them, and went towards the forest where Mlle. Lemaire waited for them. Mother waved her hand to her friend, settled comfortably upon the flat roof in the village in their rear. 'We'll come back to lean upon you when we're tired,' she signalled. But she felt no envy now. In future she would certainly never 'stay put.' Work beckoned to her—and such endless, glorious work: the whole Universe.

'What life! What a rush of splendour!' she exclaimed as they reached the great woods and heard them shouting below in the winds. 'I see now why the forest always comforted me. There's strength here I can take back into my body with me when I go.'

'The trees, yes, express visibly only a portion of their life,' he told her. 'There is an overflow we can appropriate.'

Yet their conversation was never audibly uttered. It flashed instantaneously from one to the other. All they had exchanged since leaving La Citadelle had taken place at once, it seemed. They were awake in the region of naked thought and feeling. The dictum of the materialists that thought and feeling cannot exist apart from matter did not trouble them. Matter, they saw, was everywhere, though too tenuous for any measuring instrument man's brain had yet invented.

'Come on!' he repeated; 'the Starlight Express is waiting. It will take you anywhere you please—Ireland if you like!'

They found the others waiting on the smooth layer of soft purple air that spread just below the level of the tree-tops. The crests themselves tossed wildly in the wind, but at a depth of a few feet there was peace and stillness, and upon this platform the band was grouped. 'The stars are caught in the branches to-night,' a sensitive walker on the ground might have exclaimed. The spires rose about them like little garden trees of a few years' growth, and between them ran lanes and intricate, winding thoroughfares Mother saw long, dark things like thick bodies of snakes converging down these passage-ways, filling them, all running towards the centre where the group had established itself. There were lines of dotted lights along them. They did not move with the waving of the tree-tops. They looked uncommonly familiar.

'The trains,' Jimbo was crying. He darted to and fro, superintending the embarking of the passengers.

All the sidings of the sky were full of Starlight Expresses.

The loading-up was so quickly accomplished that Mother hardly realised what was happening. Everybody carried sacks overflowing with dripping gold and bursting at the seams. As each train filled, it shot away across the starry heavens; for everyone had been to the Cave and gathered their material even before she reached the scene of action. And with every train went a *mecanicien* and a *conducteur* created by Jimbo's vivid and believing thought; a Sweep, a Lamplighter, and a Head Gardener went, too, for the children's thinking multiplied these, too, according to their needs. They realised the meaning of these Sprites so clearly now—their duties, appearance, laws of behaviour, and the rest-that their awakened imaginations thought them instantly into existence, as many as were necessary. Train after train, each with its full complement of passengers, flashed forth across that summer sky, till the people in the Observatories must have thought they had miscalculated strangely and the Earth was passing amid the showering Leonids before her appointed time.

'Where would you like to go first?' Mother heard her friend ask softly. 'It's not possible to follow all the trains at once, you know.'

'So I see,' she gasped. 'I'll just sit still a moment, and think.'

The size and freedom of existence, as she now saw it, suddenly overwhelmed her. Accustomed too long to narrow channels, she found space without railings and notice-boards bewildering. She had never dreamed before that thinking can open the gates to heaven and bring the Milky Way down into the heart. She had merely knitted stockings. She had been practical. At last the key to her husband's being was in her hand. That key at the same time opened a door through him, into her own. Hitherto she had merely criticised. Oh dear! Criticism, when she might have created!

She turned to seek him. But only her old friend was there, floating beside her in a brilliant mist of gold and white that turned the tree- tops into rows of Burning Bushes.

'Where is he?' she asked quickly.

'Hush!' was the instant reply; 'don't disturb him. Don't think, or you'll bring him back. He's filling his sack in the Star Cave. Men have to gather it,—the little store they possess is soon crystallised into hardness by Reason,—but women have enough in themselves usually to last a lifetime. They are born with it.'

'Mine crystallised long ago, I fear.'

'Care and anxiety did that. You neglected it a little. But your husband's cousin has cleaned the channels out. He does it unconsciously, but he does it. He has belief and vision like a child, and therefore turns instinctively to children because they keep it alive in him, though he hardly knows why he seeks them. The world, too, is a great big child that is crying for its Fairyland....'

'But the practical—' objected Mother, true to her type of mind-an echo rather than an effort.

'—is important, yes, only it has been exaggerated out of all sane proportion in most people's lives. So little is needed, though that little of fine quality, and ever fed by starlight. Obeyed exclusively, it destroys life. It bricks you up alive. But now tell me,' she added, 'where would you like to go first?

Whom will you help? There is time enough to cover .the world if you want to, before the interfering sun gets up.'

'*You*!' cried Mother, impulsively, then realised instantly that her friend was already developed far beyond any help that she could give. It was the light streaming from the older, suffering woman that was stimulating her own sympathies so vehemently. For years the process had gone on. It was at last effective.

'There are others, perhaps, who need it more than I,' flashed forth a lovely ray.

'But I would repay,' Mother cried eagerly, 'I would repay.' Gratitude for life rushed through her, and her friend must share it.

'Pass it on to others,' was the shining answer. 'That's the best repayment after all.' The stars themselves turned brighter as the thought flashed from her.

Then Ireland vanished utterly, for it had been mixed, Mother now perceived, with personal longings that were at bottom selfish. There were indeed many there, in the scenes of her home and childhood, whose lives she might ease and glorify by letting in the starlight while they slept; but her motive, she discerned, was not wholly pure. There was a trace in it, almost a little stain, of personal gratification— she could not analyse it quite—that dimmed the picture in her thought. The brilliance of her companion made it stand out clearly. Nearer home was a less heroic object, a more difficult case, some one less likely to reward her efforts with results. And she turned instead to this.

'You're right,' smiled the other, following her thought; 'and you couldn't begin with a better bit of work than that. Your old mother has cut herself off so long from giving sympathy to her kind that now she cannot accept it from others without feeling suspicion and distrust. Ease and soften her outlook if you can. Pour through her gloom the sympathy of stars. And remember,' she added, as Mother rose softly out of the trees and hovered a moment overhead, 'that if you need the Sweep or the Lamplighter, or the Gardener to burn away her dead leaves, you have only to summon them. Think hard, and they'll be instantly beside you.'

Upon an eddy of glowing wind Mother drifted across the fields to the corner of the village where her mother occupied a large single room in solitude upon the top floor, a solitude self-imposed and rigorously enforced.

'Use the finest quality,' she heard her friend thinking far behind her, 'for you have plenty of it. The Dustman gave it to you when you were not looking, gathered from the entire Zodiac... and from the careless meteor's track....'

The words died off into the forest.

That he keeps only
For the old and lonely,
(And is very strict about it)
Who sleep so little that they need the best—'

The words came floating behind her. She felt herself brimful—charged with loving sympathy of the sweetest and most understanding quality. She looked down a moment upon her mother's roof. Then she descended.

CHAPTER XXV

And also there's a little star—
  So white, a virgin's it must be;—
  Perhaps the lamp my love in heaven
  Hangs out to light the way for me.
    Song, THEOPHILE MARZIALS.

In this corner of Bourcelles the houses lie huddled together with an air of something shamefaced; they dare not look straight at the mountains or at the lake; they turn their eyes away even from the orchards at the back. They wear a mysterious and secret look, and their shoulders have a sly turn, as though they hid their heads in the daytime and stirred about their business only after dark.

They lie grouped about a cobbled courtyard that has no fountain in it. The fair white road goes quickly by outside, afraid to look in frankly; and the entrance to the yard is narrow. Nor does a single tree grow in it. If Bourcelles could have a slum, this would be it.

Why the old lady had left her cosy quarters in Les Glycines and settled down in this unpleasant corner of the village was a puzzle to everybody. With a shrug of the shoulders the problem was generally left unsolved. Madame Jequier discussed it volubly a year ago when the move took place, then dismissed it as one of those mysteries of old people no one can understand. To the son-in-law and the daughter, who got nearer the truth, it was a source of pain and sadness beyond their means of relief. Mrs. 'Plume'—it was a play in French upon her real name,—had been four years in the Pension, induced to come from a lonely existence in Ireland by her daughter and throw in her lot with the family, and at first had settled down comfortably enough. She was over seventy, and possessed 80 pounds a year—a dainty, witty, amusing Irish lady, with twinkling eyes and a pernicketty strong will, and a brogue she transferred deliciously into her broken French. She loved the children, yet did not win their love in return, because they stood in awe of her sarcastic criticisms. Life had gone hardly with her; she had lost her fortune and her children, all but this daughter, with whose marriage she was keenly disappointed. An aristocrat to the finger-tips, she could not accept the change of circumstances; distress had soured her; the transplanting hastened her decline; there was no sweetness left in her. She turned her heart steadily against the world.

The ostensible cause of this hiding herself away with her sorrow and disappointment was the presence of Miss Waghorn, with whom she disagreed, and even quarrelled, from morning till night. They formed a storm-centre that moved from salon to dining-room, and they squabbled acutely about everything—the weather, the heating, the opening or shutting of windows, the details of the food, the arrangement of the furniture, even the character of the cat. Miss Waghorn loved. The bickerings were incessant. They only had to meet for hot disagreement to break out. Mrs. Plume, already bent with age, would strike the floor with the ebony stick she always carried, and glare at the erect, defiant spinster—'That horrud, dirrty cat; its always in the room!' Then Miss Waghorn: 'It's a very nice cat, Madame'—she always called her Madame—'and when *I* was a young girl I was taught to be kind to animals.'—'The drawing-room is *not* the place for animals,' came the pricking answer. And then the scuffle began in earnest.

Miss Waghorn, owing to her want of memory, forgot the squabble five minutes afterwards, and even forgot that she knew her antagonist at all. She would ask to be introduced, or even come up sweetly and introduce herself within half an hour of the battle. But Madame Plume forgot nothing; her memory was keen and accurate. She did not believe in the other's failing. 'That common old woman!' she exclaimed with angry scorn to her daughter.

'It's deliberate offensiveness, that's all it is at all!' And she left the Pension.

But her attitude to the harmless old Quaker lady was really in small her attitude to humanity at large. She drew away in disgust from a world that had treated her so badly. Into herself she drew, growing smaller every day, more sour, more suspicious, and more averse to her own kind. Within the restricted orbit of her own bitter thoughts she revolved towards the vanishing point of life which is the total loss of sympathy. She felt *with* no one but herself. She belonged to that, alas, numerous type which, with large expectations unrealised, cannot accept disillusionment with the gentle laughter it deserves. She resented the universe. Sympathy was dead.

And she had chosen this unsavoury corner to dwell in because 'the poor' of the village lived there, and she wished to count herself among them. It emphasised the spite, the grudge, she felt against humanity. At first she came into *dejeuner* and *souper*, but afterwards her meals were sent over twice a day from the Pension. She discovered so many reasons for not making the little journey of a hundred yards. On Sunday the 'common people' were in the streets; on Saturday it was cleaning-day and the Pension smelt of turpentine; Monday was for letter-writing, and other days were too hot or too cold, too windy or too wet. In the end she accomplished her heart's desire. Madame Cornu, who kept the grocer's shop, and lived on the floor below with her husband, prepared the two principal meals and brought them up to her on a tray. She ate them alone. Her breakfast cup of tea she made herself, Mme. Cornu putting the jug of milk outside the door. She nursed her bitter grievance against life in utter solitude. Acidity ate its ugly pattern into her heart.

The children, as in duty bound, made dolorous pilgrimages to that upper floor from time to time, returning frightened, and Mother went regularly twice a week, coming home saddened and distressed. Her husband rarely went at all now, since the time when she told him to his face he came to taunt her. She spent her time, heaven only knows how, for she never left the building. According to Mother she was exceedingly busy doing nothing. She packed, unpacked, and then repacked all her few belongings. In summer she chased bees in her room with a wet towel; but with venom, not with humour. The Morning Post came daily from London. 'I read my paper, write a letter, and the morning's gone,' she told her daughter, by way of complaint that time was so scanty. Mme. Cornu often heard her walking up and down the floor, tapping her ebony stick and talking softly to herself. Yet she was as sane as any old body living in solitude with evil thinking well can be. She starved-because she neither gave nor *asked*.

As Mother thought of her, thus finding the way in instantly, the church clock sounded midnight. She entered a room that was black as coal and unsweetened as an airless cellar. The fair rays that had been pouring out of her returned with a little shock upon themselves— repulsed. She felt herself reduced, and the sensation was so unpleasant at first that she almost gasped. It was like suffocation. She felt enclosed with Death. That her own radiance dimmed a moment was undeniable, but it was for a moment only, for, thinking instantly of her friend, she drew upon that woman's inexhaustible abundance, and found her own stores replenished.

Slowly, as a wintry sun pierces the mist in some damp hollow of the woods, her supply of starlight lit up little pathways all about her, and she saw the familiar figure standing by the window. The figure was also black; it stood like an ebony statue in an atmosphere that was thick with gloom, turgid, sinister, and wholly rayless. It was like a lantern in a London fog. A few dim lines of sombre grey issued heavily from it, but got no farther than its outer surface, then doubled back and plunged in again. They coiled and twisted into ugly knots. Her mother's atmosphere was opaque, and as dismal as a November fog. There was a speck of light in the room, however, and it came, the visitor then perceived, from a single candle that stood beside the bed. The old lady had been reading; she rarely slept before two o'clock in the morning.

And at first, so disheartening, so hopeless seemed the task, that Mother wavered in her mission; a choking, suffocating sensation blocked all her channels of delivery. The very flowers on the window- sill, she noted, drooped in a languishing decline; they had a lifeless air as of flowers that struggle for existence in deep shadow and have never known the kiss of sunshine. Through the inch of opened window stole a soft breath of the night air, but it turned black and sluggish the moment it came in. And just then, as Mother hovered there in hesitating doubt, the figure turned and moved across to the bed, supporting herself with the ebony cane she always used. Stiffly she sank upon her knees. The habit was as strong as putting her shoes outside the door at night to be cleaned,-those shoes that never knew the stain of roadway dust-and equally devoid of spiritual significance. Yet, for a moment, as the embittered mind gabbled through the string of words that long habit had crystallised into an empty formula, Mother noticed that the lines of grey grew slightly clearer; the coil and tangle ceased; they even made an effort to emerge and leave the muddy cloud that obscured their knotted, intricate disorder.

The formula Mother recognised; it had hardly changed, indeed, since she herself had learned it at those very knees when days were brighter; it began with wholesale and audacious requests for self, then towards the end passed into vague generalities for the welfare of others. And just here it was that the lines of grey turned brighter and tried to struggle out of the murky atmosphere. The sight was pathetic, yet deeply significant. Mother understood its meaning. There was hope. Behind the prayer for others still shone at least an echo of past meaning.

'I believe in you, old, broken, disappointed heart,' flashed through her own bright atmosphere, 'and, believing, I can help you!'

Her skill, however, was slight, owing to lack of practice and experience. She moved over to the bed, trying first to force her own darting rays into the opaque, dull cloud surrounding the other; then seeking a better way-for this had no results—-she slipped somehow inside the mist, getting behind it, down at the very source. From here she forced her own light through, mixing her beams of coloured radiance with the thick grey lines themselves. She tried to feel and think as her mother felt and thought, moving beside her mind's initial working, changing the gloom into something brighter as she moved along. This was the proper way, she felt-to clean the source itself, rather than merely untie knots at the outer surface. It was a stifling business, but she persisted. Tiny channels cleared and opened. A little light shone through. She felt-with her mother, instead of arguing, as it were…

The old lady presently blew the candle out and composed herself to sleep. Mother laboured on….

'Oh dear,' she sighed, 'oh dear!' as she emerged from the gloom a moment to survey her patient and note results. To her amazement she saw that there was a change indeed, though a very curious one. The entire outer surface of the cloud seemed in commotion, with here and there a glimmering lustre as if a tiny lamp was at last alight within. She felt herself swell with happiness. Instantly, then, the grey lines shot out, fastening with wee loops and curves among her own. Some links evidently had been established. She had imparted something.

'She's dreaming! I do believe I've sown some dream of beauty in her!' she beamed to herself.

Some golden, unaccustomed sleep had fallen over the old lady. Stray shreds of darkness loosened from the general mass and floated off, yet did not melt entirely from sight. She was shedding some of her evil thoughts.

'The Sweep!' thought Mother, and turning, found him beside her in the room. Her husband, to her astonishment, was also there.

'But I didn't think of *you*!' she exclaimed.

'Not a definite thought,' he answered, 'but you needed me. I felt it. We're so close together now that we're practically one, you see.' He trailed his Pattern behind him, clothed now with all manner of rich new colouring, 'I've collected such heaps of new ideas,' he went on, 'and now I want her too. She's in the Story. I'll transfigure her as well.' He was bright as paint, and happy as a sand-boy. 'Well done, old Mother,' he added, 'you've done a lot already. See, she's dreaming small, soft, tender things of beauty that your efforts have let through.'

He glided across and poured from his own store of sympathy into that dry, atrophied soul upon the bed. 'It's a question how much she will be able to transmit, though,' he said doubtfully. 'The spiritual machinery is so stiff and out of gear from long disuse. In Miss Waghorn's case it's only physical— I've just been there—but this is spiritual blackness. We shall see to-morrow. Something will get through at any rate, and we must do this every night, you know.'

'Rather!' echoed Mother.

'Her actual self, you see, has dwindled so that one can hardly find it. It's smaller than a flea, and as hard and black.' They smiled a little sadly.

The Sweep, rushing out of the window with his heavy sack loaded to the brim, interrupted their low laughter. He was no talker, but a man of action. Busily all this time he had been gathering up the loose, stray fragments that floated off from the cloud, and stuffing them into the sack. He now flew, singing, into the night, and they barely caught the last words of his eternal song:—

'... a tremendously busy Sweep, Tossing the blacks in the Rubbish Heap Over the edge of the world.'

'Come,' whispered Daddy. 'It's getting late. The interfering sun is on the way, and you've been hours here already. All the trains are back, and every one is waiting for us.' Yet it had seemed so short a time really.

Wrapped together in the beauty of his Pattern, they left the old lady peacefully asleep, and sped across the roofs towards the forest.

But neither of them noticed, it seemed, the lovely little shining figure that hovered far in the air above and watched them go. It followed them all the way, catching even at the skirts of the flying Pattern as they went. Was it the Spirit of some unknown Star they had attracted from beyond the Milky Way? Or was it, perhaps, a Thought from some fair, exquisite heart that had been wakened by the rushing of the Expresses, and had flashed in to take a place in the wonderful story Daddy wove?

It had little twinkling feet, and its eyes were of brown flame and amber.

'No, they did not notice the starry, fluttering figure. It overtook them none the less, and with a flying leap was into the Pattern of his story—in the very centre, too!—as quickly as lightning passes through the foliage of the tree it strikes. Only the lightning stayed. The figure remained caught. The entire Pattern shivered to its outer fringes, then began to glow and shine all over. As the high harmonic crowns the end of a long cadenza on a violin, fulfilling bars of difficult effort, this point of exquisite beauty flashed life into the Pattern of the story, consummating the labour of construction with the true, inevitable climax. There was something of fairy insolence, both cheeky and delicious, in the proprietary way it chose the principal place, yet the only place still unoccupied, and sang 'I'm here. I've come!' It calmly fashioned itself a nest, as it were, curled up and made itself at home. It *was* at home. The audacity was justified. The Pattern seemed at last complete. Beauty and Truth shone at its centre. And the tiny voice continued singing, though no one seemed to know exactly whence the sound proceeded:—

'While the busy Pleiades,
Sisters to the Hyades,
Seven by seven,
Across the heaven,
Light desire
With their fire,

Flung from huge Orion's hand,
Sweetly linking
All our thinking
In the Net of Sympathy that brings back Fairyland!'

No—neither Mother nor Daddy were aware of what had happened thus in the twinkling of an eye. Certainly neither guessed that another heart, far distant as the crow flies, had felt the stream of his vital, creative thinking, and had thus delicately responded and sent out a sympathetic message of belief. But neither did Adams and Leverrier, measuring the heavens, and calculating through years of labour the delicate interstellar forces, know that each had simultaneously caught Neptune in their net of stars—three thousand million miles away. Had they been 'out,' these two big, patient astronomers, they might have realised that they really worked in concert every night. But history does not relate that they slept well or ill; their biographies make no mention of what their 'Underneaths' were up to while their brains lay resting on the pillow; and private confession, if such exists, has never seen the light of print as yet. In that region, however, where Thinking runs and plays, thought dancing hand in hand with thought that is akin to it, the fact must surely have been known and recognised. They, too, travelled in the Starlight Express.

Mother and Daddy realised it just then as little as children are aware of the loving thoughts of the parent that hovers protectingly about them all day long. They merely acknowledged that a prodigious thrill of happiness pulsed through both of them at once, feeling proud as the group in the tree-tops praised their increased brightness and admired the marvellous shining of the completed Pattern they trailed above their heads. But more than that they did not grasp. Nor have they ever grasped it perhaps. That the result came through later is proved, however, by the published story, and by the strange, sweet beauty its readers felt all over the world. But this belongs to the private working of inspiration which can never be explained, not even by the artist it has set on fire. He, indeed, probably understands it least of all.

'Where are the trains, the Starlight Expresses?' asked Mother.

'Gone!' answered Jimbo. 'Gone to Australia where they're wanted. It's evening now down there.'

He pointed down, then up. 'Don't you see? We must hurry.' She looked across the lake where the monstrous wall of Alps was dimly visible. The sky was brightening behind them. Long strata of thin cloud glimmered with faintest pink. The stars were rapidly fading. 'What ages you've been!' he added.

'And where's Tante Anna?' she inquired quickly, looking for her brilliant friend.

'She's come and gone a dozen times while you've been skylarking somewhere else,' explained Monkey with her usual exaggeration. 'She's gone for good now. She sleeps so badly. She's always waking up, you know.' Mother understood. Only too well she knew that her friend snatched sleep in briefest intervals, incessantly disturbed by racking pain.

A stream of light flashed past her, dashing like a meteor towards the village and disappearing before she could see the figure.

'There goes Jinny,' cried some one, 'always working to the very last. The interfering sun'll catch her if she doesn't look out!'

There was movement and hurry everywhere. Already the world ran loose and soft in colour. Birds, just awake, were singing in the trees below. Several passed swiftly overhead, raking the sky with a whirring rush of wings. Everybody was asking questions, urging return, yet lingering as long as possible, each according to his courage. To be caught 'out' by the sun meant waking with a sudden start that made getting out of bed very difficult and might even cause a headache.

Rogers alone seemed unperturbed, unhurried, for he was absorbed in a discovery that made him tremble. Noting the sudden perfection of his cousin's Pattern, he had gone closer to examine it, and had—seen the starry figure. Instantly he forgot everything else in the world. It seemed to him that he had suddenly found all he had ever sought. He gazed into those gentle eyes of amber and felt that he gazed into the eyes of the Universe that had taken shape in front of him. Floating up as near as he could, he spoke—

'Where do you come from—from what star?' he asked softly in an ecstasy of wonder.

The tiny face looked straight at him and smiled.

'From the Pleiades, of course,—that little group of star-babies as yet unborn.'

'I've been looking for you for ever,' he answered.

'You've found me,' sang the tiny voice. 'This is our introduction. Now, don't forget. There was a lost Pleiad, you know. Try to remember me when you wake.'

'Then why are you here?' He meant in the Pattern.

The star-face rippled with laughter.

'It's yours—your Scheme. He's given it perfect shape for you, that's all. Don't you recognise it? But it's my Story as well. ...'

A ray with crimson in it shot out just then across the shoulder of the Blumlisalp, and, falling full upon the tiny face, it faded out; the Pattern faded with it; Daddy vanished too. On the little azure winds of dawn they flashed away. Jimbo, Monkey, and certain of the Sprites alone held on, but the tree-tops to which they clung were growing more and more slippery every minute. Mother, loth to return, balanced bravely on the waving spires of a larch. Her sleep that night had been so deep and splendid, she struggled to prolong it. She hated waking up too early.

'The Morning Spiders! Look out!' cried a Sprite, as a tiny spider on its thread of gossamer floated by. It was the Dustman's voice. Catching the Gypsy with one arm and the Tramp with the other, all three instantly disappeared.

'But where's my Haystack friend?' called Mother faintly, almost losing her balance in the attempt to turn round quickly.

'Oh, she's all right,' the Head Gardener answered from a little distance where he was burning something. 'She just "stays put" and flirts with every wind that comes near her. She loves the winds. They know her little ways.' He went on busily burning up dead leaves he had been collecting all night long—dead, useless thoughts he had found clogging a hundred hearts and stopping outlets.

'Look sharp!' cried a voice that fell from the sky above them.

'Here come the Morning Spiders,
  On their gossamer outriders!'

This time it was the Lamplighter flashing to and fro as he put the stars out one by one. He was in a frantic hurry; he extinguished whole groups of them at once. The Pleiades were the last to fade.

Rogers heard him and came back into himself. For his ecstasy had carried him even beyond the region of the freest 'thinking.' He could give no account or explanation of it at all. Monkey, Jimbo, Mother, and he raced in a line together for home and safety. Above the fields they met the spiders everywhere, the spiders that bring the dawn and ride off into the Star Cave on lost rays and stray thoughts that careless minds have left scattered about the world.

And the children, as they raced and told their mother to 'please move a little more easily and slipperily,' sang together in chorus:—

'We shall meet the Morning Spiders,
  The fairy-cotton riders,
  Each mounted on a star's rejected ray;
  With their tiny nets of feather

They collect our thoughts together,
And on strips of windy weather
Bring the Day. ...'

'That's stolen from you or Daddy,' Mother began to say to Rogers—but was unable to complete the flash. The thought lay loose behind her in the air.

A spider instantly mounted it and rode it off.

Something brushed her cheek. Riquette stood rover her, fingering her face with a soft extended paw.

'But it surely can't be time yet to get up!' she murmured. 'I've only just fallen asleep, it seems.' She glanced at her watch upon the chair beside the bed, saw that it was only four o'clock, and then turned over, making a space for the cat behind her shoulder. A tremendous host of dreams caught at her sliding mind. She tried to follow them. They vanished. 'Oh dear!' she sighed, and promptly fell asleep again. But this time she slept lightly. No more adventures came. She did not dream. And later, when Riquette woke her a second time because it was half-past six, she remembered as little of having been 'out' as though such a thing had never taken place at all.

She lit the fire and put the porridge saucepan on the stove. It was a glorious July morning. She felt glad to be alive, and full of happy, singing thoughts. 'I wish I could always sleep like that!' she said. 'But what a pity one has to wake up in the end!'

And then, as she turned her mind toward the coming duties of the day, another thought came to her. It was a very ordinary, almost a daily thought, but there seemed more behind it than usual. Her whole heart was in it this time—

'As soon as the children are off to school I'll pop over to mother, and see if I can't cheer her up a bit and make her feel more happy. Oh dear!' she added, 'life is a bag of duties, whichever way one looks at it!' But she felt a great power in her that she could face them easily and turn each one into joy. She could take life more bigly, carelessly, more as a whole somehow. She was aware of some huge directing power in her 'underneath.' Moreover, the 'underneath' of a woman like Mother was not a trifle that could be easily ignored. That great Under Self, resting in the abysses of being, rose and led. The pettier Upper Self withdrew ashamed, passing over the reins of conduct into those mighty, shadowy hands.

CHAPTER XXVI

Canst thou bind the sweet influences of Pleiades,
  Or loose the bands of Orion?
        Book of Job.

The feeling that something was going to happen—that odd sense of anticipation—which all had experienced the evening before at tea-time had entirely vanished, of course, next morning. It was a mood, and it had passed away. Every one had slept it off. They little realised how it had justified itself. Jane Anne, tidying the Den soon after seven o'clock, noticed the slip of paper above the mantelpiece, read it over—'The Starlight Express will start to-night. Be reddy!'—and tore it down. 'How could that. have amused us!' she said aloud, as she tossed it into the waste-paper basket. Yet, even while she did so, some stray sensation of delight clutched at her funny little heart, a touch of emotion she could not understand that was wild and very sweet. She went singing about her work. She felt important and grown- up, extraordinarily light-hearted too. The things she sang made up their own words—such odd snatches that came she knew not whence. An insect clung to her duster, and she shook it out of the window with the crumbs and bits of cotton gathered from the table-cloth.

  'Get out, you Morning Spider,
    You fairy-cotton rider!'

she sang, and at the same minute Mother opened the bedroom door and peeped in, astonished at the unaccustomed music. In her voluminous dressing-gown, her hair caught untidily in a loose net, her face flushed from stooping over the porridge saucepan, she looked, thought Jinny, 'like a haystack somehow.' Of course she did not say it. The draught, flapping at her ample skirts, added the idea of a covering tarpaulin to the child's mental picture. She went on dusting with a half-offended air, as though Mother had no right to interrupt her with a superintending glance like this.

'You won't forget the sweeping too, Jinny?' said Mother, retiring again majestically with that gliding motion her abundant proportions achieved so gracefully.

'Of course I won't, Mother,' and the instant the door was closed she fell into another snatch of song, the words of which flowed unconsciously into her mind, it seemed—

  'For I'm a tremendously busy Sweep,
    Dusting the room while you're all asleep,

And shoving you all in the rubbish heap,
Over the edge of the tiles'

—a little wumbled, it is true, but its source unmistakable.

And all day long, with every one, it was similar, this curious intrusion of the night into the day, the sub-conscious into the conscious—a kind of subtle trespassing. The flower of forgotten dreams rose so softly to the surface of consciousness that they had an air of sneaking in, anxious to be regarded as an integral part of normal waking life. Like bubbles in water they rose, discharged their puff of fragrant air, and disappeared again. Jane Anne, in particular, was simply radiant all day long, and more than usually clear-headed. Once or twice she wumbled, but there was big sense in her even then. It was only the expression that evaded her. Her little brain was a poor transmitter somehow.

'I feel all endowed to-day,' she informed Rogers, when he congratulated her later in the day on some cunning act of attention she bestowed upon him. It was in the courtyard where they all sat sunning themselves after *dejeuner*, and before the younger children returned to afternoon school.

'I feel emaciated, you know,' she added, uncertain whether emancipated was the word she really sought.

'You'll be quite grown-up,' he told her, 'by the time I come back to little Bourcelles in the autumn.' Little Bourcelles! It sounded, the caressing way he said it, as if it lay in the palm of his big brown hand.

'But you'll never come back, because you'll never go,' Monkey chimed in. 'My hair, remember—'

'*My* trains won't take you,' said Jimbo gravely.

'Oh, a train may *take* you,' continued Monkey, 'but you can't leave. Going away by train isn't leaving.'

'It's only like going to sleep,' explained her brother. You'll come back every night in a Starlight Express—'

'Because a Starlight Express takes passengers—whether they like it or not. You take an ordinary train, but a starlight train takes you!' added Monkey.

Mother heard the words and looked up sharply from her knitting. Something, it seemed, had caught her attention vividly, though until now her thoughts had been busy with practical things of quite another order. She glanced keenly round at the faces, where all sat grouped upon the stone steps of La Citadelle. Then she smiled curiously, half to herself. What she said was clearly not what she had first meant to say.

'Children, you're not sitting on the cold stone, are you?' she inquired, but a little absent-mindedly.

'We're quite warm; we've got our thick under-neathies on,' was the reply. They realised that only part of her mind was in the, question, and that any ordinary answer would satisfy her.

Mother resumed her knitting, apparently satisfied.

But Jinny, meanwhile, had been following her own train of thought, started by her cousin's description of her as 'grown-up.' The picture grew big and gracious in her mind.

'I wonder what I shall do when my hair goes up?' she observed, apparently *a propos de bottes*. It was the day, of course, eagerly, almost feverishly, looked forward to.

'Hide your head in a bag probably,' laughed her sister. Jinny flushed; her hair was not abundant. Yet she seemed puzzled rather than offended.

'Never mind,' Rogers soothed her. 'The day a girl puts up her hair, a thousand young men are aware of it,—and one among them trembles.' The idea of romance seemed somehow in the air.

'Oh, Cousinenry!' She was delighted, comforted, impressed; but perplexity was uppermost. Something in his tone of voice prevented impudent comment from the others.

'And all the stars grow a little brighter,' he added. 'The entire universe is glad.'

'I shall be a regular company promoter!' she exclaimed, nearer to wit than she knew, yet with only the vaguest inkling of what he really meant.

'And draw up a Memorandum of Agreement with the Milky Way,' he added, gravely smiling.

He had just been going to say 'with the Pleiades,' when something checked him. A wave of strange emotion swept him. It rose from the depths within, then died away as mysteriously as it came. Like exquisite music heard from very far away, it left its thrill of beauty and of wonder, then hid behind the breath of wind that brought it. 'The whole world, you see, will know,' he added under his breath to the delighted child. He looked into her queer, flushed face. The blue eyes for a moment had, he thought, an amber tinge. It was a mere effect of light, of course; the sun had passed behind a cloud. Something that he ought to have known, ought to have remembered, flashed mockingly before him and was gone. 'One among them trembles,' he repeated in his mind. He himself was trembling.

'The Morning Spiders,' said some one quietly and softly, 'are standing at their stable doors, making faces at the hidden sun.'

But he never knew who said it, or if it was not his own voice speaking below his breath. He glanced at Jimbo. The small grave face wore an air of man-like preoccupation, as was always the case when he felt a little out of his depth in general conversation. He assumed it in self-protection. He never exposed himself by asking questions. The music of that under-voice ran on:—

'Sweet thoughts, like fine weather,
  Bind closely together
  God's stars with the heart of a boy.'

But he said it aloud apparently this time, for the others looked up with surprise. Monkey inquired what in the world he was talking about, only, not quite knowing himself, he could not answer her. Jimbo then, silent and preoccupied, found his thoughts still running on marriage. The talk about his sister's hair going up no doubt had caused it. He remembered the young schoolmistress who had her meals at the Pension, and the Armenian student who had fallen in love with, and eventually married, her. It was the only courtship he had ever witnessed. Marriage and courtship seemed everywhere this morning.

'I saw it all with Mlle. Perette,' he informed the party. 'It began already by his pouring out water for her and passing the salt and things. It *always* begins like that. He got shawls even when she was hot.'

He looked so wise and grave that nobody laughed, and his sisters even seemed impressed rather. Jinny waited anxiously for more. If Mother did make an odd grimace, it was not noticed, and anyhow was cleverly converted into the swallowing of a yawn. There was a moment's silence. Jimbo, proudly conscious that more was expected of him, provided it in his solemn little voice.

'But it must be horrid,' he announced, 'to be married—always sticked to the same woman, like that.' No sentence was complete without the inevitable 'already' or 'like that,' translated from the language he was more at home in. He thought in French. 'I shall never marry myself (*me marier*) he decided, seeing his older sister's eyes upon him wonderingly. Then, uncertain whether he had said an awfully wise or an awfully foolish thing, he added no more. Anyhow, it was the way a man should talk—with decision.

'It's bad enough to be a wife,' put in Monkey, 'but it must be worse still to have one!'

But Jane Anne seemed shocked. A man, Jimbo reflected, can never be sure how his wisdom may affect the other sex; women are not meant to know everything. She rose with dignity and went upstairs towards the door, and Monkey, rippling with laughter, smacked her as she went. This only shocked her more.

'That was a slight mistake behind,' she said reprovingly, looking back; 'you should have more reserve, I think,' then firmly shut the door.

All of which meant—so far as Jane Anne was concerned—that an important standard of conduct—grown-up, dignified, stately in a spiritual sense—was being transferred to her present behaviour, but transferred ineffectively. Elsewhere Jane Anne lived it, *was* it. She knew it, but could not get at the part of her that knew it. The transmitting machinery was imperfect. Connecting links and switches were somehow missing. Yearning was strong in her, that yearning which is common to all the world, though so variously translated. Once out of the others' sight, she made a curious face. She went into her room between the kitchen and the Den, flung herself on the bed, and burst into tears. And the fears brought relief. They oiled the machinery perhaps. At any rate, she soon felt better.

'I felt so enormous and unsettled,' she informed Mother later, when the redness of her eyes was noticed and she received breathlessly a great comforting hug. I never get anything right.'

'But you *are* right, darling,' Mother soothed her, little guessing that she told the perfect truth. 'You are all right, only you don't know it. Everybody's wumbled somewhere.' And she advised her—ah, Mother was profoundly wise instinctively—not to think so much, but just go ahead as usual and do her work.

For Mother herself felt a little queer that day, as though something very big and splendid lay hiding just beyond her reach. It surged up, vanished, then surged up again, and it came closest when she was not thinking of it. The least effort of the mind to capture it merely plunged her into an empty gulf where she could not touch bottom. The glorious thing ran instantly underground. She never ceased to be aware of it, but any attempt to focus resulted in confusion. Analysis was beyond her powers, yet the matter was very simple really, for only when thought is blank, and when the mind has forgotten to think, can inspiration come through into the heart. The intellect interprets afterwards, sets in order, regulates, examines the wonder and beauty the heart distils alchemically out of the eternal stream in which life everywhere dips its feet. If Reason interferes too soon, or during transmission, it only muddles and destroys. And Mother, hitherto, had always been so proud of being practical, prosaic, reasonable. She had deliberately suppressed the other. She could not change in a single day just because she had been 'out' and made discoveries last night. Oh, how simple it all was really, and yet how utterly most folk convert the wonder of it into wumbling!

Like Jane Anne, her miniature, she felt splendid all day long, but puzzled too. It was almost like those religious attacks she had experienced in early youth. She had no definite creed by which she could explain it. Though nominally Christian, like her husband, she could not ascribe her joy to a 'Holy Spirit,' or to a 'God' working in her. But she was reminded of her early 'religious attacks' because she now experienced that large sensation of glorious peace and certainty which usually accompanies the phenomenon in the heart called 'conversion.' She saw life whole. She rested upon some unfailing central Joy. Come what might, she felt secure and 'saved.' Something everlasting lay within call, an ever-ready help in trouble; and all day she was vaguely conscious that her life lay hid with—with what? She never found the word exactly, for 'Joy' was but one aspect of it. She fell back upon the teachings of the big religions which are the police regulations of the world. Yet all creeds shared these, and her feeling was far deeper than mere moral teachings. And then she gave up thinking about it. Besides, she had much knitting to do.

'It's come to stay anyhow; I feel in sympathy with everybody,' she said, and so dismissed vain introspection, keeping the simple happiness and peace. That was her strength, as it was also Jinny's. A re-formation had begun.

Jimbo, too, felt something in his microcosmic way, only he said little and asked no single question. It betrayed itself, however, to his Mother's widened vision. He was all stirred up. He came back again from school at three o'clock—for it was Thursday and he did not take the singing lesson from three to four—put down his books with a very business-like air, forgot to kiss his Mother—and went out.

'Where are you off to, Jimbo?' She scented mischief. He was so *affaire*.

He turned obediently at once, the face grave and puckered.

'Going over to the carpenter's house, Mummy.'

'What for, dear? Why don't you stay and play here?' She had the feeling that her husband was absorbed in his work and would not like to be disturbed.

The boy's reply was evasive too. 'I want to have a long discuss with Daddy,' he said.

'Can't you have your long discuss with me instead?' she asked.

He shook his head. 'You see,' he answered solemnly, 'it's about things.'

'But Daddy's working just now; he'll be over to tea at four. Can't it wait till then?'

She understood too well to inquire what 'things' might be. The boy wished to speak with one of his own sex—as one man to another man.

'When a man's at work,' she added, 'he doesn't like to be disturbed.'

'All right,' was the reply. 'We can wait a little,' and he settled down to other things in a corner by himself. His mind, clearly, was occupied with grave considerations he could not discuss with anybody, least of all with women and children. But, of course, busy men must not be interrupted. For a whole hour in his corner he made no sound, and hardly any movement.

But Daddy did not come at four o'clock. He was evidently deep in work. And Mother did not send for him. The carpenter's wife, she knew, would provide a cup of tea.

He came late to supper, too, at the Pension, nodded to Mother with an expression which plainly said, 'I've finished the story at last'; winked to his cousin, meaning, 'It came out all right, I'm satisfied,' and took his seat between Jinny and Mlle. Vuillemot, the governess who had earned her meal by giving a music lesson that afternoon to a *pensionnaire*. Jinny looked sideways at him in a spirit of examination, and picked the inevitable crumb deftly from his beard.

'Reminiscences!' she observed slyly. 'You did have some tea, then.' Her long word was well chosen for once; her mind unusually logical, too.

But Daddy made no reply; he went on eating whatever was set before him with an air of complete detachment; he devoured cold ham and salad automatically; and the children, accustomed to this absorption, ignored his presence. He was still in the atmosphere of his work, abstracted, lost to the outer world. They knew they would only, get wumbled answers to their questions and remarks, and they did not dare to tease him. From time to time he lifted his eyes—very bright they were—and glanced round the table, dimly aware that he was in the midst of a stream of noisy chatter, but unable to enter it successfully at any point. Mother, watching him, thought, 'He's sitting on air, he's wrapped in light, he's very happy'; and ate an enormous supper, as though an insatiable hunger was in her.

The governess, Mlle. Vuillemot, who stood in awe of the 'author' in him, seized her opportunity. She loved to exchange a *mot* with a real writer, reading all kinds of unintended subtlety into his brief replies in dreadful French. To-night she asked him the meaning of a word, title of a Tauchnitz novel she had been reading—Juggernaut; but, being on his deaf side, he caught 'Huguenot' instead, and gave her a laboured explanation, strangled by appalling grammar.

The historical allusions dazed her; the explanation ended on a date. She was sorry she had ventured, for it made her feel so ignorant.

'Shuggairnort,' she repeated bravely. She had a vague idea he had not properly heard before.

But this time he caught 'Argonaut,' and swamped her then with classical exposition, during which she never took her eyes off him, and decided that he was far more wonderful than she had ever dreamed. He was; but not for the reasons she supposed.

'Thank you,' she said with meek gratitude at the end, 'I thank you.'

'Il n'y a pas de quar,' replied Daddy, bowing; and the adventure came to an end. The others luckily had not heard it in full swing; they only caught the final phrase with which he said adieu. But it served its unwitting purpose admirably. It brought him back to the world about him. The spell was broken. All turned upon him instantly.

'Snay pas un morsow de bong.' Monkey copied his accent, using a sentence from a schoolboy's letter in *Punch*. 'It's not a bit of good.' Mother squelched her with a look, but Daddy, even if he noticed it, was not offended. Nothing could offend him to-night. Impertinence turned silvery owing to the way he took it. There was a marvellous light and sweetness about him. 'He *is* on air,' decided Mother finally. 'He's written his great Story—our story. It's finished!'

'I don't know,' he said casually to the others, as they stood talking a few minutes in the salon before going over to the Den, 'if you'd like to hear it; but I've got a new creature for the Wumble Book. It came to me while I was thinking of something else——'

'Thinking of one thing while you were thinking of another!' cried Monkey. It described exaccurately his state of mind sometimes.

'——and I jotted down the lines on my cuff. So it's not very perfect yet.'

Mother had him by the arm quickly. Mlle. Vuillemot was hovering in his neighbourhood, for one thing. It seemed to her they floated over, almost flew.

'It's a Haystack Woman,' he explained, once they were safely in the Den grouped about him. 'A Woman of the Haystack who is loved by the Wind. That is to say, the big Wind loves her, but she prefers the younger, handsomer little Winds, and——'

He was not allowed to finish. The children laid his cuff back in a twinkling, drawing up the coat sleeve.

'But surely I know that,' Mother was saying. 'I've heard of her before somewhere. I wonder where?' Others were saying the same thing. 'It's not new.'

'Impossible,' said Daddy, 'for the idea only came to me this morning while I was——'

'Thinking of something else,' Monkey again finished the sentence for him.

Mother felt that things were rushing about her from another world. She was vaguely conscious—deliciously, bewilderingly—of having heard this all before. Imaginative folk have built the certainty of a previous existence upon evidence as slight; for actual scenery came with it, and she saw dim forest trees, and figures hovering in the background, and bright atmosphere, and fields of brilliant stars. She felt happy and shining, light as a feather, too. It all was just beyond her reach, though; she could not recover it properly. 'It must have been a dream *she* told me,' was her conclusion, referring to Mlle. Lemaire. Her old friend was in it somewhere or other. She felt sure of that.

She hardly heard, indeed, the silly lines her husband read aloud to the children. She liked the sound of his voice, though; it suggested music she had known far away—in her childhood.

'It's high spirits really,' whispered Rogers, sitting beside her in the window. 'It's a sort of overflow from his story. He can't do that kind of rhyme a bit, but it's an indication——'

'You think he's got a fine big story this time?' she asked under her breath; and Cousin Henry's eyes twinkled keenly as he gave a significant nod and answered: 'Rather! Can't you feel the splendour all about him, the strength, the harmony!'

She leaped at the word. Harmony exactly described this huge new thing that had come into the family, into the village, into the world. The feeling that they all were separate items, struggling for existence one against the other, had gone for ever. Life seemed now a single whole, an enormous pattern. Every one fitted in. There was effort— wholesome jolly effort, but no longer the struggle or fighting that were ugly. To 'live carelessly' was possible and right because the pattern was seen entire. It was to live in the whole.

'Harmony,' she repeated to herself, with a great swelling happiness in her heart, 'that's the nunculus of the matter.'

'The what?' he asked, overhearing her.

'The nunculus,' she repeated bravely, seeing the word in her mind, yet unable to get it quite. Rogers did not correct her.

'Rather,' was all he said. 'Of course it is.' What did the pronunciation of a word matter at such a time? Her version even sounded better than the original. Mother saw things bigger! Already she was becoming creative!

'And you're the one who brought it,' she continued, but this time so low that he did not catch the words. 'It's you, your personality, your thinking, your atmosphere somehow that have brought this gigantic sense of peace and calm security which are *au fond* nothing but the consciousness of harmony and the power of seeing ugly details in their proper place—in a single *coup d'oeil*—and understanding them as parts of a perfect whole.'

It was her thought really running on; she never could have found the words like that. She thought in French, too, for one thing. And, in any case, Rogers could not have heard her, for he was listening now to the uproar of the children as they criticised Daddy's ridiculous effusion. A haystack, courted in vain by zephyrs, but finally taken captive by an equinoctial gale, strained nonsense too finely for their sense of what was right and funny. It was the pictures he now drew in the book that woke their laughter. He gave the stack a physiognomy that they recognised.

'But, Mother, he's making it look like you!' cried Monkey—only Mother was too far away in her magnificent reverie to reply intelligently.

I know her; she's my friend,' she answered vaguely. 'So it's all right.'

'Majestic Haystack'—it was the voice of the wind addressing her:—

'Majestic Haystack, Empress of my life,
Your ample waist
Just fits the gown I fancy for my wife,
And suits my taste;
Yet there you stand, flat-footed, square and deep,
An unresponsive, elephantine heap,
Coquetting with the stars while I'm asleep,
O cruel Stack!

Coy, silent Monster, Matron of the fields,
I sing to you;
And all the fondest love that summer yields
I bring to you;
Yet there you squat, immense in your disdain,
Heedless of all the tears of streaming rain

My eyes drip over you—your breathless swain;
O stony Stack!

Stupendous Maiden, sweetest when oblong,
Does inner flame
Now smoulder in thy soul to hear my song
Repeat thy name?
Or does thy huge and ponderous heart object
The advances of my passion, and reject
My love because it's airy and elect?
O wily Stack!

O crested goddess, thatched and top-knotted,
O reckless Stack!
Of wives that to the Wind have been allotted
There is no lack;
You've spurned my love as though I were a worm;
But next September when I see thy form,
I'll woo thee with an equinoctial storm!
I have that knack!'

'Far less wumbled than usual,' thought Rogers, as the children danced about the room, making up new ridiculous rhymes, of which 'I'll give you a whack' seemed the most popular. Only Jane Anne was quiet. A courtship even so remote and improbable as between the Wind and a Haystack sent her thoughts inevitably in the dominant direction.

'It must be nice when one is two,' she whispered ambiguously to Mother with a very anxious face, 'but I'm sure that if a woman can't cook, love flies out of the window. It's a positive calamity, you know.'

But it was Cousin Henry's last night in Bourcelles, and the spirit of pandemonium was abroad. Neither parent could say no to anything, and mere conversation in corners was out of the question. The door was opened into the corridor, and while Mother played her only waltz, Jimbo and Monkey danced on the splintery boards as though it were a parquet floor, and Rogers pirouetted somewhat solemnly with Jane Anne. She enjoyed it immensely, yet rested her hand very gingerly upon his shoulder. 'Please don't hold me *quite* so tight,' she ventured. 'I've never danced with a strange man before, you see'; and he no more laughed at her than he had laughed at Mother's 'nunculus.' Even Jane Anne, he knew, would settle down comfortably before long into the great big pattern where a particular nook awaited—aye, needed—her bizarre, odd brilliance. The most angular fragments would nest softly, neatly in. A little filing, a little polishing, and all would fit together. To force would only be to break. Hurry was of the devil. And later, while Daddy played an ancient tune that was written originally as a mazurka yet did duty now for a two-step, he danced with Mother too, and the children paused to watch out of sheer admiration.

'Fancy, Mother dancing!' they exclaimed with glee—except Jinny, who was just a little offended and went to stand by the piano till it was over. For Mother danced as lightly as a child for all her pride of measurement, and no frigate ever skimmed the waves more gracefully than Mother glided over those uneven boards.

'The Wind and the Haystack' of course, was Monkey's description.

'You'll wind and haystack to bed now,' was the reply, as Mother sat and fanned herself in the corner. The 'bed-sentence' as the children called it, was always formed in this way. Whatever the child was saying when the moment came, Mother adopted as her verb. 'Shall I put some peat on, Mother?' became 'Peat yourself off to bed-it's nine o'clock'—and the child was sorry it had spoken.

Good-byes had really been said at intervals all day long, and so to- night were slight enough; the children, besides, were so 'excitey- tired,' as Monkey put it, that they possessed no more emotion of any kind. There were various disagreeable things in the immediate future of To-morrow—getting up early, school, and so forth; and Cousin Henry's departure they lumped in generally with the mass, accepted but unrealised. Jimbo could hardly keep his eyes alight, and Monkey's hair was like a baby haystack the wind had treated to an equinoctial storm. Jinny, stiff, perplexed, and solemn with exhaustion, yet dared not betray it because she was older, in measurable distance of her hair going up.

'Why don't you play with the others, child?' asked Mother, finding her upright on a sofa while the romp went on.

'Oh, to-night,' Jinny explained, 'I sit indifferent and look on. I don't always feel like skedivvying about!'

To skedivvy was to chivvy and skedaddle—its authority not difficult to guess.

'Good-bye, Cousinenry,' each gasped, as his big arms went round them and squeezed out the exclamation. 'Oh, thank you most awfully,' came next, with another kiss, produced by his pressing something hard and round and yellow into each dirty little hand. 'It's only a bit of crystallised starlight,' he explained, 'that escaped long ago from the Cave. And starlight, remember, shines for everybody as well as for yourselves. You can buy a stamp with it occasionally, too,' he added, 'and write to me.'

'We will. Of course!'

Jimbo straightened up a moment before the final collapse of sleep.

'Your train leaves at 6.23,' he said, with the authority of exclusive information. 'You must be at the station at six to get the *bagages enregistrees*. It's a slow train to Pontarlier, but you'll find a *wagon direct* for Paris in front, next to the engine. I shall be at the station to see you off.'

'*I* shan't,' said Monkey.

Rogers realised with delight the true meaning of these brief and unemotional good-byes. 'They know I'm coming back; they feel that the important part of me is not going away at all. My thinking stays here with them.'

Jinny lingered another ten minutes for appearance's sake. It was long past her bed-time, too, but dignity forbade her retiring with the others. Standing by the window she made conversation a moment, feeling it was the proper, grown-up thing to do. It was even expected of her.

'Look! It's full moon,' she observed gravely, as though suggesting that she could, if she liked, go out and enjoy the air. 'Isn't it lovely?'

'No, yesterday was full moon,' Rogers corrected her, joining her and looking out. 'Two nights ago, to be exact, I think.'

'Oh,' she replied, as solemnly as though politics or finance were under discussion, 'then it's bigger than full moon now. It goes on, does it, getting fuller and fuller, till—'

'Now, Jinny dear, it's very late, and you'd better full-moon off to bed,' Mother interrupted gently.

'Yes, Mother; I'm just saying good-night.' She held her hand out, as though she was afraid he might kiss her, yet feared he would not. 'Good-bye, Mr. Cousin Henry, and I hope you'll have an exceedingly happy time in the train and soon come back and visit us again.'

'Thank you,' he said, 'I'm sure I shall.' He gave her a bit of solid starlight as he said it, then suddenly leaned forward and kissed her on the cheek. Making a violent movement like an experienced boxer who dodges an upper cut, Jinny turned and fled precipitately from the room, forgetting her parents altogether. That kiss, she felt, consumed her childhood in a flash of fiery flame. In bed she decided that she must lengthen her skirts the very next day, and put her hair up too. She must do something that should give her protection and yet freedom. For a long time she did not sleep. She lay thinking it over. She felt supremely happy—wild, excited, naughty. 'A man has kissed me; it was a man; it was Mr. Rogers, Daddy's cousin…. He's not *my* cousin exactly, but just "a man."' And she fell asleep, wondering how she ought to begin her letter to him when she wrote, but, more perplexing still, how she ought to—end it! That little backward brain sought the solution of the problem all night long in dreams. She felt a criminal, a dare-devil caught in the act, awaiting execution. Light had been flashed cruelly upon her dark, careful secret—the greatest and finest secret in the world. The child lay under sentence indeed, only it was a sentence of life, and not of death.

CHAPTER XXVII

Asia. ... I feel, I see
   Those eyes which burn through smiles that fade in tears,
   Like stars half quenched in mists of silver dew.
                  Prometheus Unbound, SHELLEY.

It was only ten o'clock, really, and the curfew was ringing from every village on the mountain-side. The sound of the bells, half musical, half ominous, was borne by the bise across the vineyards, for the easterly wind that brings fine weather was blowing over lake and forest, and seemed to drive before it thin sheets of moonlight that turned the whole world soft. The village lay cosily dreaming beneath the sky. Once the curfew died away there was only the rustling of the plane trees in the old courtyard. The great Citadelle loomed above the smaller houses, half in shadow half in silver, nodding heavily to the spire of the Church, and well within sight of the sentinelle poplar that guarded the village from the forest and the mountains. Far away, these mountains now lowered their enormous shoulders to let night flow down upon the sleeping world. The Scaffolding that brought it had long since sailed over France towards the sea....

Mother, still panting from the ritual of fastening the younger children into bed, had gone a moment down the passage to say good- night to Mlle. Lemaire, and when she returned, the three of them— herself, her husband, and Cousin Henry—dropped into chairs beside the window and watched the silvery world in silence for a time. None felt inclined to speak. There was drama somehow in that interval of silence—that drama which lurks everywhere and always behind life's commonest, most ordinary moments. Actions reveal it—sometimes—but it mostly lies concealed, and especially in deep silences like this, when the ticking of a cuckoo clock upon the wall may be the sole hint of its presence.

It was not the good-byes that made all three realise it so near, though good-byes are always solemn and momentous things; it was something that stirred and rose upon them from a far deeper strata of emotion than that caused by apparent separation. For no pain lay in it, but a power much more difficult to express in the sounds and syllables of speech—Joy. A great joy, creative and of big significance, had known accomplishment. Each felt it, knew it, realised it. The moonlit night was aware of it. The entire universe knew it, too. The drama lay in that. There had been creation—of more light.... The world was richer than it had been. Some one had caught Beauty in a net, and to catch Beauty is to transform and recreate all common things. It is revelation.

Through the mind of each of these three flowed the stream of casual thinking—images, reflections, and the shadowy scaffoldings of many new emotions—sweeping along between the banks of speech and silence. And this stream, though in flood, did not overflow into words for a long time. With eyes turned inwards, each watched the current pass. Clear and deep, it quietly reflected—stars. Each watched the same stream, the same calm depths, the same delicate reflections. They were in harmony with themselves, and therefore with the universe....

Then, suddenly, one of the reflections—it was the Pleiades—rose to the surface to clasp its lovely original. It was the woman who netted the golden thought and drew it forth for all to see.

'Couldn't you read it to us, Daddy?' she whispered softly across the silence.

'If it's not too long for you.' He was so eager, so willing to comply.

'We will listen till the Morning Spiders take us home,' his cousin said.

'It's only the shorter version,' Daddy agreed shiningly, 'a sketch for the book which, of course, will take a year to write. I might read *that*, perhaps.'

'Do,' urged Mother. 'We are all in it, aren't we? It's our story as well as yours.'

He rose to get the portfolio from the shelf where he had laid it, and while Rogers lit the lamp, Riquette stole in at the window, picking her way daintily across the wet tiles. She stood a moment, silhouetted against the sky; then shaking her feet rapidly each in turn like bits of quivering wire, she stepped precisely into the room. 'I am in it too,' she plainly said, curling herself up on the chair Daddy had just vacated, but resigning herself placidly enough to his scanty lap when he came back again and began to read. Her deep purring, while he stroked her absent-mindedly, became an undercurrent in the sound of his voice, then presently ceased altogether....

On and on he read, while the moon sailed over La Citadelle, bidding the stars hush to listen too. She put her silvery soft hands across their eyes that they might hear the better. The blue wind of night gathered up the meaning and spread it everywhere. The forest caught the tale from the low laughter in the crest of the poplar, and passed it on to the leagues of forest that bore it in turn across the frontiers into France. Thence snowy Altels and the giant Blumlisalp flashed it south along the crowding peaks and down among the Italian chestnut woods, who next sent it coursing over the rustling waves of the Adriatic and mixed it everywhere with the Mediterranean foam. In the morning the shadows upon bare Grecian hills would whisper it among the ancient islands, and the East catch echoes of it in the winds of dawn. The forests of the North would open their great gloomy eyes with wonder, as though strange new wild-flowers had come among them in the night. All across the world, indeed, wherever there were gardened minds tender enough to grow fairy seed, these flakes of thought would settle down in sleep, and blossom in due season into a crop of magic beauty.

He read on and on.... The village listened too, the little shadowy street, the familiar pine woods, the troubled Pension, each, as its image was evoked in the story, knew its soul discovered, and stirred in its sleep towards the little room to hear. And the desolate ridges of La Tourne and Boudry, the clefts where the wild lily of the valley grew unknown, high nooks and corners where the buzzards nested, these also knew and answered to the trumpet summons of the Thought that made them live. A fire of creation ran pulsing from this centre. All were in the Pattern of the Story.

To the two human listeners it seemed as familiar as a tale read, in childhood long ago, and only half forgotten. They always knew a little of what was coming next. Yet it spread so much further than mere childhood memories, for its golden atmosphere included all countries and all times. It rose and sang and sparkled, lighting up strange deep recesses of their unconscious and half-realised life, and almost revealing the tiny silver links that joined them on to the universe at large. The golden ladders from the Milky Way were all let down. They climbed up silvery ropes into the Moon....

'It's not my own idea,' he said; 'I'm convinced of that. It's all flocked into me from some other mind that thought it long ago, but could not write it, perhaps. No thought is lost, you see—never can be lost. Like this, somehow, I feel it:—

Now sinks to sleep the clamour of the day,
And, million-footed, from the Milky Way,
Falls shyly on my heart the world's lost Thought—
Shower of primrose dust the stars have taught
To haunt each sleeping mind,
Till it may find

A garden in some eager, passionate brain
That, rich in loving-kindness as in pain,
Shall harvest it, then scatter forth again
It's garnered loveliness from heaven caught.

Oh, every yearning thought that holds a tear,
Yet finds no mission,
And lies untold,

Waits, guarded in that labyrinth of gold,—
To reappear
Upon some perfect night,
Deathless—not old—
But sweet with time and distance,
And clothed as in a vision
Of starry brilliance
For the world's delight.'

In the pauses, from time to time, they heard the distant thunder of the Areuse as it churned and tumbled over the Val de Travers boulders. The Colombier bells, as the hours passed, strung the sentences together; moonlight wove in and out of every adventure as they listened; stars threaded little chapters each to each with their eternal golden fastenings. The words seemed written down in dew, but the dew crystallised into fairy patterns that instantly flew about the world upon their mission of deliverance. In this ancient Network of the Stars the universe lay fluttering; and they lay with it, all prisoners in Fairyland.

For the key of it all was sympathy, and the' delicate soul of it was tender human love. Bourcelles, in this magic tale, was the starting- point whence the Starlight Expresses flashed into all the world, even unto unvisited, forgotten corners that had known no service hitherto. It was so adaptable and searching, and knew such tiny, secret ways of entrance. The thought was so penetrating, true, and simple. Even old Mother Plume would wake to the recovery of some hitherto forgotten fragrance in her daily life… just as those Northern forests would wake to find new wild-flowers. For all fairytales issue first from the primeval forest, thence undergoing their protean transformation; and in similar fashion this story, so slight but so tremendous, issued from the forest of one man's underthinking—one deep, pure mind, wumbled badly as far as external things were concerned, yet realising that Bourcelles contained the Universe, and that he, in turn contained Bourcelles. Another, it is true, had shown it to him, though all unwittingly, and had cleaned in his atmosphere the channels for the entrance of the glorious pattern. But the result was the same. In his brain— perhaps by Chance, perhaps by God—lay the machinery which enabled him to give it out to others—the power and ability to transmit. It was a fairy-tale of the world, only the world had forgotten it. He brought back its fairyland again.

And this fairyland, what and where was it? And how could this tale of its recovery bring into his listeners' hearts such a sense of peace and joy that they felt suddenly secure in the world and safe mid all the confusion of their muddled lives? That there were tears in Mother's eyes seems beyond question, because the moonlight, reflected faintly from a wet cobble in the yard below, glistened like a tiny silver lantern there. They betrayed the fact that something in her had melted and flowed free. Yet there was no sadness in the fairy-tale to cause it; they were tears of joy.

Surely it was that this tale of Starlight, Starlight Expresses and Star Caves, told as simply as running water, revealed the entire Universe—as One, and that in this mighty, splendid thing each of them nested safe and comfortable. The world was really *thinking*, and all lay fluttering in the grand, magnificent old Net of Stars. What people think, they are. All can think Beauty. And sympathy—to feel with everything—was the clue; for sympathy is love, and to love a star was to love a neighbour. To be without sympathy was to feel apart, and to think apart was to cut oneself off from life, from the Whole, from God and joy—it was Death. To work at commonplace duties because they were duties to the Universe at large, this was the way to find courage, peace, and happiness, because this was genuine and successful work, no effort lost, and the most distant star aware of it. Thinking was living, whether material results were visible or not; yearning was action, even though no accomplishment was apparent; thought and sympathy, though felt but for a passing moment, sweetened the Pleiades and flashed along the Milky Way, and so-called tangible results that could prove it to the senses provided no adequate test of accomplishment or success. In the knowledge of belonging to this vast underlying unity was the liberation that brings courage, carelessness, and joy, and to admit failure in anything, by thinking it, was to weaken the entire structure which binds together the planets and the heart of a boy. Thoughts were the fairies that the world believed in when it was younger, simpler, less involved in separation; and the golden Fairyland recovered in this story was the Fairyland of lovely thinking....

In this little lamp-lit room of the Citadelle, the two listeners were conscious of this giant, delicate network that captured every flying thought and carried it streaming through the world. God became a simple thing: He fashioned Rogers's Scheme, even though it never materialised in bricks and mortar. God was behind Mother, even when she knitted or lit the fire in the Den. All were prisoners in His eternal Fairyland....

And the symbolism of the story, the so-called fantasy, they also easily understood, because they felt it true. To be 'out' of the body was merely to think and feel away from self. As they listened they realised themselves in touch with every nation and with every time, with all possible beliefs and disbeliefs, with every conceivable kind of thinking, that is, which ever has existed or ever shall exist....

The heat and radiance given out by the clear delivery of this 'inspirational' fairy-tale must have been very strong; far-reaching it certainly was....

'Ah!' sighed Rogers to himself, 'if only I could be like that!' not realising that he was so.

'Oh dear!' felt the Woman, 'that's what I've felt sometimes. I only wish it were true of me!' unaware that it could be, and even by the fact of her yearning, *was* so.

'If only I could get up and help the world!' passed like a flame across the heart of the sufferer who lay on her sleepless bed next door, listening to the sound of the droning voice that reached her through the wall, yet curiously ignorant that this very longing was already majestically effective in the world of definite action.

And even Mother Plume, pacing her airless room at the further end of the village and tapping her ebony stick upon the floor, turned suspiciously, as at a passing flash of light that warmed her for a sudden instant as it went.

'Perhaps, after all, they don't mean all these unkind things they do to me!' she thought; 'I live so much alone. Possibly I see things less clearly than I used to do!'

The spell was certainly very potent, though Daddy himself, reading out the little shining chapters, guessed as little as the rest of them how strong. So small a part of what he meant to say, it seemed, had been transferred to the paper. More than he realised, far, far more, lay between the lines, of course. There was conviction in it, because there was vision and belief. Not much was said when he put his roll of paper down and leaned back in his chair. Riquette opened her eyes and blinked narrowly, then closed them again and began to purr. The ticking of the cuckoo clock seemed suddenly very loud and noticeable.

'Thank you,' said Mother quietly in an uncertain kind of voice. 'The world seems very wonderful now—quite different.'

She moved in her chair—the first movement she had made for over two hours. Daddy rubbed his eyes, stroked his beard, and lit a cigarette; it went out almost immediately, but he puffed on at it just the same, till his cousin struck a match and stood over him to see it properly alight.

'You have caught Beauty naked in your net of stars,' he murmured; 'but you have left her as you found her—shining, silvery, unclothed. Others will see her, too. You have taken us all back into Fairyland, and I, for one, shall never get out again.'

'Nor I,' breathed some one in the shadows by the window....

The clock struck two. 'Odd,' said Mother, softly, 'but I never heard it strike once while you were reading!'

'We've all been out,' Rogers laughed significantly, 'just as you make them get out in the story'; and then, while Riquette yawned and turned a moment from the window-sill to say thank you for her long, warm sleep, Mother lit the spirit-lamp and brewed the cups of chocolate. She tiptoed in next door, and as she entered the sick-room she saw through the steam rising from the cup she carried a curious thing—an impression of brilliance about the bed, as though shafts of light issued from it. Rays pulsed and trembled in the air. There was a perfume of flowers. It seemed she stepped back into the atmosphere of the story for an instant.

'Ah, you're not asleep,' she whispered. 'We've brewed some chocolate, and I thought you might like a cup.'

'No, I'm not asleep,' answered the other woman from the bed she never would leave until she was carried from it, 'but I have been dreaming. It seemed the stars came down into my room and sang to me; this bed became a throne; and some power was in me by which I could send my thoughts out to help the world. I sent them out as a king sends messengers—to people everywhere—even to people I've never heard of. Isn't it wonderful?'

'You've had no pain?' For Mother knew that these sleepless hours at night brought usually intense suffering. She stared at her, noting how the eyes shone and glistened with unshed moisture.

'None,' was the answer, 'but only the greatest joy and peace I've ever known.' The little glass of *calmant* was untouched; it was not a drug that had soothed the exhausted nerves. In this room at any rate the spell was working still. 'I was carried through the air by stars, as though my ceaseless yearning to get up and work in the world for once was realised.'

'You can do everything from your bed,' her friend murmured, sitting down beside her. 'You do. Your thoughts go out so strongly. I've often felt them myself. Perhaps that's why God put you here in bed like this,' she added, surprised at the power in herself that made her say such things—'just to think and pray for the world.'

'I do pray sometimes for others,' the tortured woman answered modestly, 'but this time I was not conscious of praying at all. It all swept out of me of its own accord. The force in me seemed so free and inexhaustible that it overflowed. It was irresistible. I felt able to save the world.'

'You were out,' said Mother softly, 'out of yourself, I mean,' she corrected it. 'And your lovely thoughts go everywhere. You do save the world.'

There fell a long silence then between them.

'You've been reading aloud,' Mlle. Lemaire said presently. 'I heard the drone of the voice through the wall——'

'Daddy was reading his new story to us,' the other said. 'It didn't disturb you?'

'On the contrary. I think it was the voice somehow that brought the vision. I listened vaguely at first, trying to sleep; then, opening my eyes suddenly, the room, as I told you, was full of stars. Their rays caught hold of me and drew these forces out of my very heart. I yielded, giving and giving and giving ... such life flowed from me, and they carried it away in streams.... Oh, it was really like a divine sensation.' 'It was divine,' said Mother, but whether she meant the story or her friend's experience, she hardly knew herself.

'And the story—was it not about our little Bourcelles?' asked the other.

Mother held her hands up as though words failed her. She opened her arms wide. She was not quite sure of her voice.

'It was,' she said at length, 'but Bourcelles had grown into the universe. It's a fairy-tale, but it's like a great golden fire. It warmed my heart till my whole body seemed all heart, and I didn't know whether to laugh or cry. It makes you see that the whole world is *one*, and that the sun and moon and stars lie in so small and unimportant a thing as, say, Jimbo's mischief, or Monkey's impudence, or Jinny's backwardness and absurdity. All are in sympathy together, as in a network, and to feel sympathy with anything, even the most insignificant, connects you instantly with the Whole. Thought and sympathy *are* the Universe—they are life.'

While Mother paused for breath, her old friend smiled a curious, meaning smile, as though she heard a thing that she had always known.

'And all of us are in the story, and all the things we *think* are alive and active too, because we have created them. Our thoughts populate the world, flying everywhere to help or hinder others, you see.'

The sound of a door opening was heard. Mother got up to go. Shafts of light again seemed to follow her from the figure in the bed.

'Good-night,' she whispered with a full heart, while her thought ran suddenly—'You possess the secret of life and of creation, for suffering has taught it to you, and you have really known it always. But Daddy has put it into words for everybody.' She felt proud as a queen.

There were whispered good-nights then in the corridor, for Rogers and her husband were on their way home to bed.

'Your chocolate is getting cold,' said Daddy kindly.

'We thought you would probably stay in there. We're going over now. It's very late,' Rogers added. They said good-night again.

She closed and locked the great door of the Citadelle behind them, hearing their steps upon the cobbles in the yard, and for some time afterwards upon the road. But their going away seemed the same as coming nearer. She felt so close to everything that lived. Everything did live. Her heart included all that existed, that ever had existed, that ever could exist. Mother was alive all over. 'I have just been created,' she laughed, and went back into the Den to drink her cup of tepid chocolate.

CHAPTER XXVIII

See, the busy Pleiades,
Sisters to the Hyades,
Seven by seven
Across the heaven,
Light desire
With their fire,
Working cunningly together in a soft and tireless band,

Sweetly linking
All our thinking
In the Net of Sympathy that brings back Fairyland.
                    A Voice.

The prophecy of the children that Bourcelles was a difficult place to get away from found its justification next morning, for Rogers slept so heavily that he nearly missed his train. It was six o'clock when he tumbled downstairs, too late for a real breakfast, and only just in time to get his luggage upon the little char that did duty for all transport in this unsophisticated village. The carpenter pulled it for him to the station.

'If I've forgotten anything, my cousin will send it after me,' he told Mme. Michaud, as he gulped down hot coffee on the steps.

'Or we can keep it for you,' was the answer. 'You'll be coming back soon.' She knew, like the others, that one always came back to Bourcelles. She shook hands with him as if he were going away for a night or two. 'Your room will always be ready,' she added. 'Ayez la bonte seulement de m'envoyer une petite ligne d'avance.'

'There's only fifteen minutes,' interrupted her husband, 'and it's uphill all the way.'

They trundled off along the dusty road, already hot in the early July sun. There was no breath of wind; swallows darted in the blue air; the perfume of the forests was everywhere; the mountains rose soft and clear into the cloudless sky. They passed the Citadelle, where the awning was already being lowered over the balcony for Mlle. Lemaire's bed to be wheeled out a little later. Rogers waved his handkerchief, and saw the answering flutter inside the window. Riquette, on her way in, watched him from the tiles. The orchards then hid the lower floors; he passed the tinkling fountain; to the left he saw the church and the old Pension, the wistaria blossoms falling down its walls in a cascade of beauty.

The Postmaster put his head out and waved his Trilby hat with a solemn smile. 'Le barometre est tres haut...' floated down the village street, instead of the sentence of good-bye. Even the Postmaster took it for granted that he was not leaving. Gygi, standing in the door of his barn, raised his peaked hat and smiled. 'Fait beau, ce matin,' he said, 'plus tard il fera rudement chaud.' He spoke as if Rogers were off for a walk or climb. It was the same everywhere. The entire village saw him go, yet behaved as if he was not really leaving. How fresh and sweet the morning air was, keen mountain fragrance in it, and all the delicious, delicate sharpness of wet moss and dewy fields.

As he passed the courtyard near the Guillaume Tell, and glanced up at the closed windows of Mother Plume's apartment, a pattering step startled him behind, and Jimbo came scurrying up. Rogers kissed him and lifted him bodily upon the top of his portmanteau, then helped the carpenter to drag it up the hill. 'The barriers at the level crossing are down, the warning gongs are ringing. It's signalled from Auvernier.' They were only just in time. The luggage was registered and the train panting up the steep incline, when Monkey, sleep still thick in her eyes, appeared rolling along the white road. She was too breathless to speak; she stood and stared like a stuffed creature in a Museum. Jimbo was beside the engine, having a word with the *mecanicien*.

'Send a telegram, you know—like that,' he shouted, as the carriage slid past him, 'and we'll bring the *char*.' He knew his leader would come back. He took his cap off politely, as a man does to a lady—the Bourcelles custom. He did not wave his handkerchief or make undignified signs. He stood there, watching his cousin to the last, and trying to see the working of the engine at the same time. He had already told him the times and stopping places, and where he had to change; there was nothing more for a man to say.

Monkey, her breath recovered now, shouted something impudent from the road. 'The train will break down with you in it before it gets to Pontarlier, and you'll be back for tea—worse luck!' He heard it faintly, above the grinding of the wheels. She blew him a kiss; her hair flew out in a cloud of brown the sunshine turned half golden. He almost saw the shining of her eyes. And then the belt of the forest hid her from view, hid Jimbo and the village too. The last thing he saw of Bourcelles was the top of the church spire and the red roof of the towering Citadelle. The crest of the sentinel poplar topped them both for a minute longer, waved a slight and stately farewell, then lowered itself into the forest and vanished in its turn.

And Rogers came back with a start and a bump to what is called real life.

He closed his eyes and leaned back in his corner, feeling he had suddenly left his childhood behind him for the second time, not gradually as it ought to happen, but all in one dreadful moment. A great ache lay in his heart. The perfect book of fairy-tales he had been reading was closed and finished. Weeks had passed in the delicious reading, but now the last page was turned; he came back to duty—duty in London—great, noisy, overwhelming London, with its disturbing bustle, its feverish activities, its complex, artificial, unsatisfying amusements, and its hosts of frantic people. He grew older in a moment; he was forty again now; an instant ago, just on the further side of those blue woods, he had been fifteen. Life shrank and dwindled in him to a little, ugly, unattractive thing. He was returning to a flat in the dolorous edifice of civilisation. A great practical Scheme, rising in sombre bricks and mortar through a disfiguring fog, blocked all the avenues of the future.

The picture seemed sordid somewhere, the contrast was so striking. In a great city was no softness; hard, sharp angles everywhere, or at best an artificial smoothness that veiled ugliness and squalor very thinly. Human relationship worked like parts of a machine, cramped into definite orbits, each wheel, each pulley, the smallest deviation deemed erratic. In Bourcelles, the mountain village, there was more latitude, room for expansion, space. The heart leaped up spontaneously like a spring released. In the city this spring was held down rigidly in place, pressed under as by a weight; and the weight, surely, was that one for ever felt compelled to think of self—self in a rather petty, shameful way—personal safety. In the streets, in the houses, in public buildings, shops, and railway stations, even where people met to eat and drink in order to keep alive, were Notice Boards of caution and warning against their fellow kind. Instead of the kindly and unnecessary, even ridiculous little Gygi, there were big, grave policemen by the score, a whole army of them; and everywhere grinned the Notice Boards, like automatic, dummy policemen, mocking joy with their insulting warnings. The heart was oppressed with this constant reminder that safety could only be secured by great care and trouble— safety for the little personal self; protection from all kinds of robbery, depredation, and attack; beware of pickpockets, the proprietor is not responsible for overcoats and umbrellas even! And burglar alarms and doors of steel and iron everywhere—an organised defence from morning till night—against one's own kind.

He had lived among these terrible conditions all his life, proud of the personal security that civilisation provided, but he had never before viewed it from outside, as now he suddenly did. A spiritual being, a man, lives in a city as in a state of siege among his own kind. It was deplorable, it was incredible. In little Bourcelles, a mountain village most would describe pityingly as half civilised and out of the world, there was safety and joy and freedom as of the universe.... His heart contracted as he thus abruptly realised the distressing contrast. Although a city is a unit, all classes neatly linked together by laws and by-laws, by County Councils, Parliaments, and the like, the spirit of brotherhood was a mockery and a sham. There is organised charity, but there is not—Charity. In a London Square he could not ring the bell and ask for a glass of milk.... In Bourcelles he would walk into any house, since there were no bells, and sit down to an entire meal!

He laughed as the absurd comparison darted across his mind, for he recognised the foolish exaggeration in it; but behind the laughter flamed the astonishing truth. In Bourcelles, in a few weeks, he had found a bigger, richer life than all London had supplied to him in twenty years; he had found wings, inspiration, love, and happiness; he had found the universe. The truth of his cousin's story blazed upon him like an inner sun. In this new perspective he saw that it was a grander fairy-tale than he had guessed even when close to it. What was a Scheme for Disabled Thingumabobs compared to the endless, far- reaching schemes that life in Bourcelles suggested to him! There was the true centre of life; cities were accretions of disease upon the surface merely! He was leaving Fairyland behind him.

In sudden moments like this, with their synthetic bird's-eye view, the mind sometimes sees more clearly than in hours of careful reflection and analysis. And the first thing he saw now was Minks, his friendly, ridiculous little confidential secretary. From all the crowds of men and women he knew, respected, and enjoyed in London, as from the vast deluge of human mediocrity which for him *was* London, he picked out suddenly—little Minks—Herbert Montmorency Minks. His mind, that is, darting forward in swift, comprehensive survey, and searching automatically for some means whereby it might continue the happiness and sweetness recently enjoyed, selected Minks. Minks was a clue. Minks possessed—no matter how absurd the proportions of their mixing —three things just left behind: Vision, Belief, Simplicity, all products of a spiritual imagination.

And at first this was the single thought sent forward into the future. Rogers saw the fact, flash-like and true-then let it go, yielding to the greater pull that drew reflection back into the past.

And he found it rather dislocating, this abrupt stepping out of his delightful forest Fairyland.... Equilibrium was not recovered for a long time, as the train went thundering over the Jura Mountains into France, Only on the other side of Pontarlier, when the country grew unfamiliar and different, did harmony return. Among the deep blue forests he was still in Fairyland, but at Mouchard the scenery was already changing, and by the time Dole was reached it had completely changed. The train ran on among the plains and vineyards of the Burgundy country towards Laroche and Dijon. The abrupt alteration, however, was pain. His thoughts streamed all backwards now to counteract it. He roamed again among the star fields above the Bourcelles woods. It was true—he had not really left Bourcelles. His body was bumping into Dijon, but the important part of him—thought, emotion, love—lingered with the children, hovered above the Citadelle, floated through the dusky, scented forests.

And the haunting picture was ever set in its framework of old burning stars. He could not get the Pleiades in particular out of his mind. The pictures swarmed past him as upon a boy returning to school after the holidays, and each one had a background of sky with stars behind it; the faces that he knew so well had starry eyes; Jimbo flung handfuls of stars loose across the air, and Monkey caught them, fastening them like golden pins into her hair. Glancing down, he saw a long brown hair upon his sleeve. He picked it off and held his finger and thumb outside the window till the wind took it away. Some Morning Spider would ride it home—perhaps past his cousin's window while he copied out that wonderful, great tale. But, instead—how in the world could it happen in clear daylight?—a little hand shot down from above and gathered it in towards the Pleiades.

The Pleiades—the Seven Sisters—that most exquisite cluster of the eastern sky, soft, tender, lovely, clinging close together always like a group of timid children, who hide a little dimly for fear of being surprised by bolder stars upon their enormous journey—they now shone down upon all he thought and remembered. They seemed always above the horizon of his mind. They never set. In them lay souls of unborn children, children waiting to be born. He could not imagine why this particular constellation clung with such a haunting touch of beauty about his mind, or why some passion of yearning unconfessed and throbbing hid behind the musical name. Stars and unborn children had got strangely mixed!

He tried to recall the origin of the name—he had learned it once in the old Vicar's study. The Pleiades were attendants upon Artemis, the huntress moon, he recalled vaguely, and, being pursued by Orion, were set for safety among the stars. He even remembered the names of some of them; there was Maia, Tagete, Alcyone, but the other four lay in his mental lumber room, whence they could not be evoked, although Merope, he felt sure, was one of them. Of Maia, however, he felt positive.... How beautiful the names were!

Then, midway, in thinking about them, he found himself, as Monkey said, thinking of something else: of his weeks at Bourcelles again and what a long holiday it had been, and whether it was wasted time or well-used time-a kind of general stock-taking, as it were, but chiefly of how little he had accomplished after all, set down in black and white. He had enjoyed himself and let himself go, rather foolishly perhaps, but how much after all had he actually accomplished? He remembered pleasant conversations with Mother that possibly cheered and helped her—or possibly were forgotten as soon as ended. He remembered his cousin's passing words of gratitude—that he had helped him somehow with his great new story: and he remembered—this least of all-that his money had done something to relieve a case or two of suffering. And this was all! The net result so insignificant! He felt dissatisfied, eager already to make new plans, something definite and thorough that should retrieve the wasted opportunities. With a little thought and trouble, how easily he might have straightened out the tangle of his cousin's family, helped with the education of the growing children, set them all upon a more substantial footing generally. It was possible still, of course, but such things are done best on the spot, the personal touch and presence of value; arranged by correspondence it becomes another thing at once and loses spontaneity. The accent lies on the wrong details. Sympathy is watered by the post.... Importance lodges in angles not intended for it. Master of his time, with certain means at his disposal, a modicum of ability as well, he was free to work hard on the side of the angels wherever opportunity might offer; yet he had wasted all these weeks upon an unnecessary holiday, frittering the time away in enjoyment with the children. He felt ashamed and mortified as the meagre record stared him in the face.

Yet, curiously enough, when Reason had set down the figures accurately, as he fancied, and totted up the trifling totals, there flitted before him something more that refused to be set down upon the paper. The Ledger had no lines for it. What was it? Why was it pleasant, even flattering? Why did it mitigate his discontent and lessen the dissatisfied feeling? It passed hovering in and about his thoughts, though uncaught by actual words; and as his mind played with it, he felt more hopeful. He searched in vain for a definition, but, though fruitless, the search brought comfort somehow. Something *had* been accomplished and it was due to himself, because without his presence it would never have been done. This hint slipped into desire, yearning, hope—that, after all, a result *had* perhaps been achieved, a result he himself was not properly aware of—a result of that incalculable spiritual kind that escapes the chains of definite description. For he recalled—yet mortified a little the memory should flatter—that his cousin had netted Beauty in his story, and that Mother had spoken of living with greater carelessness and peace, and that each had thanked him as though he were the cause.

And these memories, half thought, half feeling, were comforting and delicious, so that he revelled in them lingeringly, and wished that they were really true. For, if true, they were immensely significant. Any one with a purse could build a hospital or pay an education fee, but to be helpful because of being oneself was a vast, incalculable power, something direct from God... and his thoughts, wandering on thus between fact and fantasy, led him back with a deep inexplicable thrill again to—the Pleiades, whose beauty, without their being aware of it, shines nightly for all who can accept it. Here was the old, old truth once more-that the left hand must not know what the right is doing, and that to be is of greater importance than to do. Here was Fairyland once more, the Fairyland he had just left. To think beauty and love is to become them, to shed them forth without realising it. A Fairy blesses because she is a Fairy, not because she turns a pumpkin into a coach and four.... The Pleiades do not realise how their loveliness may....

Rogers started. For the thought had borrowed a tune from the rhythm of the wheels and sleepers, and he had uttered the words aloud in his corner. Luckily he had the carriage to himself. He flushed. Again a tender and very exquisite thing had touched him somewhere.... It was in that involuntary connection his dreaming had found between a Fairy and the Pleiades. Wings of gauzy gold shone fluttering a moment before his inner sight, then vanished. He was aware of some one very dear and wild and tender, with amber eyes and little twinkling feet—some one whom the Great Tale brought almost within his reach.... He literally had seen stars for an instant—*a* star! Its beauty brimmed him up. He laughed in his corner. This thing, whatever it was, had been coming nearer for some time. These hints of sudden joy that breathe upon a sensitive nature, how mysterious, how wildly beautiful, how stimulating they are! But whence, in the name of all the stars, do they come? A great happiness passed flaming through his heart, an extraordinary sense of anticipation in it—as though he were going to meet some one who—who—well, what?—who was a necessity and a delight to him, the complement needed to make his life effective—some one he loved abundantly—who would love him abundantly in return. He recalled those foolish lines he had written on sudden impulse once, then thrown away....

Thought fluttered and went out. He could not seize the elusive cause of this delicious joy. It was connected with the Pleiades, but how, where, why? Above the horizon of his life a new star was swimming into glory. It was rising. The inexplicable emotion thrilled tumultuously, then dived back again whence it came... It had to do with children and with a woman, it seemed, for the next thing he knew was that he was thinking of children, children of his own, and of the deep yearning Bourcelles had stirred again in him to find their Mother... and, next, of his cousin's story and that wonderful detail in it that the principal role was filled at last, the role in the great Children's Play he himself had felt was vacant. It was to be filled by that childless Mother the writer's imagination had discovered or created. And again the Pleiades lit up his inner world and beckoned to him with their little fingers of spun gold; their eyes of clouded amber smiled into his own. It was most extraordinary and delightful. There was something— come much closer this time, almost within reach of discovery—something he ought to remember about them, something he had promised to remember, then stupidly forgotten. The lost, hidden joy was a torture. Yet, try as he would, no revelation came to clear the matter up. Had he read it somewhere perhaps? Or was it part of the Story his cousin had wumbled into his ear when he only partly listened?

'I believe I dreamed it,' he smiled to himself at last in despair. 'I do believe it was a dream—a fragment of some jolly dream I had in my Fairyland of little Bourcelles!'

Children, stars, Fairyland, dreams—these brought it somehow. His cousin's story also had to do with it, chiefly perhaps after all—this great story.

'I shall have to go back there to get hold of it completely,' he added with conviction. He almost felt as if some one were thinking hard about him— one of the characters in the story, it seemed. The mind of some one far away, as yet unknown, was searching for him in thought, sending forth strong definite yearnings which came to rest of their own accord in his own being, a garden naturally suited to their growth. The creations of his boyhood's imagination had survived, the Sweep, the Dustman, and the Lamplighter, then why not the far more powerful creations in the story...? Thought was never lost!

'But no man in his senses can believe such a thing!' he exclaimed, as the train ran booming through the tunnel.

'That's the point,' whispered a voice beside him. 'You are *out* of your senses. Otherwise you could not feel it!'

He turned sharply. The carriage was empty; there was no one there. It was, of course, another part of himself that supplied the answer; yet it startled him. The blurred reflection of the lamp, he noticed, cast a picture against the black tunnel wall that was like a constellation. The Pleiades again! It almost seemed as if the voice had issued from that false reflection in the shaking window-pane....

The train emerged from the tunnel. He rushed out into the blaze of the Interfering Sun. The lovely cluster vanished like a dream, and with it the hint of explanation melted down in dew. Fields sped past with a group of haystacks whose tarpaulin skirts spread and lifted in the gust of wind the train made. He thought abruptly of Mother.... Perhaps, after all, he had taught her something, shown her Existence as a big, streaming, endless thing in which months and years, possibly even life itself, were merely little sections, each unintelligible unless viewed as portions of the Whole, and not as separate, difficult, puzzling items set apart. Possibly he had drawn her map to bigger scale, increased her faith, given her more sense of repose and peace, more courage therefore. She thought formerly of a day, but not of its relation to all days before and behind. She stuck her husband's 'reviews' in the big book, afflicted by the poor financial results they represented, but was unable to think of his work as a stage in a long series of development and progress, no effort lost, no single hope mislaid. And that was something—*if* he had accomplished it. Only, he feared he had not. There was the trouble. There lay the secret of a certain ineffectiveness in his character. For he did not realise that fear is simply suppressed desire, vivid signs of life, and that desire is the ultimate causative agent everywhere and always. 'Behind Will stands Desire,' and Desire is Action.

And if he *had* accomplished this, how was it done? Not by preaching, certainly. Was it, then, simply by being, thinking, feeling it? A glorious thought, if true! For assuredly he had this faculty of seeing life whole, and even in boyhood he had looked ahead over its entire map. He had, indeed, this way of relating all its people, and all its parts together, instead of seeing them separate, unintelligible because the context was left out. He lived intensely in the present, yet looked backwards and forwards too at the same time. This large sympathy, this big comforting vision was his gift. Consequently he believed in Life. Had he also, then, the gift of making others feel and believe it too...?

There he was again, thinking in a circle, as Laroche flew past with its empty platforms, and warned him that Paris was getting close. He bumped out of Fairyland, yet tumbled back once more for a final reverie before the long ugly arms of the city snatched him finally out. 'To see life whole,' he reflected, 'is to see it glorious. To think one's self part of humanity at large is to bring the universe down into the heart. But to see life whole, a whole heart is necessary.... He's done it in that splendid story, and he bagged the raw idea somehow from me. That's something at any rate. ... So few think Beaaty.... But will others see it? That's the point!'

'No, it isn't,' answered the voice beside him. 'The point is that he has thought it, and the universe is richer. Even if others do not read or understand, what he has thought *is there now*, for ever and ever.'

'True,' he reflected, 'for that Beauty may float down and settle in other minds when they least are looking for it, and ignoring utterly whence comes the fairy touch. Divine! Delicious! Heavenly!'

'The Beauty he has written came through you, yet was not yours,' the voice continued very faintly. 'A far more beautiful mind first projected it into that network which binds all minds together. 'Twas thence you caught it flying, and, knowing not how to give it shape, transferred it to another—who could use it—for others…. Thought is Life, and Sympathy is living….'

The voice died away; he could not hear the remainder clearly; the passing scenery caught his attention again; during his reverie it had been unnoticed utterly. 'Thought is Life, but Sympathy is living——' it rolled and poured through him as he repeated it. Snatches of another sentence then came rising into him from an immense distance, falling upon him from immeasurable heights—barely audible:-

'… from a mind that so loved the Pleiades she made their loveliness and joy her own… Alcyone, Merope, Maia…' It dipped away into silence like a flower closing for the night, and the train, he realised, was slackening speed as it drew into the hideous Gare de Lyon.

'I'll talk to Minks about it, perhaps,' he thought, as he stood telling the Customs official that he had no brandy, cigarettes, or lace. 'He knows about things like that. At any rate, he'll sympathise.'

He went across Paris to the Gare du Nord, and caught the afternoon boat train to London. The sunshine glared up from the baking streets, but he never forgot that overhead, though invisible, the stars were shining all the time—Starlight, the most tender and least suspected light in all the world, shining bravely even when obscured by the Interfering Sun, and the Pleiades, softest, sweetest little group among them all.

And when at eleven o'clock he entered his St. James's flat, he took a store of it shining in his heart, and therefore in his eyes. Only that was no difficult matter, for all the lamps far up the heights were lit and gleaming, and caught old mighty London in their gorgeous net.

CHAPTER XXIX

Think with passion
That shall fashion
Life's entire design, well planned.
Woman of the Haystack.

'You are looking so wonderfully well, Mr. Rogers,' Minks observed at Charing Cross Station, 'the passage across the Channel, I trust, was calm.'

'And yourself and Mrs. Minks?' asked Rogers, looking into the equally sunburned face of his secretary, remembering suddenly that he had been to the sea with his family; 'Frank, too, and the other children? All well, I hope?'

'All in excellent health, Mr. Rogers, thanks to your generous thought. My wife——'

'These are the small bags,' the other interrupted, 'and here are the keys for my portmanteaux. There's nothing dutiable. You might bring them on to the flat while I run over to the Club for a bit of supper, Minks.'

'Certainly, with pleasure, Mr. Rogers,' was the beaming reply. 'And Mrs. Minks begged me to tell you——'

Only Rogers was already in his taxi-cab and out of ear-shot.

'How well he looks!' reflected Minks, dangling the keys, accustomed to these abrupt interruptions, and knowing that his message had been understood and therefore duly delivered. These cut-off sentences were like a secret code between them. 'And ten years younger! Almost like a boy again. I wonder if——' He did not permit himself to finish the thought. He tried to remember if he himself had looked like that perhaps in the days of long ago when he courted Albinia Lucy—an air of joy and secrecy and an absent-minded manner that might any moment flame into vehement, concentrated action. For this was the impression his employer had made upon him. Only he could not quite remember those far-off, happy days. There was ecstasy in them; that he knew. And there was ecstasy in Henry Rogers now; that he divined.

'He oughtn't to,' he reflected, as he hurried in another taxi with the luggage. 'All his yearnings would be satisfied if he did, his life flow into a single channel instead of into many.'

He did not think about his own position and his salary.

'He won't,' he decided as the cab stopped at the door; 'he's not that kind of man.' Minks had insight; he knew men. 'No artist ever ought to. We are so few, and the world has need of us.' His own case was an exception that had justified itself, for he was but a man of talent, and talent did not need an exclusive asceticism; whereas his employer was a man of genius, and no one woman had the right to monopolise what was intended to sweeten the entire universe.

By the time the luggage had been taken up, he had missed the last tram home, and his sleep that night must in any case be short. Yet he took no note of that. One must live largely. A small sacrifice for such a master was nothing at all. He lingered, glancing now and again at the heap of correspondence that would occupy them next morning, and sorting once more the little pile that would need immediate personal attention. He was picking a bit of disfiguring fluff from his coat sleeve when the door opened and Henry Rogers came upon him.

'Ah! I waited a moment, Mr. Rogers. I thought you might have something to say before I went, perhaps.'

'I hoped you would, Minks. I have a great deal to say. It can wait till to-morrow, really—only I wanted—but, there now, I forgot; you have to get down to Sydenham, haven't you? And it's late already——'

'That's nothing, Mr. Rogers. I can easily sleep in town. I came prepared, indeed, to do so——' as though he, too, had his Club and would take a bedroom in it.

'Clever and thoughtful of you, Minks!'

'Only you must be tired after your journey,' suggested the secretary.

'Tired!' exclaimed the other vigorously, 'not a bit! I'm as fresh as a st—a daisy, I mean. Come, draw your chair up; we'll have a smoke and a little chat. I'm delighted to see you again. How are you? And how's everything?'

Goodness! How bright his eyes were, how alert his manner! He looked so young, almost springy, thought Minks, as he obeyed decorously, feeling flattered and pleased, yet at the same time uneasy a little. Such spirits could only proceed, he feared, from one cause. He was a close observer, as all poets had need to be. He would discover some clue before he went to bed, something that should betray the true state of affairs. In any case sleep would be impossible unless he did.

'You stayed away somewhat longer than you originally intended,' he ventured at length, having briefly satisfied his employer's question. 'You found genuine recreation. You needed it, I'm sure.' He glanced with one eye at the letters.

'Re-creation, yes; the very word. It was difficult to leave. The place was so delightful,' said Rogers simply, filling his pipe and lighting it. 'A wonderful mountain village, Minks,' he added, between puffs of smoke, while the secretary, who had been waiting for the sign, then lit his own Virginian and smoked it diffidently, and with just the degree of respect he felt was becoming. He never presumed upon his master's genial way of treating him. He made little puffs and was very careful with the ashes.

'Ah, yes,' he said; 'I am sure it must have been—both delightful and —er—difficult to leave.' He recalled the Margate sands, bathing with Albinia and digging trenches with the children. He had written many lyrics during those happy weeks of holiday.

'Gave one, in fact, quite a new view of life—and work. There was such space and beauty everywhere. And my cousin's children simply would not let me go.'

There was a hint of apology and excuse in the tone and words—the merest hint, but Minks noticed it and liked the enthusiasm. 'He's been up to some mischief; he feels a little ashamed; his work—his Scheme— has been so long neglected; conscience pricks him. Ha, ha!' The secretary felt his first suspicion confirmed. 'Cousin's children,' perhaps! But who else?

'He made a tactful reference—oh, very slight and tentative—to the data he had collected for the Scheme, but the other either did not hear it, or did not wish to hear it. He brushed it aside, speaking through clouds of tobacco smoke. Minks enjoyed a bigger, braver puff at his own. Excitement grew in him.

'Just the kind of place you would have loved, Minks,' Rogers went on with zeal. 'I think you really must go there some day; cart your family over, teach the children French, you know, and cultivate a bit of vineyard. Such fine big forests, too, full of wild flowers and things—O such lovely hand-made things—why, you could almost see the hand that made 'em.' The phrase had slipped suddenly into his mind.

'Really, really, Mr. Rogers, but how very jo—delightful it sounds.' He thought of the stubble fields and treeless sea-coast where he had been. The language, however, astonished him. Enthusiasm like this could only spring from a big emotion. His heart sank a little.

'And the people all so friendly and hospitable and simple that you could go climbing with your bootmaker or ask your baker in to dine and sleep. No snobbery! Sympathy everywhere and a big free life flowing in your veins.' This settled it. Only a lover finds the whole world lovable.

'One must know the language, though,' said Minks, 'in order to enjoy the people and understand them, I suppose?'

'Not a bit, not a bit! One *feels* it all, you see; somehow one feels it and understands. A few words useful here and there, but one gets along without even these. I never knew such a place. Every one seemed to be in sympathy together. They think it, as it were. It was regular fairyland, I tell you.'

'Which means that *you* felt and thought it,' said Minks to himself. Aloud he merely remarked, though with conviction, for he was getting interested, 'Thinking is important, I know.'

Rogers laid his pipe aside and suddenly turned upon him—so abruptly that Minks started. Was this the confession coming? Would he hear now that his chief was going to be married? His wandering eyes almost drew level in the excitement that he felt. He knocked a tiny ash from his cigarette and waited. But the expected bomb did not explode. He heard instead this curious question:—

'And that's something—it reminds me now—something I particularly wanted to ask you about, my dear fellow. You are familiar, I know, with such things and theories—er—speculations, as it were. You read that sort of stuff. You are in touch with the latest ideas, I mean, and up-to-date. You can tell me, if any one can.'

He paused, hesitating a moment, as Minks, listening in some bewilderment, gazed into his eager face. He said nothing. He only committed himself to a deprecating gesture with his hands, letting his cigarette slip from his fingers on to the carpet.

'About *thought*,' continued Rogers, keeping his eyes fixed upon him while he rose with flushed face from the search to find the stump. 'What do you know about thought? Tell me what you hear about *that*— what theories are held—what people believe about it. I mean thought- transference, telepathy, or whatever it is called. Is it proved? Is it a fact?'

His voice had lowered. There was mystery in his manner. He sat back in his chair, picked up his pipe, replaced it in his mouth unlighted, and waited.

Minks pulled himself together. His admirable qualities as a private secretary now came in. Putting excitement and private speculations of his own aside, he concentrated his orderly mind upon replies that should be models of succinct statement. He had practised thought- control, and prided himself upon the fact. He could switch attention instantly from one subject to another without confusion. The replies, however, were, of course, drawn from his own reading. He neither argued nor explained. He merely stated.

'Those who have taken the trouble to study the evidence believe,' he began, 'that it is established, though its laws are as yet unknown. Personally, if I may quote myself, I do believe it.'

'Quite so, quite so. Do quote yourself—that's what I want—facts. But you refer to deliberate experiments, don't you?'

'In my own case, yes, Mr. Rogers, although the most successful thought-transference is probably unconscious and not deliberate——'

'Such as, for instance——'

'Public opinion,' replied Minks, after a moment's search, 'which is the result of waves of thought sent out by everybody—by a community; or by the joint thinking of a nation, again, which modifies every mind born into that nation, the result of centuries of common thinking along definite familiar channels. Thought-currents rush everywhere about the world, affecting every one more or less, and—er— particularly lodging in minds receptive to them.'

'Thought is dynamic, then, they hold?'

'An actual force, yes; as actual as electricity, and as little understood,' returned the secretary, proud that he had read these theories and remembered them. 'With every real thought a definite force goes forth from you that modifies every single person, and probably every single object as well, in the entire world. Thought is creative according to its intensity. It links everybody in the world with everybody else——'

'Objects too, you say?' Rogers questioned.

Minks glanced up to make sure there was no levity in the question, but only desire for knowledge.

'Objects too,' he replied, apparently satisfied, 'for science tells us that the movement of a body here affects the farthest star. A continuous medium— ether—transmits the vibrations without friction— and thought-force is doubtless similarly transmitted—er——'

'So that if I think of a flower or a star, my thought leaps into them and affects them?' the other interrupted again.

'More, Mr. Rogers,' was the reply, 'for your thought, being creative, enriches the world with images of beauty which may float into another mind across the sea, distance no obstacle at all. You make a mental image when you think. There's imagination in all real thinking—if I make myself clear. "Our most elaborate thoughts," to quote for a moment, "are often, as I think, not really ours, but have on a sudden come up, as it were, out of hell or down out of heaven." So what one thinks affects everybody in the world. The noble thinkers lift humanity, though they may never tell their thoughts in speech or writing.'

His employer stared at him in silence through the cloud of smoke. The clock on the mantelpiece struck half-past twelve.

'That is where the inspiration of the artist comes in,' continued the secretary after a moment's hesitation whether he should say it or not, 'for his sensitive soul collects them and gives them form. They lodge in him and grow, and every passionate longing for spiritual growth sets the whole world growing too. Your Scheme for Disabled——'

'Even if it never materialises——' Rogers brusquely interposed.

'Sweetens the world—yes—according to this theory,' continued Minks, wondering what in the world had come over his chief, yet so pleased to state his own views that he forgot to analyse. 'A man in a dungeon earnestly praying would accomplish more than an active man outside who merely lived thoughtlessly, even though beneficently—if I make myself clear.'

'Yes, yes; you make yourself admirably clear, Minks, as I knew you would.' Rogers lit his pipe again and puffed hard through a minute's silence. The secretary held his peace, realising from the tone of the last sentence that he had said enough. Mr. Rogers was leading up to other questions. Hitherto he had been clearing the ground.

It came then, through the clouds of smoke, though Minks failed to realise exactly why it was—so important:

'So that if I thought vividly of anything, I should. actually create a mental picture which in turn might slip into another's mind, while that other would naturally suppose it was his own?'

'Exactly, Mr. Rogers; exactly so.' Minks contrived to make the impatience in his voice sound like appreciation of his master's quickness. 'Distance no obstacle either,' he repeated, as though fond of the phrase.

'And, similarly, the thought I deemed my own might have come in its turn from the mind of some one else?'

'Precisely; for thought binds us all together like a network, and to think of others is to spread oneself about the universe. When we think thus we get out—as it were—into that medium common to all of us where spirit meets spirit——'

'Out!' exclaimed Rogers, putting down his pipe and staring keenly, first into one eye, then into the other. 'Out?'

'Out—yes,' Minks echoed faintly, wondering why that particular word was chosen. He felt a little startled. This earnest talk, moreover, stirred the subconsciousness in him, so that he remembered that unfinished sonnet he had begun weeks ago at Charing Cross. If he were alone now he could complete it. Lines rose and offered themselves by the dozen. His master's emotion had communicated itself to him. A breath of that ecstasy he had already divined passed through the air between them.

'It's what the Contemplative Orders attempt——' he continued, yet half to himself, as though a little bemused.

'Out, by George! Out!' Rogers said again.

So emphatic was the tone that Minks half rose from his chair to go.

'No, no,' laughed his chief; 'I don't mean that you're to get out. Forgive my abruptness. The fact is I was thinking aloud a moment. I meant—I mean that you've explained a lot to me I didn't understand before—had never thought about, rather. And it's rather wonderful, you see. In fact, it's *very* wonderful, Minks,' he added, with the grave enthusiasm of one who has made a big discovery, 'this world *is* a very wonderful place.'

'It is simply astonishing, Mr. Rogers,' Minks answered with conviction, 'astonishingly beautiful.'

'That's what I mean,' he went on. 'If I think beauty, that beauty may materialise——'

'Must, will, does materialise, Mr. Rogers, just as your improvements in machinery did. You first thought them out!'

'Then put them into words; yes, and afterwards into metal. Strong thought is bound to realise itself sooner or later, eh? Isn't it all grand and splendid?'

They stared at one another across the smoky atmosphere of the London flat at the hour of one in the morning in the twentieth century.

'And when I think of a Scaffolding of Dusk that builds the Night,' Rogers went on in a lower tone to himself, yet not so low that Minks, listening in amazement, did not catch every syllable, 'or of a Dustman, Sweep, and Lamplighter, of a Starlight Express, or a vast Star Net that binds the world in sympathy together, and when I weave all these into a story, whose centre somehow is the Pleiades—all this is real and actual, and—and——'

'May have been projected by another mind before it floated into your own,' Minks suddenly interposed almost in a whisper, charmed wholly into the poet's region by these suggestive phrases, yet wondering a little why he said it, and particularly how he dared to say it.

His chief turned sharply upon him.

'My own thought exactly!' he exclaimed; 'but how the devil did you guess it?'

Minks returned the stare with triumph.

'Unconscious transference!' he said.

'You really think *that*?' his master asked, yet not mockingly.

Minks turned a shade pinker.

'I do, indeed, sir,' he replied warmly. 'I think it probable that the thoughts of people you have never seen or heard of drop into your mind and colour it. They lodge there, or are rejected, according to your mood and the texture of your longings—what you want to be, that is. What you want, if I may say so, is emptiness, and that emptiness invites. The flying thought flits in and makes itself at home. Some people overflow with thoughts of kindness and beauty that radiate from them, of love and tenderness and desire to help. These thoughts, it may be, find no immediate object; but they are not lost. They pour loose about the world of men and women, and sooner or later find the empty heart that needs them. I believe, sir, that to sit in a chair and think such things strongly brings comfort to thousands who have little idea whence comes the sudden peace and happiness. And any one who happens to be praying for these things at the moment attracts them instantly. The comfort, the joy, the relief come—'

'What a good idea, Minks,' said Rogers gently, 'and how helpful if we all believed it. No one's life need be a failure then. Those who want love, for instance, need it, crave it, just think what an army they are!'

He stared thoughtfully a moment at his little secretary.

'You might write a book about it, you know—try and make people believe it—convince them. Eh? Only, you'd have to give your proofs, you know. People want proofs.'

Minks, pinker than before, hesitated a moment. He was not sure how far he ought to, indulge his private theories in words. The expression in his chief's blue eyes apparently encouraged him.

'But, indeed, Mr. Rogers, the proofs are there. Those moments of sudden strength and joy that visit a man, catching him unawares and unexplained— every solitary man and woman knows them, for every solitary man and woman in the world craves first of all—to *be* loved. To love another, others, an impersonal Cause, is not enough. It is only half of life; to *be* loved is the other half. If every single person—I trust, sir, I do not tire you?—was loved by some one, the happiness of life would be enormously greater than it is, for each one loved would automatically then give out from his own store, and to receive love makes one overflow with love for every one else. It is so, is it not, sir?'

Rogers, an odd thrill catching him unawares, nodded. 'It is, Minks, it is,' he agreed. 'To love one person makes one half prepared to love all, and to be loved in turn may have a similar effect. It is nice to think so anyhow.'

'It is true, sir——' and Minks sat up, ready with another deluge.

'But you were saying something just now,' interrupted the other, 'about these sudden glimpses of joy and beauty that—er—come to one— er—inexplicably. What d'ye mean by that precisely?'

Minks glowed. He was being listened to, and understood by his honoured chief, too!

'Simply that some one, perhaps far away—some sweet woman probably—has been thinking love,' he replied with enthusiasm, yet in a low and measured voice, 'and that the burning thoughts have rushed into the emptiness of a heart that needs them. Like water, thought finds its level. The sudden gush—all feel it more or less at times, surely!— may rise first from her mind as she walks lonely upon the shore, pacing the decks at sea, or in her hillside rambles, thinking, dreaming, hoping, yearning—to pour out and find the heart that needs these very things, perhaps far across the world. Who knows? Heart thrills in response to heart secretly in every corner of the globe, and when these tides flood unexplained into your soul——'

'Into *my* soul——!' exclaimed his chief.

'I beg your pardon, sir,' Minks hurried to explain; 'I mean to any lonely soul that happens to crave such comfort with real longing—it implies, to my mind at least, that these two are destined to give and take from one another, and that, should they happen to meet in actual life, they will rush together instantly like a pair of flames——'

'And if they never—meet?' asked Rogers slowly, turning to the mantel-piece for the matches.

'They will continue to feed each other in this delicious spiritual way from a distance, sir. Only—the chances are—that they will meet, for their thought already connects them vitally, though as yet unrealised.'

There was a considerable pause. Rogers lit his pipe. Minks, feeling he ought to stand while his master did so, also rose from his chair. The older man turned; they faced each other for a moment, Rogers putting smoke violently into the air between them.

'Minks, my dear fellow,' he observed, 'you are, as I have always thought, a poet. You have ideas, and, whether true or not, they are rather lovely. Write them out for others to read. Use your spare time writing them out. I'll see to it that you have more leisure.'

With a laugh the big man moved abruptly past his chair and knocked his pipe on the edge of the ash-bowl. His eye, as he did so, fell upon the pile of letters and papers arranged so neatly on the table. He remembered the lateness of the hour—and other things besides.

'Well, well,' he said vaguely with a sigh; 'so here we are again back at work in London.'

Minks had turned, too, realising that the surprising conversation was over. A great excitement was in him. He did not feel in the least tired. An unusual sense of anticipation was in the air. He could not make it out at all. Reviewing a dozen possibilities at once, he finally rejected the romantic one he had first suspected, and decided that the right moment had at last come to say something of the Scheme. He had worked so hard to collect data. All was in perfect order. His chief could not feel otherwise than pleased.

'Then I'll be saying good-night, Mr. Rogers,' he began, 'for you must be very tired, and I trust you will enjoy a long night's rest. Perhaps you would like me to come a little later in the morning than usual.'

He stood looking affectionately at the formidable pile of correspondence, and, as his chief made no immediate reply, he went on, with more decision in his voice:

'Here,' he said, touching the papers he had carefully set on one side, 'are all the facts you wanted referring to your great Scheme——'

He jumped. His master's fist had come down with a bang upon the table. He stepped back a pace. They stared at one another.

'Damn the Scheme!' cried Rogers. 'have done and finished with it. Tear up the papers. Cancel any arrangements already made. And never mention the thing again in my hearing. It's all unreal and wrong and unnecessary!'

Minks gasped. The man was so in earnest. What could it mean?

'Wrong—unnecessary—done with!' he faltered. Then, noticing the flashing eyes that yet betrayed a hint of merriment in their fire, he added quickly, 'Quite so, Mr. Rogers; I understand. You've got an improvement, you mean?'

It was not his place to ask questions, but he could not contain himself. Curiosity and disappointment rushed over him.

'A bigger and a better one altogether, Minks,' was the vehement reply. He pushed the heap of papers towards the secretary. Minks took them gingerly, reluctantly.

'Burn 'em up,' Rogers went on, 'and never speak to me again about the blessed thing. I've got a far bigger Scheme than that.'

Minks slowly gathered the papers together and put them in his biggest pocket. He knew not what to think. The suddenness of the affair dazed him. Thought-transference failed this time; he was too perturbed, indeed, to be in a receptive state at all. It seemed a catastrophe, a most undesirable and unexpected climax. The romantic solution revived in him—but only for a passing moment. He rejected it. Some big discovery was in the air. He felt that extraordinary sense of anticipation once again.

'Look here, my dear fellow, Minks,' said Rogers, who had been watching his discomfiture with amusement, 'you may be surprised, but you need not be alarmed. The fact is, this has been coming for a long time; it's not an impulsive decision. You must have felt it—from my letters. That Scheme was all right enough, only I am not the right man for it. See? And our work,' he added laughingly, 'won't go for nothing either, because our thought will drop into another mind somewhere that will accomplish the thing far better than I could have accomplished it.'

Minks made an odd gesture, as who should say this might not be true. He did not venture upon speech, however. This new plan must be very wonderful, was all he thought just then. His faith in his employer's genius was complete.

'And in due time you shall hear all about it. Have a little patience. Perhaps you'll get it out of my thoughts before I tell it to you,' he smiled, 'but perhaps you won't. I can only tell you just now that it has beauty in it—a beauty of the stars.'

Yet what his bigger Scheme was he really had no clear idea. He felt it coming-that was all!

And with that Minks had to be content. This was dismissal. Good-nights were said, and the secretary went out into the street.

'Go to a comfortable hotel,' was the last thing he heard, 'and put it down to me, of course. Sleep well, sleep well. To-morrow at two o'clock will do.'

Minks strolled home, walking upon air. The sky was brilliant with its gorgeous constellations—the beauty of the stars. Poems blazed upon him. But he was too excited to compose. Even first lines evaded capture. 'Stars,' besides, was a dreadful word to rhyme with, for all its charm and loveliness.

He knew of old that the only word was 'wars,' most difficult to bring in naturally and spontaneously, and with the wrong sound in any case.

'He must have been writing poetry out there,' he reflected finally, 'or else living it. Living it, probably. He's a grand fellow anyhow, grand as a king.' Stars, wars, kings, thrones-=the words flew in and out among a maze of unaccomplished lines.

But the last thing in his mind as he curled up to sleep in the strange bed was that he had delivered his wife's message, but that he could not tell her about this sudden collapse of the great, long-talked-of Scheme. Albinia would hardly understand. She might think less of his chief. He would wait until the new one dawned upon the horizon with its beauty of the stars. Then he would simply overwhelm her with it, as his temperament loved to do.

CHAPTER XXX

Lo, every yearning thought that holds a tear,
Yet finds no mission
And lies untold,
Waits, guarded in that labyrinth of gold,—
To reappear
Upon some perfect night,
Deathless—not old—
But sweet with time and distance,
And clothed as in a vision
Of starry brilliance
For the world's delight.
                    JOHN HENRY CAMPDEN.

Then, as the days passed, practical life again caught Henry Rogers in its wholesome grip. Fairyland did not fade exactly, but it dipped a little below the horizon. Like hell and heaven, it was a state of mind, open potentially to all, but not to be enjoyed merely for the asking. Like other desirable things, it was to be 'attained.' Its remoteness and difficulty of access lent to it a haunting charm; for though its glory dimmed a little, there was a soft afterglow that shed its radiance even down Piccadilly and St. James's Street. He was always conscious of this land beyond the sunset; the stars shone brightly, though clouds or sunlight interfered to blur their message.

London life, however, by the sheer weight of its grinding daily machinery, worked its slow effect upon him. He became less sensitive to impressions. These duller periods were interrupted sometimes by states of brilliant receptiveness, as at Bourcelles; but there was a fence between the two—a rather prickly frontier, and the secret of combining them lay just beyond his reach. For his London mind, guided by reason, acted in a logical plane of two dimensions, while imagination, captained by childhood's fairy longings, cantered loose in all directions at once—impossibly. The first was the world; the second was the universe. As yet, he was unable to co-ordinate them. Minks, he was certain, could—and did, sailing therefore upon an even keel. There was this big harmony in little Minks that he envied. Minks had an outlet. Sydenham, and even the City, for him were fairyland; a motor-bus fed his inspiration as surely as a starlit sky; moon always rhymed with June, and forget with regret. But the inner world of Henry Rogers was not yet properly connected with the outer. Passage from one to the other was due to chance, it seemed, not to be effected at will. Moods determined the sudden journey. He rocked. But for his talks with little Minks, he might have wrecked.

And the talks with Minks were about—well, he hardly knew what, but they all played round this map of fairyland he sought to reduce to the scale of everyday life. They discussed thought, dreams, the possibility of leaving the body in sleep, the artist temperament, the source of inspiration as well as the process of the imaginative faculty that created. They talked even of astronomy. Minks held that the life of practical, daily work was the bed-rock of all sane production, yet while preaching this he bubbled over with all the wild, entrancing theories that were in the air to-day. They were comical, but never dangerous—did not upset him. They were almost a form of play.

And his master, listening, found these conversations an outlet somehow for emotions in himself he could not manage—a scaffolding that provided outlines for his awakening dreams to build upon. He found relief. For Minks, with his delightful tact, asked no awkward questions. He referred neither to the defunct Scheme, nor mentioned the new one that held 'a beauty of the stars.' He waited. Rogers also waited.

And, while he waited, he grew conscious more and more of an enormous thing that passed, driving behind, *below*, his daily external life. He could never quite get at it. In there, down out of sight somewhere, he knew everything. His waking existence was fed invisibly from below. In the daytime he now frequently caught himself attempting to recover the memory of things that went on elsewhere, things he was personally involved in, vital things. This daylight effort to recover them was as irksome as the attempt to draw a loose hair that has wound about the tongue. He spoke at length to Minks about it.

'Some part of you,' replied the imperturbable secretary, after listening carefully to his master's vague description of the symptoms, 'is being engaged elsewhere—very actively engaged——'

'Eh?' asked Rogers, puzzled.

'Probably at night, sir, while your brain and body sleep,' Minks elaborated, 'your energetic spirit is out—on the plane of causes——'

The other gasped slightly, 'While my body lies unconscious?'

'Your spirit may be busy at all kinds of things. *That* can never be unconscious,' was the respectful answer. 'They say——'

'Yes, what do they say?' He recognised a fairy theory, and jumped at it.

'That in sleep,' continued the other, encouraged, 'the spirit knows a far more concentrated life—dips down into the deep sea of being—our waking life merely the froth upon the shore.'

Rogers stared at him. 'Yes, yes,' he answered slowly, 'that's very pretty, very charming; it's quite delightful. What ideas you have, my dear Minks! What jolly, helpful ideas!'

Minks beamed with pleasure.

'Not my own, Mr. Rogers, not my own,' he said, with as much pride as if they *were* his own, 'but some of the oldest in the world, just coming into fashion again with the turn of the tide, it seems. Our daily life—even the most ordinary—is immensely haunted, girdled about with a wonder of incredible things. There are hints everywhere to-day, though few can read the enormous script complete. Here and there one reads a letter or a word, that's all. Yet the best minds refuse to know the language, not even the ABC of it; they read another language altogether—'

'The best minds!' repeated Rogers. 'What d'you mean by that!' It sounded, as Minks said it, so absurdly like best families.

'The scientific and philosophical minds, sir. They think it's not worth learning, this language. That's the pity of it—ah, the great pity of it!' And he looked both eager and resentful—his expression almost pathetic. He turned half beseechingly to his employer, as though *he* might alter the sad state of things. 'As with an iceberg, Mr. Rogers,' he added, 'the greater part of everything—of ourselves especially—is invisible; we merely know the detail banked against an important grand Unseen.'

The long sentence had been suffered to its close because the audience was busy with thoughts of his own instead of listening carefully. Behind the wild language stirred some hint of meaning that, he felt, held truth. For a moment, it seemed, his daylight searching was explained—almost.

'Well and good, my dear fellow, and very picturesque,' he said presently, gazing with admiration at his secretary's neat blue tie and immaculate linen; 'but thinking, you know, is not possible without matter.' This in a tone of '*Do* talk a little sense.' 'Even if the spirit does go out, it couldn't think apart from the brain, could it now, eh?'

Minks took a deep breath and relieved himself of the following:

'Ah, Mr. Rogers'—as much as to say 'Fancy *you* believing that!'— 'but it can experience and know *direct*, since it passes into the region whence the material that feeds thought issues in the first instance—causes, Mr. Rogers, causes.'

'Oho!' said his master, 'oho!'

'There is no true memory afterwards,' continued the little dreamer, 'because memory depends upon how much the spirit can bring back into the brain, you see. We have vague feelings, rather than actual recollection—feelings such as you were kind enough to confess to me you had been haunted by yourself—'

'All-overish feelings,' Rogers helped him, seeing that he was losing confidence a little, 'vague sensations of joy and wonder and—well—in a word, strength.'

'Faith,' said Minks, with a decision of renewed conviction, 'which is really nothing but unconscious knowledge—knowledge unremembered. And it's the half-memory of what you do at night that causes this sense of anticipation you now experience; for what is anticipation, after all, but memory thrown forward?'

There was a pause then, during which Rogers lit a cigarette, while Minks straightened his tie several times in succession.

'You are a greater reader than I, of course,' resumed his employer presently; 'still, I have come across one or two stories which deal with this kind of thing. Only, in the books, the people always remember what they've done at night, out of the body, in the spirit, or whatever you like to call it. Now, *I* remember nothing whatever. How d'you account for that, pray?'

Minks smiled a little sadly. 'The books,' he answered very softly, 'are wrong there—mere inventions—not written from personal experience. There can be no detailed memory unless the brain has been 'out' too—which it hasn't. That's where inaccuracy and looseness of thought come in. If only the best minds would take the matter up, you see, we might—'

Rogers interrupted him. 'We shall miss the post, Minks, if we go on dreaming and talking like this,' he exclaimed, looking at his watch and then at the pile of letters waiting to be finished. 'It is very delightful indeed, very—but we mustn't forget to be practical, too.'

And the secretary, not sorry perhaps to be rescued in time from the depths he had floundered in, switched his mind in concentration upon the work in hand again. The conversation had arisen from a chance coincidence in this very correspondence—two letters that had crossed after weeks of silence.

Work was instantly resumed. It went on as though it had never been interrupted. Pride and admiration stirred the heart of Minks as he noticed how keenly and accurately his master's brain took up the lost threads again. 'A grand fellow!' he thought to himself, 'a splendid man! He lives in both worlds at once, yet never gets confused, nor lets one usurp his powers to the detriment of the other. If only I were equally balanced and effective. Oh dear!' And he sighed.

And there were many similar conversations of this kind. London seemed different, almost transfigured sometimes. Was this the beginning of that glory which should prove it a suburb of Bourcelles?

Rogers found his thoughts were much in that cosy mountain village: the children capered by his side all day; he smelt the woods and flowers; he heard the leaves rustle on the poplar's crest; and had merely to think of a certain room in the tumble-down old Citadelle for a wave of courage and high anticipation to sweep over him like a sea. A new feeling of harmony was taking him in hand. It was very delightful; and though he felt explanation beyond his reach still, his talks with Minks provided peep-holes through which he peered at the enormous thing that brushed him day and night.

A great settling was taking place inside him. Thoughts certainly began to settle. He realised, for one thing, that he had left the theatre where the marvellous Play had been enacted. He stood outside now, able to review and form a judgment. His mind loved order. Undue introspection he disliked, as a form of undesirable familiarity; a balanced man must not be too familiar with himself; it endangered self-respect.

He had been floundering rather. After years of methodical labour the freedom of too long a holiday was disorganising. He tried to steady himself. And the Plan of Life, answering to control, grew smaller instantly, reduced to proportions he could examine reasonably. This was the beginning of success. The bewildering light of fairyland still glimmered, but no longer so diffused. It focused into little definite kernels he could hold steady while he scrutinised them.

And these kernels he examined carefully as might be: in the quiet, starry evenings usually, while walking alone in St. James's Park after his day of board meetings, practical work with Minks, and the like.

Gradually then, out of the close survey, emerged certain things that seemed linked together in an intelligible sequence of cause and effect. There was still mystery, for subconscious investigation ever involves this background of shadow. Question and Wonder watched him. But the facts emerged.

He jotted them down on paper as best he could. The result looked like a Report drawn up by Minks, only less concise and—he was bound to admit it—less intelligible. He smiled as he read them over....

'My thoughts and longings, awakened that night in the little Crayfield garden,' he summed it up to himself, having read the Report so far, 'went forth upon their journey of realisation. I projected them— according to Minks—vividly enough for that! I thought Beauty—and this glorious result materialised! More—my deepest, oldest craving of all has come to life again—the cry of loneliness that yearns to—that seeks—er——'

At this point, however, his analysis grew wumbled; the transference of thought and emotion seemed comprehensible enough; though magical, it was not more so than wireless telegraphy, or that a jet of steam should drive an express for a hundred miles. It was conceivable that Daddy had drawn thence the inspiration for his wonderful story. What baffled him was the curious feeling that another was mixed up in the whole, delightful business, and that neither he nor his cousin were the true sponsors of the fairy fabric. He never forgot the description his cousin read aloud that night in the Den—how the Pattern of his Story reached its climax and completeness when a little starry figure with twinkling feet and amber eyes had leaped into the centre and made itself at home there. From the Pleiades it came. The lost Pleiad was found. The network of thought and sympathy that contained the universe had trembled to its uttermost fastenings. The principal role was filled at last.

It was here came in the perplexing thing that baffled him. His mind sat down and stared at an enormous, shadowy possibility that he was unable to grasp. It brushed past him overhead, beneath, on all sides. He peered up at it and marvelled, unconvinced, yet knowing himself a prisoner. Something he could not understand was coming, was already close, was watching him, waiting the moment to pounce out, like an invisible cat upon a bewildered mouse. The question he flung out brought no response, and he recalled with a smile the verse that described his absurd position:—

Like a mouse who, lost in wonder,
Flicks its whiskers at the thunder!

For, while sprites and yearning were decidedly his own, the interpretation of them, if not their actual origin, seemed another's. This other, like some dear ideal on the way to realisation, had taken him prisoner. The queer sense of anticipation Bourcelles had fostered was now actual expectation, as though some Morning Spider had borne his master-longing, exquisitely fashioned by the Story, across the Universe, and the summons had been answered-from the Pleiades. The indestructible threads of thought and feeling tightened. The more he thought about his cousin's interpretation the more he found in it a loveliness and purity, a crystal spiritual quality, that he could credit neither to the author's mind nor to his own. This soft and starry brilliance was another's. Up to a point the interpretation came through Daddy's brain, just as the raw material came through his own; but there-after this other had appropriated both, as their original creator and proprietor. Some shining, delicate hand reached down from its starry home and gathered in this exquisite form built up from the medley of fairy thought and beauty that were first its own. The owner of that little hand would presently appear to claim it.

'We were but channels after all then—both of us,' was the idea that lay so insistently in him. 'The sea of thought sends waves in all directions. They roll into different harbours. I caught the feeling, he supplied the form, but this other lit the original fire!'

And further than this wumbled conclusion he could not get. He went about his daily work. however, with a secret happiness tugging at his mind all day, and a sense of expectant wonder glancing brightly over everything he thought or did. He was a prisoner in fairyland, and what he called his outer and his inner world were, after all, but different ways of looking at one and the same thing. Life everywhere was one.

CHAPTER XXXI

Es stehen unbeweglich
Die Sterne in der Hoh'
Viel tausend Jahr', und schauen
Sich an mit Liebesweh.

Sie sprechen eine Sprache,
Die ist so reich, so schon;
Doch keiner der Philologen
Kann diese Sprache verstehen.

Ich aber hab' sie gelernet,
Und ich vergesse sie nicht;
Mir diente als Grammatik
Der Herzallerliebsten Gesicht.
                    HEINE.

One evening in particular the sense of expectation in him felt very close upon delivery. All day he had been aware of it, and a letter received that morning from his cousin seemed the cause. The story, in its shorter version, had been accepted. Its reality, therefore, had already spread; one other mind, at least, had judged it with understanding. Two months from now, when it appeared in print, hundreds more would read it. Its beauty would run loose in many hearts. And Rogers went about his work that day as though the pleasure was his own. The world felt very sweet. He saw the good in every one with whom he came in contact. And the inner excitement due to something going to happen was continuous and cumulative.

Yet London just then—it was August—was dull and empty, dusty, and badly frayed at the edges. It needed a great cleaning; he would have liked to pour sea water over all its streets and houses, bathed its panting parks in the crystal fountains of Bourcelles. All day long his thoughts, indeed, left London for holidays in little Bourcelles. He was profoundly conscious that the Anticipation he first recognised in that forest village was close upon accomplishment now. On the journey back to England he recalled how urgent it had been. In London, ever since, it had never really left him. But to-day it now suddenly became more than expectation—he felt it in him as a certainty that approached fulfilment. It was strange, it was bewildering; it seemed to him as though something from that under-self he could never properly reach within him, pushed upwards with a kind of aggressive violence towards the surface. It was both sweet and vital. Behind the 'something' was the 'some one' who led it into action.

At half-past six he strolled down a deserted St. James's Street, passed the door of his club with no temptation to go in, and climbed the stairs slowly to his rooms. His body was languid though his mind alert. He sank into an arm-chair beside the open window. 'I must *do* something to-night,' he thought eagerly; 'mere reading at the club is out of the question. I'll go to a theatre or—or—.' He considered various alternatives, deciding finally upon Richmond Park. He loved long walks at night when his mind was restless thus; the air in Richmond Park was peculiarly fresh and scented after dark. He knew the little gate that was never closed. He would dine lightly, and go for a ten-mile stretch among the oaks, surprise the deer asleep, listen to the hum of distant London, and watch the fairy battle between the lurid reflection of its million lights and the little stars…. There were places in the bracken where….

The rumbling clatter of a railway van disturbed the picture. His mind followed the noise instead. Thought flashed along the street to a station. He saw trains…

'Come at once! You're wanted here—some one calls you!' sounded a breathless merry voice beside him. 'Come quickly; aussi schnell que moglich!'

There was a great gulp of happiness in him; his spirit plunged in joy. He turned and looked about him swiftly. That singing voice, with its impudent mingling of languages was unmistakable.

'From the Pleiades. Look sharp! You've been further off than ever lately, and further is further than farther—much! Over the forests and into the cave, that is the way we must all behave—-!'

He opened an eye.

Between him and a great gold sunset ran the wind. It was a slender violet wind. The sunset, however, was in the act of disappearing for the Scaffolding of Dusk was passing through the air—he saw the slung trellis-work about him, the tracery of a million lines, the guy-ropes, uprights, and the feathery threads of ebony that trailed the Night behind them like a mighty cloth. There was a fluttering as of innumerable wings.

'You needn't tug like that,' he gasped. 'I'm coming all right. I'm out!'

'But you're so slow and sticky,' she insisted. 'You've been sticky like this for weeks now!'

He saw the bright brown eyes and felt the hair all over his face like a bath of perfume. They rushed together. His heart beat faster....

'Who wants me in such a hurry?' he cried, the moment he was disentangled. Laughter ran past him on every side from the world of trees.

'As if you didn't know! What *is* the good of pretending any longer! You're both together in the Network, and you know it just as well as she does!'

Pretending! Just as well as *she* does!

As though he had eyes all over his body he saw the Net of Stars above him. Below were forests, vineyards, meadows, and the tiny lights of houses. In the distance shimmered the waters of a familiar lake. Great purple mountains rolled against the sky line. But immediately over his head, close yet also distant, filling the entire heavens, there hung a glittering Pattern that he knew, grown now so vast that at first he scarcely recognised its dazzling loveliness. From the painted western horizon it stretched to other fastenings that dipped below the world, where the East laid its gulfs of darkness to surprise the sun. It swung proudly down, as though hung from the Pole Star towards the north, and while the Great Bear 'pointers' tossed its embroidery across Cassiopeia, the Pleiades, just rising, flung its further fringes down to Orion, waiting in wonder to receive them far below the horizon. Old Sirius wore one breadth of it across his stupendous shoulder, and Aldebaran, with fingers of bronze and fire, drew it delicately as with golden leashes over the sleeping world.

When first he saw it, there was this gentle fluttering as of wings through all its intricate parts, but the same moment four shooting stars pierced its outlying edges with flying nails of gold. It steadied and grew taut.

'There she is!' cried Monkey, flashing away like a comet towards the Cave. 'You'll catch it now—and you deserve to!' She turned a brilliant somersault and vanished.

Then, somehow, the vast Pattern settled into a smaller scale, so that he saw it closer, clearer, and without confusion. Beauty and wonder focused for his sight. The perfected design of Daddy's fairy story floated down into his heart without a hint of wumbling. Never had he seen it so luminous and simple. For others, of course, meanwhile had known and understood it. Others believed. Its reality was more intense, thus, than before.

He rose from the maze of tree-tops where he floated, and stretched his arms out, no fear or hesitation in him anywhere. Perched in the very centre of the Pattern, seated like a new-born star upon its throne, he saw that tiny figure who had thrilled him months ago when he caught it in a passing instant, fluttering in the web of Daddy's story,—both its climax and its inspiration. The twinkling feet were folded now. He saw the soft little eyes that shone like starlight through clear amber. The hands, palms upwards, were stretched to meet his own.

'You, of course, must come up—to me,' he heard.

And climbing the lace-like tracery of the golden web, he knelt before her. But, almost before both knees were bent, her hands had caught him—the touch ran like a sheath of fire through every nerve—and he was seated beside her in that shining centre.

'But why did it suddenly grow small?' he asked at once. He felt absolutely at home. It was like speaking to a child who loved him utterly, and whom he, in his turn, knew intimately inside out.

'Because you suddenly understood,' was the silvery, tiny answer. 'When you understand, you bring everything into yourself, small as a toy. It is size that bewilders. Men make size. Fairy things, like stars and tenderness, are always small.'

'Of course,' he said; 'as if I didn't know it already!'

'Besides,' she laughed, half closing her brilliant eyes and peering at him mischievously, 'I like everything so tiny that you can find it inside a shell. That makes it possible to do big things.'

'Am *I* too big——?' he exclaimed, aware of clumsiness before this exquisite daintiness.

'A little confused, that's all,' her laughter rippled. 'You want smoothing down. I'll see to that.'

He had the feeling, as she said it, that his being included the entire Pattern, even to its most distant edges where it fastened on to the rim of the universe. From this huge sensation, he came back swiftly to its tiny correspondence again. His eyes turned to study her. But she seemed transparent somehow, so that he saw the sky behind her, and in it, strangely enough—just behind her face—the distant Pleiades, shining faintly with their tender lustre. They reached down into her little being, it seemed, as though she emanated from them. Big Aldebaran guided strongly from behind. For an instant he lost sight of the actual figure, seeing in its place a radiant efflorescence, purified as by some spiritual fire—the Spirit of a Star.

'I'm here, quite close beside you,' whispered the tiny voice. 'Don't let your sight get troublesome like your size. Inside-sight, remember, is the thing!'

He turned, or rather he focused sight again to find her. He was startled a little. For a moment it seemed like his own voice speaking deep down within himself.

'Make yourself at home,' it continued, 'you belong here—almost as much as I do.' And at the sound of her voice all the perplexities of his life lay down. It brushed him smooth, like a wind that sets rough feathers all one way,

He remembered again where he was, and what was going on.

'I do,' he answered, happy as a boy. 'I am at home. It is perfect.'

'Do you, indeed! You speak as though this story were your own!'

And her laugh was like the tinkle of hare-bells in the wind.

'It is,' he said; 'at least I had—I *have*, rather, a considerable hand in the making of it.'

'Possibly,' she answered, 'but the story belongs to the person who first started it. And that person is myself. The story is mine really!'

'Yours!' he gasped.

'Because—I am the story!'

He stared hard to find the face that said this thing. Thought stopped dead a moment, blocked by a marvel that was impossible, yet true.

'You mean—-?' he stammered.

'You heard perfectly what I said; you understood it, too. There's no good pretending,' impatience as well as laughter in the little voice. 'I am the story,—the story that you love.'

A sudden joy burst over him in a flood. Struggle and search folded their wings and slept. An immense happiness wrapped him into the very woof of the pattern wherein they sat. A thousand loose and ineffective moods of his life found coherence, as a thousand rambling strands were gathered home and fastened into place.

And the Pattern quivered and grew brighter.

'I am the story because I thought of it first. You, as a version of its beauty—a channel for its delivery—belong utterly to me. You can no more resist me than a puddle can resist the stars' reflection. You increase me. We increase each other.'

'You say you thought it first,' he cried, feeling the light he radiated flow in and mingle with her own. 'But who are you? Where do you come from?'

'Over there somewhere, I think,' she laughed, while a ray like fire flashed out in the direction of the Pleiades that climbed the sky towards the East. 'You ought to know. You've been hunting for me long enough!'

'But who *are* you?' he insisted again, 'for I feel it's you that have been looking for me—I've so often heard you calling!'

She laughed again till the whole web quivered. Through her eyes the softness of all the seven Pleiades poured deliciously into him.

'It's absurd that such a big thing as you could hide so easily,' she said. 'But you'll never hide again. I've got you fast now. And you've got me! It's like being reflected together in the same puddle, you see!'

The dazzling radiance passed as she said it into a clearer glow, and across the fire of it he caught her eyes steadily a moment, though he could not see the face complete. Two brilliant points of amber shone up at him, as stars that peep from the mirror of a forest pool. That mental daylight-searching seemed all explained, only he could not remember now that there was any such thing at all as either searching or daylight. When 'out' like this, waking was the dream——the sunlight world forgotten.

'This Pattern has always been my own,' she continued with infinite softness, yet so clearly that his whole body seemed a single ear against her lips, 'for I've thought it ever since I can remember. I've lived it. This Network of Stars I made ages ago in a garden among far bigger mountains than these hills, a garden I knew vividly, yet could not always find—almost as though I dreamed it. The Net included the— oh, included everything there is, and I fastened it to four big pines that grew on the further side of the torrent in that mountain garden of my dream—fastened it with nails of falling stars. And I made the Pleiades its centre because I loved them best of all. Oh! Orion, Orion, how big and comforting your arms are! Please hold me tight for ever and ever!'

'But I know it, too, that lovely dream,' he cried. 'It all comes back to me. I, too, have dreamed it with you then somewhere—somewhere——!' His voice choked. He had never known that life could hold such sweetness, wonder, joy. The universe lay within his arms.

'All the people I wanted to help I used to catch in my Net of Stars,' she went on. 'There was a train that brought them up to its edges, and once I got the passengers into the web, and hung them loose in it till they were soaked with starlight, I could send them back happier and braver than they came. It's been my story ever since I can remember anything—my adventure, my dream, my life. And when the great Net faded a little and wanted brightening, we knew an enormous cavern in the mountains where lost starlight collected, and we used to gather this in thousands of sacks, and wash and paint the entire web afresh. That made it sticky, so that the passengers hung in it longer. Don't you remember?

They came back with starlight in their hair and eyes and voices—and in their hearts.'

'And the way you—*we* got them into the Net,' he interrupted excitedly, 'was by understanding them—by feeling with them——'

'Sympathy,' she laughed, 'of course! Only there were so many I could not reach and could not understand, and so could never get in. In particular there was some one who ought to have been there to help me. If I could find that some one I could do twice as much. I searched and searched. I hunted through every corner of the garden, through forest, cavern, sky, but never with success. Orion never overtook me! My longing cried every where, but in vain. Oh, Orion, my lost Orion, I have found you now at last!... The Net flashed messages in all directions, but without response. This some one who could make my work complete existed—that I *knew*— only he was hidden somewhere out of sight—concealed in some corner or other, veiled by a darkness that he wove about himself—as though by some funny kind of wrong thinking that obscured the light I searched for and made it too dim to reach me properly. His life or mind—his thought and feeling, that is—were wumbled——'

'*Wumbled!*' he cried, as the certainty burst upon him with the password. He stood close to her, opening his arms.

Instantly she placed her golden palm upon his mouth, with fingers that were like soft star-rays. Her words, as she continued, were sweeter than the footfalls of the Pleiades when they rise above the sea.

'Yet there were times when we were so close that we could feel each other, and each wondered why the other did not actually appear. I have been trying,' she whispered, oh so dearly, 'to find you always. And you knew it, too, for I've felt you searching too....'

The outlying skirts of the Pattern closed in a little, till the edges gathered over them like a tent of stars. Alone in the heart of the universe they told their secret very softly....

'There are twin-stars, you know,' she whispered, when he released her, 'that circle so close about each other that they look like one. I wonder, oh, I wonder, do they ever touch!'

'They are apart in order to see one another better,' he murmured. 'They watch one another more sweetly so. They play at separation for the joy of coming together again.'

And once more the golden Pattern hid them for a moment from the other stars.... The shafts of night-fire played round and above their secret tent in space.... Most marvellously their beings found each other in the great whispering galleries of the world where Thought and Yearning know that first fulfilment which is the source of action later....

'So, now that I have found you,' her voice presently went on, 'our Network shall catch everybody everywhere. For the Pattern of my story, woven so long ago, has passed through you as through a channel—to another who can give it forth. It will spread across every sky. All, all will see it and climb up.'

'My scheme——' he cried, with eager delight, yet not quite certain what he meant, nor whence the phrase proceeded.

'Was my thought first,' she laughed, 'when you were a little boy and I was a little girl—somewhere in a garden very long ago. A ray from its pattern touched you into beauty. Though I could do nothing with it myself, one little ray shot into the mirror of your mind and instantly increased itself. But then, you hid yourself; the channel closed——'

'It never died, though,' he interrupted; 'the ray, I mean.'

'It waited,' she went on, 'until you found children somewhere, and the channel cleared instantly. Through you, opened up and cleaned by them, my pattern rushed headlong into another who can use it. It could never die, of course. And the long repression—I never ceased to live it— made its power irresistible.'

'Your story!' he cried. 'It *is* indeed your story.'

The eyes were so close against his own that he made a movement that was like diving into a deep and shining sea to reach them.... The Pleiades rushed instantly past his face.... Soft filaments of golden texture stroked his very cheeks. That slender violet wind rose into his hair. He saw other larger winds behind it, deeply coloured.... Something made him tremble all over like a leaf in a storm. He saw, then, the crest of the sentinel poplar tossing between him and the earth far, far below. A mist of confusion caught him, so that he knew not where he was.... He made an effort to remember... a violent effort.... Some strange sense of heaviness oppressed him.... He was leaving her.

'Quick!' he tried to cry; 'be quick! I am changing. I am drowsy with your voice and beauty. Your eyes have touched me, and I am—falling asleep!' His voice grew weaker as he said it.

Her answer sounded faint, and far above him:

'Give me... your... hand. Touch me. Come away with me... to... my ... garden ... in the mountains.... We may wake together ... You are waking now...!'

He made an effort to find her little palm. But the wind swept coldly between his opened fingers.

'Waking!—what is it?' he cried thinly. He thought swiftly of something vague and muddy—something dull, disordered, incomplete. Here it was all glass-clear. 'Where are you? I can't find you. I can't see!'

A dreadful, searching pain shot through him. He was losing her, just when he had found her. He struggled, clung, fought frantically to hold her. But his fingers seized the air.

'Oh, I shall find you—even when you wake,' he heard far away among the stars. 'Try and remember me—when I come. *Try and remember....*'

It dipped into the distance. He had lost her. He caught a glimpse of the Pleiades as he fell at a fearful speed. Some one behind them picked up stars and tossed them after him. They dimmed as they shot by—from gold to white, from white to something very pale. Behind them rose a wave of light that hurt his eyes.

'Look out! The Interfering Sun!' came a disappearing voice that was followed by a peal of laughter. 'I hope you found her, and I hope you caught it well. You deserved to....'

There was a scent of hair that he loved, a vision of mischievous brown eyes, an idea that somebody was turning a somersault beside him—and then he landed upon the solid earth with a noise like thunder.

The room was dark. At first he did not recognise it. Through the open window came the clatter of lumbering traffic that passed heavily down St. James's Street. He rose stiffly from his chair, vexed with himself for having dozed. It was more than a doze, though; he had slept some thirty minutes by his watch. No memory of any dreams was in him— nothing but a feeling of great refreshing lightness and peace....

It was wonderful, he reflected, as he changed into country clothes for his walk in Richmond Park, how even the shortest nap revives the brain and body. There was a sense that an immense interval had elapsed, and that something very big had happened or was going to happen to him very soon....

And an hour later he passed through the Richmond Gate and found the open spaces of the Park deserted, as they always were. The oaks and bracken rustled in a gentle breeze. The swishing of his boots through the wet grass was the only sound he heard, for the boom and purr of distant London reached him more as touch than as something audible. Seated on a fallen tree, he watched the stars and listened to the wind. That hum and boom of the city seemed underground, the flare it tossed into the sky rose from vast furnaces below the world. The stars danced lightly far beyond its reach, secure and unafraid. He thought of children dancing with twinkling feet upon the mountains....

And in himself there was hum and light as well. Too deep, too far below the horizon for full discovery, he caught the echo, the faint, dim flashings of reflection that are called by men a Mood. These, rising to the surface, swept over him with the queer joy of intoxicating wonder that only children know. Some great Secret he had to tell himself, only he had kept it so long and so well that he could not find it quite. He felt the thrill, yet had forgotten what it was.

Something was going to happen. A new footfall was coming across the world towards him. He could almost hear its delicate, swift tread. Life was about to offer him this delicious, thrilling secret—very soon. Looking up he saw the Pleiades, and the single footfall became many. He remembered that former curious obsession of the Pleiades... and as Thought and Yearning went roaming into space, they met Anticipation, who took them by the hand. It seemed, then, that children came flocking down upon him from the sky, led by a little figure with starry eyes of clearest amber, a pair of tiny twinkling feet, and a voice quite absurdly soft and tender.

'Your time is coming,' he heard behind the rustling of the oak leaves overhead, 'for the children are calling to you—children of your own. And this is the bravest Scheme in all the world. There is no bigger. How can there be? For all the world is a child that goes past your windows crying for its lost Fairyland...!'

It was after midnight when at length he slipped through the Robin Hood Gate, passed up Priory Lane, and walked rapidly by the shuttered houses of Roehampton. And, looking a moment over Putney Bridge; he saw the reflections of the stars in the muddy, dawdling Thames. Nothing anywhere was thick enough to hide them. The Net of Stars, being in his heart, was everywhere. No prisoner could be more securely caught than he was.

CHAPTER XXXII

Asia. The point of one white star is quivering still
    Deep in the orange light of widening morn
    Beyond the purple mountains: through a chasm
    Of wind-divided mist the darker lake
    Reflects it: now it wanes: it gleams again
    As the waves fade, and as the burning threads
    Of woven cloud unravel in the pale air:
    'Tis lost! and through yon peaks of cloud-like snow
    The roseate sunlight quivers: hear I not
    The Æolian music of her sea-green plumes
    Winnowing the crimson dawn?
        Prometheus Unbound, SHELLEY.

August had blazed its path into September, and September had already trimmed her successor's gown with gold and russet before Henry Rogers found himself free again to think of holidays. London had kept its grip upon him all these weeks while the rest of the world was gay and irresponsible. He was so absurdly conscientious. One of his Companies had got into difficulties, and he was the only man who could save the shareholders' money. The Patent Coal Dust Fuel Company, Ltd., had bought his invention for blowing fine coal dust into a furnace whereby an intense heat was obtainable in a few minutes. The saving in material, time, and labour was revolutionary. Rogers had received a large sum in cash, though merely a nominal number of the common shares. It meant little to him if the Company collapsed, and an ordinary Director would have been content with sending counsel through the post in the intervals of fishing and shooting. But Henry Rogers was of a different calibre. The invention was his child, born by hard labour out of loving thought. The several thousand shareholders believed in him: they were his neighbours. Incompetence and extravagance threatened failure. He took a room in the village near the Essex factories, and gave his personal energy and attention to restoring economical working of every detail. He wore overalls. He put intelligence into hired men and foremen; he spent his summer holiday turning a system of waste into the basis of a lucrative industry. The shareholders would never know whose faithfulness had saved them loss, and at the most his thanks would be a formal paragraph in the Report at the end of the year. Yet he was satisfied, and worked as though his own income depended on success. For he knew—of late this certainty had established itself in him, influencing all he did—that faithful labour, backed by steady thinking, must reach ten thousand wavering characters, merge with awakening tendencies in them, and slip thence into definite daily action. Action was thought materialised. He helped the world. A copybook maxim thus became a weapon of tempered steel. His Scheme was bigger than any hospital for disabled bodies. It would still be cumulative when bodies and bricks were dust upon the wind. It must increase by geometrical progression through all time.

It was largely to little Minks that he owed this positive conviction and belief, to that ridiculous, high-souled Montmorency Minks, who, while his master worked in overalls, took the air himself on Clapham Common, or pored with a wet towel round his brow beneath the oleograph of Napoleon in the attempt to squeeze his exuberant emotion into tripping verse. For Minks admired intensely from a distance. He attended to the correspondence in the flat, and made occasional visits down to Essex, but otherwise enjoyed a kind of extra holiday of his own. For Minks was not learned in coal dust. The combustion was in his eager brain. He produced an amazing series of lyrics and sonnets, though too high-flown, alas, to win a place in print. Love and unselfishness, as usual, were his theme, with a steady sprinkling of 'the ministry of Thought,' 'true success, unrecognised by men, yet noted by the Angels,' and so forth. His master's labour seemed to him a 'brilliant form of purity,' and 'the soul's security' came in admirably to close the crowded, tortuous line. 'Beauty' and 'Duty' were also thickly present, both with capitals, but the verse that pleased him most, and even thrilled Albinia to a word of praise, was one that ended—'Those active powers which are the Doves of Thought.' It followed 'neither can be sold or bought,' and Mrs. Minks approved, because, as she put it, 'there, now, is something you can *sell*; it's striking and original; no editor could fail to think so.' The necessities of Frank and Ronald were ever her standard of praise or blame.

Thus, it was the first week in October before Rogers found himself free to leave London behind him and think of a change of scene. No planning was necessary.... Bourcelles was too constantly in his mind all these weary weeks to admit of alternatives. Only a few days ago a letter had come from Jinny, saying she was going to a Pension in Geneva after Christmas, and that unless he appeared soon he would not see her again as she 'was,' a qualification explained by the postscript, 'My hair will be up by that time. Mother says I can put it up on Xmas Day. So please hurry up, Mr. Henry Rogers, if you want to see me as I am.'

But another thing that decided him was that the great story was at last in print. It was published in the October number of the Review, and the press had already paid considerable attention to it. Indeed, there was a notice at the railway bookstall on the day he left, to the effect that the first edition was exhausted, and that a large second edition would be available almost immediately. 'Place your orders at once' was added in bold red letters. Rogers bought one of these placards for his cousin.

'It just shows,' observed Minks, whom he was taking out with him.

'Shows what?' inquired his master.

'How many more thoughtful people there are about, sir, than one had any idea of,' was the reply. 'The public mind is looking for something of that kind, expecting it even, though it hardly knows what it really wants. That's a story, Mr. Rogers, that must change the point of view of all who read it—with understanding. It makes the commonest man feel he is a hero.'

'You've put our things into a non-smoker, Minks,' the other interrupted him. 'What in the world are you thinking about?'

'I beg your pardon, I'm sure, sir; so I have,' said Minks, blushing, and bundling the bags along the platform to another empty carriage, 'but that story has got into my head. I sat up reading it aloud to Mrs. Minks all night. For it says the very things I have always longed to say. Sympathy and the transference of thought—to say nothing of the soul's activity when the body is asleep—have always seemed to me——'

He wandered on while his companion made himself comfortable in a corner with his pipe and newspaper. But the first thing Rogers read, as the train went scurrying through Kent, was a summary of the contents of this very Review. Two-thirds of the article was devoted to the 'Star Story' of John Henry Campden, whose name 'entitled his work to a high standard of criticism.' The notice was well written by some one evidently of intelligence and knowledge; sound judgment was expressed on style and form and general execution, but when it came to the matter itself the criticism was deplorably misunderstanding. The writer had entirely missed the meaning. While praising the 'cleverness' he asked plainly between the lines of his notice 'What does it mean?' This unconscious exposure of his own ignorance amused his reader while it also piqued him. The critic, expert in dealing with a political article, was lamentably at sea over an imaginative story.

'Inadequate receiving instrument,' thought Rogers, smiling audibly.

Minks, deep in a mysterious looking tome in the opposite corner, looked up over his cigarette and wondered why his employer laughed. He read the article the other handed to him, thinking how much better he could have done it himself. Encouraged by the expression in Mr. Rogers's eyes, he then imparted what the papers call 'a genuine contribution to the thought upon the subject.'

'The writer quarrels with him,' he observed, 'for not giving what is expected of him. What he has thought he must go on thinking, or be condemned. He must repeat himself or be uncomprehended.

Hitherto'—Minks prided himself upon the knowledge—'he has written studies of uncommon temperaments. Therefore to indulge in fantasy now is wrong.'

'Ah, you take it that way, do you?'

'Experience justifies me, Mr. Rogers,' the secretary continued. 'A friend of mine, or rather of Mrs. Minks's, once wrote a volume of ghost stories that, of course, were meant to thrill. His subsequent book, with no such intention, was judged by the object of the first— as a failure. It must make the flesh creep. Everything he wrote must make the flesh creep. One of the papers, the best—a real thunderer, in fact—said "Once or twice the desired thrill comes close, but never, alas, quite comes off."'

'How wumbled,' exclaimed his listener.

'It is indeed,' said Minks, 'in fact, one of the thorns in the path of literature. The ordinary clever mind is indeed a desolate phenomenon. And how often behind the "Oxford manner" lurks the cultured prig, if I may put it so.'

'Indeed you may,' was the other's rejoinder, 'for you put it admirably.'

They laughed a little and went on with their reading in their respective corners. The journey to Paris was enlivened by many similar discussions, Minks dividing his attentions between his master, his volume of philosophy, and the needs of various old ladies, to whom such men attach themselves as by a kind of generous, manly instinct. Minks was always popular and inoffensive. He had such tact.

'Ah! and that reminds me, Minks,' said Rogers, as they paced the banks of the Seine that evening, looking at the starry sky over Paris. 'What do you know about the Pleiades? Anything—eh?'

Minks drew with pride upon his classical reading.

'The seven daughters of Atlas, Mr. Rogers, if I remember correctly, called therefore the Atlantides. They were the virgin companions of Artemis. Orion, the great hunter, pursued them in Boeotia, and they called upon the gods for help.'

'And the gods turned 'em into stars, wasn't it?'

'First into doves, sir—Peleiades means doves—and then set them among the Constellations, where big Orion still pursues, yet never overtakes them.'

'Beautiful, isn't it? What a memory you've got, Minks. And isn't one of 'em lost or something?'

'Merope, yes,' the delighted Minks went on. He knew it because he had looked it up recently for his lyric about 'the Doves of Thought.' 'She married a mortal, Sisyphus, the son of Aeolus, and so shines more dimly than the rest. For her sisters married gods. But there is one who is more luminous than the others——'

'Ah! and which was that?' interrupted Rogers.

'Maia,' Minks told him pat. 'She is the most beautiful of the seven. She was the Mother, too, of Mercury, the Messenger of the gods. She gave birth to him in a cave on Mount Cyllene in Arcadia. Zeus was the father——'

'Take care; you'll get run over,' and Rogers pulled him from the path of an advancing taxi-cab, whose driver swore furiously at the pair of them. 'Charming, all that, isn't it?'

'It is lovely, sir. It haunts the mind. I suppose,' he added, 'that's why your cousin, Mr. Campden, made the Pleiades the centre of his Star Net in the story—a cluster of beautiful thoughts as it were.'

'No doubt, no doubt,' his tone so brusque suddenly that Minks decided after all not to mention his poem where the Pleiades made their appearance as the 'doves of thought.'

'What a strange coincidence,' Rogers said as they turned towards the hotel again.

'Subconscious knowledge, probably, sir,' suggested the secretary, scarcely following his meaning, if meaning indeed there was.

'Possibly! One never knows, does one?'

'Never, Mr. Rogers. It's all very wonderful.'

And so, towards six o'clock in the evening of the following day, having passed the time pleasantly in Paris, the train bore them swiftly beyond Pontarlier and down the steep gradient of the Gorges de l'Areuse towards Neuchatel. The Val de Travers, through which the railway slips across the wooded Jura into Switzerland, is like a winding corridor cleft deep between savage and precipitous walls. There are dizzy glimpses into the gulf below. With steam shut off and brakes partly on, the train curves sharply, hiding its eyes in many tunnels lest the passengers turn giddy. Strips of bright green meadow- land, where the Areuse flows calmly, alternate with places where the ravine plunges into bottomless depths that have been chiselled out as by a giant ploughshare. Rogers pointed out the chosen views, while his secretary ran from window to window, excited as a happy child. Such scenery he had never known. It changed the entire content of his mind. Poetry he renounced finally before the first ten minutes were past. The descriptions that flooded his brain could be rendered only by the most dignified and stately prose, and he floundered among a welter of sonorous openings that later Albinia would read in Sydenham and retail judiciously to the elder children from 'Father's foreign letters.'

'We shall pass Bourcelles in a moment now! Look out! Be ready with your handkerchief!' Rogers warned him, as the train emerged from the final tunnel and scampered between thick pine woods, emblazoned here and there with golden beeches. The air was crystal, sparkling. They could smell the forests.

They took their places side by side at the windows. The heights of Boudry and La Tourne, that stand like guardian sentries on either side of the mountain gateway, were already cantering by. The precipices flew past. Beyond lay the smiling slopes of vineyard, field, and orchard, sprinkled with farms and villages, of which Bourcelles came first. The Areuse flowed peacefully towards the lake. The panorama of the snowy Alps rolled into view along the farther horizon, and the slanting autumn sunshine bathed the entire scene with a soft and ruddy light. They entered the Fairyland of Daddy's story.

'Voila la sentinelle deja!' exclaimed Rogers, putting his head out to see the village poplar. 'We run through the field that borders the garden of the Pension. They'll come out to wave to us. Be ready.'

'Ah, oui,' said Minks, who had been studying phrase books, 'je vwa.' But in reality he saw with difficulty, for a spark had got into his eye, and its companion optic, wandering as usual, was suffused with water too.

The news of their arrival had, of course, preceded them, and the row of waving figures in the field gave them a welcome that went straight to Minks's heart. He felt proud for his grand employer. Here was a human touch that would modify the majesty of the impersonal mountain scenery in his description. He waved his handkerchief frantically as the train shot past, and he hardly knew which attracted him most—the expression of happiness on Mr. Rogers's face, or the line of nondescript humanity that gesticulated in the field as though they wished to stop the Paris 'Rapide.'

For it was a *very* human touch; and either Barnum's Circus or the byeways and hedges of Fairyland had sent their picked representatives with a dance seen usually only in shy moonlit glades. His master named them as the carriage rattled by. The Paris Express, of course, did not stop at little Bourcelles. Minks recognised each one easily from the descriptions in the story.

The Widow Jequier, with garden skirts tucked high, and wearing big gauntlet gloves, waved above her head a Union Jack that knocked her bonnet sideways at every stroke, and even enveloped the black triangle of a Trilby hat that her brother-in-law held motionless aloft as though to test the wind for his daily report upon the condition of le barometre. The Postmaster never waved. He looked steadily before him at the passing train, his small, black figure more than usually dwarfed by a stately outline that rose above the landscape by his side, and was undoubtedly the Woman of the Haystack. Telling lines from the story's rhymes flashed through Minks's memory as, chuckling with pleasure, he watched the magnificent, ample gestures of Mother's waving arms. She seemed to brush aside the winds who came a-courting, although wide strokes of swimming really described her movements best. A little farther back, in the middle distance, he recognised by his peaked cap the gendarme, Gygi, as he paused in his digging and looked up to watch the fun; and beyond him again, solid in figure as she was unchanging in her affections, he saw Mrs. Postmaster, struggling with a bed sheet the *pensionnaires des Glycines* helped her shake in the evening breeze. It was too close upon the hour of *souper* for her to travel farther from the kitchen. And beside her stood Miss Waghorn, waving an umbrella. She was hatless. Her tall, thin figure, dressed in black, against the washing hung out to dry, looked like a note of exclamation, or, when she held the umbrella up at right angles, like a capital L the fairies had set in the ground upon its head.

And the fairies themselves, the sprites, the children! They were everywhere and anywhere. Jimbo flickered, went out, reappeared, then flickered again; he held a towel in one hand and a table napkin in the other. Monkey seemed more in the air than on the solid earth, for one minute she was obviously a ball, and the next, with a motion like a somersault, her hair shot loose across the sunlight as though she flew. Both had their mouths wide open, shouting, though the wind carried their words all away unheard. And Jane Anne stood apart. Her welcome, if the gesture is capable of being described at all, was a bow. She moved at the same time sedately across the field, as though she intended to be seen separately from the rest. She wore hat and gloves. She was evidently in earnest with her welcome. But Mr. John Henry Campden, the author and discoverer of them all, Minks did not see.

'But I don't see the writer himself!' he cried. 'I don't see Mr. Campden.'

'You can't,' explained Rogers, 'he's standing behind his wife.'

And the little detail pleased the secretary hugely. The true artist, he reflected, is never seen in his work.

It all was past and over—in thirty seconds. The spire of the church, rising against a crimson sky, with fruit trees in the foreground and a line of distant summits across the shining lake, replaced the row of wonderful dancing figures. Rogers sank back in his corner, laughing, and Minks, saying nothing, went across to his own at the other end of the compartment. It all had been so swift and momentary that it seemed like the flash of a remembered dream, a strip of memory's pictures, a vivid picture of some dazzling cinematograph. Minks felt as if he had just read the entire story again from one end to the other—in thirty seconds. He felt different, though wherein exactly the difference lay was beyond him to discover. 'It must be the spell of Bourcelles,' he murmured to himself. 'Mr. Rogers warned me about it. It is a Fairyland that thought has created out of common things. It is quite wonderful!' He felt a glow all over him. His mind ran on for a moment to another picture his master had painted for him, and he imagined Albinia and the family out here, living in a little house on the borders of the forest, a strip of vineyards, sunlight, mountains, happy scented winds, and himself with a writing-table before a window overlooking the lake… writing down Beauty.

CHAPTER XXXIII

We never meet; yet we meet day by day
Upon those hills of life, dim and immense:
The good we love, and sleep-our innocence.
O hills of life, high hills! And higher than they,

Our guardian spirits meet at prayer and play.
Beyond pain, joy, and hope, and long suspense,
Above the summits of our souls, far hence,
An angel meets an angel on the way.

Beyond all good I ever believed of thee
Or thou of me, these always love and live.
And though I fail of thy ideal of me,

My angel falls not short. They greet each other.
Who knows, they may exchange the kiss we give,
Thou to thy crucifix, I to my mother.
ALICE MCYNELL.

The arrival at the station interrupted the reverie in which the secretary and his chief both were plunged.

'How odd,' exclaimed Minks, ever observant, as he leaped from the carriage, 'there are no platforms. Everything in Switzerland seems on one level, even the people—everything, that is, except the mountains.'

'Switzerland *is* the mountains,' laughed his chief.

Minks laughed too. 'What delicious air!' he added, filling his lungs audibly. He felt half intoxicated with it.

After some delay they discovered a taxi-cab, piled the luggage on to it, and were whirled away towards a little cluster of lights that twinkled beneath the shadows of La Tourne and Boudry. Bourcelles lay five miles out.

'Remember, you're not my secretary here,' said Rogers presently, as the forests sped by them. 'You're just a travelling companion.'

'I understand,' he replied after a moment's perplexity. 'You have a secretary here already.'

'His name is Jimbo.'

The motor grunted its way up the steep hill above Colombier. Below them spread the vines towards the lake, sprinkled with lights of farms and villages. As the keen evening air stole down from forest and mountain to greet them, the vehicle turned into the quiet village street. Minks saw the big humped shoulders of La Citadelle, the tapering church spire, the trees in the orchard of the Pension. Cudrefin, smoking a cigar at the door of his grocery shop, recognised them and waved his hand. A moment later Gygi lifted his peaked hat and called 'bon soir, bonne nuit,' just as though Rogers had never gone away at all. Michaud, the carpenter, shouted his welcome as he strolled towards the Post Office farther down to post a letter, and then the motor stopped with a jerk outside the courtyard where the fountain sang and gurgled in its big stone basin. Minks saw the plane tree. He glanced up at the ridged backbone of the building. What a portentous looking erection it was. It seemed to have no windows. He wondered where the famous Den was. The roof overlapped like a giant hood, casting a deep shadow upon the cobbled yard. Overhead the stars shone faintly.

Instantly a troop of figures shot from the shadow and surrounded them. There was a babel of laughter, exclamations, questions. Minks thought the stars had fallen. Children and constellations were mingled all together, it seemed. Both were too numerous to count. All were rushing with the sun towards Hercules at a dizzy speed.

'And this is my friend, Mr. Minks,' he heard repeated from time to time, feeling his hand seized and shaken before he knew what he was about. Mother loomed up and gave him a stately welcome too.

'He wears gloves in Bourcelles!' some one observed audibly to some one else.

'Excuse me! This is Riquette!' announced a big girl, hatless like the rest, with shining eyes. 'It's a she.'

'And this is my secretary, Mr. Jimbo,' said Rogers, breathlessly, emerging from a struggling mass. Minks and Jimbo shook hands with dignity.

'Your room is over at the Michauds, as before.'

'And Mr. Mix is at the Pension—there was no other room to be had—'

'Supper's at seven—'

'Tante Jeanne's been *grand-cieling* all day with excitement. She'll burst when she sees you!'

'She's read the story, too. Elle dit que c'est le bouquet!'

'There's new furniture in the salon, and they've cleaned the sink while you've been away!...'

The author moved forward out of the crowd. At the same moment another figure, slight and shadowy, revealed itself, outlined against the white of the gleaming street. It had been hidden in the tangle of the stars. It kept so quiet.

'Countess, may I introduce him to you,' he said, seizing the momentary pause. There was little ceremony in Bourcelles. 'This is my cousin I told you about—Mr. Henry Rogers. You must know one another at once. He's Orion in the story.'

He dragged up his big friend, who seemed suddenly awkward, difficult to move. The children ran in and out between them like playing puppies, tumbling against each in turn.

'They don't know which is which,' observed Jinny, watching the introduction. Her voice ran past him like the whir of a shooting star through space—far, far away. 'Excuse me!' she cried, as she cannoned off Monkey against Cousinenry. 'I'm not a terminus! This is a regular shipwreck!'

The three elder ones drew aside a little from the confusion.

'The Countess,' resumed Daddy, as soon as they were safe from immediate destruction, 'has come all the way from Austria to see us. She is staying with us for a few days. Isn't it delightful? We call her the little Grafin.' His voice wumbled a trifle thickly in his beard. 'She was good enough to like the story—our story, you know— and wrote to me—'

'My story,' said a silvery, laughing voice.

And Rogers bowed politely, and with a moment's dizziness, at two bright smiling eyes that watched him out of the little shadow standing between him and the children. He was aware of grandeur.

He stood there, first startled, then dazed. She was so small. But something about her was so enormous. His inner universe turned over and showed its under side. The hidden thing that so long had brushed his daily life came up utterly close and took him in its gigantic arms. He stared like an unmannered child.

Something had lit the world....

'This *is* delicious air,' he heard Minks saying to his cousin in the distance— to his deaf side judging by the answer:

'Delicious here—yes, isn't it?'

Something had lit the stars....

Minks and his cousin continued idly talking. Their voices twittered like birds in empty space. The children had scattered like marbles from a spinning-top. Their voices and footsteps sounded in the cobbled yard of La Citadelle, as they scampered up to prepare for supper. Mother sailed solemnly after them, more like a frigate than ever. The world, on fire, turned like a monstrous Catherine wheel within his brain.

Something had lit the universe....

He stood there in the dusk beneath the peeping stars, facing the slender little shadow. It was all he saw at first—this tiny figure. Demure and soft, it remained motionless before him, a hint of childhood's wonder in its graceful attitude. He was aware of something mischievous as well—that laughed at him.... He realised then that she waited for him to speak. Yet, for the life of him, he could find no words, because the eyes, beneath the big-brimmed hat with its fluttering veil, looked out at him as though some formidable wild creature watched him from the opening of its cave. There was a glint of amber in them. The heart in him went thumping. He caught his breath. Out, jerked, then, certain words that he tried hard to make ordinary—

'But surely—we have met before—I think I know you—'

He just said it, swallowing his breath with a gulp upon the unfinished sentence. But he said it—somewhere else, and not here in the twilight street of little Bourcelles. For his sight swam somehow far away, and he was giddy with the height. The roofs of the houses lay in a sea of shadow below him, and the street wound through them like a ribbon of thin lace. The tree-tops waved very softly in a wind that purred and sighed beneath his feet, and this wind was a violet little wind, that bent them all one way and set the lines and threads of gold a-quiver to their fastenings. For the fastenings were not secure; any minute he might fall. And the threads, he saw, all issued like rays from two central shining points of delicate, transparent amber, radiating forth into an exquisite design that caught the stars. Yet the stars were not reflected in them. It was they who lit the stars....

He *was* dizzy. He tried speech again.

'I told you I *should*—' But it was not said aloud apparently.

Two little twinkling feet were folded. Two hands, he saw, stretched down to draw him close. These very stars ran loose about him in a cloud of fiery sand. Their pattern danced in flame. He picked out Sirius, Aldebaran—the Pleiades! There was tumult in his blood, a wild and exquisite confusion. What in the world had happened to him that he should behave in this ridiculous fashion? Yet he was doing nothing. It was only that, for a passing instant, the enormous thing his life had been dimly conscious of so long, rose at last from its subterranean hiding-place and overwhelmed him. This picture that came with it was like some far-off dream he suddenly recovered. A glorious excitement caught him. He felt utterly bewildered.

'Have we?' he heard close in front of him. 'I do not think I have had the pleasure'—it was with a slightly foreign accent—'but it is so dim here, and one cannot see very well, perhaps.'

And a ripple of laughter passed round some gigantic whispering gallery in the sky. It set the trellis-work of golden threads all trembling. He felt himself perched dizzily in this shaking web that swung through space. And with him was some one whom he knew.... He heard the words of a song:

'Light desire With their fire.'

Something had lit his heart....

He lost himself again, disgracefully. A mist obscured his sight, though with the eyes of his mind he still saw crystal-clear. Across this mist fled droves and droves of stars. They carried him out of himself—out, out, out!... His upper mind then made a vehement effort to recover equilibrium. An idea was in him that some one would presently turn a somersault and disappear. The effort had a result, it seemed, for the enormous thing passed slowly away again into the caverns of his under-self, ... and he realised that he was conducting himself in a foolish and irresponsible manner, which Minks, in particular, would disapprove. He was staring rudely—at a shadow, or rather, at two eyes in a shadow. With another effort—oh, how it hurt!—he focused sight again upon surface things. It seemed his turn to say something.

'I beg your pardon,' he stammered, 'but I thought—it seemed to me for a moment—that I—remembered.'

The face came close as he said it. He saw it clear a moment. The figure grew defined against the big stone fountain—the little hands in summer cotton gloves, the eyes beneath the big brimmed hat, the streaming veil. Then he went lost again—more gloriously than before. Instead of the human outline in the dusky street of Bourcelles, he stared at the host of stars, at the shimmering design of gold, at the Pleiades, whose fingers of spun lustre swung the Net loose across the world....

'Flung from huge Orion's hand...'

he caught in a golden whisper,

'Sweetly linking
  All our thinking....'

His cousin and Minks, he was aware vaguely, had left him. He was alone with her. A little way down the hill they turned and called to him. He made a frantic effort—there seemed just time—to plunge away into space and seize the cluster of lovely stars with both his hands. Headlong, he dived off recklessly... driving at a fearful speed, ... when—the whole thing vanished into a gulf of empty blue, and he found himself running, not through the sky to clutch the Pleiades, but heavily downhill towards his cousin and Minks.

It was a most abrupt departure. There was a curious choking in his throat. His heart ran all over his body. Something white and sparkling danced madly through his brain. What must she think of him?

'We've just time to wash ourselves and hurry over to supper,' his cousin said, as he overtook them, flustered and very breathless. Minks looked at him—regarded him, rather—astonishment, almost disapproval, in one eye, and in the other, apparently observing the vineyards, a mild rebuke.

He walked beside them in a dream. The sound of Colombier's bells across Planeyse, men's voices singing fragments of a Dalcroze song floated to him, and with them all the dear familiar smells:—

Le coeur de ma mie
Est petit, tout petit petit,
J'en ai l'ame ravie....

It was Minks, drawing the keen air noisily into his lungs in great draughts, who recalled him to himself.

'I could find my way here without a guide, Mr. Campden,' he was saying diffidently, burning to tell how the Story had moved him. 'It's all so vivid, I can almost see the Net. I feel in it,' and he waved one hand towards the sky.

The other thanked him modestly. 'That's your power of visualising then,' he added. 'My idea was, of course, that every mind in the world is related with every other mind, and that there's no escape—we are all prisoners. The responsibility is vast.'

'Perfectly. I've always believed it. Ah! if only one could *live* it!'

Rogers heard this clearly. But it seemed that another heard it with him. Some one very close beside him shared the hearing. He had recovered from his temporary shock. Only the wonder remained. Life was sheer dazzling glory. The talk continued as they hurried along the road together. Rogers became aware then that his cousin was giving information—meant for himself.

'... A most charming little lady, indeed. She comes from over there,' and he pointed to where the Pleiades were climbing the sky towards the East, 'in Austria somewhere. She owns a big estate among the mountains. She wrote to me—I've had *such* encouraging letters, you know, from all sorts of folk— and when I replied, she telegraphed to ask if she might come and see me. She seems fond of telegraphing, rather.' And he laughed as though he were speaking of an ordinary acquaintance.

'Charming little lady!' The phrase was like the flick of a lash. Rogers had known it applied to such commonplace women.

'A most intelligent face,' he heard Minks saying, 'quite beautiful, *I* thought—the beauty of mind and soul.'

'... Mother and the children took to her at once,' his cousin's voice went on. 'She and her maid have got rooms over at the Beguins. And, do you know, a most singular coincidence,' he added with some excitement, 'she tells me that ever since childhood she's had an idea like this— like the story, I mean—an idea of her own she always wanted to write but couldn't———'

'Of course, of course,' interrupted Rogers impatiently; and then he added quickly, 'but how *very* extraordinary!'

'The idea that Thought makes a network everywhere about the world in which we all are caught, and that it's a positive duty, therefore, to think beauty—as much a duty as washing one's face and hands, because what you think *touches* others all day long, and all night long too— in sleep.'

'Only she couldn't write it?' asked Rogers. His tongue was like a thick wedge of unmanageable wood in his mouth. He felt like a man who hears another spoil an old, old beautiful story that he knows himself with intimate accuracy.

'She can telegraph, she says, but she can't write!'

'An expensive talent,' thought the practical Minks.

'Oh, she's very rich, apparently. But isn't it odd? You see, she thought it vividly, played it, lived it. Why, she tells me she even had a Cave in her mountains where lost thoughts and lost starlight collected, and that she made a kind of Pattern with them to represent the Net. She showed me a drawing of it, for though she can't write, she paints quite well. But the odd thing is that she claims to have thought out the main idea of my own story years and years ago with the feeling that some day her idea was bound to reach some one who *would* write it——'

'Almost a case of transference,' put in Minks.

'A fairy tale, yes, isn't it!'

'Married?' asked Rogers, with a gulp, as they reached the door. But apparently he had not said it out loud, for there was no reply.

He tried again less abruptly. It required almost a physical effort to drive his tongue and frame the tremendous question.

'What a fairy story for her children! How *they* must love it!' This time he spoke so loud that Minks started and looked up at him.

'Ah, but she has no children,' his cousin said.

They went upstairs, and the introductions to Monsieur and Madame Michaud began, with talk about rooms and luggage. The mist was over him once more. He heard Minks saying:—

'Oui, je comprongs un poo,' and the clatter of heavy boots up and down the stairs, ... and then found himself washing his hands in stinging hot water in his cousin's room.

'The children simply adore her already,' he heard, 'and she won Mother's confidence at the very start. They can't manage her long name. They just call her the Little Countess—die kleine Gräfin. She's doing a most astonishing work in Austria, it seems, with children... the Montessori method, and all that....'

'By George, now; is it possible? Bourcelles accepted her at once then?'

'She accepted Bourcelles rather—took it bodily into herself—our poverty, our magic boxes, our democratic intimacy, and all the rest; it was just as though she had lived here with us always. And she kept asking who Orion was—that's you, of course—and why you weren't here——'

'And the Den too?' asked Rogers, with a sudden trembling in his heart, yet knowing well the answer.

'Simply appropriated it—came in naturally without being asked; Jimbo opened the door and Monkey pushed her in. She said it was her Star Cave. Oh, she's a remarkable being, you know, rather,' he went on more gravely, 'with unusual powers of sympathy. She seems to feel at once what you are feeling. Takes everything for granted as though she knew. I think she *does* know, if you ask me——'

'Lives the story in fact,' the other interrupted, hiding his face rather in the towel, 'lives her belief instead of dreaming it, eh?'

'And, fancy this!' His voice had a glow and softness in it as he said it, coming closer, and almost whispering, 'she wants to take Jinny and Monkey for a bit and educate them.' He stood away to watch the effect of the announcement. 'She even talks of sending Edward to Oxford, too!' He cut a kind of wumbled caper in his pleasure and excitement.

'She loves children then, evidently?' asked the other, with a coolness that was calculated to hide other feelings. He rubbed his face in the rough towel as though the skin must come off. Then, suddenly dropping the towel, he looked into his cousin's eyes a moment to ensure a proper answer.

'Longs for children of her own, I think,' replied the author; 'one sees it, feels it in all she says and does. Rather sad, you know, that! An unmarried mother——'

'In fact,' put in Rogers lightly, 'the very character you needed to play the principal role in your story. When you write the longer version in book form you'll have to put her in.'

'And find her a husband too—which is a bore. I never write love stories, you see. She's finer as she is at present—mothering the world.'

Rogers's face, as he brushed his hair carefully before the twisted mirror, was not visible.

There came a timid knock at the door.

'I'm ready, gentlemen, when you are,' answered the voice of Minks outside.

They went downstairs together, and walked quickly over to the Pension for supper. Rogers moved sedately enough so far as the others saw, yet inwardly he pranced like a fiery colt in harness. There were golden reins about his neck. Two tiny hands directed him from the Pleiades. In this leash of sidereal fire he felt as though he flew. Swift thought, flashing like a fairy whip, cut through the air from an immense distance, and urged him forwards. Some one expected him and he was late—years and years late. Goodness, how his companions crawled and dawdled!

'... she doesn't come over for her meals,' he heard, 'but she'll join us afterwards at the Den. You'll come too, won't you, Mr. Minks?'

'Thank you, I shall be most happy—if I'm not intruding,' was the reply as they passed the fountain near the courtyard of the Citadelle. The musical gurgle of its splashing water sounded to Rogers like a voice that sang over and over again, 'Come up, come up, come up! You must come up to me!'

'How brilliant your stars are out here, Mr. Campden,' Minks was saying when they reached the door of La Poste. He stood aside to let the others pass before him. He held the door open politely. 'No wonder you chose them as the symbol for thought and sympathy in your story.' And they climbed the narrow, creaking stairs and entered the little hall where the entire population of the Pension des Glycines awaited them with impatience.

The meal dragged out interminably. Everybody had so much to say. Minks, placed between Mother and Miss Waghorn, talked volubly to the latter and listened sweetly to all her stories. The excitement of the Big Story, however, was in the air, and when she mentioned that she looked forward to reading it, he had no idea, of course, that she had already done so at least three times. The Review had replaced her customary Novel. She went about with it beneath her arm. Minks, feeling friendly and confidential, informed her that he, too, sometimes wrote, and when she noted the fact with a deferential phrase about 'you men of letters,' he rose abruptly to the seventh heaven of contentment. Mother meanwhile, on the other side, took him bodily into her great wumbled heart. 'Poor little chap,' her attitude said plainly, 'I don't believe his wife half looks after him.' Before the end of supper she knew all about Frank and Ronald, the laburnum tree in the front garden, what tea they bought, and Albinia's plan for making coal last longer by mixing it with coke.

Tante Jeanne talked furiously and incessantly, her sister-in-law told her latest dream, and the Postmaster occasionally cracked a solemn joke, laughing uproariously long before the point appeared. It was a merry, noisy meal, and Henry Rogers sat through it upon a throne that was slung with golden ropes from the stars. He was in Fairyland again. Outside, the Pleiades were rising in the sky, and somewhere in Bourcelles—in the rooms above Beguin's shop, to be exact—some one was waiting, ready to come over to the Den. His thoughts flew wildly. Passionate longing drove behind them. 'You must come up to me,' he heard. They all were Kings and Queens.

He played his part, however; no one seemed to notice his preoccupation. The voices sounded now far, now near, as though some wind made sport with them; the faces round him vanished and reappeared; but he contrived cleverly, so that none remarked upon his absent-mindedness. Constellations do not stare at one another much.

'Does your Mother know you're "out"?' asked Monkey once beside him—it was the great joke now, since the Story had been read—and as soon as she was temporarily disposed of, Jimbo had serious information to impart from the other side. 'She's a real Countess,' he said, speaking as man to man. 'I suppose if she went to London she'd know the King— visit him, like that?'

Bless his little heart! Jimbo always knew the important things to talk about.

There were bursts of laughter sometimes, due usually to statements made abruptly by Jane Anne—as when Mother, discussing the garden with Minks, reviled the mischievous birds:—

'They want thinning badly,' she said.

'Why don't they take more exercise, then?' inquired Jinny gravely.

And in these gusts of laughter Rogers joined heartily, as though he knew exactly what the fun was all about. In this way he deceived everybody and protected himself from discovery. And yet it seemed to him that he shouted his secret aloud, not with his lips indeed, but with his entire person. Surely everybody knew it...! He was self- conscious as a schoolgirl.

'You must come up—to me,' rang continuously through his head like bells. 'You must come up to me.'

CHAPTER XXXIV

How many times do I love thee, dear?
  Tell me how many thoughts there be
    In the atmosphere
    Of a new fall'n year,
Whose white and sable hours appear
  The latest flake of Eternity:—
So many times do I love thee, dear.

How many times do I love again?
  Tell me how many beads there are
    In a silver chain
    Of evening rain,
Unravelled from the tumbling main,
  And threading the eye of a yellow star:—
So many times do I love again.
                THOMAS LOVELL BEDDOES.

A curious deep shyness settled upon Henry Rogers as they all trooped over to the Den. The others gabbled noisily, but to him words came with difficulty. He felt like a boy going up for some great test, examination, almost for judgment. There was an idea in him that he must run and hide somewhere. He saw the huge outline of Orion tilting up above the Alps, slanting with the speed of his eternal hunt to seize the Pleiades who sailed ever calmly just beyond his giant arms. Yet what that old Hunter sought was at last within his reach. He knew it, and felt the awe of capture rise upon him.

'You've eaten so much supper you can't speak,' said Monkey, whose hand was in his coat-pocket for loose chicken-feed, as she called centimes. 'The Little Countess will *regler ton affaire* all right. Just wait till she gets at you.'

'You love her?' he asked gently, feeling little disposed to play.

The child's reply was cryptic, yet uncommonly revealing:—

'She's just like a relation. It's so funny she didn't know us long, long ago—find us out, I mean.'

'Mother likes her awfully,' added Jimbo, as though that established the matter of her charm for ever. 'It's a pity she's not a man'—just to show that Cousinenry's position was not endangered.

They chattered on. Rogers hardly remembers how he climbed the long stone steps. He found himself in the Den. It came about with a sudden jump as in dreams. *She* was among them before the courtyard was crossed; she had gone up the steps immediately in front of him.... Jinny was bringing in the lamp, while Daddy struggled with a load of peat for the fire, getting in everybody's way. Riquette stood silhouetted against the sky upon the window sill. Jimbo used the bellows. A glow spread softly through the room. He caught sight of Minks standing rather helplessly beside the sofa talking to Jane Anne, and picking at his ear as he always did when nervous or slightly ill at ease. He wondered vaguely what she was saying to him. He looked everywhere but at the one person for whose comfort the others were so energetic.

His eyes did not once turn in her direction, yet he knew exactly how she was dressed, what movements she made, where she stood, the very words, indeed, she used, and in particular the expression of her face to each in turn. For he was guilty of a searching inner scrutiny he could not control. And, above all, he was aware, with a divine, tumultuous thrill, that she, for her part, also neither looked at him nor uttered one sentence that he could take as intended for himself.

Because, of course, all she said and did and looked *were* meant for him, and her scrutiny was even closer and more searching than his own.

In the Den that evening there was one world within another, though only these two, and probably the intuitive and diabolically observant Minks, perceived it. The deep furnaces of this man's inner being, banked now so long that mere little flames had forgotten their way out, lay open at last to that mighty draught before whose fusing power the molten, fluid state becomes inevitable.

'You must come up to me' rang on in his head like a chime of bells. 'O think Beauty: it's your duty....'

The chairs were already round the open fireplace, when Monkey pushed him into the big one with the broken springs he always used, and established herself upon his knee. Jimbo was on the other in a twinkling. Jane Anne plumped down upon the floor against him. Her hair was up, and grown-ups might sit as they pleased. Minks in a hard, straight-backed chair, firmly assured everybody that he was exceedingly comfortable and really preferred stiff chairs. He found safety next to Mother who, pleased and contented, filled one corner of the sofa and looked as though she occupied a pedestal. Beyond her perched Daddy, on the music stool, leaning his back against the unlighted fourneau. The Wumble Book was balanced on his knees, and beside him sat the little figure of the visitor who, though at the end, was yet somehow the true centre of the circle. Rogers saw her slip into her unimportant place. She took her seat, he thought, as softly as a mouse. For no one seemed to notice her. She was so perfectly at home among them. In her little folded hands the Den and all its occupants seemed cared for beyond the need of words or definite action. And, although her place was the furthest possible remove from his own, he felt her closer to him than the very children who nestled upon his knees.

Riquette then finally, when all were settled, stole in to complete the circle. She planted herself in the middle of the hearth before them all, looked up into their faces, decided that all was well, and began placidly to wash her face and back. A leg shot up, from the middle of her back apparently, as a signal that they might talk. A moment later she composed herself into that attitude of dignified security possible only to the feline species. She made the fourth that inhabited this world within a world. Rogers, glancing up suddenly from observing her, caught—-for the merest fraction of an instant—a flash of starfire in the air. It darted across to him from the opposite end of the horse- shoe. Behind it flickered the tiniest smile a human countenance could possibly produce.

'Little mouse who, lost in wonder,
Flicks its whiskers at the thunder.'

It was Jane Anne repeating the rhyme for Minks's benefit. How appropriately it came in, he thought. And voices were set instantly in motion; it seemed that every one began to speak at once.

Who finally led the conversation, or what was actually said at first, he has no more recollection than the man in the moon, for he only heard the silvery music of a single voice. And that came rarely. He felt washed in glory from head to foot. In a dream of happy starlight he swam and floated. He hid his face behind the chair of Monkey, and his eyes were screened below the welcome shelter of Jimbo's shoulder.

The talk meanwhile flowed round the horse-shoe like a river that curves downhill. Life ran past him, while he stood on the banks and watched. He reconstructed all that happened, all that was said and done, each little movement, every little glance of the eye. These common things he recreated. For, while his body sat in the Den before a fire of peat, with children, a cat, a private secretary, three very ordinary people and a little foreign visitor, his spirit floated high above the world among the immensities of suns and starfields. He was in the Den, but the Den was in the universe, and to the scale of the universe he set the little homely, commonplace picture. Life, he realised, *is* thought and feeling; and just then he thought and felt like a god. He was Orion, and Orion had at last overtaken the Pleiades. The fairest of the cluster lay caught within his giant arms. The Enormous Thing that so long had haunted him with hints of its approach, rose up from his under-self, and possessed him utterly. And, oh, the glory of it, the splendour, the intoxication!

In the dim corner where *she* sat, the firelight scarcely showed her face, yet every shade of expression that flitted across her features he saw unobscured. The sparkling, silvery sentences she spoke from time to time were volumes that interpreted life anew. For years he had pored over these thick tomes, but heavily and without understanding. The little things she said now supplied the key. Mind and brain played no part in this. It was simply that he heard—and knew. He re- discovered her from their fragments, piece by piece....

The general talk flowed past him in a stream of sound, cut up into lengths by interrupting consonants, and half ruined by this arbitrary division; but what *she* said always seemed the living idea that lay behind the sound. He could not explain it otherwise. With herself, and with Riquette, and possibly with little, dreaming Minks, he sat firmly at the centre of this inner world. The others, even the children, hovered about its edges, trying to get in. That tiny smile had flashed its secret, ineffable explanation into him. Starlight was in his blood....

Mother, for instance, he vaguely knew, was speaking of the years they all had lived in Bourcelles, of the exquisite springs, of the fairy, gorgeous summers. It was the most ordinary talk imaginable, though it came sincerely from her heart.

'If only you had come here earlier,' she said, 'when the forest was so thick with flowers.' She enumerated them one by one. 'Now, in the autumn, there are so few!'

The little sparkling answer lit the forest glades afresh with colour, perfume, wonder:—

'But the autumn flowers, I think, are the sweetest; for they have the beauty of all the summer in them.'

A slight pause followed, and then all fell to explaining the shining little sentence until its lustre dimmed and disappeared beneath the smother of their words. In himself, however, who heard them not, a new constellation swam above the horizon of his inner world. Riquette looked slyly up and blinked. She purred more deeply, but she made no stupid sign....

And Daddy mentioned then the forest spell that captured the entire village with its peace and softness—'all so rough and big and tumbled, and yet every detail so exquisitely finished and thought out, you know.'

Out slipped the softest little fairy phrase imaginable from her dim corner then:—

'Yes, like hand-made things—you can almost see the hand that made them.'

And Rogers started so perceptibly that Jimbo shifted his weight a little, thinking he must be uncomfortable. He had surely used that very phrase himself! It was familiar. Even when using it he remembered wondering whence its sweetness had dropped into his clumsier mind. Minks uncrossed his legs, glanced up at him a moment, then crossed them again. He made this sign, but, like Riquette, he said nothing....

The stream flowed on and on. Some one told a story. There was hushed attentive listening, followed suddenly by bursts of laughter and delight. Who told it, or what it was about, Rogers had no notion. Monkey dug him in the ribs once because apparently he grunted at the wrong moment, and Jimbo chided her beneath his breath—'Let him have a nap if he wants to; a man's always tired after a long journey like that...!' Some one followed with another story—Minks, was it, this time?—for Rogers caught his face, as through a mist, turning constantly to Mother for approval. It had to do with a vision of great things that had come to a little insignificant woman on a bed of sickness. He recognised the teller because he knew the tale of old. The woman, he remembered, was Albinia's grandmother, and Minks was very proud of it.

'That's a *very* nice story,' rippled from the dim corner when it was over. 'For I like everything so tiny that you can find it inside a shell. That's the way to understand big things and to do them.'

And again the phrase was as familiar to him as though he had said it himself—heard it, read it, dreamed it, even. Whatever its fairy source, he knew it. His bewilderment increased absurdly. The things she said were so ordinary, yet so illuminating, though never quite betraying their secret source. Where had he heard them? Where had he met this little foreign visitor? Whence came the singular certainty that she shared this knowledge with him, and might presently explain it, all clear as daylight and as simple? He had the odd impression that she played with him, delayed purposely the moment of revelation, even expected that *he* would be the first to make it known. The disclosure was to come from himself! She provided him with opportunities—these little sparkling sentences! But he hid in his corner, silent and magically excited, afraid to take the lead. These sentences were addressed to him. There was conversation thus between the two of them; but his replies remained inaudible. Thought makes no sound; its complete delivery is ever wordless.... He felt very big, and absurdly shy.

It was gesture, however, that infallible shorthand of the mind, which seemed the surest medium of this mute delightful intercourse. For each little gesture that she made—unconsciously, of course—expressed more than the swiftest language could have compassed in an hour. And he noted every one: the occasional flourish of the little hands, the bending of the graceful neck, the shadowy head turned sideways, the lift of one shoulder, almost imperceptible, and sometimes the attitude of the entire body. To him they were, one and all, eloquently revealing. Behind each little gesture loomed a yet larger one, the scale increasing strangely, till his thoughts climbed up them as up a ladder into the region where her ideas lay naked before casual interpretation clothed them. Those, he reflected, who are rich in ideas, but find words difficult, may reveal themselves prodigally in gesture. Expression of one kind or another there must be; yet lavish action, the language of big souls, seems a man's expression rather than a woman's.... He built up swiftly, surely, solidly his interpretation of this little foreign visitor who came to him thus suddenly from the stars, whispering to his inmost thought, 'You must come up to me.' The whole experience dazed him. He sat in utter dumbness, shyer than a boy, but happier than a singing star!... The Joy in his heart was marvellous.

Yet how could he know all this?

In the intervals that came to him like breathing spaces he asked himself this childish question. How could he tell that this little soft being with the quiet unobtrusive manners had noble and great beauty of action in her anywhere? A few pretty phrases, a few significant gestures, these were surely a slight foundation to build so much upon! Was there, then, some absolute communion of thought between the two of them such as his cousin's story tried to show? And had their intercourse been running on for years, neither of them aware of it in the daytime? Was this intimate knowledge due to long acquaintance? Had her thought been feeding him perhaps since childhood even?

In the pause of his temporary lunacy he asked himself a dozen similar questions, but before the sign of any answer came he was off again, sweeping on outstretched wings among the stars. He drank her in. He knew. What was the good of questions? A thirsty man does not stop midway in his draught to ask when his thirst began, its cause, or why the rush of liquid down his throat is satisfying. He knows, and drinks. It seemed to Henry Rogers, ordinary man of business and practical affairs, that some deep river which so long had flowed deep out of sight, hidden below his daily existence, rose now grandly at the flood. He had heard its subterranean murmurs often. Here, in the Den, it had reached his lips at last. And he quenched his thirst.... His thought played round her without ceasing, like flowing water....

This idea of flux grew everywhere about him. There was fluid movement in this world within a world. All life was a flowing past of ceaseless beauty, wonder, splendour; it was doubt and question that dammed the rush, causing that stoppage which is ugly, petty, rigid. His being flowed out to mingle with her own. It was all inevitable, and he never really doubted once. Only before long he would be compelled to act—to speak—to tell her what he felt, and hear her dear, dear answer.... The excitement in him became more and more difficult to control. Already there was strain and tension below his apparent outer calmness. Life in him burst forward to a yet greater life than he had ever known....

The others—it was his cousin's voice this time—were speaking of the Story, and of his proposed treatment of it in its larger version as a book. Daddy was saying, apparently, that it must fail because he saw no climax for it. The public demanded a cumulative interest that worked up to some kind of thrilling denouement that they called a climax, whereas his tale was but a stretch of life, and of very ordinary life. And Life, for the majority, knew no such climax. How could he manage one without inventing something artificial?

'But the climax of life comes every day and every minute,' he heard her answer—and how her little voice rang out above the others like a bell!—'when you deny yourself for another, and that other does not even know it. A day is lost that does not pin at least one sweet thought against each passing hour.'

And his inner construction took a further prodigious leap, as the sentence showed him the grand and simple motive of her being. It had been his own as well, though he had stupidly bungled it in his search to find something big enough to seem worth doing. She, he divined, found neighbours everywhere, losing no time. He had known a few rare, exquisite souls who lived for others, but here, close beside him at last, was one of those still rarer souls who seem born to—die for others.... They give so unsparingly of their best.... To his imaginative interpretation of her he gave full rein.... And it was instantaneous as creation....

The voices of Minks and Mother renewed the stream of sound that swept by him then, though he caught no words that were comparable in value to these little singing phrases that she used from time to time. Jimbo, bored by the grown-up talk that took the place of expected stories, had fallen asleep upon his shoulder; Monkey's hair, as usual, was in his eyes; he sat there listening and waiting with a heart that beat so loudly he thought the children must feel it and ask him what was the matter. Jinny stirred the peat from time to time. The room was full of shadows. But, for him, the air grew brighter every minute, and in this steady brilliance he saw the little figure rise and grow in grandeur till she filled all space.

'You called it "getting out" while the body is asleep,' came floating through the air through the sound of Jimbo's breathing, 'whereas *I* called it getting away from self while personal desire is asleep. But the idea is the same....'

His cousin's words that called forth this criticism he had not heard. It was only her sentence that seemed to reach him.

From the river of words and actions men call life she detained, it seemed to him, certain that were vital and important in some symbolical sense; she italicised them, made them her own—then let them go to join the main stream again. This selection was a kind of genius. The river did not overwhelm her as it overwhelms most, because the part of it she did not need for present action she ignored, while yet she swam in the whole of it, shirking nothing.

This was the way he saw her—immediately. And, whether it was his own invention, or whether it was the divination of a man in the ecstasy of sudden love, it was vital because he felt it, and it was real because he believed it. Then why seek to explain the amazing sense of intimacy, the certainty that he had known her always? The thing was *there*; explanation could bring it no nearer. He let the explanations go their way; they floated everywhere within reach; he had only to pocket them and take them home for study at his leisure afterwards— with her.

'But, we *shall* come to it in time,' he caught another flying sentence that reached him through the brown tangle of Monkey's hair. It was spoken with eager emphasis. 'Does not every letter you write begin with *dear*?....'

All that she said added something to life, it seemed, like poetry which, he remembered, 'enriches the blood of the world.' The selections were not idle, due to chance, but belonged to some great Scheme, some fairy edifice she built out of the very stuff of her own life. Oh, how utterly he understood and knew her. The poison of intellectuality, thank heaven, was not in her, yet she created somehow; for all she touched, with word or thought or gesture, turned suddenly alive in a way he had never known before. The world turned beautiful and simple at her touch....

Even the commonest things! It was miraculous, at least in its effect upon himself. Her simplicity escaped all signs of wumbling. She had no favourite and particular Scheme for doing good, but did merely what was next her at the moment to be done. She *was* good. In her little person glowed a great enthusiasm for life. She created neighbours. And, as the grandeur of her insignificance rose before him, his own great Scheme for Disabled Thingumabobs that once had filled the heavens, shrank down into the size of a mere mouse-trap that would go into his pocket. In its place loomed up another that held the beauty of the Stars. How little, when announcing it to Minks weeks and weeks ago, had he dreamed the form it was to take!

And so, wrapped in this glory of the stars, he dreamed on in his corner, fashioning this marvellous interpretation of a woman he had never seen before, and never spoken with. It was all so different to ordinary falling in love at sight, that the phrase never once occurred to him. It was consummated in a moment—out there, beside the fountain when he saw her first, shadowy, with brilliant, peering eyes. It seemed perfect instantly, a recovery of something he had always known. And who shall challenge the accuracy of his vision, or call its sudden maturity impossible? For where one sees the surface only, another sees the potentialities below. To believe in these is to summon them into activity, just as to think the best of a person ever brings out that best. Are we not all potential splendours?

Swiftly, in a second, he reviewed the shining sentences that revealed her to him: The 'autumn flowers'—she lived, then, in the Present, without that waste of energy which is regret! In 'a little shell' lay the pattern of all life,—she saw the universe in herself and lived, thus, in the Whole! To be 'out' meant forgetting self; and life's climax is at every minute of the day—she understood, that is, the growth of the soul, due to acceptance of what every minute brings, however practical, dull, uninteresting. By recreating the commonest things, she found a star in each. And her world was made up of neighbours—for 'every letter that one writes begins with *dear*!'

The Pattern matured marvellously before his eyes; and its delicate embroideries, far out of sight, seemed the arabesques that yearnings, hitherto unfulfilled, had traced long long ago with the brush of tender thinking. Together, though at opposite ends of the world, these two had woven the great Net of sympathy, thought, and longing in which at last they both were prisoners … and with them all the earth.

The figure of Jane Anne loomed before him like an ogress suddenly.

'Cousinenry, *will* you answer or will you *not?* Daddy's already asked you twenty times at least!' Then, below her breath, as she bent over him, 'The Little Countess will think you awf'ly rude if you go to sleep and snore like this.'

He looked up. He felt a trifle dazed. For a moment he had forgotten where he was. How dark the room had grown! Only—he was sure he had not snored.

'I beg your pardon,' he stammered, 'but I was only thinking—how wonderful you—how wonderful it all is, isn't it? I was listening. I heard perfectly.'

'You were dozing,' whispered Monkey. 'Daddy wants the Countess to tell you how she knew the story long ago, or something. *Ecoute un peu, man vieux!*'

'I should love to hear it,' he said, louder, sitting up so abruptly in his chair that Jimbo tilted at a dangerous angle, though still without waking. 'Please, please go on.'

And he listened then to the quiet, silvery language in which the little visitor described the scenery of her childhood, when, without brothers or sisters, she was forced to play alone, and had amused herself by imagining a Net of Constellations which she nailed by shooting stars to four enormous pine trees that grew across the torrent. She described the great mountains that enclosed her father's estate, her loneliness in this giant garden, due to his morose severity of character, her yearnings to escape and see the big world beyond the ridges. All her thought and longing went to the fashioning of this Net, and every night she flung it far across the peaks and valleys to catch companions with whom she might play. The characters in her fairy books came out of the pages to help her, and sometimes when they drew it in, it was so heavy with the people entangled in its meshes that they could scarcely move it. But the moment all were out, the giant Net, relieved of their weight, flew back into the sky. The Pleiades were its centre, because she loved the Pleiades best of all, and Orion pursued its bright shape with passion, yet could never quite come up with it.

'And these people whom you caught,' whispered Rogers from his corner, listening to a tale he knew as well as she did, 'you kept them prisoners?'

'I first put into them all the things I longed to do myself in the big world, and then flung them back again into their homes and towns and villages——'

'Excepting one,' he murmured.

'Who was so big and clumsy that he broke the meshes and so never got away.' She laughed, while the children stared at their cousin, wondering how he knew as much as she did. 'He stayed with me, and showed me how to make our prisoners useful afterwards by painting them all over with starlight which we collected in a cave. Then they went back and dazzled others everywhere by their strange, alluring brilliance. We made the whole world over in this way——'

'Until you lost him.'

'One cloudy night he disappeared, yes, and I never found him again. There was a big gap between the Pleiades and Orion where he had tumbled through. I named him Orion after that; and I would stand at night beneath the four great pine trees and call and call, but in vain. "You must come up to me! You must come up to me!" I called, but got no answer—'

'Though you knew quite well where he had fallen to, and that he was only hiding—'

'Excuse me, but *how* did she know?' inquired Jinny abruptly.

The Little Countess laughed. 'I suppose—because the threads of the Net were so sensitive that they went on quivering long after he tumbled out, and so betrayed the direction—'

'And afterwards, when you got older, Grafin,' interrupted Daddy, who wished his cousin to hear the details of the extraordinary coincidence, 'you elaborated your idea—'

'Yes, that thought and yearning always fulfil themselves somewhere, somehow, sooner or later,' she continued. 'But I kept the imagery of my Star Net in which all the world lies caught, and I used starlight as the symbol of that sympathy which binds every heart to every other heart. At my father's death, you see, I inherited his property. I escaped from the garden which had been so long my prison, and I tried to carry out in practical life what I had dreamed there as a child. I got people together, where I could, and formed Thinkers' Guilds— people, that is, who agreed to think beauty, love, and tolerance at given hours in the day, until the habit, once formed, would run through all their lives, and they should go about as centres of light, sweetening the world. Few have riches, fewer still have talent, but all can think. At least, one would *think* so, wouldn't one?'— with a smile and a fling of her little hands.

She paused a moment, and then went on to describe her failure. She told it to them with laughter between her sentences, but among her listeners was one at least who caught the undertone of sadness in the voice.

'For, you see, that was where I made my mistake. People would do anything in the world rather than think. They would work, give money, build schools and hospitals, make all manner of sacrifices—only—they would not think; because, they said, there was no visible result.' She burst out laughing, and the children all laughed too.

'I should think not indeed,' ventured Monkey, but so low that no one heard her.

'And so you went on thinking it all alone,' said Rogers in a low voice.

'I tried to write it first as a story,' she answered softly, 'but found that was beyond me; so I went on thinking it all alone, as you say—'

'Until the Pattern of your thought floated across the world to me,' said Daddy proudly. 'I imagined I was inspired; instead I was a common, unoriginal plagiarist!'

'Like all the rest of us,' she laughed.

'Mummie, what *is* a plagiarist?' asked Jinny instantly; and as Rogers, her husband, and even Minks came hurriedly to her aid, the spell of the strange recital was broken, and out of the turmoil of voices the only thing distinctly heard was Mother exclaiming with shocked surprise:—

'Why, it's ten o'clock! Jimbo, Monkey, please plagiarise off to bed at once!'—in a tone that admitted of no rejoinder or excuses.

'A most singular thing, isn't it, Henry?' remarked the author, coming across to his side when the lamp was lit and the children had said their good-nights.

'I really think we ought to report it to the Psychical Society as a genuine case of thought-transference. You see, what people never properly realise is——'

But Henry Rogers lost the remainder of the sentence even if he heard the beginning, for his world was in a state of indescribable turmoil, one emotion tumbling wildly upon the heels of another. He was elated to intoxication. The room spun round him. The next second his heart sank down into his boots. He only caught the end of the words she was saying to Mother across the room:—

'... but I must positively go to-morrow, I've already stayed too long. So many things are waiting at home for me to do. I must send a telegram and....'

His cousin's wumbling drowned the rest. He was quite aware that Rogers was not listening to him.

'... your great kindness in writing to him, and then coming yourself,' Mother was saying. 'It's such an encouragement. I can't tell you how much he—we—'

'And you'll let me write to you about the children,' she interrupted, 'the plans we discussed, you know....'

Rogers broke away from his cousin with a leap. It felt at least like a leap. But he knew not where to go or what to say. He saw Minks standing with Jane Anne again by the fourneau, picking at his ear. By the open window with Mother stood the little visitor. She was leaving to-morrow. A torturing pain like twisting knives went through him. The universe was going out!... He saw the starry sky behind her. Daddy went up and joined them, and he was aware that the three of them talked all at once for what seemed an interminable time, though all he heard was his cousin's voice repeating at intervals, 'But you *can't* send a telegram before eight o'clock to-morrow morning in any case; the post is closed....'

And then, suddenly, the puzzle reeled and danced before his eyes. It dissolved into a new and startling shape that brought him to his senses with a shock. There had been a swift shuffling of the figures.

Minks and his cousin were helping her into her cloak. She *was* going.

One of them—he knew not which—was offering politely to escort her through the village.

It sounded like his own sentence of exile, almost of death. Was he forty years of age, or only fifteen? He felt awkward, tongue-tied, terrified.

They were already in the passage. Mother had opened the door into the yard.

'But your way home lies down the hill,' he heard the silver voice, 'and to go with me you must come up. I can easily——'

Above the leaves of the plane tree he saw the stars. He saw Orion and the Pleiades. The Fairy Net flung in and caught him. He found his voice.

In a single stride he was beside her. Minks started at his sudden vehemence and stepped aside.

'*I* will take you home, Countess, if I may,' and his tone was so unnecessarily loud and commanding that Mother turned and stared. 'Our direction lies together. I will come up—with you.'

She did not even look at him. He saw that tiny smile that was like the flicker of a star—no more. But he heard her answer. It seemed to fill the sky.

'Thank you. I might lose my way alone.'

And, before he realised how she managed it, they had crossed the cobbled yard, Daddy was swinging away downhill towards the carpenter's, and Minks behind them, at the top of the stone steps, was saying his last good-night to Mother. With the little visitor beside him, he passed the singing fountain and led her down the deserted village street beneath the autumn stars.

Three minutes later they were out of sight... when Minks came down the steps and picked his way among the shadows after Daddy, who had the latch-key of the carpenter's house. He ran to overtake him.

> And he ran upon his toes
> As softly as a saying does,
> For so the saying goes!

His thoughts were very active, but as clear as day. He was thinking whether German was a difficult language to acquire, and wondering whether a best man at a wedding ought to wear white gloves or not. He decided to ask Albinia. He wrote the letter that very night before he went to sleep.

And, while he slept, Orion pursued the Pleiades across the sky, and numerous shooting stars fastened the great Net of thought and sympathy close over little Bourcelles.

THE END

Milton Keynes UK
Ingram Content Group UK Ltd.
UKHW030622061024
449204UK00004B/407